Industry 5.0's Impact on Economic Innovation

Mohammad Mehdi Oskounejad
Azad University of the Emirates, UAE

Hamed Nozari
https://orcid.org/0000-0002-6500-6708
Azad University in the Emirates, UAE

IGI Global
Scientific Publishing
Publishing Tomorrow's Research Today

Published in the United States of America by
IGI Global Scientific Publishing
701 East Chocolate Avenue
Hershey, PA, 17033, USA
Tel: 717-533-8845 | Fax: 717-533-7115
Website: https://www.igi-global.com E-mail: cust@igi-global.com

Library of Congress Cataloging-in-Publication Data

Names: Oskounejad, Mohammad Mehdi, 1952- editor. | Nozari, Hamed, 1984- editor.
Title: Industry 5.0's impact on economic innovation / edited by Mohammad Mehdi Oskounejad, Hamed Nozari.
Description: Hershey, PA : Business Science Reference, [2026] | Includes bibliographical references and index. | Summary: "In this book, an attempt is made to explain various financial and economic processes in the context of Industry 5.0. The use of the Internet of Things and Blockchain technologies in data extraction and creating transparent and intelligent systems will be evaluated. Financial systems and software are also examined in the context of Industry 5.0. This book tries to provide a deep insight into understanding economic innovations in Industry 5.0"-- Provided by publisher.
Identifiers: LCCN 2024038658 (print) | LCCN 2024038659 (ebook) | ISBN 9798369345252 (hardcover) | ISBN 9798369345269 (paperback) | ISBN 9798369345276 (ebook)
Subjects: LCSH: Economic development--Technological innovations. | Industry 5.0.
Classification: LCC HD82 .I34123 2024 (print) | LCC HD82 (ebook) | DDC 338.9--dc23/eng/20240925
LC record available at https://lccn.loc.gov/2024038658
LC ebook record available at https://lccn.loc.gov/2024038659

British Cataloguing in Publication Data
A Cataloguing in Publication record for this book is available from the British Library.

Table of Contents

Detailed Table of Contents

This research examines the role of value networks and ecosystem innovation in the formation of Industry 5.0 organizations. The main focus is on the interaction between smart technologies, organizational structures, human capital, and sustainability principles. The conceptual framework presented shows that value in Industry 5.0 is created not linearly, but through synergies between technological, human, and social layers. The results show that adaptive governance, knowledge management, open innovation, and learning decision-making are key elements for the successful implementation of value networks and the development of human-centered and sustainable ecosystems.

This research introduces a new framework called "Neuromorphic-Cognitive Economics," which combines the principles of brain-inspired computing with the foundations of cognitive economics. The proposed model simulates the economic decision-making process in a dynamic, adaptive, and self-learning manner using spiking neural networks, memristive memory, and reinforcement learning. The simulation results show that economic agents can learn, adapt, and reproduce complex behaviors such as skepticism, trust, and risk-taking, just like biological neurons. This model opens up new horizons for designing smart, self-organizing economies.

This chapter examines the role of AI in the transformation of economic forecasting in the context of Industry 5.0, demonstrating that economic forecasting is no longer a linear analytical activity but rather part of a dynamic, human-centered cognitive system. By integrating multi-source data, adaptive learning models, and decision-support architectures, forecasting is elevated from the level of future estimation to the level of future design. Various applications in supply chains, sustainable manufacturing, financial services, and policymaking demonstrate that AI not only increases forecasting accuracy, but also turns it into a tool for resilience, sustainability, and competitive advantage.

This study aims to explain the role of urban digital twin in shaping the 5.0 economy, and presents a data-driven and human-centered framework for smart city management. The proposed model shows that the integration of data flow, dynamic simulation, cognitive decision-making engines, and citizen feedback can lead to improved governance, increased resilience, optimized infrastructure, and improved quality of life. The findings suggest that urban digital twin is not a single technology, but a strategic infrastructure for sustainable development, accurate decision-making, and value creation in future cities. This approach guides the path of urban transformation toward predictive, efficient, and human-centered management.

Industry 5.0 signifies the forthcoming advancement in industrial transformation, shifting away from the automation-focused model of Industry 4.0 to emphasise collaboration between humans and machines, as well as the creation of sustainable value. Industry 4.0 focused on enhancing efficiency via cyber-physical systems, artificial intelligence, and the Internet of Things, whereas Industry 5.0 aims to re-establish the importance of humans in production processes Unlike Industry 4.0, which emphasized precision farming through IoT, drones, AI, and big data, Industry 5.0 integrates these technologies with human creativity, intuition, and local knowledge to build value-driven agricultural enterprises. Agripreneurs adopting Industry 5.0 approaches leverage robotics, AI-assisted decision tools, and digital twins alongside traditional farming wisdom to achieve sustainable intensification, resource optimization, and climate-resilient cultivation practices.

This research presents a novel framework for green and circular finance supply chains, which is designed based on carbon twin accounting in the context of Industry 5.0. By integrating real-time environmental data, financial indicators, and digital twin technology, the proposed model enables sustainable, transparent, and adaptive decision-making. This framework not only helps reduce carbon emissions and optimize financial resources, but also provides a basis for data-driven policymaking and the formation of a cognitive carbon-finance ecosystem in the future. The research results show that Industry 5.0 can become the driving force of the green economy and intergenerational justice.

This research presents a new framework for AI-based economic intelligence in adaptive supply chains. The proposed model, by utilizing machine learning, predictive analytics, and intelligent feedback, enhances economic decision-making ability from static to dynamic. The results show that using this model reduces costs, increases capital efficiency, and improves economic flexibility. By combining the concepts of adaptive economics, data analytics, and AI, the present research presents a practical model for intelligent supply chain management in the era of Industry 5.0.

This study investigates the implementation of Industry 5.0 technologies in Tamil Nadu's automotive manufacturing sector, focusing on their impact on economic innovation, productivity, and sustainability. Utilizing a mixed-methods approach, the research combined qualitative insights from interviews and focus groups with quantitative survey data from 188 respondents across 58 companies. Key findings revealed that gender and experience significantly influence perceived challenges and opportunities, while gender and age affect perceptions of technology implementation

Apparel waste has significantly increased, becoming a global issue amid concerns about landfills in many countries. The solution lies in collaborative apparel consumption, provided a suitable structure is established for its implementation. The research investigates the correlation between apparel and collaborative consumption through comprehensive literature assessment, including bibliometric and text analysis, to identify shared characteristics and underlying theories. The resulting conceptual framework defines apparel consumption through collaborative practices. This study provides a solid basis for scholars and researchers exploring novel opportunities in fashion marketing via collaborative consumption. It examines the characteristics and relationships of publications in collaborative consumption during the study period, offering a comprehensive understanding. The study aims to guide industry players, policymakers, and scholars toward creative and sustainable cooperation models in the apparel sector.

This research examines human-centric business models in the era of Industry 5.0, an era in which technology is put at the service of humans and economic value is redefined based on meaning, well-being, and sustainability. By combining human and artificial intelligence, Industry 5.0 offers a model of creative collaboration between humans and machines that leads to multidimensional value creation, ethical decision-making, and sustainable development. The conceptual framework presented introduces three key dimensions of human empowerment, intelligent human-machine interaction, and sustainable value systems as the foundation for future business transformation.

Preface

On the threshold of a new era of industrial transformation, fundamental questions are being raised about the relationship between humans, technology, and the economy; questions that not only concern how new technologies are used, but also redefine the nature of value creation, sustainability, and human interactions. Industry 5.0 emerges at such a point; a point where technology is no longer simply a tool for increasing productivity, but rather a platform for the creative coexistence of human intelligence and advanced computing capacities. In this context, the economy—as the driving force of any society—is faced with a range of technological, environmental, and social innovations that are not limited to a single industry or business model, but permeate the fabric of entire production, service, and urban ecosystems.

This book is an attempt to understand this historical transition more deeply; A transition that not only reflects the acceleration of technological change, but also presents a clear picture of a future in which economic value is created from different paths: from the integration of artificial and neuromorphic intelligence into decision-making mechanisms to the creation of collaborative value networks, from urban digital twins that strengthen the data-driven economy to carbon-based accounting that brings the link between the economy and the environment closer than ever before. This series attempts to present a unified picture of the transformations that are changing not only large industries, but also the smallest production and service units, and even the way people consume, work, and live.

The aim of this book is not to provide definitive answers; it is an invitation to think, discuss, and rethink about an economic future that is simultaneously becoming more complex, more human-centered, and more intelligent. In the following lines, the reader will encounter trends that each play a decisive role in the formation of the emerging economy: from explaining new patterns of value creation and the smartization of supply chains to examining the transformation of traditional industries and the emergence of business models based on collaboration and sustainability. This series attempts to be a bridge between theoretical knowledge and practical experience, and to provide a tool for researchers, policymakers, managers, and all those who want to contribute to building the future of the human-centered economy of Industry 5.0.

OVERVIEW OF CHAPTERS

Chapter 1: Value Networks and Ecosystem Innovation in Industry 5.0 Enterprises

This research examines the role of value networks and ecosystem innovation in the formation of Industry 5.0 organizations. The main focus is on the interaction between smart technologies, organizational structures, human capital, and sustainability principles. The conceptual framework presented shows that value in Industry 5.0 is created not linearly, but through synergies between technological, human, and social layers. The results show that adaptive governance, knowledge management, open innovation, and learning decision-making are key elements for the successful implementation of value networks and the development of human-centered and sustainable ecosystems.

Chapter 2: Neuromorphic Computing and Cognitive Economics

This research introduces a new framework called "Neuromorphic-Cognitive Economics," which combines the principles of brain-inspired computing with the foundations of cognitive economics. The proposed model simulates the economic decision-making process in a dynamic, adaptive, and self-learning manner using spiking neural networks, memristive memory, and reinforcement learning. The simulation results show that economic agents can learn, adapt, and reproduce complex behaviors such as skepticism, trust, and risk-taking, just like biological neurons. This model opens up new horizons for designing smart, self-organizing economies.

Chapter 3: AI-Driven Economic Forecasting for Industry 5.0 Enterprises

This chapter examines the role of AI in the transformation of economic forecasting in the context of Industry 5.0, demonstrating that economic forecasting is no longer a linear analytical activity but rather part of a dynamic, human-centered cognitive system. By integrating multi-source data, adaptive learning models, and decision-support architectures, forecasting is elevated from the level of future estimation to the level of future design. Various applications in supply chains, sustainable manufacturing, financial services, and policymaking demonstrate that AI not only increases forecasting accuracy, but also turns it into a tool for resilience, sustainability, and competitive advantage.

Chapter 4: Urban Digital Twins and Data-Centric Architectures for the Emergent Economy 5.0

This study aims to explain the role of urban digital twin in shaping the 5.0 economy, and presents a data-driven and human-centered framework for smart city management. The proposed model shows that the integration of data flow, dynamic simulation, cognitive decision-making engines, and citizen feedback can lead to improved governance, increased resilience, optimized infrastructure, and improved quality of life. The findings suggest that urban digital twin is not a single technology, but a strategic infrastructure for sustainable development, accurate decision-making, and value creation in future cities. This approach guides the path of urban transformation toward predictive, efficient, and human-centered management.

Chapter 5: A Human-Centric Technological Revolution in Agriculture-Industry 5.0 for Sustainable Agripreneurship

Industry 5.0 signifies the forthcoming advancement in industrial transformation, shifting away from the automation-focused model of Industry 4.0 to emphasise collaboration between humans and machines, as well as the creation of sustainable value. Industry 4.0 focused on enhancing efficiency via cyber-physical systems, artificial intelligence, and the Internet of Things, whereas Industry 5.0 aims to re-establish the importance of humans in production processes Unlike Industry 4.0, which emphasized precision farming through IoT, drones, AI, and big data, Industry 5.0 integrates these technologies with human creativity, intuition, and local knowledge to build value-driven agricultural enterprises. Agripreneurs adopting Industry 5.0 approaches leverage robotics, AI-assisted decision tools, and digital twins alongside traditional farming wisdom to achieve sustainable intensification, resource optimization, and climate-resilient cultivation practices.

Chapter 6: Green & Circular Supply Chain Finance Supported by Carbon-Twin Accounting

This research presents a novel framework for green and circular finance supply chains, which is designed based on carbon twin accounting in the context of Industry 5.0. By integrating real-time environmental data, financial indicators, and digital twin technology, the proposed model enables sustainable, transparent, and adaptive decision-making. This framework not only helps reduce carbon emissions and optimize financial resources, but also provides a basis for data-driven policymaking and the formation of a cognitive carbon-finance ecosystem in the future. The research results show that Industry 5.0 can become the driving force of the green economy and intergenerational justice.

Chapter 7: AI-Driven Economic Intelligence for Adaptive Supply Chain Ecosystems

This research presents a new framework for AI-based economic intelligence in adaptive supply chains. The proposed model, by utilizing machine learning, predictive analytics, and intelligent feedback, enhances economic decision-making ability from static to dynamic. The results show that using this model reduces costs, increases capital efficiency, and improves economic flexibility. By combining the concepts of adaptive economics, data analytics, and AI, the present research presents a practical model for intelligent supply chain management in the era of Industry 5.0.

Chapter 8: Harnessing Industry 5.0 for Economic Innovation: A Case Study of the Automotive Manufacturing Sector in Tamil Nadu

This study investigates the implementation of Industry 5.0 technologies in Tamil Nadu's automotive manufacturing sector, focusing on their impact on economic innovation, productivity, and sustainability. Utilizing a mixed-methods approach, the research combined qualitative insights from interviews and focus groups with quantitative survey data from 188 respondents across 58 companies. Key findings revealed that gender and experience significantly influence perceived challenges and opportunities, while gender and age affect perceptions of technology implementation effectiveness. The study underscores the need for targeted strategies in workforce development, data security, and policy advocacy. Regression analysis highlighted that addressing key challenges and leveraging opportunities are crucial for driving economic innovation and productivity. The study concludes with recommendations for demographic-specific strategies to maximize Industry 5.0 benefits.

Chapter 9: Circular and Regenerative Economy in Industry 5.0: Human-Centric Innovation for Sustainable Industrial Transformation

This research examines the role of the circular and regenerative economy within the framework of Industry 5.0, and shows that the synergy between smart technologies, sustainable policymaking, and human values can form the foundation of the economy of the future. Relying on technologies such as digital twins, artificial intelligence, and blockchain, Industry 5.0 provides a platform in which economic growth, resource recovery, and social well-being can be realized simultaneously. The results show that the transition to a regenerative economy leads not only to environmental sustainability, but also to increased productivity and industrial innovation.

Chapter 10: Exploring the Dimensions and Indicators of the Digital Economy in the Age of Industry 5.0

The 5th industrial revolution is a pioneer in the industry adjusting for both advanced technologies and human-centric-sustainable solutions, playing an important role that also brings us to a highly skilled workforce besides its adaptability. In this paper, the essence and its parts of the digital economy in Industry 5.0 have been analyzed. Besides, light is shed on important indicators that can lead industry to productivity improvement and enhance/GDP growth and economic development. These are all based around the three core pillars of sustainability, human-centricity, and resilience - demanding industrial progression to be more sustainable, being contextually matched with environmental responsibility, and valuing worker welfare. Capital investment in artificial intelligence (AI), the Internet of Things (IoT), robotics, additive manufacturing, and augmented reality (AR) can seem essential to this advancement. It utilizes AI and machine learning for real-time production, predictive maintenance, and quality control.

Chapter 11: Future Trends in Apparel Consumption through Collaborative Models: A Systematic Literature Review and Bibliometric Framework

Apparel waste has significantly increased, becoming a global issue amid concerns about landfills in many countries. The solution lies in collaborative apparel consumption, provided a suitable structure is established for its implementation. The research investigates the correlation between apparel and collaborative consumption through comprehensive literature assessment, including bibliometric and text analysis, to identify shared characteristics and underlying theories. The resulting conceptual framework defines apparel consumption through collaborative practices. This study provides a solid basis for scholars and researchers exploring novel opportunities in fashion marketing via collaborative consumption. It examines the characteristics and relationships of publications in collaborative consumption during the study period, offering a comprehensive understanding. The study aims to guide industry players, policymakers, and scholars toward creative and sustainable cooperation models in the apparel sector.

Chapter 12: Human–Centric Business Models in Industry 5.0: Redefining Economic Value Creation

This research examines human-centric business models in the era of Industry 5.0, an era in which technology is put at the service of humans and economic value is redefined based on meaning, well-being, and sustainability. By combining human and artificial intelligence, Industry 5.0 offers a model of creative collaboration between humans and machines that leads to multidimensional value creation, ethical decision-making, and sustainable development. The conceptual framework presented introduces three key dimensions of human empowerment, intelligent human-machine interaction, and sustainable value systems as the foundation for future business transformation.

Chapter 13: Revolutionizing Work from Home and Technological Transformation in the Age of Industry 5.0

This study explores the transformative impact of Industry 5.0 on business operations, emphasizing how this new industrial era is redefining traditional business models, and the global economic landscape. By examining the confluence of advanced technologies and human creativity, the study illustrates how Industry 5.0 promotes sustainable and localized production, thereby fostering a more resilient and adaptable economy. The research methodology includes a historical review of the industrial revolution from Industry 1.0 to Industry 5.0, highlighting the critical developments that have shaped modern manufacturing and business practices. Additionally, it delves into the principles of human-machine collaboration and the growing emphasis on sustainability. The study reveals that the integration of human skills with advanced technologies leads to more innovative and efficient production processes This briefing offers a novel perspective on the synergistic relationship between WFH and Industry 5.0.

It is hoped that this book can provide a basis for deepening the view, expanding the boundaries of thought, and providing inspiration for future research and innovations; because the economy of the future is not the product of a single technology, but rather the result of dynamic and creative interactions between humans, data, and technology, interactions that today form the foundation of tomorrow's new economy.

Hamed Nozari
Azad University of the Emirates, UAE

Chapter 1
Value Networks and Ecosystem Innovation in Industry 5.0 Enterprises

Azam Hajiaghajani
https://orcid.org/0000-0001-8993-7649
Department of Management, Cha.C., Islamic Azad University, Chalus, Iran

ABSTRACT

This research examines the role of value networks and ecosystem innovation in the formation of Industry 5.0 organizations. The main focus is on the interaction between smart technologies, organizational structures, human capital, and sustainability principles. The conceptual framework presented shows that value in Industry 5.0 is created not linearly, but through synergies between technological, human, and social layers. The results show that adaptive governance, knowledge management, open innovation, and learning decision-making are key elements for the successful implementation of value networks and the development of human-centered and sustainable ecosystems.

1- INTRODUCTION

In the era of transition to a more complex industry than ever before, the concept of Value Networks and innovation in ecosystems has reached a central position in the literature of the innovative economy and Industry 5.0. Industry 5.0, which is considered the continuation and evolution of Industry 4.0, emphasizes the three fundamental components of human-centeredness, sustainability and resilience and, from this perspective, is considered a turning point in the transformation of industrial and economic systems . In this context, automation and intelligent connection of

DOI: 10.4018/979-8-3693-4525-2.ch001

machines are no longer enough; it is also necessary that shared human capacities, inter-organizational interactions, and the sharing of knowledge and resources are also at the center of value creation.

Value networks are defined as a set of actors, knowledge flows, resources, and dynamic relationships in which value is created not only within the boundaries of a firm but also in the interactions between firms, suppliers, customers, technologists, and societal stakeholders (Nozari et al., 2025). Such networks form the basis of innovation ecosystems, where collaboration, trust, and collective learning replace mere competition, and the flow of information and resources is directed toward the creation of shared value.

Meanwhile, the shift toward Industry 5.0 has fundamentally redefined the role of technologies in these networks. Enabling technologies such as artificial intelligence (AI), the Internet of Things (IoT), digital twins, and edge computing are not only productivity tools but also infrastructures for the synergy of humans and machines in the innovation process (Adel, 2022). In other words, Industry 5.0, by emphasizing the collaboration of humans and technology, provides the basis for the emergence of a value ecosystem in which data, knowledge, and human experience are simultaneously effective in creating value.

The fundamental difference between the value chain and the value network also stems from this. While the value chain model has a linear structure and activities flow sequentially from the supply of materials to the delivery of the final product, the value network model has a nonlinear, dynamic, and interactive structure in which value is formed within multilateral links and collaborations (Ghobakhloo, 2023). From this perspective, organizations in Industry 5.0 can no longer simply focus on internal optimization; they must also incorporate the ability to collaborate intelligently, contribute data-drivenly, and align with global sustainability goals into their structure.

As a result, value networks have become structures in which economy, technology, and society operate in an integrated manner. Collaboration between humans and machines not only increases productivity but also incorporates ethical, social, and environmental values into decision-making. This trend, especially in Industry 5.0-based enterprises, has led to the emergence of a concept called Symbiotic Innovation, in which diverse actors use cognitive technologies to create shared value.

From a policy and management perspective, these developments require the development of new models of network governance in which trust, transparency, and continuous learning are central. To be present in innovative ecosystems, companies must simultaneously benefit from advanced technologies, creative human resources, and ethical frameworks in order to maximize economic and social value together. Industry 5.0 has thus evolved from a purely technological project into a human-centered, knowledge-based, and value-driven model for the future of the global economy.

Focusing on the role of value networks and innovation ecosystems in Industry 5.0 firms, this chapter seeks to answer the question of how firms can benefit from the collaboration and interaction between technology, people, and organizations to create shared value. This chapter attempts to provide a conceptual framework through which the structure, dynamics, and mechanisms of innovation in value-driven ecosystems can be explained. In doing so, it emphasizes that the future of industry lies not in individual competition but in intelligent collaboration and technological and human coexistence.

2- THEORETICAL FOUNDATIONS OF VALUE NETWORKS

In the organizational and innovative economics literature, the concept of a "value network" has been proposed as a framework beyond the traditional value chain; one that views the interaction between different actors, the exchange of knowledge and resources, and the creation of shared value in a more dynamic and multifaceted network context. According to Allee (2008), a value network can be considered "any set of roles and interactions" in which individuals or organizations carry out both tangible (commercial, contractual) and intangible (knowledge, credit, ideas) exchanges to achieve an economic or social goal. In this view, the network is not only a platform for value transfer, but also a mechanism for transforming different values into each other (Allee, 2008).

One of the key theoretical principles in this context is the need to move from the single firm perspective to the space of inter-firm interactions: value is no longer produced within the boundaries of a single firm but rather in the interactions between actors, in continuous and collective flows. For example, Corsaro et al.'s (2012) research showed that network configuration has a direct impact on value recipients, value creation paths, and outcomes. They found that different network structures (such as open/closed, or producer/consumer networks) provide different outcomes from a value creation perspective. This finding highlights the importance of paying attention to the structural design of the network in understanding value networks (Nozari et al., 2025).

In addition, theories related to innovation and networks are also noteworthy in this context; In particular, theories that consider innovation as a network process in which interactions between organizations, recombination of ideas, and sharing of resources play a fundamental role (Nozari, 2025). In this view, value networks are not simply a platform for collaboration, but also the engine for the production and diffusion of innovation; because cognitive and technological resources are shared through nodes and links, and new value is formed through this path.

A theoretical distinctive feature of value networks compared to traditional value chains is the emphasis on the dynamism, non-linearity, and reconfigurableness of these structures. In other words, value networks in complex and dynamic environments provide the possibility of flexibility, adaptation, and co-creation; a process that linear value chains hardly cover. This point is clearly raised in Alleli's work; He believes that intangible resources – such as knowledge, trust, collaboration – need a network structure that allows these resources to be exchanged and transformed into negotiable value (Allee, 2008).

From an operational perspective, a conceptual model for analyzing value networks can include roles, transactions, and tangible and intangible values. Roles – whether within or across organizations – carry specific assets (experience, technology, customers) and, through interactions with other roles, convert these assets into value. This value conversion is the key point of the theory: when, for example, an organization converts its technological expertise into a marketable service, it has activated the value network and undergone a value creation process (Allee, 2008).

In addition to the role of conversion, the interactions between actors and the paths of value flows in the network are also central to the theory. Value networks can be formed with open or closed structures, with a focus on the producer or the consumer, and with different degrees of resource sharing, each of which determines a different path of value creation (Li et al., 2024). These structures, depending on the industrial and technological environment, determine how data, knowledge, technology, and human resources flow and value is produced.

Finally, the theory of value networks also aligns with the innovation ecosystem literature; in the sense that firms and stakeholders interact in a networked environment, share resources, and create value based on common goals. This theoretical convergence allows for the analysis of synergies between actors and technologies and can be the basis of a model for the analysis of value networks in the Industry 5.0 space.

3- ECOSYSTEM INNOVATION IN INDUSTRY 5.0

In the era of transformation known as Industry 5.0, the concept of "Ecosystem Innovation" has become one of the main topics of technological, economic and social discussions, because value production is no longer carried out in the closed space of individual enterprises, but is formed in an interactive, networked and context-oriented framework. In this view, the innovation ecosystem means a range of actors, resources, knowledge and technology flows that, in their mutual interaction with each other, create opportunities for innovation and sustainable value creation.

In this framework, Industry 5.0, with its three main pillars (human-centeredness, sustainability and resilience) has left behind the traditional approach based solely on technology and is moving towards combining the interactions between technology and people, enterprise and ecosystem, and production and environment to create a "value-creating ecosystem". As a result, ecosystem innovation in this context is realized when firms, while utilizing advanced technologies, become active actors in a dynamic network; a network in which synergies between actors, resource sharing, and collective learning emerge as fundamental structures.

One of the distinctive aspects of innovation in Industry 5.0 ecosystems is the emphasis on an ecosystem that integrates human and machine interactions with the aim of ethical, social, and environmental productivity. Studies show that these types of ecosystems not only respond to the speed of technology but also have the capacity to adapt to uncertain conditions, continuous learning, and co-creation of value (Kumar et al., 2024). In other words, ecosystemic innovation in Industry 5.0 is not necessarily limited to the introduction of new technology; it also incorporates the combination of human intelligence, data networks, connected technologies, and a collaborative mindset.

From a structural perspective, an innovation ecosystem can be understood as a system in which a network of stakeholders (including manufacturing firms, suppliers, customers, universities, technological institutions and policymakers) are engaged in a reciprocal flow of interaction, learning and value creation. In the Industry 5.0 environment, technologies such as the Internet of Things (IoT), artificial intelligence, digital twin and edge computing are not just tools but also platforms for connectivity, synergy and sharing that facilitate the linkage between firms and stakeholders (Voropai et al., 2025). In such an environment, the innovation ecosystem becomes an engine of shared value creation, where value is derived from the interaction between nodes rather than from the individual activity of each actor.

In addition, ecosystem innovation in Industry 5.0 requires a network governance architecture that ensures synergy, collaboration, and learning. This network governance can include trust-building mechanisms, transparency in data flows, coordination between stakeholders, and resource optimization, which is especially important in complex, changing, and technological environments (Babkin et al., 2025). Without such governance frameworks, innovation ecosystems may be relegated to insular interactions or pure competition, and opportunities for co-creation may be lost.

Finally, it should be emphasized that ecosystem innovation in Industry 5.0 means a transition from an "enterprise-based" approach to "network-based value creation," meaning that firms should not only think about producing new goods but also about participating in value networks, sharing knowledge, and co-designing systems. This shift not only increases competitiveness but also enables the creation of human-centered and nature-friendly socio-economic structures. This chapter seeks to examine this theoretical and structural transformation in detail, so that firms in the era of Industry 5.0 can play an active role in creating networked and long-term value in innovative ecosystems.

4- INTEGRATIVE FRAMEWORK FOR VALUE NETWORK–DRIVEN ECOSYSTEMS

This section presents and explains an integrated conceptual framework for value network ecosystems; a framework that attempts to combine technological, organizational, cognitive, and sustainability dimensions into a single model to explain the mechanism of value creation, distribution, and re-creation in the Industry 5.0 environment. This framework emphasizes the interaction of layers and value flows in a dynamic and multidimensional system.

At the core of this model is the Technological Layer, which forms the main infrastructure of the innovation ecosystem. This layer includes a set of intelligent, data-driven, and connected technologies that enable information flow, real-time analytics, and adaptive decision-making. Technologies such as artificial intelligence, the Internet of Things, digital twins, and cloud computing play a driving role at this level because they provide the ability to observe, predict, and optimize value-creating processes. In fact, this layer is the "perceptual infrastructure" of the ecosystem that collects data from different points and transforms it into usable knowledge. Without this technological platform, synergy and interaction at higher levels are not possible and the value flow in the network is disrupted.

Above this structure is the Organizational Layer, which acts as a space for cooperation, coordination and synergy between different firms, institutions and stakeholders. This layer focuses on the design of value networks, governance models, division of roles and inter-organizational trust. In the Industry 5.0 ecosystem, firms do not engage in pure competition but in co-opetition; meaning that competition and cooperation occur simultaneously on a common platform so that the entire ecosystem benefits from the creation of collective value. At this level, the coordination of data and resources between different actors and the creation of common standards are of particular importance. The higher the level of organizational and communication maturity in this layer, the greater the ecosystem's ability to respond to environmental changes and create sustainable value.

After that, the Human–Cognitive Layer is introduced as the defining dimension of the model. Unlike previous generations of industry, Industry 5.0 emphasizes not only automation but also "human-technology coexistence." At this level, human interaction with machines and algorithms is the main source of idea creation, moral judgment, and cognitive innovation. Humans are no longer simply users of technology; they are designers, interpreters, and complements. Hence, tacit knowledge, practical experience, and human creativity are directly incorporated into decision-making and value creation processes. This layer also includes dimensions of organizational learning, knowledge transfer, and emotional intelligence in interpersonal interactions that give the ecosystem the ability to adapt and be resilient.

Finally, the Sustainability Layer is the most comprehensive level of the model, encompassing all other layers and acting as a sphere of economic, environmental and social alignment. Industry 5.0 seeks to create value-creating systems that ensure not only financial returns but also a balance between economic profit, social responsibility and environmental protection. This layer elevates the concept of value from short-term profitability to long-term well-being and ecosystem sustainability. Technological and organizational decisions will be meaningful and sustainable when they are aligned with indicators of sustainable development, social justice and green productivity.

The relationship between these four layers is explained in the form of a multi-level value stream. Data and signals start from the technological layer and are transformed into shared knowledge and strategies through the organizational layer. They are then interpreted, recreated and enriched in the human-cognitive layer to return to the flow in the form of new ideas and decisions. All these interactions ultimately make sense within the framework of the sustainability layer, because real value in Industry 5.0 is only achieved when economic, social and environmental impacts are balanced.

This integrated structure shows that value-driven ecosystems are not a linear system, but a self-adaptive and reflective network; that is, changes in any layer can change the value flow in the entire structure. For example, innovation in data-driven technologies can transform the organizational collaboration model, or changes in human behavior and organizational culture can affect the efficiency of the technological infrastructure. Therefore, the dynamics between layers are the most important feature of the model, and there is no clear boundary between technology, organization, people and sustainability.

Overall, the proposed framework is an attempt to understand in an integrated way how people, technology and organization coexist in Industry 5.0 ecosystems. This model allows managers and policymakers to identify and assess the path of value flow across different layers and, through alignment between them, increase the capacity for innovation, sustainability, and competitiveness. Figure 1 visually depicts this synergy between layers, demonstrating that value in future ecosystems will emerge not through the dominance of one layer, but through a constant dialogue between them all.

Figure 1. Integrated framework for value network-based ecosystems in Industry 5.0

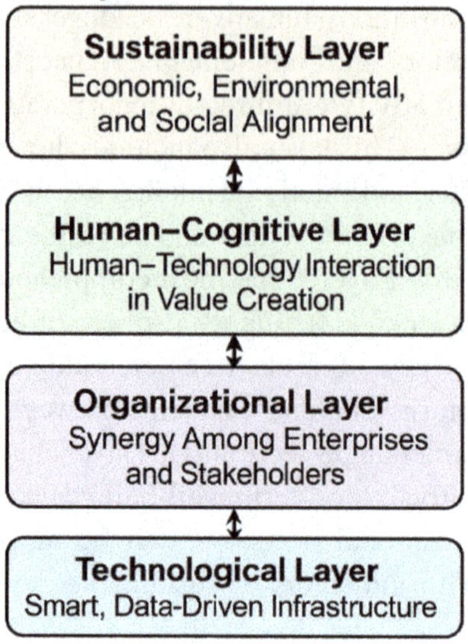

Figure 1 shows the four-layer conceptual structure of Industry 5.0 ecosystems, which are formed by the interaction between smart technologies, synergistic organizations, creative people, and sustainable systems. This framework states that value in future ecosystems will result from the synergy between the technological, organizational, human, and sustainable layers, rather than the independent functioning of each of them.

5- GOVERNANCE AND POLICY DIMENSIONS

In the era of Industry 5.0, the concept of governance has moved away from the linear and bureaucratic structures of the past and towards networked, data-driven and human-centered models. In such an environment, policy and decision-making are not the exclusive domain of governments but rather in the form of multi-stakeholder ecosystems composed of industries, universities, technological institutions and civil society (Slavic et al., 2024). This transformation is the result of a new understanding of value; a value that is no longer limited to economic productivity, but also includes social resilience, environmental responsibility and synergy between humans and technology. Industry 5.0 is therefore considered a civilizational project to recreate the relationship between innovation, ethics and governance, rather than being a purely technological stage.

In this framework, adaptive governance and responsible innovation are two main pillars of policymaking. Rather than imposing top-down control, policies should be interactive and feedback-driven to adapt to rapid technological and social changes. For example, regulations related to artificial intelligence, digital twins, and industrial data should be dynamically reviewed so that they do not constrain innovation on the one hand, and on the other, they should maintain security, ethics, and transparency (Molina, 2024). Such a policy guides technology rather than prohibits it, and strikes a balance between freedom of innovation and risk control.

In Industry 5.0 ecosystems, data plays a vital role as the main source of value creation, and effective governance is not possible without a data-driven system. Data collected from machines, supply chains, and human users must be managed in a transparent, secure, and trust-based environment. For this reason, policymakers must develop new frameworks for data ownership, inter-organizational exchange, and privacy protection (Nozari et al., 2025). These frameworks must allow for technological collaboration without violating individual rights so that the ecosystem can grow harmoniously and ethically.

From a macro-governance perspective, Industry 5.0 requires a "power network configuration" in which decision-making is distributed across sectors. In this model, the government changes its role from being a regulator and regulator to a facilitator of innovation and synergy. The role of governments is not to limit but to support collaboration among different actors; from financing joint projects and creating open data platforms to developing international standards on technological ethics and sustainable production (Nassa et al., 2025). The government must shape policy frameworks that are flexible, transparent, and learning, together with the private sector and academic institutions.

A key feature of Industry 5.0 is governance based on trust and transparency. In such a system, trust is built not through coercion but through data sharing, algorithmic transparency, and shared accountability among stakeholders. In other words, successful governance occurs when all members of the ecosystem feel part of the decision-making and its benefits. This kind of networked trust can be strengthened by tools such as AI ethical auditing, green data certificates, or blockchain-based smart contracts (Nozari et al., 2024).

Alongside these developments, Industry 5.0 policymaking must also take into account international dimensions. New technologies have made national borders meaningless; as a result, policy coordination between countries is crucial to counter the risks of regulatory incoherence. Issues such as cross-border data transfers, AI standardization, and global sustainability indicators require multi-level governance that spans from the local to the global (Ionescu, 2025). Regional cooperation between the EU, Asia, and other regions could establish a new paradigm of "symbiotic policymaking" that combines technological competition with ethical cooperation.

Overall, Industry 5.0 requires a complete redefinition of the roles of government, industry, and society in the innovation process. This transformation means a shift from control governance to enabling governance, where policymaking builds capacity rather than restricts and guides technology towards the creation of human value. The future of governance in this industry depends on the ability of policymakers to integrate three key dimensions: technology ethics, data transparency, and human participation. If these three axes are properly aligned, Industry 5.0 will not only increase industrial productivity, but also be a factor in the formation of a smart, sustainable, and human-centered civilization.

6- MANAGERIAL AND STRATEGIC IMPLICATIONS

In the context of Industry 5.0, the role of managers has changed from being process controllers to designers and coordinators of value networks. Organizations no longer operate in a vacuum, but are part of a broader ecosystem of customers, suppliers, technology partners, and knowledge institutions. In such an environment, value is not created within the boundaries of an organization, but in the interaction and synergy between different actors. Therefore, Industry 5.0 managers must have the ability to create, guide, and maintain value networks across interconnected organizations.

Value Network implementation strategies in Industry 5.0 organizations require a rethinking of traditional business models and the design of mechanisms for value co-creation. These strategies usually begin with creating an "open architecture" in the organization's structure; meaning that data, knowledge, and innovation must flow transparently between internal departments and external partners. For example, companies that use digital twins to connect manufacturing processes and supply chains are able to make more coordinated decisions and improve the quality of their products through real-time data exchange. This type of synergy not only increases productivity but also strengthens the organization's resilience to market fluctuations.

In such a framework, knowledge and data management play a vital role in value co-creation. The data generated in industrial processes must not only be stored and analyzed, but also transformed into "decision-making knowledge." Industry 5.0 managers must create systems for the circulation of knowledge that allow employees and different units to access the information they need in real time and use it for evidence-based decision-making. Also, combining human data (such as feedback, experience, and creativity) with machine data (sensors, IoT, or AI) creates multi-layered insights that help improve performance and predict trends.

Another key dimension in managing Industry 5.0 value networks is open innovation. In the past, innovation mostly occurred within organizational boundaries; now, the most successful companies are those that collaborate with external actors (from startups and universities to user communities) to create value. These collaborations allow organizations to benefit from diverse ideas, shorten product development cycles, and be more flexible in responding to technological and market changes. Implementing open innovation requires creating a culture of trust, transparency, and shared benefits so that knowledge and data can be exchanged between parties with minimal friction.

At the decision-making level, Industry 5.0 organizations require adaptive and learning decision-making models. These models adjust decision-making not linearly, but based on continuous feedback from data, the environment, and user behavior. Managers should use advanced analytical tools, machine learning systems, and dynamic simulation models to be able to predict different scenarios and choose the appropriate response. Such a model allows the organization to learn from mistakes, update strategies, and remain resilient to market uncertainties.

In the meantime, the role of learning and agile leadership is also very prominent. Industry 5.0 managers must have an adaptive mindset and see their employees as intellectual collaborators in the decision-making process, not just as executors of orders. This type of leadership focuses on creating a culture of collaboration, continuous learning, and mutual trust. Successful leaders, by combining technological intelligence with human intelligence, create an environment where innovation occurs naturally and spontaneously.

The managerial implications of these developments for manufacturing, service, and technology companies are significant. In manufacturing companies, the focus has shifted from mere productivity to flexibility, sustainability, and customized production. These companies must optimize their processes in real time using digital twins, smart sensors, and deep learning algorithms. In service industries, value is created through customer experience and data-driven services, where personalization and rapid response to customer needs are key to competitiveness. In technology companies, the focus on designing open platforms and creating collaborative ecosystems between users and developers has become a key driver of growth.

From a strategic perspective, Industry 5.0 organizations must balance three axes: technological efficiency, human creativity, and social sustainability. Managers who can simultaneously institutionalize these three dimensions in their decision-making structure will be able to build flexible, innovative, and value-driven organizations. In other words, strategy in the era of Industry 5.0 no longer means following a fixed plan, but rather "the ability to intelligently adapt to the future."

Ultimately, the successful implementation of value networks in Industry 5.0 requires alignment between technology, people, and the organization. Managers must learn that true value lies not in owning technology, but in the ability to use it creatively to improve human and societal lives. Such a view elevates management from the art of control to the art of collaboration, learning, and co-creation of value. This is the true essence of Industry 5.0.

7- CONCLUSION

The transition from Industry 4.0 to Industry 5.0 is not just a technological change, but also a transformation in the logic of value creation, governance structures, and the role of humans in the industrial system. Focusing on the concept of value networks and ecosystem innovation, this research showed that the future of industries is not shaped by complete automation, but by intelligent interaction between technology, organization, and humans. Industry 5.0, with a human-centered, sustainable, and resilient approach, seeks to create a model of production and services in which value is created collectively and inter-organizationally.

The results of this chapter showed that value networks are the fundamental infrastructure for the formation of innovation ecosystems in Industry 5.0. Unlike traditional value chains, whose flow was linear and centralized, value networks rely on interaction, synergy, and resource sharing among different actors. This structure provides a context for multifaceted value creation in which technological innovation, human knowledge, and social responsibility operate simultaneously.

In the theoretical foundations section, it was explained that value networks are in fact dynamic and self-organizing structures that create new value from the combination of tangible and intangible resources (such as data, knowledge, trust, and experience). In the Industry 5.0 ecosystem, these resources are strengthened in the interaction between humans and technology, leading to the creation of a culture of collective learning and continuous innovation. Meanwhile, the integrated conceptual framework presented in this research shows that four key layers (technological, organizational, human-cognitive, and sustainability) are interconnected in a network and value is produced in the dynamic flow between these layers.

On the other hand, the analysis of the governance and policy dimensions revealed that there is a need for a kind of multilevel and adaptive governance to realize Industry 5.0. This system must be able to balance freedom of innovation and ethical control, while keeping pace with the pace of technological change. Governments and regulators must move away from linear models of regulation and toward networked, data-driven, and collaborative models. In such an environment, policymakers will be not only regulators but also facilitators of value co-creation a role on which the future of industry and technology depends.

At the managerial level, Industry 5.0 also requires leaders to move from mere control and competition to collaboration, trust, and adaptive decision-making. Managers must learn how to turn data into insight, technology into empowerment, and collaboration into sustainable innovation. Among these, knowledge management, open innovation, and learning decision-making are three key axes that enable organizations to operate effectively in complex, dynamic, and uncertain environments.

In general, Industry 5.0 represents the convergence of three fundamental dimensions: technological intelligence, human wisdom, and social responsibility. The future of industry and the global economy depends on our ability to integrate these three dimensions into value-driven ecosystems. Thus, value is no longer limited to a product or service, but rather to processes of knowledge sharing, human-machine collaboration, and adherence to ethical and environmental principles.

Finally, we can conclude that Industry 5.0 is an invitation to rethink the meaning of innovation and progress; an invitation to build a world in which technology does not replace humans, but rather assists and enhances them. In such a world, value networks will not only be the engine of the economy, but also the pillars of sustainability, justice, and human development. This vision is the fundamental orientation that distinguishes Industry 5.0 from the past and connects it to a human-centered and value-driven future.

REFERENCES

Adel, A. (2022). Future of industry 5.0 in society: Human-centric solutions, challenges and prospective research areas. *J Cloud Comp*, *11*, 40. DOI: 10.1186/s13677-022-00314-5

Babkin, A., Shkarupeta, E., Mamrayeva, D., Tashenova, L., Umarov, A., & Karimov, D. (2025). A Structural-Functional Model for Managing Digital Maturity in a Cluster-Based, Innovation-Active Industrial Ecosystem within Industry 5.0. *Int. J. Technol*, *16*, 1209–1219.

Corsaro, D., Ramos, C., Henneberg, S. C., & Naudé, P. (2012). The impact of network configurations on value constellations in business markets—The case of an innovation network. *Industrial Marketing Management*, *41*(1), 54–67.

Ghobakhloo, M., Iranmanesh, M., Tseng, M. L., Grybauskas, A., Stefanini, A., & Amran, A. (2023). Behind the definition of Industry 5.0: A systematic review of technologies, principles, components, and values. *Journal of Industrial and Production Engineering*, *40*(6), 432–447. DOI: 10.1080/21681015.2023.2216701

Li, J., Sun, B., & Yu, B. (2024). Suitable innovation in Industry 5.0: The moderating mechanism of innovation transmission types in innovation ecosystem. *IEEE Transactions on Engineering Management*, *71*, 6031–6043.

Molina, R. I. R., Ruiz, M. J. S., Molina, R. J. R., Raby, N. D. L., & Severino-González, P. (2024). Innovation systems in industry 5.0: Theoretical and methodological bases. *Procedia Computer Science*, *231*, 595–600.

Nozari, H., Abdi, H., Szmelter-Jarosz, A., & Rahmaty, M. (2025). A digital twin-based neutrosophic multi-objective optimization model for smart supply chains in the food industry. *Journal of Intelligent Manufacturing*, •••, 1–15.

Nozari, H., Ghahremani-Nahr, J., & Szmelter-Jarosz, A. (2024). AI and machine learning for real-world problems. [). Elsevier.]. *Advances in Computers*, *134*, 1–12.

Nozari, H., Szmelter-Jarosz, A., & Weiland, D. (2025). A Fuzzy Multi-Objective Sustainable and Agile Supply Chain Model Based on Digital Twin and Internet of Things with Adaptive Learning Under Environmental Uncertainty. *Applied Sciences (Basel, Switzerland)*, *15*(19), 10399.

Nozari, H. (2025). Integrating Neuromorphic Intelligence with Fuzzy Multi-Objective Models in Resilient Green Supply Chain Design. Process Integration and Optimization for Sustainability, 1-14.

Slavic, D., Marjanovic, U., Medic, N., Simeunovic, N., & Rakic, S. (2024). The evaluation of Industry 5.0 concepts: Social network analysis approach. *Applied Sciences (Basel, Switzerland)*, *14*(3), 1291.

Verna Allee. (2008, January 18). Value network analysis and value conversion of tangible and intangible assets. *Journal of Intellectual Capital*, *9*(1), 5–24. DOI: 10.1108/14691930810845777

Voropai, O., & Antoniouk, O. (2025). Innovation Ecosystem Models: Defining the Role of the University in the Industry 5.0 Perspective. *Humanities and Social Sciences*, *32*(1), 143–152.

Chapter 2
Neuromorphic Computing and Cognitive Economics

Hamed Nozari
https://orcid.org/0000-0002-6500-6708
Azad University of the Emirates, Dubai, UAE

ABSTRACT

This research introduces a new framework called "Neuromorphic-Cognitive Economics," which combines the principles of brain-inspired computing with the foundations of cognitive economics. The proposed model simulates the economic decision-making process in a dynamic, adaptive, and self-learning manner using spiking neural networks, memristive memory, and reinforcement learning. The simulation results show that economic agents can learn, adapt, and reproduce complex behaviors such as skepticism, trust, and risk-taking, just like biological neurons. This model opens up new horizons for designing smart, self-organizing economies.

1- INTRODUCTION

In recent decades, the emergence of brain-inspired computing has created new approaches to understanding and recreating human cognitive processes in economic decision-making. While classical economics was based on the assumption of perfect rationality and rational behavior, cognitive economics attempted to incorporate human mental, emotional, and perceptual dimensions into economic models. However, the complexity of human neural and cognitive processes has made traditional models unable to accurately reflect the dynamics of real decision-making. In the meantime, neuromorphic computing, as an emerging approach in intelligent systems

DOI: 10.4018/979-8-3693-4525-2.ch002

engineering, has enabled the biological structures of the brain, including neurons, synapses, and spiking dynamics, to be reproduced at the hardware and algorithmic levels (Ye et al., 2025).

Neuromorphic computing not only aims to model the human brain, but also is an attempt to create systems that can operate like the brain, simultaneously, in parallel, and adaptively with the environment. These features are particularly valuable in the field of cognitive economics, as real-world economic decisions are the result of complex interactions between memory, learning, risk perception, and cognitive constraints. In this regard, the use of neuromorphic architectures can lead to the creation of models that not only better simulate human behavior, but also have the ability to learn and dynamically adapt in unstable economic environments (Smolka et al., 2024).

Cognitive economics seeks to understand how people make decisions under conditions of uncertainty, time pressure, and lack of information. In this view, humans are limited in terms of cognitive capacity who use approximate and intuitive strategies in their decisions. On the other hand, neuromorphic computing, by imitating these limited but efficient mechanisms, provides a platform for economic models to operate not only based on numerical calculations but also on neural dynamics. In other words, in such a model, "economic rationality" gives way to "neural rationality"; Rationality that makes decisions not based on abstract formulas, but on experience, learning, and neural patterns formed over time (Nozari et al., 2024).

One reason for the importance of combining these two fields is the growing need for models that can analyze the behavior of markets, consumers, and investors in complex and nonlinear situations. In the real world, decisions are always made in a context of emotions, trust, expectations, and social interactions; factors that cannot be quantified in traditional models. But using a neuromorphic approach, decision-making processes can be reconstructed as a network of interacting neurons, in which synaptic dynamics reflect changes in trust, motivation, or subjective value. This approach can help develop cognitive economics at a completely new level; a level in which the unit of analysis is not a hypothetical rational human, but a computational neural system that performs decision-making like the brain (Nozari et al., 2025).

From a philosophical and interdisciplinary perspective, the convergence of neuromorphic computing and cognitive economics reflects a deeper movement in contemporary science: an attempt to understand the economy as a living, dynamic entity, not as a mechanical machine. Just as the human brain is constantly adapting to environmental changes, the economy is a network of actors, information, and motivations that is constantly learning and adjusting itself. From this perspective, markets can be thought of as neural networks that reach new equilibrium through behavioral feedback, price signals, and reward mechanisms. Thus, the use of neuromorphic computing is not just a technical tool but a scientific metaphor for redefining the nature of the economy; one defined by cognitive dynamism and intelligent adaptation rather than linear prediction.

In practical terms, this link can lead to the design of intelligent decision-support systems in the fields of policy-making, investment, and risk management. For example, by using spiking networks in the analysis of financial market behavior, it is possible to simulate neural responses to sudden changes in supply and demand and create more robust forecasting models. At a larger level, neuromorphic-based economics can help to better understand collective behavior in markets, the emergence of price bubbles, and mass reactions to economic shocks. This capability is doubly important, especially in the era of big data and cognitive artificial intelligence; because modern economic systems are faced with more complex information flows and unpredictable decisions than ever before (Vineyard et al., 2024).

Ultimately, the goal of this chapter is to create a theoretical and computational framework that can redefine the foundations of cognitive economics while simultaneously utilizing neuromorphic principles. This framework aims to show how neural learning mechanisms, adaptive memory, and event-driven processing can be used to model economic behavior. This combination is expected to lead to the emergence of "neurocognitive economics" in the future, a system in which decision-making, adaptation, and learning are based not on pure mathematical rules but on simulated cognitive processes. In this way, the boundary between mind and market is disappearing, and the economy of the future will resemble the human brain more than ever before.

2- THEORETICAL BACKGROUND

The theoretical foundation of this chapter is based on two complementary axes: neuromorphic computing as a brain-inspired architecture for intelligent information processing, and cognitive economics as a framework for analyzing human decision-making based on mental, perceptual processes, and cognitive constraints. Both fields, despite their apparent differences, pursue a common goal: understanding and modeling decision-making under uncertainty, adaptation, and learning. On the one hand, neuromorphic seeks to imitate biological neural networks in the form of hardware and algorithmic systems, and on the other hand, cognitive economics seeks to explain human economic behavior based on cognition, memory, and emotion.

Neuromorphic computing emerged from the limitations of classical computer architecture. The von Neumann architecture, which has been the foundation of digital computing for decades, has suffered from a transmission bottleneck due to the separation between memory and processor. In contrast, neuromorphic architecture, inspired by the human brain, integrates processing and storage into a single, dynamic platform. In this structure, signals are exchanged in the form of spikes or short electrical pulses, which is similar to the behavior of biological neurons. This type of processing, in addition to reducing energy consumption, allows for adaptive learning and interaction with the environment (Jaeger, 2020). As a result, neuromorphic systems can not only make decisions independently but also understand environmental patterns without explicit programming.

In this regard, cognitive economics was also proposed as a reaction to classical economic models that assumed humans to be completely rational decision-makers with complete information. Cognitive economics believes that humans use heuristics, mental biases, and past experiences in the decision-making process. In other words, economic decisions are not the result of precise mathematical calculations but rather the result of the interaction between memory, perception, emotion, and mental predictions. In the meantime, the neuromorphic structure provides a natural platform for recreating such decisions; Because in this architecture, information is encoded not in an algebraic manner but in the form of continuous excitations and synaptic changes (Nozari et al., 2025).

One of the fundamental concepts in the integration of these two fields is the concept of "simultaneous learning". The human brain, relying on synapses, regulates the connections between neurons based on past experiences. This is the same principle of Hebbian learning that is also implemented in neuromorphic systems. In cognitive economics, the human agent also modifies his behavior based on experience, feedback, and rewards. As a result, any economic decision can be considered as the output of a neural learning process in which synaptic weights are equivalent to the individual's subjective preferences and values. Such a view interprets the economy not as a system of equations but as a dynamic network of cognitive interactions.

In addition, neuromorphic architecture has the ability to model nonlinear and adaptive behaviors, features that play a central role in real human decision-making. For example, a sudden change in the price of a commodity or the occurrence of a financial crisis leads to complex emotional and cognitive reactions that cannot be predicted by classical models. However, in neuromorphic models, such reactions can be reflected in the form of changes in the intensity of spikes or the adjustment of synaptic dynamics. This process creates a kind of "artificial cognitive flexibility" that allows the system to display human-like behaviors in the face of economic shocks (Smith et al., 2022). On the other hand, cognitive economics, by introducing concepts such as "cognitive load", "adaptive learning" and "mental reward", provides a platform for analyzing economic phenomena from the perspective of psychology and neuroscience. In this field, the economic value of a decision is not limited to its financial outcome, but also involves the degree of subjective satisfaction, trust or sense of justice. Such phenomena can be modeled at the neuromorphic level by changing the firing rate of neurons or the synchronous intensity of network activity.

Thus, cognitive economics and neuromorphic computing naturally converge at a point: the point where both human and machine minds make decisions based on neural dynamics.

This convergence has important implications for understanding future economies. Digital economies in the age of artificial intelligence no longer rely on static data and mere statistical analysis; they require systems that can dynamically identify and process patterns of behavior, trust, and social interaction. In this context, neuromorphic computing can serve as the hardware and cognitive infrastructure for creating "neuroeconomic agents" that not only analyze data but also, like humans, learn from experience and modify their strategies (Nozari et al., 2025).

At the theoretical level, the combination of these two approaches leads to the emergence of a new paradigm that can be called "neuromorphic economics." In this paradigm, economic phenomena are represented in the form of complex networks of decision-making neurons, rather than linear variables. The dynamics of these networks reflect market changes, consumer preferences, and social interactions. Such an approach not only allows for more accurate prediction of market behavior but can also lead to the development of self-organizing economic systems; systems that, like the brain, are able to maintain their equilibrium through cognitive and adaptive feedback (Raikar et al., 2024).

In summary, the theoretical basis for the link between neuromorphic computing and cognitive economics lies in a deeper understanding of the human decision-making process. By combining neural models, adaptive learning principles, and cognitive frameworks, we can envision an economy that not only simulates human behavior but also has the ability to understand and predict the hidden motivations behind every decision. Such a model paves the way for the design of a new generation of economic systems in which the boundary between human rationality and machine computation is gradually erased, and the economy becomes a cognitive, living structure.

3- CONCEPTUAL FRAMEWORK: THE NEUROMORPHIC-COGNITIVE ECONOMY MODEL

The conceptual framework of "neuromorphic-cognitive economics" is an attempt to redefine the foundations of economic decision-making from the computational to the cognitive level, in such a way that the mechanisms of the human brain are recreated in the form of a computational system. This framework sees the economy not as a set of static equations and equilibria, but as a dynamic network of neural, perceptual, and adaptive processes in which economic agents, like neurons, are in constant interaction. Every economic decision is the result of a momentary balance between perception, cognition, motivation, and environmental feedback. In this view, markets, like the brain, have a distributed structure formed by thousands of synaptic connections between actors, and decision-making is not done centrally, but throughout the network (Rajendran & Alibart, 2016).

Figure 1 shows the conceptual framework of the neuromorphic-cognitive economics model. The framework consists of four main layers: Perception, Cognitive Processing, Decision Encoding, and Adaptive Economy. These four layers are modeled after the neural structure of the brain and interact with each other in a recursive manner. Information enters through the perception layer, is processed and filtered in the cognitive layer, then encoded into economic decisions, and finally absorbs environmental feedback through adaptive mechanisms. This creates a closed, self-learning loop that allows the system to learn, adapt, and optimize like a living organism (Tsur, 2021).

In the perception layer, economic data is modeled as neural signals. This data can include prices, supply, demand, market sentiment, or even non-quantitative information such as trust or collective anxiety. This stage acts like the sensory cortex of the brain, which collects raw information from the environment. In neuromorphic architecture, this stage is implemented by spiking networks, where each spike is equivalent to an economic event. The intensity and frequency of the spikes represent the importance and urgency of that event. This data is then passed to the cognitive layer to be interpreted in the form of mental models.

In the cognitive processing layer, the input data is analyzed based on memory, experience, and adaptive learning rules. At this stage, the concept of "cognitive load" and "mental reward" is introduced into the model. The system, like humans, weights different options, forms biases, and constructs mental probabilities for outcomes. In the neuromorphic framework, this process is done by regulating synapses; that is, just as the brain learns by strengthening or weakening neural connections, the system also reaches a new cognitive equilibrium by increasing or decreasing synaptic weights over time. This is the heart of the model, showing how the economy can learn and correct itself cognitively.

The third part is decision encoding. In this stage, cognitive output is translated into actionable decisions. Just as the brain translates the output of neural activity into physical action, the neuromorphic-cognitive system translates cognitive analysis into economic choices, such as making purchases, investing, or changing consumption patterns. Decisions are encoded in the form of neural pulses, the intensity and frequency of which indicate the level of economic confidence, motivation, or fear. This introduces the concept of a "cognitive utility function" a function defined not in terms of absolute profit, but in terms of subjective satisfaction and psychological adaptation. This part can be used to model the behavior of complex markets, such as stock fluctuations or reactions to macro policies.

The fourth layer is economic adaptation, which acts as a feedback loop. At this stage, the results of decisions are fed back into the system to modify the synaptic weights and learning rules. If a decision leads to a positive reward or outcome, the associated neural connections are strengthened; otherwise, they are weakened. This mechanism is the equivalent of reinforcement learning in neural networks but operates at the economic level. In other words, the system learns from the results of its decisions and adjusts future behavior according to past experiences. This learning cycle allows the model to constantly evolve and perform optimally in dynamic environments.

A key aspect of this framework is the concept of the "synaptic map of the economy." This map represents the pattern of communication between economic agents in cognitive space. Each node in this network corresponds to an economic agent, and each synaptic connection represents the flow of information, trust, or reward between them. The dynamics of this network cause small changes in behavior or information to cascade throughout the system; Just like how signals propagate in the brain, the economy, in this framework, is considered a self-organizing cognitive organism capable of collective learning.

Figure 1. Conceptual framework of the neuromorphic-cognitive economic model

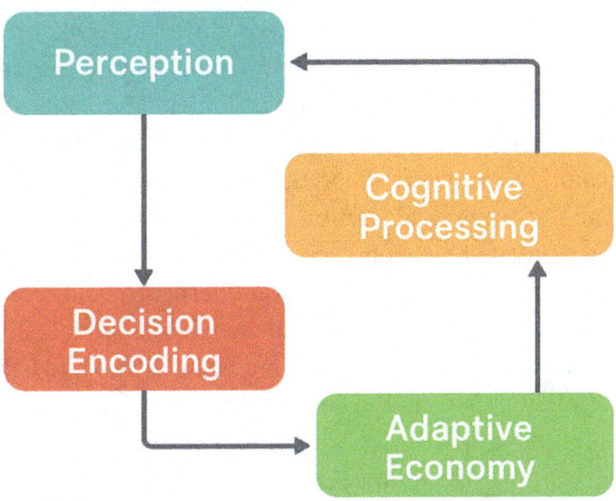

Economic input data enters from the left, is processed in the center by the cognitive layer, and is converted into economic decisions on the right. Feedback flows back from the bottom up to complete the learning process. At each point in the network, spiking signals flow, representing the transfer of knowledge, rewards, and experience.

The application of this model is wide-ranging in various economic areas. From analyzing consumer behavior and building trust in online markets to investor decision-making in critical situations, the neuromorphic-cognitive framework can be used as a basis for designing intelligent forecasting and control systems. It also paves the way for combining neuromorphic computing with cognitive artificial intelligence, reinforcement learning, and even quantum models. In such a horizon, the future economy is not simply a set of indicators and mathematical relationships, but a living, learning system that, like the human brain, is capable of perceiving, making decisions, and adapting to environmental changes.

Overall, the conceptual framework of neuromorphic-cognitive economics suggests that economic understanding can move beyond the level of data analysis to the level of computational consciousness. This development paves the way for a convergence between neuroscience, economics, and AI engineering that could lead to a generation of economic systems that think, learn, and adapt in much the same way that the human brain does.

4- COMPUTATIONAL MODELING AND SYSTEM DESIGN

The computational modeling and system design section of the neuromorphic-cognitive economics framework aims to reproduce the dynamics of economic decision-making based on neural principles and brain-inspired architectures. In this model, economic agents are represented not as logical and computational entities, but as decision-making neurons in a dynamic and learning network. The aim of this section is to explain how previous theoretical concepts such as perception, cognitive processing, and economic adaptation can be transformed into computational structures that can simulate real economic behavior. In such a model, the economic decision-making process is recreated based on interneuronal interactions, synaptic regulation, and subjective rewards (Tathavadekar & Mahankale, 2025).

At the computational level, each economic agent is modeled as a neural node that receives multiple inputs from the environment. These inputs can include price signals, market sentiment, trust indicators, or even cognitive patterns such as risk appetite or social learning. Each input is transmitted to the decision neuron in the form of a spiking signal (a short electrical pulse), and its intensity or frequency indicates the importance of that variable. The output of each neuron indicates the corresponding economic action, such as buying, investing, or postponing a decision. This structure is implemented using spiking neural networks and memristor-based memory models that allow for dynamic storage and learning (Li et al., 2019).

In the next step, the relationships between these neurons are defined through synaptic weights. The weight of each connection indicates the degree of influence of one factor on another; for example, in market conditions, an increase in public confidence can have a reinforcing effect on purchasing behavior. Learning in this model is carried out through reward and punishment algorithms. If the output of the network leads to a desirable economic outcome (such as increased profits or cognitive satisfaction), synaptic connections are strengthened; Otherwise, they are weakened. This process is similar to Hebbian learning in the human brain, in which the simultaneous stimulation of two neurons strengthens their connection.

The proposed model consists of two main subsystems: the perception subsystem and the decision-making subsystem. The perception subsystem includes layers for receiving environmental data and filtering noise, while the decision-making subsystem is responsible for generating economic choices in the form of logical outputs by relying on short-term and long-term memory. These subsystems operate in a feedback manner; meaning that the result of each decision is recorded again as a new input in the system to modify future behaviors. In this way, a self-learning system is created that is able to readjust its decision-making strategies in the face of environmental changes.

To better understand the main components of the model, Table 1 shows the key components of the neuromorphic-cognitive system.

Table 1. Key components of the computational model of neuromorphic-cognitive economics

System Component	Functional Description	Modeling Level	Input Data Type	Generated Output
Perception Layer	Receives economic, psychological, and social data from the environment and converts them into processable signals	Artificial sensory neurons	Prices, market sentiments, trust indices	Spiking signals (encoded neural pulses)
Cognitive Processing	Analyzes data, performs adaptive learning, and updates synaptic weights based on rewards and experience	Spiking networks and memristive memory	Filtered perceptual signals	Cognitive decision-making patterns
Decision Encoding	Translates cognitive outputs into real economic actions	Neural decision units	Weighted vectors produced by cognitive processing	Economic actions such as purchase, investment, or decision postponement
Adaptive Economy	Evaluates decision outcomes, learns from environmental feedback, and adjusts synaptic weights	Reinforcement feedback loop	Data from decision outcomes and environmental rewards	Adjusted learning parameters and improved system performance

As the table shows, the designed system uses multi-source inputs and recreates the decision-making process in several neural stages. The perception layer converts raw data into encoded signals. The cognitive layer then interprets and weights these data into decision patterns. Finally, the results are converted into real economic actions through the decision encoding layer, and the economic adaptation layer is responsible for modifying the network based on feedback.

From a system design perspective, the model operates based on an event-driven architecture; meaning that the system is activated only when a change occurs or a new input is received. This feature saves energy and increases computational efficiency, similar to how the human brain works, which only works in response to stimuli. For the practical implementation of this architecture, existing neuromorphic platforms such as Intel Loihi or SpiNNaker can be used. These chips allow for the parallel execution of thousands of artificial neurons with low power consumption and are well suited for modeling dynamic economic behavior.

At the algorithmic level, unsupervised and reinforcement learning methods are used. In unsupervised learning, the system discovers hidden patterns in the data without having the correct answer, while in reinforcement learning, decisions are gradually modified based on environmental rewards. The combination of these two methods allows the model to both learn from past experiences and create new behavior as conditions change. This type of learning leads to the formation of a "dynamic cognitive utility function" that adapts to the economic and psychological state of the environment at any given moment (Nozari, 2026).

In the mathematical dimension, the system can be expressed as a set of nonlinear differential equations that describe the firing rates of neurons and the changes in synaptic weights. These equations represent the collective behavior of neurons at a macro level in the form of dynamic fluctuations. Analysis of these fluctuations can be used to predict market behavior, identify patterns of instability, and assess the impact of economic policies.

The result is that the neuromorphic-cognitive computational model is a step towards a more realistic representation of human economic behavior. This model is able to combine emotional, experiential, and cognitive elements alongside objective economic data and make adaptive and intelligent decisions through neural learning. By expanding this framework, we can move towards designing "artificial neural economies" that not only process data but also learn, feel, and adapt to environmental changes like the brain.

5- SIMULATION AND CASE ILLUSTRATION

To practically evaluate the neuromorphic-cognitive economic model and measure its effectiveness in representing human decision-making behaviors, a computational simulation was designed to show the interaction between perception, cognition, and adaptation in the form of a dynamic economic system. The purpose of this simulation was to investigate how economic agents learn, adapt, and react in the face of environmental and information changes. The proposed model was implemented based on the architecture of spiking neural networks and memristive systems to use the biological properties of the brain in processing sequential signals and memory dependence (Nozari, 2025).

In this simulation, a set of economic agents were placed in an artificial environment whose main variables included commodity prices, demand, public confidence, and the intensity of market fluctuations. Each economic agent acted as a decision-making neuron that received input signals from the environment and responded to them based on its synaptic weights. Inputs were fed into the system in the form of spike pulses of different intensities to perceive the level of importance of information. Agents could modify their preferences based on past experiences and adopt new strategies for interacting with the environment. Thus, the decision-making process was formed not only based on instantaneous data, but also relying on memory and previous feedback (Murthy & Mehra, 2021).

To implement the model, the simulation environment was designed in three time stages: the initial learning stage, the response to fluctuation stage, and the long-term adaptation stage. In the first stage, economic agents made random decisions without prior knowledge of the environment, and the system adjusted synaptic weights through reward or punishment feedback. In the second stage, an artificial shock was introduced into the market, such as a sudden increase in price or a decrease in consumer confidence. This shock caused an immediate change in the network behavior, as the decision-making neurons automatically changed their firing pattern. In the third stage, the system gradually reached a new equilibrium in which the behavior of the agents had adapted to the new market conditions.

Simulation results showed that the neuromorphic-cognitive model is able to reproduce adaptive decision-making patterns without the need for predefined rules. One of the outstanding features of the model was that economic agents learned over time to balance immediate and long-term rewards, a behavior that is difficult to represent in classical economic models. It was also observed that when faced with noisy data or incomplete information, the system naturally uses a cognitive filtering mechanism and processes only important stimuli. This phenomenon is similar to the brain's function in eliminating irrelevant data and indicates the system's inherent ability to manage complexity and reduce cognitive load (Nozari et al., 2025).

To better understand the dynamics of the system, the behavior of a specific scenario was analyzed as a "case study." In this scenario, 100 economic agents operated in a simulated market with five types of goods. Environmental parameters, including the rate of price change, the level of trust, and consumer psychological fluctuations, varied randomly but within specified intervals. Over 5,000 time steps, the model showed that the synaptic connections between agents were organized into a self-organizing network. Initially, the system had a scattered and unstable behavior, but after about 1,500 steps, stable patterns of coordination and synchrony in decisions were formed. These patterns represented a kind of "collective learning" among economic agents, achieved through mutual feedback and synaptic strengthening.

From a quantitative perspective, the analysis of neuronal firing rates showed that the intensity of neural activity increased significantly during economic shocks and then returned to a new equilibrium level over time. This behavior closely resembles the oscillatory patterns observed in real financial market data, where initial emotional reactions are gradually replaced by cognitive adaptation. Also, comparing the performance of the neuromorphic model with a conventional model based on deep neural networks showed that the proposed model performs better not only in convergence speed but also in decision stability and resilience to uncertain data. This advantage is due to its event-driven structure and synaptic dynamics, which cause the system to be activated only when a change occurs (Zheng, 2023).

Conceptually, the simulations performed showed that neuromorphic-cognitive economics is able to reflect complex human behaviors such as hesitation, regret, and long-term preference. In parts of the simulation, some agents showed less willingness to accept risk after experiencing unsuccessful decisions, while others, learning from positive feedback, became more inclined to bold behaviors. This behavioral diversity made the entire economic network more resilient to environmental fluctuations, as the presence of agents with different tendencies reduced the co-oscillation of behaviors.

Another interesting point was that on a macro scale, the simulated market behavior reached a kind of collective self-regulation. This phenomenon, which can be called "economic synchrony," is similar to the coordinated fluctuations in biological neural networks. With the increase in synaptic connections between agents, the overall market pattern automatically moved towards a new equilibrium in which the average decision rate, price volatility, and trust level reached relative stability. Such a phenomenon shows that economic systems can reach equilibrium through cognitive mechanisms and collective learning, without the need for central control.

In conclusion, the simulation and case study showed that the neuromorphic-cognitive approach has a high ability to represent economic processes not only from a theoretical but also from a practical perspective. This model bridges computational neuroscience and cognitive economics, leading to the design of systems that can recreate human decision-making in dynamic, uncertain, and multidimensional situations. In the future, this framework could be used to analyze phenomena such as trust formation in virtual markets, collective reactions to news, and even the design of self-organizing economic policies. Thus, neuromorphic-cognitive economics is proposed as a new generation of adaptive decision-making models that establish a real link between the human mind and machine logic.

6- DISCUSSION

The results obtained show that the integration of neuromorphic computing principles with the foundations of cognitive economics is not only a conceptual innovation in economics, but also provides a new framework for understanding human behavior in dynamic and multi-layered environments. Unlike classical approaches that consider decision-making to be a function of linear computation and explicit optimization, this model shows that cognitive and neural processes affect economic decision-making at a deeper and more dynamic level. Humans are not computational machines, but rather adaptive and learning systems that rewrite their decision-making rules in continuous interaction with the environment.

In this framework, simulation findings showed that the behavior of economic agents can be dynamically shaped from the bottom up; that is, individual decisions, as a result of synaptic interactions between agents, become macro-behavioral patterns. This phenomenon depicts a kind of collective emergence at the economic level, in which market stability or volatility arises not due to central control, but rather through cognitive learning and feedback mechanisms. Such an approach could be an answer to one of the important gaps in behavioral economics, namely how micro-behavior is translated into macro-phenomena. In the neuromorphic model, this translation is realized through synaptic dynamics and synchrony in decision-making networks; just as in the brain, coordination between neurons leads to the emergence of complex cognitive behaviors.

From a theoretical perspective, this research redefines the boundary between neuroscience and economics in such a way that economics is no longer considered simply a science of resource allocation, but also a science of collective perception, decision, and learning. This paradigm shift makes it possible to understand economic processes from a biological and cognitive perspective. For example, the concept of "cognitive utility" in this model replaces the traditional utility function; So that decision-making is no longer based solely on profit maximization, but on subjective satisfaction, a sense of control, or the reduction of cognitive uncertainty. Such an approach can explain why in many real-world cases, humans make decisions that seem irrational from the perspective of economic rationality, but are completely consistent and optimal from a mental and neurological perspective.

On the other hand, this model helps to better understand nonlinear and adaptive behaviors in economic systems. In many classical models, market dynamics are considered linear and predictable, while in reality, human decision-making is influenced by memory, emotion, and social interactions. The neuromorphic-cognitive model allows these complexities to be reproduced naturally in a computational framework. The behavior of agents in this model is not fixed, but depends on the history of previous decisions and experiences; Just like learning in biological neural networks, synaptic connections are rearranged with each new experience. This can be used to analyze phenomena such as trust formation in digital markets, unexpected price fluctuations, or even group behavior in social networks.

From a comparative perspective, the proposed model has advantages over classical neural networks or deep learning models. In neuromorphic systems, processing is event-driven, meaning that the system is activated only when receiving new stimuli. In addition to saving computational energy, this feature is also consistent with the reality of human cognitive behavior; the brain is activated only during meaningful stimuli and remains relatively quiescent in the rest of the time. This allows the model to handle uncertain and noisy data without losing efficiency. In the simulation, this feature was clearly observed, as the system was able to filter out irrelevant stimuli and focus only on key information.

On a larger scale, the results of this research imply the possibility of designing "artificial cognitive economies"; systems in which intelligent economic agents can learn, adapt, and modify their relationships like living organisms. Such systems could in the future be used to manage financial markets, set dynamic policies, or predict consumer behavior. Also, in the context of explainable AI, the neuromorphic-cognitive model can provide a framework for explaining why decisions are made, because in this system, the decision-making process is not followed inside a "black box," but through transparent cognitive and neural pathways.

Another discussion concerns the nature of collective learning in this model. It was observed that economic agents, in continuous interaction with each other, achieve a kind of group adaptation that is very similar to collective behavior in neural networks of the brain. This behavior creates a kind of "economic synchrony" that can explain macro phenomena such as relative market stability or sudden crises. In fact, just as excessive coordination of neurons can lead to the emergence of neural abnormalities, excessive coordination of economic agents may also cause severe fluctuations in the market. Therefore, the proposed model can be a tool for identifying critical levels of synchrony and designing policies to maintain the stability of the system.

Finally, it should be noted that the neuromorphic-cognitive model does not replace traditional models, but complements them. The goal of this research is to present a perspective that can introduce deeper layers of human behavior into economic analysis. There are also limitations, including the difficulty in tuning synaptic parameters, the need for accurate behavioral data, and the challenge of empirically validating the results. However, the potential of this model in combining adaptive learning, memory, and human cognition has opened up a new path in the study of smart economics and decision-support systems. In the future, it seems that smart economies will move towards models that not only analyze data, but also think and learn from experience, like the brain.

7- CONCLUSION

In conclusion, it can be said that the integration of neuromorphic computing with the foundations of cognitive economics has opened a new horizon in understanding and modeling economic behavior. Inspired by the neural mechanisms of the brain, this approach attempts to reconstruct the human decision-making process not as a set of static equations, but as a dynamic, learning, and adaptive system. The research findings showed that economic agents in the neuromorphic framework are able to learn from the environment, respond to stimuli, and modify their strategies based on experience, just like biological neurons. Such a model shows that economic decision-making is actually a multi-layered cognitive process in which perception, memory, reward, and feedback operate simultaneously.

The presented model was able to simulate behaviors that could not previously be explained in classical economic theories. Phenomena such as risk preference, emotional decisions, social learning, and even cognitive hesitation were all represented within the framework of neuromorphic networks. Simulation results showed that such a system can automatically adapt to market fluctuations and find a more optimal decision-making path through synaptic strengthening. This dynamic is reminiscent of the behavior of the human brain, which reorganizes its neural patterns in response to new conditions to perform more optimally. Therefore, it can be said that neuromorphic-cognitive economics is a type of living economy in which decision-makers are in constant interaction as a network of learning neurons.

Conceptually, this research helps to move from views of absolute rationality to neural rationality; a rationality in which decisions are the result of the interaction between objective data and mental states. Such an approach paves the way for a more realistic understanding of human economic behavior and can be used in the design of economic policies, financial markets, and intelligent decision-support systems. In addition, by providing a platform for reinforcement learning, the neuromorphic framework allows researchers to simulate long-term dynamics in the behavior of economic agents without the need to explicitly model complex behaviors.

One of the most important achievements of this research is the demonstration of the ability of brain-inspired computational systems to manage noisy, incomplete, and uncertain data. Unlike classical models that require a large amount of information to accurately process data, the neuromorphic model is able to extract meaningful patterns through gradual learning and cognitive filtering. This feature can be the basis for designing a new generation of digital economies and smart platforms that make optimal decisions with minimal input data.

In practical terms, the presented framework has the potential to be used in areas such as market behavior prediction, consumer sentiment analysis, trust modeling in economic networks, and even financial crisis management. In the future, by developing neuromorphic chips and combining them with deep learning algorithms, it will be possible to achieve systems that implement economic decision-making in real time and rely on cognitive mechanisms. Such systems can be effective decision-making tools not only at the firm or market level, but also at the macro-level of policy-making.

Of course, this research also has limitations. One of the main challenges is the accurate calibration of synaptic parameters and ensuring the stability of the model on larger scales. Also, to generalize the results to real environments, there is a need for accurate and experimental behavioral data. However, the path outlined in this research has provided a foundation for future research to develop a new generation of human decision-making models by combining neuroscience, behavioral economics, and intelligent computing.

Ultimately, it can be said that neuromorphic-cognitive economics is not just a theory, but a step towards recreating human rationality in the form of intelligent computing. Rather than focusing on absolute prediction, this approach emphasizes understanding, learning, and adaptation) features that are at the heart of human decision-making. For this reason, we can expect this framework to become a major research direction in computational economics, cognitive science, and the design of intelligent decision-support systems in the coming decades) because the future of economics will likely lie not in machines that compute, but in systems that think.

REFERENCES

Jaeger, H. (2020). Exploring the landscapes of" computing": digital, neuromorphic, unconventional—and beyond. arXiv preprint arXiv:2011.12013.

Li, Z., Ma, X., Li, J., Qiu, Q., & Wang, Y. (2019, June). Efficient cloud resource management using neuromorphic modeling and prediction for virtual machine resource utilization. In *2019 IEEE International Conference on Embedded Software and Systems (ICESS)* (pp. 1-8). IEEE.

Murthy, P., & Mehra, A. (2021). Exploring neuromorphic computing for ultra-low latency transaction processing in edge database architectures. *Journal of Emerging Technologies and Innovative Research*, *8*(1), 25–26.

Nozari, H. (2025). Integrating Neuromorphic Intelligence with Fuzzy Multi-Objective Models in Resilient Green Supply Chain Design. Process Integration and Optimization for Sustainability, 1-14.

Nozari, H. (2026). Neuromorphic Models for Dynamic Customer Segmentation in Digital Marketing. In Improving Consumer Engagement in Digital Marketing Through Cognitive AI (pp. 311-326). IGI Global Scientific Publishing.

Nozari, H., Abdi, H., Szmelter-Jarosz, A., & Rahmaty, M. (2025). A digital twin-based neutrosophic multi-objective optimization model for smart supply chains in the food industry. *Journal of Intelligent Manufacturing*, •••, 1–15.

Nozari, H., Ghahremani-Nahr, J., & Szmelter-Jarosz, A. (2024). AI and machine learning for real-world problems. [). Elsevier.]. *Advances in Computers*, *134*, 1–12.

Nozari, H., Nassar, S., & Szmelter-Jarosz, A. (2025). Fuzzy multi-objective optimization model for resilient supply chain financing based on blockchain and IoT. *Digital*, *5*(3), 32.

Nozari, H., Szmelter-Jarosz, A., & Samadi, S. (2025). Machine Learning Models for Energy Optimization and Resource Consumption in Smart Factories. In *Artificial Intelligence of Everything and Sustainable Development* (pp. 175–189). Springer Nature Singapore.

Nozari, H., Szmelter-Jarosz, A., & Weiland, D. (2025). A Fuzzy Multi-Objective Sustainable and Agile Supply Chain Model Based on Digital Twin and Internet of Things with Adaptive Learning Under Environmental Uncertainty. *Applied Sciences (Basel, Switzerland)*, *15*(19), 10399.

Raikar, A. S., Andrew, J., Dessai, P. P., Prabhu, S. M., Jathar, S., Prabhu, A., & Raikar, G. V. S. (2024). Neuromorphic computing for modeling neurological and psychiatric disorders: Implications for drug development. *Artificial Intelligence Review*, *57*(12), 318.

Rajendran, B., & Alibart, F. (2016). Neuromorphic computing based on emerging memory technologies. *IEEE Journal on Emerging and Selected Topics in Circuits and Systems*, *6*(2), 198–211.

Smith, J. D., Hill, A. J., Reeder, L. E., Franke, B. C., Lehoucq, R. B., Parekh, O., & Aimone, J. B. (2022). Neuromorphic scaling advantages for energy-efficient random walk computations. *Nature Electronics*, *5*(2), 102–112.

Smolka, M., Stoepel, L., Quill, J., Wahlbrink, T., Floehr, J., Böschen, S., & Lemme, M. (2024). Transdisciplinary development of neuromorphic computing hardware for Artificial Intelligence applications: technological, economic, societal, and environmental dimensions of transformation in the NeuroSys Cluster4Future. In *Transformation Towards Sustainability: A Novel Interdisciplinary Framework from RWTH Aachen University* (pp. 271–301). Springer International Publishing.

Tathavadekar, V. P., & Mahankale, N. R. (2025). Neuromorphic Computing-Enabled Digital Twin Framework for Sustainable IT Supply Chain Integration in Smart Urban Ecosystems. *Frontiers in Digital Twin Urban Ecosystems*, *1*(1), 1–8.

Tsur, E. E. (2021). *Neuromorphic Engineering: The Scientist's, Algorithms Designer's and Computer Architect's Perspectives on Brain-Inspired Computing*. CRC Press.

Vineyard, C. M., Severa, W. M., & Aimone, J. B. (2024, July). Strategic Considerations for Neuromorphic Computing. In *2024 International Conference on Neuromorphic Systems (ICONS)* (pp. 161-168). IEEE.

Ye, A., Xu, D., Li, Y., Du, J., Wu, Z., & Tang, J. (2025). Neuromorphic energy economics: Toward biologically inspired and sustainable power market design. *Frontiers in Computational Neuroscience*, *19*, 1597038. PMID: 40495879

[] Zheng, N. (2023). "Cognitive Computing of Visual and Auditory Information": State of the Art. Cognitive Computing of Visual and Auditory Information, 29-40.

Chapter 3
AI-Driven Economic Forecasting for Industry 5.0 Enterprises

Mohammadhossein Shakerian
University of Sussex, UK

Hamidreza Keihani
https://orcid.org/0000-0001-9140-8455
Åbo Akademi University, Finland

ABSTRACT

This chapter examines the role of AI in the transformation of economic forecasting in the context of Industry 5.0, demonstrating that economic forecasting is no longer a linear analytical activity but rather part of a dynamic, human-centered cognitive system. By integrating multi-source data, adaptive learning models, and decision-support architectures, forecasting is elevated from the level of future estimation to the level of future design. Various applications in supply chains, sustainable manufacturing, financial services, and policymaking demonstrate that AI not only increases forecasting accuracy, but also turns it into a tool for resilience, sustainability, and competitive advantage.

1- INTRODUCTION

In recent decades, technological evolution has blurred the boundaries between artificial intelligence, the digital economy, and advanced manufacturing systems. In this context, the emergence of Industry 5.0 is not simply a natural continuation of Industry 4.0, but rather a cognitive shift in the logic of value creation in organi-

DOI: 10.4018/979-8-3693-4525-2.ch003

zations, one that emphasizes the coexistence of humans and machines, intelligent decision-making, environmental sustainability, and economic flexibility. In this new system, economic forecasting plays a central role, as industrial enterprises face an environment full of volatility, uncertainty, complexity, and interdependence, an environment that traditional forecasting methods, such as linear or statistical averaging models, cannot adequately address (Abdi et al., 2025).

The increasing dependence of production and value-creation processes on real-time data, connected ecosystems, adaptive supply chains, and the smart economy has made decision-making no longer based on the past, but on dynamic and explainable forecasting. In such a situation, AI-driven economic forecasting is not only a new analytical approach, but also a foundation for resilience, agility, and competitive advantage in the era of Industry 5.0. This transformation becomes especially meaningful when enterprises are exposed to global economic shocks, supply chain disruptions, sudden changes in demand, sustainability regulations, and ESG pressures; issues that are difficult to predict with classical models (Singh & Kumar, n.d.).

What distinguishes Industry 5.0 from previous generations is not only automation or the use of robots, but also its human-centric nature; This means that economic forecasting is no longer just a machine mission, but must also form the framework for human-AI interaction. In this regard, deep learning models, recurrent neural networks, and reinforcement learning-based approaches provide the ability to predict dynamic behavior in multidimensional markets, but these models will lose their practical value until they are embedded in transparent, interpretable, and human-logic-aligned decision-support systems. Therefore, AI in Industry 5.0 is used not as a replacement for humans, but as an enhancer of their cognitive capacity. This change in attitude has led to the concept of "economic forecasting" being elevated from the level of data analysis to the level of shared human-machine architectures.

On the other hand, the growth of economic data from sensors, digital transactions, supply chain platforms, social networks, blockchain, and IoT has caused enterprises to face not a shortage of data, but its abundance and heterogeneity. This situation doubles the need for intelligent algorithms, as new data structures are time-space, market sentiment, real-time production signals, environmental data, and resilience indicators. In such a context, artificial intelligence, with its ability to extract hidden patterns, identify structural changes, and predict behavior, provides the opportunity to move beyond the linear and unstable models of the past. In other words, if traditional economics relied on analyzing the past, the Industry 5.0 economy relies on predicting a dynamic, adaptive, and learnable future (Hu et al., 2025).

Despite these advantages, there are also significant challenges. First, excessive dependence on the output of AI models may distance economic decision-making from human judgment. Second, the existence of a conflict between the accuracy of predictions and the interpretability of models can reduce the trust of managers.

Third, the issue of ethics, algorithmic transparency, and data bias can lead to unfair or wrong decisions. Hence, new research approaches seek to design models that are simultaneously explainable, robust to uncertainty, and aligned with human values. This is where Industry 5.0 and AI-driven forecasting become a future-oriented paradigm rather than a mere technological response.

The aim of this chapter is to explain the role of AI in new economic forecasting architectures for organizations operating in the Industry 5.0 ecosystem, organizations that not only seek profitability but also emphasize sustainability, resilience, and human-machine synergy. The chapter will first review the conceptual foundations of Industry 5.0 and the evolution of economic forecasting, then present a proposed AI-based framework, and finally discuss challenges, applications, and future research directions.

2- BACKGROUND & CONCEPTUAL FOUNDATIONS

The history of economic forecasting cannot be separated from the evolution of manufacturing and digital systems. In previous decades, economic forecasting was based on linear models, limited historical data, and static behavioral assumptions; models that relied mainly on statistical patterns such as trend, seasonality, moving averages, or linear regression, and were suitable for environments with slow and predictable changes. However, with the expansion of the digital economy, the emergence of data-driven platforms, and the increasing speed of global disruptions, these models lost their ability to predict nonlinear, time-dependent, and multidimensional feedback phenomena (Nozari & Samadi, 2025). As a result, the need to move from "past-based forecasting" to "future-adaptive forecasting" emerged; a shift that was reinforced by the emergence of a new generation of technologies such as artificial intelligence, deep learning, real-time processing, and digital twins.

Conceptually, Industry 4.0 is usually associated with automation, the Internet of Things, cyber-physical systems, and smart production lines, but Industry 5.0 shifts the focus from "machine intelligence" to "human-machine coexistence." Industry 5.0 is fundamentally a data-driven but value-driven economy; that is, it focuses on human empowerment, ethical decision-making, sustainability, and resilience, unlike the previous generation that emphasized productivity and speed. In such a framework, economic forecasting is not a management support tool, but a core component of a future-oriented decision-making architecture. Industry 5.0 seeks to transform economic forecasting models from being univariate, financially-driven, and outsourced to multi-source, human-centered, and interactive structures (Dmitrieva et al., 2024). This transformation has led to forecasting no longer being simply a numerical estimate of the future, but rather part of the "cognitive system of the organization."

At a technical level, traditional economic forecasting models relied mainly on the analysis of stable time series, but the growth of irregular, correlated, network-based data and real-time variables has made statistical approaches alone insufficient. This is where machine learning and deep learning come in. Random forest models, support vector machines, long-term memory (LSTM)-based neural networks or more advanced structures such as Transformer are able to extract temporal dependencies, nonlinear patterns, interactions between variables and structural fluctuations. Alongside this progress, a move is taking shape from "numerical forecasting" to "cognitive forecasting"; that is, models that not only produce outputs but also explain the decision logic. This evolution has led to increased attention to issues such as model interpretability, forecasting ethics, data bias detection and the combination of statistical models and artificial intelligence.

From an economic perspective, AI-based modeling in Industry 5.0 is characterized by three key differences from the past: first, the data used is not limited to economic indicators, but also includes operational data, IoT sensors, market sentiment indicators, energy consumption, and sustainability indicators. second, the goal of forecasting is not simply profit maximization or cost reduction, but encompasses a multi-objective set of objectives including sustainability, resilience, supply chain agility, and human satisfaction. third, forecasting is transformed from a separate analytical activity into a permanent layer of industrial decision support systems; systems that learn, modify, and dynamically reproduce future behavior with new data (Nozari, Nassar, & Szmelter-Jarosz, 2025).

For this reason, in modern approaches, economic forecasting relies not only on machine learning techniques, but also operates in interaction with digital twins, scenario-based simulation, uncertainty analysis, and adaptive control. Digital twins allow the output of predictive models to be tested in a virtual environment and then implemented in a real environment, which reduces the risk of economic decisions. Also, the combination of fuzzy logic, probabilistic risk analysis, and multi-layered AI structures allows Industry 5.0 models to cope with ambiguity, latency, volatility, and non-stationary data.

However, there are still challenges such as the trade-off between accuracy and interpretability, data quality limitations, the conflict between human logic and algorithmic output, and ethical issues such as model transparency. The fundamental question is whether Industry 5.0 organizations should rely on fully automated predictions, or whether a hybrid structure between "machine prediction" and "human interpretation" is the best option. This question is at the heart of today's discussions and is where the "AI-driven but Human-aligned" approach comes into play.

In short, the future vision of economic forecasting in Industry 5.0 is based on the combination of several key elements: multi-source data, self-learning algorithms, simulation architectures, and collaborative human-machine frameworks. This integration will not only improve forecast accuracy, but also shape a new ecosystem of collaborative decision-making, sustainability, and economic innovation.

3- THE ROLE OF AI IN NEXT-GENERATION ECONOMIC FORECASTING

The role of AI in the new generation of economic forecasting should be analyzed in relation to three fundamental developments in the business environment: first, the fundamental transformation of the nature of economic data; second, the transition from linear forecasting to adaptive and collaborative forecasting; and third, the convergence of human decision-making and algorithmic processing. In this perspective, AI acts not simply as a computational tool, but as a "cognitive forecasting engine"; an engine capable of transforming the complexity, uncertainty, and dynamism of the Industry 5.0 economy into decision-making patterns (Bakator et al., 2025).

In the past, economic forecasting was based on the assumption that market behavior, demand, financial rates, and macro indicators were somewhat predictable and that their patterns remained relatively stable. But in the Industry 5.0 world, the pace of change has increased so much that the data life cycle is shorter than the traditional decision-making cycle. For this reason, models that rely solely on historical data are ineffective in the face of sudden disruptions, systematic shocks, or structural changes. This is where AI, with its ability to learn in real time, discover hidden patterns, and adapt to new data, becomes a key element in the design of predictive systems. In this approach, the model no longer provides only a "numerical forecast," but also produces a "decision signal," meaning that the model's output can be directly translated into management action.

The first key role of AI is to manage the diversity and heterogeneity of data. In the Industry 5.0 economy, data is collected not only from financial or statistical sources, but also from industrial sensors, supply chain platforms, user behavior, environmental data, and even market sentiment patterns. This data is not regular, static, or homogeneous, and is structured at different levels in time, space, and semantics. Techniques such as deep learning, transfer learning, and graph neural networks can extract nonlinear relationships and network dependencies from this data, enabling a new level of multidimensional forecasting (Nozari, Szmelter-Jarosz, & Weiland, 2025).

A second role for AI is to create adaptive forecasting systems. Unlike classic models that were trained once and then used over a long period of time, AI models in Industry 5.0 are dynamically updated with new data. This process, sometimes referred to as "live forecasting," allows the system to analyze unexpected scenarios and correct its course without relying entirely on past assumptions. This feature is critical for organizations dealing with supply chain shocks, energy price fluctuations, or non-stationary demand.

In addition to accuracy, AI has introduced another dimension to economic forecasting: interpretability and alignment with human decision-making. One of the serious criticisms of AI models was that they act like "black boxes" and their output cannot be trusted unless they are explained. In Industry 5.0, where decisions are based on shared responsibility between humans and intelligent systems, forecasting models must be able to explain the reasons and structure of their relationships. New techniques such as XAI (Explainable AI), layered transparency models, and sensitivity analysis of variables have helped to move economic forecasting from a purely algorithmic state to a "reasonable" state.

Ethical dimensions have also become important. If economic forecasting is the basis for resource allocation, pricing, or policymaking, model errors can lead to discrimination, systemic risk, or failure in resilience. Industry 5.0 therefore emphasizes the need for responsible forecasting; A forecast that is not only accurate, but also transparent, unbiased, and auditable (Hammad et al., 2025).

The third role of AI is to transform economic forecasting into a feedback learning system. In this case, the model not only predicts the future based on the past, but also receives actual future outcomes as input and modifies its internal structure. This is the "forecast → decision → result → retraining" loop that is at the heart of AI-driven forecasting systems. Such a structure guides organizational economics from static models to self-organizing patterns that are resilient to uncertainty.

Finally, it can be said that the role of AI in the new generation of economic forecasting is not only to improve accuracy, but also to change the nature of forecasting from an analytical activity to an organization-wide neurocognitive process. AI enables economic forecasting to simultaneously understand complexity, model uncertainty, integrate multi-source data, and provide decisions that are aligned with human logic and the goals of Industry 5.0.

4- PROPOSED FRAMEWORK / ARCHITECTURE

The proposed framework section in this chapter aims to provide an integrated architecture for AI-based economic forecasting in the context of Industry 5.0; an architecture that defines not just a computational model, but a cognitive and adaptive decision support system. In this framework, economic forecasting is no longer a separate activity in the analysis unit, but becomes part of the "organizational nervous system"; a system that senses data, simulates the future, gives meaning to human decisions, and learns from past results to modify future behavior. This approach is a combination of three key layers: the data layer, the predictive intelligence layer, and the human-machine synergy layer.

In the first layer, data is collected not only from financial reports or economic indicators, but also from a wide range of sources, based on the logic of Industry 5.0: digital transactions, environmental data, IoT sensors on production lines, logistics data, customer behavior patterns, energy indicators, financial market signals, and even socio-emotional flows. This layer, relying on cloud, edge, or hybrid computing infrastructures, transforms raw data into learnable data. At this stage, the data architecture must have three characteristics: temporal continuity, semantic convergence, and real-time updateability. Data is not an archive, but a living entity that is constantly being reproduced.

In the second layer, the predictive intelligence core, machine learning algorithms, deep learning, and hybrid models operate. This core is designed based on multi-model logic; This means that time series models, recurrent networks, graph-based models, scenario-based analysis, and reinforcement learning can simultaneously or in combination simulate the future in different economic dimensions. This part does not simply learn from data, but retrains itself to deal with structural changes. The forecasting system operates adaptively, and each forecast iteration produces a new version of the system's understanding of the future. The fundamental difference between this architecture and traditional models is that the forecast output is not just a number, but also includes the "range of uncertainty", "explanation of effective variables", and "sensitivity analysis on the decision". As a result, the model output is not only reliable, but also discussable and interpretable by humans.

In the third layer, the connection between artificial intelligence and human decision is established; where the forecast becomes a decision. Industry 5.0 emphasizes that AI should augment human judgment, not replace it. Therefore, the human-machine interface should be designed as a "cognitive decision-making dashboard." This interface can include self-explanatory dashboards, scenario-based alerts, predictive maps of the future, and even interactive dialogue. At this point, XAI models come into play to explain why the algorithm reached a certain conclusion, which variable played the most role, and what impact changing a parameter will have on the possible future.

The proposed framework is not simply a static picture, but a dynamic cycle. A prediction is made, a decision is made, the actual result is recorded, and then it is fed back to the system as feedback data. This learning cycle turns prediction from a time-consuming analysis into a living process that becomes more accurate, more realistic, and more in line with human logic each time. In this sense, the forecasting system is upgraded from a mathematical model to a "neuro-economic system".

The framework also has the ability to connect to the economic digital twin. In this case, the forecast is implemented not only in the form of data, but also in a simulated way in a virtual environment to observe the possible effects of decisions before they are implemented in the real world. This feature allows organizations to reduce the cost of error and test high-risk scenarios first in the digital twin.

In summary, the proposed architecture for economic forecasting in Industry 5.0 is not based on reliance on past data, but on a combination of algorithmic intelligence, continuous learning and human interpretation. Rather than replacing humans, the model enhances the decision-making structure and uses forecasting as a cognitive infrastructure for the organization of the future.

5- APPLICATION DOMAINS & CASE EXAMPLES

The application of AI-based economic forecasting in the context of Industry 5.0 is not limited to finance or market analysis, but plays a role in a diverse range of industrial systems, supply chains, manufacturing systems, real-time demand-driven services, and even economic policymaking. The main feature of these models is that they elevate forecasting from a numerical level to a "future-intervention capability" level; that is, the model not only describes the future, but also allows it to be redesigned. In the following, several key areas where the use of AI-based forecasting has become a strategic advantage are examined.

One of the first areas of exploitation is smart supply chains. In the Industry 5.0 ecosystem, the supply chain is not a linear path for transporting goods, but a dynamic, self-organizing network that must be resilient to demand fluctuations, logistical shocks, environmental changes, and global disruptions. AI-based forecasting can detect hidden patterns in consumer demand behavior, order timing, price changes, and transportation conditions, and simulate future scenarios. This capability allows organizations to proactively adjust inventory, design alternative routes, or adjust production capacity rather than reacting to a crisis. In cases where reliance on traditional data has led to computational errors, the use of multi-source forecasting models has been shown to improve resilience (Nozari, Abdi, et al., 2025).

A second application is seen in sustainability-oriented manufacturing industries. Unlike the previous generation, which focused primarily on automation and productivity, Industry 5.0 emphasizes the combination of productivity, human-centeredness, and environmental sustainability. AI-based economic forecasting is used in this sector to estimate energy costs, predict raw material prices, analyze production line efficiency, and optimize cost-carbon simultaneously. For example, a factory can adjust its production schedule to reduce costs and minimize its carbon footprint by combining data on energy consumption, current electricity prices, ambient temperature, and market demand. These models can even simulate long-term economic scenarios such as changing environmental regulations, carbon taxes, or resource market fluctuations, so that decision-making is not based solely on short-term profits (Ardanta et al., 2025).

The third area concerns financial services and economic risk prediction. In a data-driven economy, banks, investment funds, and smart financing platforms must be able to predict market behavior not only based on historical indicators, but also on real-time data, digital sentiment, network dependencies, and volatility indicators. AI models can analyze the nonlinear behavior of financial markets, chain failure patterns, and domino effects in the digital economy ecosystem. The result is that forecasting is being upgraded from indicator analysis to "systemic risk" analysis, enabling adaptive decision-making to allocate resources and control volatility. This transformation has led to the shift in economic risk management from a descriptive to a predictive and interventionist mode (Gorobynskaya & Krivtsova, 2025).

A fourth application is in the service economy and customer experience. In industries based on personalization, such as e-commerce, digital health, or smart tourism, predicting demand based on demographic patterns or past behavior is not enough. AI models can combine environmental data, sentiment variables, social patterns in digital networks, and situational indicators to predict when, which group of customers, and which product or service will be preferred at what price. This type of economic forecasting shifts from "demand forecasting" to "value forecasting"; that is, the goal is not to predict sales volume, but to predict the highest possible level of economic impact. The result is the creation of dynamic pricing models, flexible product designs, and real-time improvements in customer experience.

In economic policymaking, AI-driven forecasting has also become a tool for analyzing the future of population, employment, resources, and macroeconomic sustainability. Using hybrid models, governments can simulate the possible consequences of climate change, migration, labor market transformation, or financial crises and develop alternative scenarios. The difference in this approach is that the model no longer just "predicts the outcome," but also shows which interventions can correct the undesirable future.

In short, AI-driven economic forecasting in Industry 5.0 acts not as an analysis tool, but as a cognitive biotechnology for the economy; a biotechnology that can connect data, decisions, and the future in a learning loop. This feature has led organizations to ask, instead of asking, "What will happen?" Get to the question "What can we change?"

6- METHODOLOGICAL CONSIDERATIONS

The study and implementation of AI-based economic forecasting in the context of Industry 5.0 requires simultaneous attention to technical, cognitive, data, and decision-making dimensions. Unlike traditional models that were usually limited to choosing a statistical method or determining numerical parameters, new approaches require the design of a multilayer methodological logic; a logic that can integrate heterogeneous data, model uncertainty, have the ability to continuously learn, and ultimately provide its output in the form of a reliable and explainable decision to humans. For this reason, the methodological discussion in this chapter is not limited to the choice of algorithm, but also includes fundamental questions about the nature of the data, validation criteria, human-machine coexistence, and the level of model reliability.

The first methodological issue relates to the selection and structuring of data. In Industry 5.0 economic forecasting, data is no longer only obtained from the macroeconomic past or financial data of companies, but is also extracted from diverse sources such as production sensors, platform flows, socio-emotional indicators, climate data, automated logistics signals, and even human interactions. These data may be heterogeneous, non-stationary, noisy, or time-invariant. Therefore, it is necessary to design a mechanism for filtering, time-alignment, eliminating systematic errors, and creating a common semantic structure among the data before entering the modeling phase. Data fusion approaches based on deep learning, common component analysis, and multi-source data mining methods can play a key role in this phase (Nozari, 2025).

The second methodological challenge is related to the choice of model type and forecasting logic. In the real world, no single algorithm is able to simulate all types of economic behavior. For this reason, the Industry 5.0 methodology recommends the use of hybrid or multi-model models instead of single models. For example, combining time series models and recurrent neural networks to analyze dynamic trends, integrating graph models to analyze network connections in financial markets, or combining reinforcement learning algorithms with scenario-based simulation to compensate for the lack of historical data are some of these solutions. At this point, the forecast is no longer based solely on probability calculations, but on "adaptive learning from the environment." This feature allows the model to modify its internal logic in the face of shocks and changing conditions.

The concept of uncertainty is the third important dimension in the methodology of this field. In traditional models, it was assumed that the data were relatively stable and errors could be controlled. However, in the economic forecast of Industry 5.0, uncertainty comes in the form of fluctuations, structural disruption, unpredictable human behavior, and nonlinear interactions. Therefore, the forecasting methodology should be able to specify not only the forecast value, but also the “confidence limit” and “decision sensitivity”. In this context, the use of fuzzy models, forecasting variance analysis, deep learning-based Bayesian, and AI-enhanced Monte Carlo simulation are among the solutions that can make uncertainty not hidden, but measurable and decision-able (Nozari & Nassar, 2025).

The fourth consideration is the issue of algorithmic interpretability and accountability. While many deep learning models have high accuracy, the main issue in the Industry 5.0 environment is that the model output must be trusted by the human decision maker. As a result, the methodology should contain a mechanism that shows the reason for the forecast, the weighting of variables, and the possible effects of human intervention. XAI models, key variable impact analysis, and layered transparency algorithms are used for this purpose. This step marks the boundary between “numerical forecasting” and “decision-making forecasting.”

The fifth layer of the methodology concerns model evaluation and validation. In classical models, forecast accuracy was often measured by indicators such as RMSE, MAPE, or R^2. In Industry 5.0, however, the evaluation criteria must be multidimensional: accuracy, stability under non-stationary conditions, decision-making value of the output, robustness to error, interpretability, and the speed of adaptation of the model to new data. This evolution has also changed the validation logic, so that the model is tested not only against past data, but also against simulated future data and improbable scenarios (Fernández-Miguel et al., 2025).

Finally, the Industry 5.0 economic forecasting methodology must have a living feedback loop; that is, the forecast output shapes the decision, the decision leads to the actual outcome, and the actual outcome feeds back into the model to refine the forecast logic. This continuous learning cycle is what transforms forecasting from a static process into a self-improving system.

In short, building an economic forecasting model in Industry 5.0 is not simply a computational problem, but rather the design of a social-cognitive system that must simultaneously learn from data, understand uncertainty, enhance decision-making, and maintain human trust. Such a view blurs the line between economic analysis and artificial intelligence, making forecasting part of the macro intelligence of the organization.

7- CONCLUSION

The conclusion of this chapter is based on the fact that economic forecasting in the era of Industry 5.0 is no longer a separate analytical activity or a tool for estimating future values, but is part of the cognitive architecture of organizations; an architecture in which humans, machines, data and decisions interact with each other in an intelligent and synergistic cycle. By emphasizing the coexistence of humans and artificial intelligence, Industry 5.0 has elevated the status of forecasting from the level of "numerical forecasting" to the level of "future-affecting forecasting" and has made it one of the central elements of economic resilience, sustainability and innovation. This transformation is not only due to the advancement of algorithms, but also the result of a shift in perspective from a reactive economy to a predictive economy; an economy that not only asks "what will happen?" but also asks "how can the future be redesigned?" In this perspective, artificial intelligence, as the main engine of forecasting, plays a role beyond time series analysis or learning from historical patterns. Deep learning models, adaptive systems, and multi-source algorithms have made it possible to understand the complex, nonlinear, and dynamic relationships between economic variables; variables that are no longer simply financial in today's world, but are linked to environmental, demographic, technical, emotional, logistical, and even human behavioral data. Thus, economic forecasting in Industry 5.0 is more of a "pattern-based understanding of future dynamics" than a reflection of the past.

However, the transition to intelligence-driven forecasting is not without its challenges. First, the issue of trust and interpretability of algorithms remains a critical issue. Although the accuracy of AI models has surpassed classical methods in many cases, as long as the decision-making logic of the model is not explainable to humans, the forecast cannot become a valid decision. This shows that interpretability and transparency are not a complementary layer, but a condition for the survival of the model in the Industry 5.0 ecosystem. Second, the issue of data and its quality also plays a decisive role. In AI-based economic forecasting, data is not only the fuel of the model, but also determines the scope of its knowledge. Incomplete, biased or unreliable data can lead even the most accurate models to strategic errors.

Another challenge is the issue of uncertainty and unpredictable behavior of socio-economic systems. While classical models tried to linearize the future, Industry 5.0 accepts the fact that the future is in many cases subject to "rare but influential events" and that forecasting must be accompanied by a continuous cognitive flow and corrective feedback. For this reason, economic forecasting is no longer an output file, but a living process that must be continuously executed, compared, retrained and refined.

From an applied perspective, the experience of various industries shows that the value of economic forecasting lies not in the predicted number, but in the capacity to "make uncertainty decisive". Smart supply chains, dynamic pricing systems, data-driven investing, energy management, economic policymaking, and even personalized services all benefit from forecasting when the model output can not only describe but also guide future behavior. In this sense, economic forecasting becomes the backbone of intelligent decision-making.

This chapter has shown that the proposed architecture in Industry 5.0 is based on three principles: multi-source data integration, algorithmic adaptive learning, and human-machine cognitive interaction. The fundamental difference between this approach and traditional models is that forecasting becomes the "beginning of decision" rather than the "end of analysis." Organizations seek not only to know the future, but also to control it, and AI acts as an augmentation of human capacity, not a substitute.

Ultimately, the future direction of research and implementation in this area will be to integrate economic forecasting with concepts such as digital twins, autonomous economies, explainable artificial intelligence, scenario-based forecasting, and multi-agent cognitive architectures. In this direction, the most important distinction between proactive and reactive organizations will be their ability to use forecasting not as a report, but as a tool to design the future. If Industry 4.0 was the revolution of smart manufacturing, Industry 5.0 is the revolution of smart decision-making; and economic forecasting is at the core of this revolution.

Given this perspective, it can be said that the future belongs to organizations that consider forecasting not as a part of data analysis, but as a living part of their decision-support system; organizations that do not just accept the future, but create it.

REFERENCES

Abdi, H., Jahanian, A., & Nozari, H. (2025). Digital Twin-Enabled Bioreactors: Transforming Industrial Biotechnology in Smart Economies. In Dynamic and Safe Economy in the Age of Smart Technologies (pp. 105-120). IGI Global Scientific Publishing.

Ardanta, M. A., Fauzi, A., Patimah, P., Khadijah, F., Yunandi, S. R., & Ghowe, A. M. (2025). Human-AI Collaboration in Supply Chain Industry 5.0 to Build a Human-Centered Autonomous Ecosystem. [SIJDB]. *Siber International Journal of Digital Business*, *2*(4), 357–368.

Bakator, M., Ćoćkalo, D., Ugrinov, S., & Premčevski, V. (2025). Industry 5.0 with AI Applications for Smart and Sustainable Production. In International Conference "New Technologies, Development and Applications" (pp. 56-63). Springer, Cham.

Dmitrieva, E., Balmiki, V., Lakhanpal, S., Lavanya, G., & Bhandari, P. (2024). AI evolution in Industry 4.0 and Industry 5.0: an experimental comparative assessment. In BIO Web of Conferences (Vol. 86, p. 01069). EDP Sciences.

Fernández-Miguel, A., García-Muiña, F. E., Ortíz-Marcos, S., Jiménez-Calzado, M., Fernández del Hoyo, A. P., & Settembre-Blundo, D. (2025). AI-Driven Transformations in Manufacturing: Bridging Industry 4.0, 5.0, and 6.0 in Sustainable Value Chains. *Future Internet*, *17*(9), 430.

Gorobynskaya, M., & Krivtsova, T. (2025). The Impact of Industry 5.0 on Enterprise Resilience in the Digital Environment. *FINANCIAL AND CREDIT SYSTEMS: PROSPECTS FOR DEVELOPMENT*, *2*(17), 167–179.

Hammad, M. Y., Rahamaddulla, S. R., Muhamad Tamyez, P. F., & Fauzi, M. A. (2025). From Industry 4.0 to 5.0: leveraging AI and IoT for sustainable and human-centric operations. International Journal of Industrial Engineering and Operations Management, 1-19.

Hu, J. L., Li, Y., & Chew, J. C. (2025). Industry 5.0 and Human-Centered Energy System: A Comprehensive Review with Socio-Economic Viewpoints. *Energies*, *18*(9), 2345.

Nozari, H. (2025). Integrating Neuromorphic Intelligence with Fuzzy Multi-Objective Models in Resilient Green Supply Chain Design. Process Integration and Optimization for Sustainability, 1-14.

Nozari, H., Abdi, H., Szmelter-Jarosz, A., & Rahmaty, M. (2025). A digital twin-based neutrosophic multi-objective optimization model for smart supply chains in the food industry. *Journal of Intelligent Manufacturing*, •••, 1–15.

Nozari, H., & Nassar, S. (2025). Real-time data-driven multi-objective optimization in B2B marketing using digital twins. OPSEARCH, 1-27.

Nozari, H., Nassar, S., & Szmelter-Jarosz, A. (2025). Fuzzy multi-objective optimization model for resilient supply chain financing based on blockchain and IoT. *Digital*, *5*(3), 32.

Nozari, H., & Samadi, S. (2025). Digital Twin-Enhanced Sentiment Analysis for Targeted Marketing Optimization. In Dynamic and Safe Economy in the Age of Smart Technologies (pp. 121-138). IGI Global Scientific Publishing.

Nozari, H., Szmelter-Jarosz, A., & Weiland, D. (2025). A Fuzzy Multi-Objective Sustainable and Agile Supply Chain Model Based on Digital Twin and Internet of Things with Adaptive Learning Under Environmental Uncertainty. *Applied Sciences (Basel, Switzerland)*, *15*(19), 10399.

Singh, V., & Kumar, R. The Rise of Industry 5.0: how artificial intelligence is shaping the future of manufacturing. In *Artificial Intelligence and Communication Techniques in Industry 5.0* (pp. 26–46). CRC Press.

Chapter 4
Urban Digital Twins and Data-Centric Architectures for the Emergent Economy 5.0

Hamed Nozari
https://orcid.org/0000-0002-6500-6708
Azad University of the Emirates, Dubai, UAE

ABSTRACT

This study aims to explain the role of urban digital twin in shaping the 5.0 economy, and presents a data-driven and human-centered framework for smart city management. The proposed model shows that the integration of data flow, dynamic simulation, cognitive decision-making engines, and citizen feedback can lead to improved governance, increased resilience, optimized infrastructure, and improved quality of life. The findings suggest that urban digital twin is not a single technology, but a strategic infrastructure for sustainable development, accurate decision-making, and value creation in future cities. This approach guides the path of urban transformation toward predictive, efficient, and human-centered management.

1- INTRODUCTION

The emergence of a new wave of smart urbanization in the last decade has transformed the landscape of urban management in such a way that reliance on traditional planning models is no longer adequate to address the complexities of the urban environment, fluctuating service demand, environmental pressures, and the growing need for sustainability. In such an environment, urban digital twins

DOI: 10.4018/979-8-3693-4525-2.ch004

have emerged as a key technology for the intelligent regeneration of infrastructure; tools that enable advanced analysis, prediction, and decision-making by digitally representing the physical elements of the city and connecting them to real-time data streams. The combination of this technology with data-driven architectures enables the establishment of a new generation of urban governance that is aligned with the principles of Economy 5.0. Economy 5.0 is an approach based on human-centeredness, social resilience, environmental sustainability, and the pervasive use of cognitive technologies, and seeks to put technology at the service of human value creation and the long-term well-being of citizens (Nozari, 2023).

The exponential growth of urban data and the evolution of IoT, 5G, edge computing and cloud infrastructures suggest that future cities will not be simply equipped with smart systems, but will become "digital entities" in which data flows will play the same role as physical infrastructures played for traditional cities. This vision can only be realized with a data-centric architecture; one that can collect, cleanse, integrate, standardize and then organize scattered data from sensors, platforms, traffic, environment and infrastructure into a coherent digital chain. Such an architecture forms the foundation for creating a city digital twin, because without a unified data platform, simulation models or predictive capabilities cannot reflect the complex reality of the city (Nassar et al., 2025).

In Economy 5.0, the role of data goes beyond a mere information source and becomes a strategic asset; An asset that plays a decisive role in the decision-making process, urban policy design, energy optimization, traffic management, development planning, risk management and the creation of new services for citizens. By enabling interaction between physical and virtual models, digital twins offer an effective solution for the value-added use of urban data and help managers evaluate scenarios and analyze possible future paths before crises occur. In this approach, the city is not only monitored in real time, but its future is also simulated and managed. This feature distinguishes digital twins from other smart technologies and makes them a key tool in realizing sustainable and human-centered cities.

On the other hand, the increasing complexities of urban life in areas such as transportation, energy, air quality, waste management, water infrastructure and urban security require systems that can operate with a high level of autonomy, adaptation and prediction. By integrating data-driven models and predictive algorithms, the urban digital twin enables the behavior of systems to be not only observed, but also analyzed and optimized. From this perspective, data-driven architecture is not just a technical layer, but also the main infrastructure for the formation of "cognitive governance" in future cities; a governance in which decisions are made based on continuous data analysis, machine learning, and citizen feedback, resulting in increased productivity, reduced urban costs, and improved quality of life.

As the world's digitalization continues to expand, cities are forced to design complementary digital layers, rather than focusing solely on developing physical infrastructure; layers that can make decision-making more accurate with a comprehensive and continuous picture of the city's state. In such a context, the urban digital twin is not just a technological tool, but a transformational platform that can connect stakeholders, data, and decision-making models. With its interactive and iterative nature, this technology enables the constant improvement of simulations and models, allowing the city to continuously learn from past experiences and current data.

The importance of this issue becomes even more clear when we realize that the 5.0 economy is not only about intelligence, but also about creating a structure that uses technology to achieve human well-being, spatial justice, and urban resilience. With its ability to generate actionable insights and strengthen decision-making, the digital twin enables the city to move towards this goal. Energy consumption management, environmental impact reduction, efficient transportation planning, land use optimization, and data-driven policy design are just some examples of digital twin value creation on the path to Economy 5.0 (Mazzetto, 2024).

In light of these developments, this study examines the role of urban digital twins and data-driven architectural design as the foundation for realizing Economy 5.0, and attempts to show how data integration and predictive modeling can provide a platform for future-oriented governance and sustainable urban development. In this regard, presenting a comprehensive picture of the relationship between data, simulation, cognitive technologies, and economic value creation can open a new path for understanding and designing future cities; a path in which urban decision-making is not based on reacting to events, but on predicting and intelligently guiding trends.

2- THEORETICAL FOUNDATIONS OF ECONOMY 5.0 AND THE NEED FOR DATA-DRIVEN ARCHITECTURE

The conceptual evolution of Economy 5.0 has been shaped along the macro-currents of technological and social change and represents the transition from an economy based on efficiency and automation to a human-centered, hyper-intelligent and sustainable economy. Unlike previous models that focused on production, competition or digitalization, this concept attempts to put emerging technologies at the service of human development, social resilience and improving the quality of life. Economy 5.0 not only focuses on the integration of digital technologies into economic contexts, but also emphasizes the creation of a structure in which data-based decision-making, participatory policy-making and sustainable value creation establish an organic link. Such a view has caused cities in this paradigm to become complex, data-driven and learning units; units that require coherent, standardized and scalable data architectures to move in the future (Nozari, Szmelter-Jarosz, & Weiland, 2025).

In this framework, data is considered the main infrastructure for economic value creation. The forces shaping the 5.0 economy, such as the Internet of Things, predictive analytics, cloud computing, edge computing, and artificial intelligence, can only play an effective role in development when there is an integrated platform for collecting, storing, processing, and applying data. In the absence of such a platform, the capacities available in smart cities will operate in a dispersed, inefficient, and unreliable manner. Therefore, a data-centric architecture is not a choice, but a structural requirement for realizing the principles of the 5.0 economy.

In Figure 1, a data-centric architecture is shown in a layered manner. In this architecture, the data flow starts from the real environment and, after passing through layers of processing, integration, and analysis, reaches intelligent decision-making engines. This image shows that the urban digital twin is not just a simulation model, but a comprehensive mechanism for transforming raw data into actionable insights. This architecture is designed to establish the interaction between the physical elements of the city, digital systems, predictive models and human policy-making in a continuous feedback loop. Such a loop forms the core of Economy 5.0, as it enables the move from "reactive management" to "predictive management".

Figure 1. Data-Driven Architecture of the Urban Digital Twin for Economy 5.0

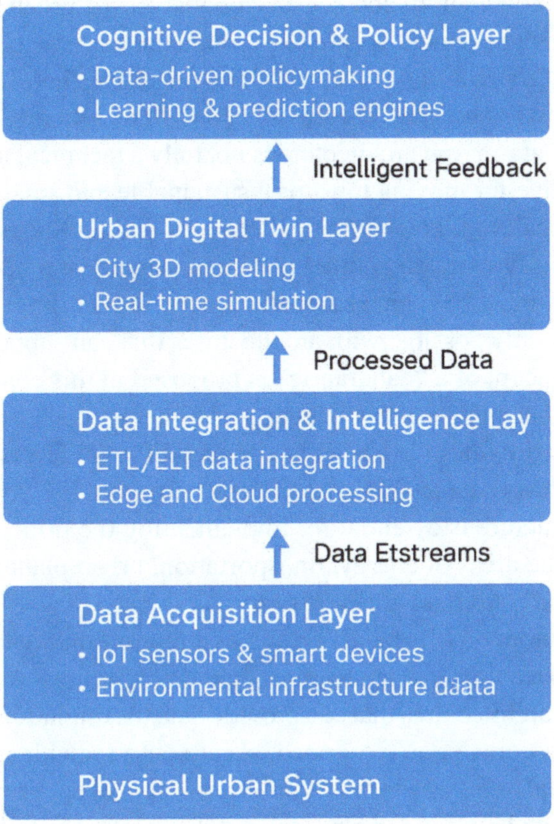

In addition to the integration of technology, the concept of human-machine synergy is also of particular importance in the Economy 5.0 paradigm; this means that intelligent systems must work to enhance human decision-making, reduce errors, accelerate analytics and increase spatial justice. This is not possible without a reliable data-centric architecture, as data must be provided to cognitive engines in a structured, traceable and standardized format. Although the vast volume of urban data can potentially be a valuable resource for cities, without the right architecture, this data can easily increase complexity, error, and chaos. Thus, data-driven architecture is a kind of "soft infrastructure" that, like water and electricity networks, supports the functioning of the entire urban system and ensures the stability of decision-making (Omar, 2025).

Economy 5.0 also emphasizes resilience to environmental, social, and technological crises. This has led cities to move towards designing systems that have the ability to predict, self-regulate, and recover quickly in the face of disruptions. The urban digital twin, which is a direct output of data-driven architecture, is an important tool for achieving such goals, as it allows for large-scale scenario building, policy testing before implementation, and sensitivity analysis of urban events. With this mechanism, urban management is able to examine the possible effects of decisions in a simulated environment and select options that have the lowest cost and the highest effectiveness. These features are fully consistent with the spirit of Economy 5.0 and show that data-driven architecture is not only a technical necessity, but also a strategic imperative for moving towards a sustainable and smart future.

On the other hand, rapid technological changes and the increasing complexity of urban ecosystems have made traditional data management models ineffective. In Economy 5.0, data must be managed continuously, in real time, and in a scalable manner, and this is only possible with architectures that can support heterogeneous data flows. The concept of a "data fabric" is proposed in this context as a comprehensive approach that enables the connection and interaction between data sources. This approach also provides the ability to connect different layers of the city to the digital twin and allows data to flow in a specific path from IoT devices to cognitive models. Such a structure is essential for implementing the principles of Economy 5.0, especially in the areas of energy, transportation, urban planning, and resource management (Nozari, Abdi, et al., 2025).

In general, Economy 5.0 is based on the assumption that data and technology are not used to replace humans, but to enhance their capacities. Achieving this goal requires designing architectures that can provide data to simulation, forecasting, and decision-making systems in an integrated, secure, and scalable manner. In such a context, urban digital twins, as the most important output of data-driven architecture, play the role of a link between the physical and digital worlds and pave the way for economic value creation, infrastructure optimization, and quality of life improvement. Therefore, the theoretical foundations of Economy 5.0 would be incomplete without considering data-driven architecture, because the basis of this economy's functioning is transparency, continuous learning, deep analysis, and data-driven decision-making; elements that are only possible with a data architecture that is compatible with the needs of the new era.

3- THE CONCEPT AND EVOLUTION OF THE URBAN DIGITAL TWIN

In recent years, the urban digital twin has become one of the main pillars of the digital transformation in urban governance and, as a dynamic and intelligent model that represents the digital and online version of the city, plays a fundamental role in the transition to next-generation cities. The concept of the digital twin was first proposed in the manufacturing and engineering industries, but with the expansion of data infrastructure, the Internet of Things, cloud computing and artificial intelligence, its scope has also been transferred to urban management and today it is recognized as one of the key enablers in urban analysis and decision-making. The urban digital twin is not just a static simulation, but a living and continuous system that collects real-time data from the city, processes and integrates it, and then presents it in the form of an updatable model. This interactive feature has made the digital twin an essential platform for planning, forecasting and managing urban flows (Tu et al., 2024).

The evolution of this concept has been simultaneous with the advancement of technology and the changing needs of cities. Early cities used only geometric models or 2D maps that did not have the ability to analyze behavior or intra-city dynamics. With the advent of GIS and 3D tools, more realistic representations of the city became possible, but the models still lacked real-time data and the ability to interact with real systems. With the development of IoT networks and the use of data that continuously flows from infrastructure, sensors, traffic, weather, and transportation systems, the ground was prepared for the transition to a true digital twin; a model that not only reflects the current state of the city, but also predicts the future behavior of the systems. In new generations, the urban digital twin has become part of the city's data-driven ecosystem and, through connections to analytics, machine learning, and predictive scenario-building engines, provides the ability to assess the consequences of decisions before they are implemented (Nozari, 2025a).

Urban digital twin can be considered as a multi-layered framework that is formed by the connection between the physical and digital worlds. Data from the real environment is first placed in the collection layer, then it enters the integration, cleaning and processing process and is finally used in the digital twin model. This model not only represents the geometric image of the city, but also models the behavior of urban systems, flows and actions. Such a structure has made digital twin as a comprehensive tool, enabling complex analyses on a city scale; for example, understanding traffic patterns, predicting energy consumption, crisis management, monitoring air quality, evaluating urban development scenarios or analyzing the effects of land use changes are among the capabilities that are made possible with the help of digital twin.

One of the most important features of urban digital twin is the ability to interact and learn from real data. Traditional models were based on fixed assumptions and did not change much after design, but digital twins can modify their parameters and adjust their behavior according to real conditions by receiving updated data. This learning capability reduces the gap between the model and reality and makes the system more suitable for managing complex and dynamic cities. On the other hand, digital twins enable the implementation of "what if" analyses and allow city managers to examine the consequences of their policies and decisions before implementation and without real costs.

The evolution of urban digital twins has not only been driven by technological advances, but also by a change in the approach to governance in cities. In the past, decision-making was based more on intuition, experience, and limited studies, but with the increase in urban complexity and environmental instability, the need for tools for data-driven decision-making and predictive analytics has intensified. As a bridge between the world of data and urban governance, digital twins enable managers to make policies with greater precision, greater flexibility, and less risk. This is particularly important in areas such as crisis management, where rapidly changing conditions require instant and intelligent decisions.

In recent years, urban digital twins have been seen as more than a simulation tool and have emerged as a central platform for coordinating urban systems. They can integrate data from different systems such as transportation, buildings, energy, water, the environment, and urban health, providing a unified and analyzable picture. The result is increased transparency, improved efficiency of urban operations, easier asset management, and reduced maintenance costs. Furthermore, digital twinning plays a pivotal role in improving citizen engagement, as it can make urban data and models available to the public in a visually understandable format, helping to increase awareness and participation in urban decision-making (Aliahmadi et al., 2022).

Urban digital twinning is also directly aligned with the goals of Economy 5.0, as it creates a platform in which human decision-making and artificial intelligence work together in a complementary manner. With this model, the city becomes an intelligent, forward-looking, and human-centered system that is able to improve sustainable development and quality of life with a data-driven approach. This alignment has made digital twinning increasingly important not only from a technical perspective, but also from an economic and social perspective, and has become a fundamental element of next-generation cities.

4- DATA-DRIVEN ARCHITECTURE FOR CREATING AN URBAN DIGITAL TWIN

Creating an effective city digital twin requires a data-centric architecture that can collect, process, and deliver a continuous, diverse, and massive stream of city data in a structured manner to simulation and decision-making models. This architecture is the backbone of the digital twin, because without a stable and integrated platform for data management, it is not possible to create a living and dynamic model of the city. The data-centric architecture not only helps organize and standardize data, but also provides a link between physical infrastructure, digital systems, analysis models, and governance layers. In Figure 2, this architecture is depicted as layered and flow-oriented; in such a way that data starts from the real city environment, passes through processing and integration layers, reaches the digital twin model, and finally reaches the decision-making engines (Nozari & Nassar, 2025).

Figure 2. Data-Centric Layered Architecture for Building an Urban Digital Twin

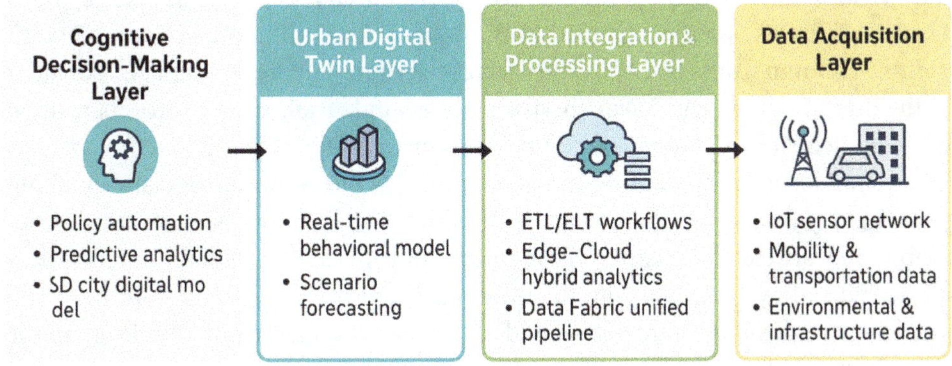

In the first layer of this architecture, the data collection layer, all raw information is collected from sensors, smart systems, cameras, transportation networks, energy and environmental infrastructure, and other data sources. This layer is the direct point of contact between the physical city and its digital structure, and is responsible for transferring different parts of the data with the lowest latency and highest accuracy. The main challenge of this stage is the diversity and heterogeneity of the data; because urban data can be structured, semi-structured, or completely unstructured, and have very different production rates. The data-driven architecture must function in a way that can support this data in various formats and prepare it for processing.

After data collection, this information enters the integration, processing, and intelligence layer. In this layer, the data is cleaned, filtered, standardized, and transformed into usable formats. This part of the architecture is particularly important because raw data is often noisy, repetitive, inconsistent, or fragmented, and only after processing can it be fed into digital twin models. Edge and cloud computing technologies also play a key role in this layer; edge processing enables rapid data analysis at the point of production, and cloud computing enables the management of large amounts of data and the execution of complex algorithms. Another key component of this layer is the Data Fabric, which, like a data flow engine, enables the simultaneous connection of different data sources and their transfer to the digital twin model. This part makes the data-driven architecture resilient to system changes and highly scalable.

Next, the processed data enters the modeling and digital twin layer. This layer is the heart of the system and is responsible for transforming real data into an interpretable digital model. In this model, the geometric structure of the city, the infrastructure components and the dynamic behavior of the systems are represented in the form of multidimensional simulations. The data transmitted from the lower layers allows for real-time updating of the model, and this combination makes the digital twin not a static image, but a "living digital city". The model can analyze different scenarios, predict future behaviors and show the connections between systems. The importance of this layer becomes more apparent when we consider that the digital twin in the 5.0 economy is not a single tool, but a central part of an intelligent decision-making ecosystem (Aliahmadi & Nozari, 2023).

The final layer of the data-driven architecture is the cognitive decision-making layer. This layer receives the output of the digital twin analyses and provides actionable and efficient decisions through learning models, predictive algorithms, data-driven policy tools and intelligent control engines. This is where data and analytics are translated into policy and action. A key feature of this layer is the feedback loop, which allows the results of decisions to be fed back into the digital twin model, allowing the system to correct or optimize itself. This learning loop is the foundation of smart governance in future cities.

From an operational perspective, data-driven architecture brings wide-ranging benefits to cities. For example, in transportation management, real-time data from sensors and cameras is processed into a digital twin model to represent current traffic conditions. The model can then predict future traffic flows and provide recommendations for optimal management. In energy, data from buildings and distribution networks can be analyzed in a digital twin model to allow the city to optimize consumption patterns and prevent waste. In crisis management, digital twins can predict emergencies such as floods, fires, or air pollution and identify rapid response routes.

Importantly, data-driven architecture is not simply a technical structure, but a governance framework that defines how data, technology, and urban decision-making interact. This architecture plays a very prominent role in Economy 5.0, because the new economy is based on the free flow of data, transparency, citizen participation and smart value creation. Data-driven architecture creates a context in which all these elements work together, and the result will be to improve the resilience, productivity and sustainability of the city (Nozari & Yordanova, 2025).

In general, data-driven architecture for creating an urban digital twin not only provides the necessary technical platform for simulation and intelligent analysis, but also creates conditions for the city to operate as a dynamic, learning and forward-looking system. This architecture enables cities to cope with complex challenges and make more accurate and effective decisions through intelligent data processing.

For this reason, the design and implementation of data-driven architecture is one of the most important elements of the development of digital twins and the transition to cities based on Economy 5.0.

5- LINKING URBAN DIGITAL TWIN WITH ECONOMY 5.0

The digital transformation of cities in the last decade has not only been limited to making infrastructures smarter, but has also moved towards creating systems that create a value-creating cycle between technology, humans, and the urban environment. In this regard, urban digital twinning, as one of the most advanced modeling and decision-making tools, plays a key role in realizing Economy 5.0; an economy based on human-centeredness, sustainability, resilience, and the intelligent use of technology to improve the quality of life. Unlike previous models that focused solely on productivity, Economy 5.0 attempts to apply new technologies in a way that also strengthens the social, environmental, and welfare dimensions of urban development. Urban digital twinning is considered one of the most important tools of this transition due to its integrated, learning, and forward-looking nature (Bhatia & Kumar, 2026).

In Economy 5.0, data is considered a strategic asset. The value of this data increases when it can be transformed into actionable insights for decision-making, policy design, and urban activity management. By providing a platform for integrating, processing, and analyzing real-time data from infrastructure, the environment, and citizen behavior, urban digital twins enable cities to make decisions based not on guesswork but on accurate and predictive analysis. This is in line with the spirit of Economy 5.0, in which systems must be able to operate more intelligently and efficiently by combining data and cognitive technologies. In such a context, Digital Twins play the role of a connecting link between data and urban governance.

On the other hand, Economy 5.0 emphasizes urban sustainability and resilience. Today's cities face challenges such as climate change, population growth, pressure on infrastructure, and environmental crises. By enabling forecasting, identifying vulnerabilities, and analyzing different scenarios, urban digital twins help city managers make decisions that increase city resilience. For example, in energy management, digital twins can analyze actual consumption, behavioral patterns, and waste points, and provide suggestions that reduce consumption and increase sustainability. In such a case, digital twins are a valuable tool not only from a technological perspective, but also from an economic and environmental perspective (Nozari et al., 2021).

Economy 5.0 also emphasizes the integration of humans and technology; that is, instead of replacing humans with machines, it tries to increase the synergy between human capabilities and technological processing power. Urban digital twins achieve this synergy in two ways: first, by providing visual and understandable models, it empowers citizens, managers, and stakeholders to better understand the state of the city; Second, it translates the results of complex analytics into a language that can be used for human decision-making. This feature makes the governance process in Economy 5.0 more participatory, transparent, and efficient than ever before. When citizens can see the state of their neighborhoods, traffic, pollution, and other urban indicators in the form of digital models, their participation in the decision-making process increases, which leads to strengthening social capital and public trust.

From an economic perspective, urban digital twins act as a value-generating infrastructure. Through the optimal use of data, cities can reduce operating costs, increase infrastructure efficiency, and improve public services. For example, in waste management, digital twins can optimize collection routes; in transportation, they can predict traffic patterns and facilitate traffic decongestion; and in urban development, they can simulate the effects of projects before they are implemented. Together, these functions lead to increased economic productivity and pave the way for smart growth. Economy 5.0 also seeks to create new business models, such as providing data as a service or using digital platforms to manage assets. The city digital twin strengthens this opportunity by creating a huge source of structured data and paves the way for the development of innovative ecosystems.

Another important aspect of the link between digital twinning and Economy 5.0 is its role in spatial and social justice. Economy 5.0 is not only about improving efficiency, but also pursuing equitable development and reducing inequalities. By providing a comprehensive picture of the situation in different parts of the city, digital twinning can help identify gaps, deprived areas and patterns of inequality. These analyses pave the way for policies designed to improve public services, reduce pollution, promote safety or increase access to facilities. In fact, digital twinning can be a practical tool for achieving urban justice in Economy 5.0.

The link between urban digital twinning and Economy 5.0 is also evident in crisis and emergency management. In critical situations, the speed and accuracy of decision-making are of vital importance. Digital twinning enables faster and more effective responses by modeling and predicting conditions, identifying sensitive areas and analyzing the possible effects of decisions. This is fully in line with the principles of Economy 5.0, which emphasizes resilience, flexibility, and proactive management (Nozari & Tavakkoli-Moghaddam, 2026).

Ultimately, urban digital twinning is not just a technology, but a transformative framework on the path to Economy 5.0. By integrating data, analytics, and decision-making, it enables cities to move away from traditional, reactive models and toward smart, sustainable, and people-centered governance. This transition will shift the trajectory of urban development from quantitative to qualitative growth, resulting in cities that are not only more efficient, but also more livable, sustainable, and equitable.

6- KEY APPLICATIONS OF URBAN DIGITAL TWIN IN ECONOMY 5.0

Digital transformation in cities makes sense when technology can actually improve quality of life, infrastructure efficiency, urban resilience and social justice. This is precisely why urban digital twinning has become crucial in Economy 5.0. By providing an intelligent, data-driven and real-time simulation environment, this technology allows cities not only to better understand their current situation, but also to predict the future and guide their development path. The applications of urban digital twinning in Economy 5.0 are broad and multidimensional, encompassing a combination of technological innovation and social value creation. These applications can be seen in areas such as transport, energy, environment, crisis management, urban development and digital governance, each of which is directly aligned with the goals of Economy 5.0 (Nozari et al., 2022).

In the field of transportation, urban digital twinning is one of the most effective tools for traffic management, optimizing traffic flow and predicting travel patterns. Digital models can represent the state of transportation networks in real time and examine the effects of changes in infrastructure, traffic light timing, new route development or transportation policies before implementation. This capability will not only reduce congestion and energy consumption, but will also increase safety, reduce accidents and improve citizen satisfaction. In the 5.0 economy, which emphasizes human-centeredness and sustainability, this type of intelligent management is vital and will increase efficiency and equity of access.

In the energy sector, urban digital twinning also plays a special role. This model can analyze energy consumption patterns in buildings, distribution networks, urban lighting and industries and identify points where energy is wasted the most. Using these models, the city can adopt solutions to reduce consumption, manage grid load, increase efficiency and develop renewable energies. Digital twins are also able to simulate the effects of energy development plans before implementation to reduce the risk of decisions. Such an approach, which is based on data, forecasting and scientific analysis, is precisely in line with the Economy 5.0 approach, which aims to optimize resource consumption and reduce the environmental impact of urban development (Imandi et al., 2025).

The environment is another key area of application of urban digital twins. Today's cities face challenges such as air pollution, climate change, resource scarcity and environmental threats. Urban digital twins allow patterns of environmental changes to be identified and the effects of different actions on air quality, temperature, vegetation or noise pollution to be analyzed. With the help of real-time data from environmental sensors, the digital twin model can predict the response of the environment to different scenarios; For example, the effect of changing traffic routes on air pollution, the impact of installing ventilation systems in densely populated areas, or the impact of developing green areas on reducing urban temperatures. These types of analyses are important in Economy 5.0, because environmental sustainability is one of its main pillars.

Digital twins can also play a very important role in the field of crisis management and urban security. Crises such as floods, earthquakes, urban fires or industrial accidents require rapid response and accurate decision-making. Using digital twins, managers can assess critical situations before they occur in a simulated environment, identify infrastructure weaknesses and optimize emergency response routes. The model can predict population behavior, transport network capacity, potential bottlenecks and safe evacuation routes. After a crisis, digital twins can also play an effective role in damage assessment and urban recovery management. These analyses are fully consistent with the principles of Economy 5.0, which emphasizes resilience and a proactive approach.

Another important application of digital twins is in urban development and planning. Urban designs are often complex and costly, and their consequences may not be apparent for years. Using urban digital twins allows designers to analyze the effects of land use development, the construction of new areas, the rerouting of streets, or the creation of public spaces before they are implemented. The model can predict the behavior of different systems in response to new development and provide solutions to mitigate negative impacts. Such capabilities help city managers make decisions that are aligned with the long-term vision and principles of Economy 5.0.

One of the most innovative applications of digital twins in Economy 5.0 is the development of data-driven services and new economic models. Using structured and analytical data, cities can create new services, from optimizing energy consumption at the neighborhood level to intelligent management of transportation fleets and even providing data as a service. These capacities lead to the development of an innovative economy, increased productivity and the creation of new job opportunities. In addition, the private sector can also use digital twins to design services based on the real needs of the city; services such as asset management, smart building maintenance and customer behavior analysis (Nozari, 2026).

On the social side, digital twins can increase citizen participation and awareness. Visual and understandable digital twin models can show citizens how the city is doing, how management decisions affect their lives and what options are available for improvement. This transparency increases public trust and strengthens urban democracy. In Economy 5.0, the active role of citizens is very important and digital twins can be an effective participation tool.

Overall, urban digital twins offer a wide range of impactful applications that affect both the economic, social and environmental dimensions of urban development. This technology not only increases the productivity and sustainability of cities, but also helps to shape smart and human-centered governance. Linking these capabilities with the goals of Economy 5.0, Digital Twin has become one of the essential tools of the cities of the future; tools that transform cities from a passive state to a predictive, learning and value-creating state.

7- PROPOSED CONCEPTUAL MODEL

Designing a conceptual model for implementing urban digital twin in the context of economy 5.0 requires a deep understanding of the multi-layered interactions between data, technology, urban infrastructure, decision-making, and human participation. This model should be developed in a way that can, on the one hand, cover the inherent complexities of the city in physical, functional, and behavioral dimensions, and, on the other hand, be aligned with the principles of economy 5.0 that emphasize human-centeredness, sustainability, resilience, and digital value creation. In the proposed approach, urban digital twin is considered not only as a technical tool, but also as a cognitive-social system that creates a continuous learning loop between the real and digital worlds. The conceptual model presented in this research consists of four fundamental components: data flow, digital modeling layer, cognitive decision-making engine, and human-centered feedback loop. These components interact in an integrated and dynamic structure and lead to the formation of an efficient architecture for smart city management (Shafik, 2025).

In the first step, the data flow is considered as the fundamental element of the model. Data is collected from the city level and through a wide network of sensors, transportation systems, infrastructure equipment, energy systems, environment, cameras and smart devices. This data is constantly changing and evolving, providing a live picture of the city's situation. The proposed model feeds this raw data into the processing layer, where cleaning, standardization, integration and knowledge extraction operations are performed. In this step, the Data Fabric structure plays a key role and allows diverse data sources to enter the digital flow without creating a break. This processing layer provides the basis for updating the digital twin and establishes the connection between the physical infrastructure and the digital model.

In the second step, the processed data is fed into the modeling layer and creates the digital twin. This layer is the heart of the conceptual model because it transforms real-world data into a multidimensional digital structure. The digital model includes a three-dimensional representation of the city, dynamic behaviors, relationships between subsystems, and performance patterns. The model not only reflects the current state of the city, but is also able to predict the future behavior of the systems based on predictive analytics, learning algorithms, and scenario simulations. The digital twin acts as an “urban laboratory” at this stage, where the consequences of decisions, actions, and development projects can be investigated without real costs. This predictive capability is a critical element of Economy 5.0, as it guides the system from reactive to intelligent and proactive management (Nozari, 2024).

The third component of the conceptual model is the cognitive decision-making engine, which receives the output of the digital twin and uses it to generate recommendations, policies, and intelligent decisions. This component is a combination of advanced analysis algorithms, machine learning, predictive models, decision support systems and intelligent monitoring tools. The cognitive decision-making engine is not only able to analyze the city's situation, but also to provide suggestions for optimizing resource consumption, crisis management, improving infrastructure performance and improving the quality of life. This component is also able to analyze social, environmental and economic indicators alongside technical data and adjust decisions within the framework of the human-centered economy 5.0. The distinctive feature of this component is its ability to continuously learn; meaning that it adjusts and optimizes itself by receiving new feedback.

Finally, the fourth component of the conceptual model is the human-centered feedback loop. Unlike previous approaches that replaced humans with technology, Economy 5.0 emphasizes the synergy of humans and technology. In this model, feedback from citizens, managers, and end-users enters the system as part of the data flow and enriches the digital twin. This feedback can include citizens' needs, priorities, perceptions, and assessments of the city's situation. By integrating this human feedback, the proposed conceptual model guides the system towards spatial justice, social well-being, and participatory governance. This feedback loop also increases transparency and public trust, as citizens see that decisions are made based on data and their real needs.

The interaction between these four components makes the urban digital twin function as an integrated and dynamic system. The model not only has the ability to analyze the past and present, but also predicts the future, helping the city make decisions based on science, data, and foresight. In the field of transportation, the model can analyze traffic patterns and suggest optimal routes; in the energy sector, it can identify network loads and waste points; in urban development, it can predict the impacts of projects; and in crisis management, it can provide the best response scenarios. These capabilities show that the conceptual model is not just a theoretical construct, but can also be a practical basis for designing next-generation urban systems (Mazzetto, 2024).

Overall, the proposed conceptual model attempts to redefine urban digital twin within the framework of Economy 5.0; a framework in which data, technology, people, and policy interact in a continuous and intelligent learning cycle. This model emphasizes the connection between data layers, digital modeling, and decision-making, with the ultimate goal of creating a resilient, sustainable, innovative, and human-centered city. In such an approach, digital twinning will not be an auxiliary tool but a strategic infrastructure in the path of future urban development.

8- CONCLUSION

The digital transformation in urban management has reached a point where it can no longer be considered a mere technological trend; it has become a fundamental paradigm shift in the way cities are understood, analyzed, and managed. In this regard, urban digital twinning, as one of the most pivotal transformative technologies, plays a decisive role in creating smart, resilient, and human-centered cities. Focusing on Economy 5.0, this research showed that urban digital twinning is not just a technological model, but a cognitive-social framework that is able to create a dynamic link between data, people, and urban policymaking. The result is a city that is managed not based on guesswork, but on data-driven analysis, predictive simulation, and human feedback.

In the first parts of the research, it became clear that Economy 5.0, unlike previous generations that focused mainly on industrial optimization and automation, follows a human-centered, sustainable, and value-oriented approach. In this framework, technology is not a substitute for humans but a complement; data is used not only for economic efficiency but also to improve the quality of life; and decision-making is not solely at the disposal of machine systems, but is shaped in an interactive cycle of human participation, artificial intelligence, and data-driven policymaking. Urban digital twins operate precisely with this logic. This technology is able to simulate the city as a living and dynamic organism, predict the behavior of systems, test different scenarios, and enable informed, rapid, and responsible decision-making.

A review of the theoretical foundations and evolution of digital twins showed that this concept initially entered the urban sphere from manufacturing industries, but in cities it acquired much more complex dimensions. Cities are multilayered, dynamic systems influenced by social, environmental, and economic factors. Digital twins can transform this complexity into an analyzable structure and allow managers to predict the future behavior of the city. This capability is particularly important in crisis management, infrastructure optimization, urban development planning, and traffic management. At the same time, the Digital Twin is also an educational and participatory tool because it provides citizens with a clear and understandable picture of the city's situation and allows them to play a more active role in urban decisions.

In the data-driven architecture section, it was also clear that without a unified data structure, the Digital Twin will not be able to function effectively. The layers of collection, processing, integration, modeling, and decision-making must operate in a coherent architecture to transform raw data into usable knowledge. Here, the role of the Data Fabric, edge processing, cloud computing, machine learning algorithms, and real-time data streams is very key. Such a data-driven architecture allows the Digital Twin to adapt to the reality of the city moment by moment and provide an accurate and dynamic picture of the current situation.

The connection between urban digital twin and Economy 5.0 showed that this technology can serve as the main infrastructure for smart governance in future cities. Digital twin realizes the values of Economy 5.0 by enhancing transparency, accountability, and social participation. On the other hand, by reducing operating costs, increasing energy efficiency, improving asset management, and developing innovative data-driven services, this technology can contribute to sustainable economic growth. Finally, Economy 5.0's emphasis on social justice and public welfare is aligned with the capabilities of Digital Twin, as it can reveal urban inequalities, service gaps, vulnerabilities, and the real needs of citizens, and provide a basis for equitable policymaking.

The conceptual model proposed in this study provided a comprehensive and practical framework in which four main components (data flow, Digital Twin layer, cognitive decision-making engine, and human-centered feedback) are defined in an integrated and cyclical structure. This model shows that digital twinning is only effective when a continuous learning cycle is formed between technology and humans. In other words, data is transformed into a model, model into analysis, analysis into decision, and decision into human feedback; and this feedback is fed back into the data stream to improve the system itself. Such a cycle creates a learning urban system that is able to continuously adapt and move towards sustainable development.

Finally, this research showed that urban digital twinning can be one of the most effective tools to achieve the goals of Economy 5.0. This technology allows cities to experience the future before it happens, make decisions more accurately, increase social participation and improve public services. As a result, the path of future cities will be clearer, more scientific and more human-centered through digital twinning. The development of this technology in the coming years is expected to not only improve the quality of urban life, but also create a new foundation for governance, urban development, and the smart economy, a foundation in which data, technology, and humans work together to build a better future.

REFERENCES

Aliahmadi, A., & Nozari, H. (2023, January). Evaluation of security metrics in AIoT and blockchain-based supply chain by Neutrosophic decision-making method. In Supply chain forum: an international journal (Vol. 24, No. 1, pp. 31-42). Taylor & Francis.

Aliahmadi, A., Nozari, H., Ghahremani-Nahr, J., & Szmelter-Jarosz, A. (2022). Evaluation of key impression of resilient supply chain based on artificial intelligence of things (AIoT). arXiv preprint arXiv:2207.13174.

Bhatia, M., & Kumar, V. (2026). The role of digital twin in urban infrastructure and building management: A global scientometric perspective. *Cluster Computing*, *29*(1), 38.

Imandi, R., Chethana, B., Prasad, B. P., Sethi, K., & Kumar, B. P. (2025). Enhancing Data Management in Industry 5.0: The Role of Digital Twins in Optimizing Industrial Operations. In *Industry 5.0: Key Technologies and Drivers* (pp. 211–236). Springer Nature Switzerland.

Mazzetto, S. (2024). A review of urban digital twins integration, challenges, and future directions in smart city development. *Sustainability*, *16*(19), 8337.

Mazzetto, S. (2024). A review of urban digital twins integration, challenges, and future directions in smart city development. *Sustainability*, *16*(19), 8337.

Nassar, S., Nozari, H., & Samadi, S. (2025). AIoE-Based Multi-objective Optimization for Smart and Sustainable Warehouse Management. In *Artificial Intelligence of Everything and Sustainable Development* (pp. 241–255). Springer Nature Singapore.

Nozari, H. (Ed.). (2023). *Building Smart and Sustainable Businesses with Transformative Technologies*. IGI Global.

Nozari, H. (2024). Green supply chain management based on artificial intelligence of everything. *Journal of Economics and Management*, *46*, 171–188.

Nozari, H. (2025). Integrating Neuromorphic Intelligence with Fuzzy Multi-Objective Models in Resilient Green Supply Chain Design. Process Integration and Optimization for Sustainability, 1-14.

Nozari, H. (2026). Neuromorphic-driven energy optimization in smart urban logistics. In *Energy-Efficient Transformative Technologies for Data-Driven Smart Cities* (pp. 211–228). Elsevier.

Nozari, H., Abdi, H., Szmelter-Jarosz, A., & Rahmaty, M. (2025). A digital twin-based neutrosophic multi-objective optimization model for smart supply chains in the food industry. *Journal of Intelligent Manufacturing*, •••, 1–15.

Nozari, H., Fallah, M., Kazemipoor, H., & Najafi, S. E. (2021). Big data analysis of IoT-based supply chain management considering FMCG industries. *Бизнес-информатика*, *15*(1 (eng)), 78–96.

Nozari, H., & Nassar, S. (2025). Real-time data-driven multi-objective optimization in B2B marketing using digital twins. OPSEARCH, 1-27.

Nozari, H., Szmelter-Jarosz, A., & Ghahremani-Nahr, J. (2022). Analysis of the challenges of artificial intelligence of things (AIoT) for the smart supply chain (case study: FMCG industries). *Sensors (Basel)*, *22*(8), 2931. PMID: 35458916

Nozari, H., Szmelter-Jarosz, A., & Weiland, D. (2025). A Fuzzy Multi-Objective Sustainable and Agile Supply Chain Model Based on Digital Twin and Internet of Things with Adaptive Learning Under Environmental Uncertainty. *Applied Sciences (Basel, Switzerland)*, *15*(19), 10399.

Nozari, H., & Tavakkoli-Moghaddam, R. (2026). Edge computing for an energy-efficient super-smart city. In *Energy-Efficient Transformative Technologies for Data-Driven Smart Cities* (pp. 197–210). Elsevier.

Nozari, H., & Yordanova, Z. (2025). An intelligent digital twin approach for optimizing multi-channel supply chains in uncertain environments. Green Technologies and Sustainability, 100309.

Omar, O. (2025). Digital twins for climate-responsive urban development: Integrating zero-energy buildings into smart city strategies. *Sustainability*, *17*(15), 6670.

SHAFIK, W. (2025). Navigating Artificial Intelligence and Digital Twin for Smart Cities. Driving Innovation through AI and Digital Twin for 6G Powered Sustainable Ultra Smart Cities, 1-26.

Tu, X., Ala-Laurinaho, R., Yang, C., Autiosalo, J., & Tammi, K. (2024). Architecture for data-centric and semantic-enhanced industrial metaverse: Bridging physical factories and virtual landscape. *Journal of Manufacturing Systems*, *74*, 965–979.

Chapter 5
A Human-Centric Technological Revolution in Agriculture-Industry 5.0 for Sustainable Agripreneurship

Pawan Prabhakar
https://orcid.org/0000-0002-3665-9486
Woxsen University, Hyderabad, India

ABSTRACT

Industry 5.0 signifies the forthcoming advancement in industrial transformation, shifting away from the automation-focused model of Industry 4.0 to emphasise collaboration between humans and machines, as well as the creation of sustainable value. Industry 4.0 focused on enhancing efficiency via cyber-physical systems, artificial intelligence, and the Internet of Things, whereas Industry 5.0 aims to re-establish the importance of humans in production processes Unlike Industry 4.0, which emphasized precision farming through IoT, drones, AI, and big data, Industry 5.0 integrates these technologies with human creativity, intuition, and local knowledge to build value-driven agricultural enterprises. Agripreneurs adopting Industry 5.0 approaches leverage robotics, AI-assisted decision tools, and digital twins alongside traditional farming wisdom to achieve sustainable intensification, resource optimization, and climate-resilient cultivation practices.

DOI: 10.4018/979-8-3693-4525-2.ch005

INTRODUCTION

The concept of Industry 5.0 has gained prominence as a progressive response to the limitations and challenges posed by Industry 4.0.The Industry 4.0 was largely characterized by the integration of cyber-physical systems, the Internet of Things (IoT), Artificial Intelligence (AI), big data analytics, and widespread automation often aimed at maximizing efficiency, reducing costs, and minimizing human intervention (Aheleroff, Huang, Xu & Zhong, 2022; Narkhede, Pasi, Rajhans & Kulkarni, 2023). Industry 5.0 brings a transformative shift by re-centering the role of humans in the industrial landscape. It challenges the notion that machines alone should drive progress and instead promotes a synergistic partnership between humans and advanced technologies. This evolution is not merely technological, but also philosophical and ethical, focusing on how innovation can serve broader social goals (Adel, 2022). Industry 5.0 advocates for a more human-centric approach where technological development is aligned with values such as well-being, social equity, and environmental sustainability. It reflects a significant philosophical and operational shift in how we perceive the role of technology in society. Unlike Industry 4.0, which primarily prioritized efficiency, speed, and automation through artificial intelligence, robotics, and data, Industry 5.0 acknowledges that industrial progress must also be measured in terms of its impact on people and the planet (Islam et al., 2025; Hu et al., 2025).

A human-centric approach means putting people not machines at the heart of innovation. It recognizes that technology should serve humanity rather than replace it. In practical terms, this means designing work environments that enhance employee satisfaction, safety, and mental health. For instance, collaborative robots (cobots) are used not to eliminate human jobs but to assist workers in physically demanding or repetitive tasks, allowing them to focus on creative and decision-making roles. This improves both productivity and job satisfaction, thereby promoting human well-being (Matheson et al., 2019). Social equity in Industry 5.0 addresses the need to ensure that technological advancements do not deepen societal inequalities. Social equity in Industry 5.0 means more than just opening the door to new technologies about building an industrial transformation that actively dismantles existing barriers and ensures everyone shares in its benefits. In practical terms, this starts with bridging the digital divide: rural communities, women, persons with disabilities, and economically underprivileged groups must have affordable access to high-speed internet, smart devices, and digital literacy programs. Without these foundations, any AI-driven process or IoT-enabled workflow only magnifies the gap between the "haves" and the "have-nots." Industry 5.0 therefore calls for public–private partnerships to invest in community training centres, mobile tech labs, and scholarship schemes so that people from all backgrounds can acquire the skills to operate, maintain, and even co-create advanced manufacturing systems (Adel, 2022; Fogaca et al., 2025). Beyond access, social equity demands inclusive design. The Products, interfaces, and workstations should be developed with diverse users in mind from cobots with adjustable heights to software dashboards that support multiple languages (including local Indian languages), voice commands, and accessibility features for the visually and hearing impaired. When factories and service platforms are co-designed with feedback from frontline workers especially women and those with disabilities, they become more usable, safer, and ultimately more productive. This participatory approach also builds a sense of ownership and pride among workers, reducing attrition and fostering a culture of continuous improvement (Muratovski, 2015; Cheng et al., 2024).

Industry 5.0 promotes equitable opportunity and reward by fundamentally reshaping the relationship between technology, people, and the economy. Unlike previous industrial revolutions that prioritized efficiency, automation, and mass production, Industry 5.0 centers on a human-centric approach where technological advancement serves human needs rather than replacing them. This means creating work environments where humans and intelligent machines collaborate rather than compete. In doing so, it opens opportunities for a broader segment of society to participate meaningfully in the innovation economy (Gamberini & Pluchino, 2024). For example, while Industry 4.0 might have replaced manual roles with automation, Industry 5.0 leverages human creativity, emotional intelligence, craftsmanship, and decision-making alongside AI and robotics, recognizing these human contributions as invaluable and irreplaceable. It seeks to bridge digital divides by making advanced tools more accessible to workers in marginalized or low-income communities, rural areas, and developing countries. This democratization of access ensures that not only tech-savvy urban populations benefit from digital growth, but also those traditionally left behind in earlier industrial transitions (Erol et al., 2019). Furthermore, by aligning with principles of social equity, inclusion, and sustainability, Industry 5.0 supports policies and systems that promote fair wages, safe working conditions, and lifelong learning, thus enabling continuous upskilling and reskilling across diverse populations. Governments and businesses embracing this model are encouraged to adopt ethical frameworks where productivity gains do not just increase corporate profits but are fairly distributed in the form of job creation, social welfare improvements, and reduced economic inequality. Ultimately, Industry 5.0 envisions a regenerative and inclusive economy where technological progress goes hand in hand with human dignity, empowerment, and equitable reward. While Industry 5.0 offers many promising opportunities for innovation and sustainability, its application in agripreneurship entrepreneurship in the agriculture sector faces several key challenges and problems like digital divide and lack of infrastructure, technology gap, high cost of adoption, lack of customized solutions that limit its effective implementation (Kashinatahan et al., 2022; Narkhede, Pasi, Rajhans & Kulkarni, 2025). By embedding these measures into their core operating model, Industry 5.0 makes sure that technological progress does not concentrate wealth and opportunities at the top, but spreads them throughout the entire workforce and the wider business ecosystem. The result is a more motivated, innovative, and socially cohesive industry one where everyone has a real stake in success. As automation takes over repetitive tasks, organizations must pair technology deployment with robust upskilling and reskilling initiatives ideally funded or subsidized by industry consortia so that employees can transition into higher-value roles in quality control, data analysis, or collaborative robotics (Raja Santhi & Muthuswamy, 2023). The wage policies must reflect the increased skill levels and not penalize workers displaced by automation. Moreover, small, and medium enterprises (SMEs) should have access to shared "innovation hubs" or "micro-factory as a service" models, enabling them to experiment with cutting-edge technologies without prohibitive capital expenditure (Prabhakar et al., 2025).

Therefore, by integrating these principles access, inclusion, and fair reward into the very blueprint of industrial development and Industry 5.0 ensures that technological progress becomes a true engine of social upliftment, rather than a force that widens existing inequalities. Access to new technologies, training programs, and economic opportunities should be distributed fairly across different demographics including women, rural populations, and underprivileged communities so that no one is left behind in the industrial transformation (Prabhakar & Nimesh, 2022). This approach aims to bridge the digital divide, promote inclusive growth, and build resilient communities. Environmental sustainability, the third pillar, means that industries must operate within ecological limits and use resources responsibly. Industry 5.0 supports innovations that reduce carbon emissions, minimize waste, and promote circular economy models where materials are reused and recycled. For example, using AI not just for optimizing production lines, but for monitoring environmental impact, predicting equipment wear to reduce energy waste, or enhancing supply chain transparency to ensure ethical sourcing. In essence, Industry 5.0 reframes the purpose of technology from merely generating profit and efficiency to co-creating a future that is sustainable, fair, and humane (Nishant et al., 2020; Gundeti et al., 2024). Therefore, integrating ethical considerations, social responsibility, and long-term ecological impact into the core of industrial advancement, Industry 5.0 does not discard the achievements of Industry 4.0 but rather builds upon them to forge a future where human dignity and the planet are prioritized alongside productivity and growth. This chapter deals with the role and importance of industry 5.0 in agripreneurship together with several issues and obstacles that hinder the successful implementation of Industry 5.0 in agripreneurship. Such as elevated implementation expenses and restricted access to new technology inhibit smallholder involvement., deficiencies in digital literacy and insufficient training pose obstacles for rural youth and women entrepreneurs. Although, Industry 5.0 possesses revolutionary potential for agripreneurship, it is imperative to surmount these economic, social, and infrastructural obstacles to achieve a human-centric, inclusive, and sustainable agricultural future.

BACKGROUND

Key Drivers of Industry 5.0

Industry 5.0 represents the subsequent advancement in industrial development, emphasising not just efficiency and automation but also human-centricity, sustainability, and resilience. In contrast to Industry 4.0, which focused on smart factories and machine-to-machine communication, Industry 5.0 repositions humans at the core of innovation by facilitating collaboration between humans and intelligent machines (Singh et al., 2023). As it anticipates an economy in which technical progress is harmonised with social, ethical, and environmental principles. Therefore, it is important to discover the significant factors responsible for driving and promoting the industry 5.0 in current scenario. The key drivers for a sustainable and effective industry 5.0 are:

Human-Centric Innovation

Human-centric innovation denotes the design, development, and deployment of technologies, systems, and solutions that prioritise human requirements, values, and experiences. In the framework of Industry 5.0, this signifies that technology is engineered to accommodate human needs rather than the reverse empowering individuals, augmenting their capacities, and promoting overall well-being in both professional and personal spheres (Nahavandi, 2019). At the core of Industry 5.0 lies a transformative shift in how we perceive the role of technology: instead of people adapting to machines, technology is adapted to serve people. This core principle reimagines innovation not just as a tool for productivity, but to uplift the human experience, emphasizing well-being, purpose, and creativity over pure efficiency or automation (Carayannis et al., 2022).

In practical terms, this means that the design and implementation of industrial systems must prioritize human values, such as dignity, inclusion, safety, and personal fulfilment. For example, in a manufacturing plant, rather than completely automating every process, cobots (collaborative robots) can be used to assist workers by handling heavy, dangerous, or repetitive tasks freeing up human workers to focus on tasks that require critical thinking, empathy, artistic judgment, or problem-solving. This not only increases job satisfaction but also creates more meaningful work environments where humans are not replaced by machines but are empowered by them. Furthermore, this approach recognizes that humans possess unique strengths like emotional intelligence, ethical reasoning, contextual understanding, and creativity that no machine can replicate. As such, Industry 5.0 emphasizes customization over standardization, allowing businesses to create personalized products and services that reflect individual consumer needs and values, something only humans can truly understand and deliver with care. This people-first mindset also applies beyond the factory floor (Matheson et al., 2019). In sectors like healthcare, education, agriculture, and design, Industry 5.0 technologies are being developed with a focus on enhancing human potential rather than automating it away. Decision-support systems, for instance, do not replace doctors or teachers, but help them make better, faster, and more personalized decisions (Basulo-Ribeiro & Teixeira, 2024). Ultimately, Industry 5.0 promotes a vision of progress where technological advancement is balanced with social impact. It calls for industries to move beyond profit-maximization and instead build systems that foster human flourishing—where machines do what they do best (precision, speed, repetition), and humans do what only they can do best (connect, create, care). This synergy not only boosts productivity but builds a more equitable, innovative, and sustainable future (Rashid & Kausik, 2024).

Integration of Modern Technologies

In Industry 5.0, sophisticated technologies such AI, Robotics, and IoT constitute the technological foundation that underpins a more human-centric, resilient, and sustainable industrial future. In contrast to Industry 4.0, which prioritised automation and intelligent machinery for enhanced efficiency, Industry 5.0 underscores a synergistic partnership between humans and advanced technologies. AI is essential for analysing vast information to generate actionable insights, facilitate real-time decision-making, customise customer experiences, and predict trends, so augmenting human judgement instead than supplanting it (Czeczot et al., 2023). It facilitates industries in advancing towards mass customisation, wherein products and services are adapted to individual requirements on a large scale. Robotics, especially collaborative robots or cobots, are engineered to operate safely and intuitively in conjunction with human workers. These machines assume repetitive, hazardous, or physically arduous activities, enabling humans to concentrate on creative, strategic, and emotionally intelligent roles—resulting in enhanced job satisfaction and productivity (Pietrantoni et al., 2024). Simultaneously, the IoT integrates the physical and digital realms by incorporating sensors into machinery, equipment, and goods that gather real-time data, facilitating remote monitoring, predictive maintenance, and astute resource management. This connectivity enables enterprises to function more efficiently and sustainably by reducing waste, conserving energy, and optimising logistics. Collectively, these technologies convert conventional workflows into dynamic, intelligent ecosystems that enhance human understanding rather than supplant it. The integration of AI, Robotics, and IoT in Industry 5.0 guarantees that technology advances as a collaborator with humanity, fostering innovation while honouring human values, ethical principles, and environmental consequences. These technologies enable smart automation without replacing the human touch (Allioui and Mourdi, 2023).

Personalisation and Mass Customization

Personalisation and mass customisation are fundamental attributes of Industry 5.0, embodying its essential principle of human-centric innovation. While conventional mass production emphasises uniformity and efficiency, Industry 5.0 shifts towards the customisation of products and services to meet individual consumer requirements, all while maintaining the scale and pace of industrial production. Personalisation denotes the creation of distinctive, user-specific experiences or products, such as bespoke footwear, skincare, or digital services that cater to individual preferences. Mass customisation integrates the adaptability of personalisation with the productivity of mass production, enabling organisations to provide bespoke solutions while maintaining size and cost efficiency (Adel, 2022). Industry 5.0 facilitates this with sophisticated technologies such artificial intelligence, machine learning, 3D printing, robotics, and the Internet of Things, enabling swift modifications in design, materials, and production processes. For example, AI may assess consumer behaviour and preferences to recommend product modifications; robotic systems can be configured to adapt their functions in real time; and IoT sensors can track user feedback or environmental data to optimise production immediately. This method generates significant value, enhancing customer happiness and brand loyalty while minimising waste, preventing overproduction, and augmenting operational flexibility. Mass customisation significantly impacts sectors such as fashion, automotive, furniture, healthcare, and agriculture, as consumers increasingly seek products that embody their personalities, health requirements, local demands, or sustainability preferences. In healthcare, personalised medication informed by genetic profiles is increasingly attainable. In retail, people can collaboratively design apparel or furnishing items that align with their preferences and aesthetics (Rani et al., 2024). Industry 5.0 technologies enable this achievement without sacrificing the requisite speed and scale for maintaining competitiveness. Ultimately, personalisation and mass customisation embody the human-centric ethos of Industry 5.0. They enable consumers to become co-creators instead of passive purchasers, transition the emphasis from "one size fits all" to "one size fits one," and guarantee that contemporary production corresponds with individual beliefs, tastes, and lifestyles—at scale, with efficiency, and with compassion (Sarıoğlu, 2023).

Sustainability and the Circular Economy in Industry 5.0

In Industry 5.0, sustainability and the circular economy are not just supplementary goals—they form the foundation of how industries are reimagined to serve both people and the planet. Unlike the linear "take-make-dispose" model of past industrial revolutions, Industry 5.0 champions a circular economic framework, where resources are designed to be reused, regenerated, and reintegrated into the production cycle. This approach emphasizes eco-friendly design, minimizing environmental impact by enabling repairability, recyclability, and longer product lifespans. Advanced technologies such as AI, IoT, robotics, and digital twins enable real-time monitoring of resources, predictive maintenance, and energy optimization, all of which contribute to reducing waste and emissions (Atif, 2023; Payer et al., 2024). At the same time, Industry 5.0 fosters human-centric innovation, ensuring that sustainability efforts support not only environmental goals but also social equity and worker well-being. For example, smart factories in Industry 5.0 prioritize renewable energy, localized production, and closed-loop systems that recover materials from end-of-life products. This reduces dependency on virgin raw materials and mitigates the negative impacts of extraction and waste disposal. Ultimately, the integration of sustainability and circular economy principles in Industry 5.0 signals a transformative shift towards resilient, inclusive, and regenerative industrial ecosystems, where technological progress is in harmony with nature and humanity (Rejeb et al., 2025; Santiago et al., 2025).

Resilience and Adaptability

In the context of Industry 5.0, resilience and adaptability refer to the ability of industrial systems to withstand disruptions, recover quickly, and adapt to changing conditions—whether those changes come from market demands, environmental challenges, technological shifts, or global crises like pandemics and climate change. Unlike Industry 4.0, which primarily emphasized efficiency and automation, Industry 5.0 is built around the idea that future-ready industries must be flexible, human-centric, and prepared for uncertainty. Resilience in Industry 5.0 is achieved through distributed and decentralized systems, where smart manufacturing units are not dependent on a single centralized process. Technologies like artificial intelligence, IoT, and edge computing enable factories to make real-time decisions and operate independently if needed. For example, if one part of a global supply chain is disrupted, the system can reroute resources or shift production to another node, minimizing downtime and financial loss (Ivanov, 2023). Adaptability is closely linked, highlighting the need for businesses to respond quickly to changing customer needs and global trends. Through human-machine collaboration, workers supported by intelligent technologies can reconfigure production lines, customize products, and switch to new workflows with ease. This adaptability not only boosts innovation and personalization but also makes organizations more competitive and future-proof. Moreover, Industry 5.0 promotes the use of predictive analytics and digital twins to simulate scenarios and plan responses in advance. These tools allow businesses to foresee potential disruptions—such as material shortages or climate-related events—and prepare contingency plans. In doing so, they move from being reactive to proactive. Overall, resilience and adaptability in Industry 5.0 are about creating industrial ecosystems that are flexible, intelligent, human-focused, and sustainable, ensuring that businesses can thrive in a fast-changing and often unpredictable world (Alojaiman, 2023; Jäpel et al., 2024).

Learning and Skills Development

In the context of Industry 5.0, resilience and adaptability refer to the ability of industrial systems to withstand disruptions, recover quickly, and adapt to changing conditions—whether those changes come from market demands, environmental challenges, technological shifts, or global crises like pandemics and climate change. Unlike Industry 4.0, which primarily emphasized efficiency and automation, Industry 5.0 is built around the idea that future-ready industries must be flexible, human-centric, and prepared for uncertainty. Resilience in Industry 5.0 is achieved through distributed and decentralized systems, where smart manufacturing units are not dependent on a single centralized process. Technologies like artificial intelligence, IoT, and edge computing enable factories to make real-time decisions and operate independently if needed (Leng et al., 2023). For example, if one part of a global supply chain is disrupted, the system can reroute resources or shift production to another node, minimizing downtime and financial loss. Adaptability is closely linked, highlighting the need for businesses to respond quickly to changing customer needs and global trends. Through human-machine collaboration, workers supported by intelligent technologies can reconfigure production lines, customize products, and switch to new workflows with ease. This adaptability not only boosts innovation and personalization but also makes organizations more competitive and future-proof. Moreover, Industry 5.0 promotes the use of predictive analytics and digital twins to simulate scenarios and plan responses in advance. These tools allow businesses to foresee potential disruptions such as material shortages or climate-related events and prepare contingency plans (Habibi et al., 2023). In doing so, they move from being reactive to proactive. Overall, resilience and adaptability in Industry 5.0 are about creating industrial ecosystems that are flexible, intelligent, human-focused, and sustainable, ensuring that businesses can thrive in a fast-changing and often unpredictable learning and skills development in Industry 5.0. In Industry 5.0, the focus shifts from purely automating tasks to enhancing human potential, making learning and skills development a cornerstone of this new industrial era. Unlike Industry 4.0, which emphasized technical and digital literacy to work with smart machines, Industry 5.0 promotes a balanced development of both technical and human-centric skills, recognizing that innovation thrives when machines and humans collaborate intelligently. This era demands a workforce that is not only skilled in technologies like AI, robotics, IoT, data analytics, and cybersecurity, but also excels in creative thinking, emotional intelligence, adaptability, problem-solving, and ethical reasoning (Rame et al., 2024).

Learning in Industry 5.0 is continuous, personalized, and embedded into the work environment. With the help of AI-driven learning platforms, workers can receive real-time feedback, customized training modules, and on-the-job upskilling that evolves with changing roles and responsibilities. Virtual reality (VR) and augmented reality (AR) are being used to create immersive training environments, allowing employees to safely simulate complex procedures, improve performance, and reduce training costs. Furthermore, Industry 5.0 promotes a culture of lifelong learning, where employees are encouraged to reskill and upskill regularly to stay relevant. Organizations are moving from fixed job descriptions to flexible, role-based models, where learning agility becomes more important than static qualifications. Educational institutions and industries are increasingly collaborating to create modular, interdisciplinary curricula that blend STEM (Science, Technology, Engineering, Math) with humanities, ethics, and design thinking, preparing learners for the hybrid roles of the future (Tusquellas et al., 2025). Importantly, Industry 5.0 emphasizes inclusive learning ensuring that all demographics, including women, rural workers, and older employees, are equipped to participate in the digital economy. Policies and technologies are being designed to reduce digital inequality and provide equal access to training opportunities through online platforms, local centers, and mobile-based learning. In essence, learning and skills development in Industry 5.0 are about empowering individuals to grow alongside machines, fostering a human-machine symbiosis where continuous education, emotional intelligence, and technical proficiency collectively drive innovation, adaptability, and social well-being (Alves et al., 2023).

INDUSTRY 5.0 IN THE AGRIPRENEURSHIP

Agripreneurship involves taking risks and devising creative solutions within the agricultural industry to enhance production, sustainability, and profitability. The objective is to convert farms into sustainable enterprises and develop value-added products and services (Prabhakar et al., 2023a, b). Industry 5.0 marks a significant evolution in how industries, especially agriculture, are transforming not just through automation and efficiency, but by prioritizing human values, environmental sustainability, and social inclusion. In the context of sustainable agripreneurship, Industry 5.0 plays a pivotal role by merging cutting-edge technology with human creativity, enabling farmers and agripreneurs to build agricultural businesses that are profitable, resilient, eco-friendly, and inclusive. Industry 5.0 reimagines agriculture by integrating technology, sustainability, ethics, and human values. It empowers farmers with intelligent tools while respecting their expertise, aiming for high productivity, environmental care, and social inclusion. In a world facing climate challenges and rising food demand, Industry 5.0 provides a balanced, future-ready model for global agriculture. The role of Industry 5.0 in the agricultural context, divided into three major areas.

Industry 5.0 for Human-Centric Precision Agriculture

Industry 5.0 introduces a human-centric approach to precision agriculture, where technology and human intelligence work together to make farming more efficient, sustainable, and meaningful. Unlike Industry 4.0, which focused on automation and machine-to-machine communication, Industry 5.0 emphasizes collaboration between humans and machines, placing the farmer at the heart of innovation (Raja Santhi & Muthuswamy, 2023). This fusion of cutting-edge technology with human insight is what defines Human-Centric Precision Agriculture. In this model, advanced tools like AI, IoT sensors, robotics, and drones are used not to replace the farmer, but to empower them. For example, IoT-based soil sensors provide real-time data on moisture, pH, and nutrient content, helping farmers understand exactly what their soil needs. AI systems analyze this data and recommend specific actions such as targeted irrigation, crop rotation, or fertilization. But the decision to act is not left to machines alone (Hassoun et al., 2024; Victor et al., 2024). The farmer's local knowledge, experience, and judgment are essential in customizing and executing these decisions according to on-ground conditions like market demand, traditional practices, or unexpected weather changes. Drones are used for crop monitoring, detecting pests, and spraying with pinpoint accuracy, reducing chemical use and protecting the environment. However, farmers still decide when and where to deploy these technologies based on their understanding of crop cycles and field conditions.

This collaborative decision-making process preserves the farmer's agency and ensures that technology is used ethically, effectively, and in harmony with nature. Moreover, Industry 5.0 supports the creation of user-friendly platforms and interfaces in local languages, making advanced agricultural technologies accessible even to small and marginal farmers. These platforms provide customized insights, voice-based instructions, and visual dashboards, allowing farmers to understand and benefit from complex data without needing technical expertise (Holzinger et al., 2024).

In essence, Human-Centric Precision Agriculture in Industry 5.0 is about creating a balance between digital intelligence and human wisdom. It enhances productivity while protecting the environment, respects traditional knowledge while embracing innovation, and ensures that farmers are not left behind in the race toward modernization. This approach not only improves yield and efficiency but also restores dignity and autonomy to farming communities, making agriculture a smarter, more sustainable, and more inclusive profession in the 21st century. Industry 5.0 enables precision farming by using technologies like AI, IoT, drones, and satellite mapping to make agriculture more targeted and efficient (Kaur et al., 2023). Agripreneurs can now monitor real-time data on soil health, water levels, weather, and crop conditions, which helps them make smarter decisions. This minimizes resource wastage, optimizes input use (like fertilizers, water, and pesticides), and reduces environmental damage, supporting the goal of sustainable resource management. For example, AI-powered irrigation systems can reduce water consumption by up to 50%, while smart spraying systems apply only the necessary amount of chemicals, lowering costs and preventing pollution (Shahab et al., 2024).

Sustainability and Resource Optimization

Industry 5.0 brings a transformative shift in how we approach sustainability and resource optimization, especially in agriculture, by moving beyond automation to incorporate human values, environmental consciousness, and intelligent collaboration between humans and machines. This evolution emphasizes not just profit and productivity, but also planet and people, aligning closely with global sustainability goals. In the context of resource optimization, Industry 5.0 leverages precision agriculture tools such as IoT sensors, AI analytics, drones, and robotics to minimize the overuse of water, fertilizers, pesticides, and energy (Kuar et al., 2023; Oyekunle et al., 2024). For example, smart irrigation systems use real-time soil moisture and weather data to deliver water only when and where it is needed, avoiding waste and preserving groundwater. Similarly, variable-rate application of fertilizers and pesticides ensures that inputs are used only in the required quantity and in specific zones of the farm, drastically reducing chemical runoff and soil degradation. From a sustainability standpoint, Industry 5.0 encourages a circular economy in agriculture turning agricultural waste into valuable by-products. Crop residues, organic waste, and livestock manure are transformed into biogas, organic fertilizers, or compost, promoting zero-waste farming systems. This reduces dependency on synthetic chemicals and fossil fuels while improving soil health and biodiversity. Moreover, renewable energy integration like solar-powered pumps and wind-driven energy for farm operations further reduces the carbon footprint of farming practices (Et-taibi et al., 2024). Predictive AI models also help farmers make informed decisions about planting cycles, harvest timing, and market demands, thus reducing food loss and optimizing supply chains. Importantly, Industry 5.0 places a strong emphasis on ethical and inclusive innovation, ensuring that these sustainable technologies are accessible and scalable for smallholders, not just large agribusinesses. Through localized, user-friendly platforms, farmers can adopt green practices without the burden of complex systems or high costs (Mana et al., 2024).

Resilience to Climate Change

Industry 5.0 plays a critical role in building resilience to climate change, especially in climate-sensitive sectors like agriculture. Unlike its predecessor, Industry 5.0 goes beyond automation and efficiency by emphasizing human-centric innovation, ethical responsibility, and sustainable technology. This new paradigm empowers farmers and communities to adapt to climate risks with intelligent, inclusive, and responsive systems. One of the key contributions of Industry 5.0 to climate resilience is the use of AI-driven predictive modelling and big data analytics. These tools analyze massive datasets including historical weather patterns, satellite imagery, and soil health data to predict extreme climate events like droughts, floods, heatwaves, or unseasonal rainfall (Adel et al., 2022; Kumar et al., 2024). Early warnings help farmers and planners take proactive measures such as adjusting planting dates, selecting climate-resilient crop varieties, or reinforcing irrigation infrastructure thus minimizing losses and ensuring food security (Shabur et al., 2025; Prabhakar et al., 2025). In addition, IoT sensors deployed in the fields continuously monitor environmental parameters such as temperature, humidity, soil moisture, and wind speed. This real-time monitoring enables adaptive management farmers can change irrigation schedules, apply mulch, or erect shade nets depending on immediate field conditions. When combined with human decision-making, these systems create a dynamic response mechanism that is both smart and context-sensitive (Sahab et al., 2024). Another important pillar of resilience is diversification, and Industry 5.0 supports this through smart crop planning tools that suggest alternative crops or mixed farming systems based on climate adaptability, market demand, and local resources. These technologies reduce overdependence on a single crop and spread risk, making farming systems more robust under uncertain climatic conditions.

Furthermore, blockchain and traceability systems ensure transparent tracking of food from farm to market, which strengthens supply chains during disruptions caused by climate events. This improves consumer trust and secures better prices for farmers, contributing to economic resilience (Mihrete and Mihretu, 2025). Most importantly, Industry 5.0 ensures that resilience-building technologies are accessible to all, including small and marginal farmers. Through mobile-based platforms, local language interfaces, and community-driven innovation hubs, even resource-poor regions can implement climate-smart practices without requiring high-tech infrastructure or deep technical knowledge. Industry 5.0 fosters climate resilience not only by using advanced technologies, but by aligning them with human values, local wisdom, and inclusive growth. It prepares agricultural systems to withstand, adapt to, and recover from climate-related shocks, creating a future where food production remains secure, ecosystems stay healthy, and vulnerable communities are empowered to thrive in the face of climate uncertainty (Bissadu et al., 2025; Majumdar et al., 2025).

Customization and Inclusion indued by Industry 5.0

Industry 5.0 champions a shift from mass production and rigid automation toward personalized, inclusive, and human-centric innovation. In agriculture, this means designing solutions that not only increase efficiency but also respect local contexts, empower diverse users, and bridge inequality. By integrating advanced technologies like AI, IoT, and machine learning with human insight and social values, Industry 5.0 creates a new ecosystem where every farmer, regardless of scale or literacy level, can benefit (Adel, 2022). At the heart of Industry 5.0 is the idea of customization. Unlike one-size-fits-all approaches of the past, modern agricultural tools can now offer farm-specific, crop-specific, and even plot-specific advice. For instance, AI-based platforms can analyze soil health, past yield data, rainfall patterns, and market trends to provide personalized recommendations on which crops to plant, when to sow, and what inputs to use. These insights are tailored to the unique needs of each farmer, improving productivity and reducing input costs (Islam, 2025; Rejeb et al., 2025). Industry 5.0 ensures that these intelligent systems are not just available to large agribusinesses but are also accessible to small and marginal farmers, women farmers, and those in remote or underdeveloped regions. Through mobile apps in regional languages, voice-based commands, visual dashboards, and offline functionality, technology becomes easier to use even for those with limited literacy or technical skills. This democratization of innovation helps close the digital divide in rural areas. Industry 5.0 also fosters community-level solutions. Shared machinery models, farmer co-operatives, digital marketplaces, and local knowledge hubs allow even the poorest farmers to access modern tools and training. Inclusive design ensures that people with different abilities, education levels, and resources can participate in and benefit from the agricultural transformation. Moreover, these solutions respect cultural diversity and traditional knowledge. Instead of erasing indigenous practices, Industry 5.0 enables their integration with modern data-driven insights. For example, a tribal farmer using traditional seed-saving methods can receive alerts on climate risks or pest outbreaks while still preserving ancestral farming techniques (Haloui et al., 2024; Victor et al., 2024).

Ethical, Safe, and Transparent Food Systems

Industry 5.0 advocates for technology progress alongside ethical principles, safety, and openness, particularly within the food and agriculture industry. In contrast to earlier industrial revolutions that prioritised efficiency and profit, Industry 5.0 adopts a human-centric and value-oriented approach to food systems, guaranteeing that our agricultural practices, processing methods, and consumption are safe, traceable, inclusive, and mindful of environmental and social responsibilities (Ghobakhloo et al., 2023). Blockchain technology is a disruptive tool that facilitates complete tracking of food from production to consumption. Each phase from seed procurement, agricultural methods, harvesting, logistics, storage, to retail can be digitally documented and securely archived. This enables consumers to scan a product and immediately ascertain its origin, processing methods, the usage of pesticides or chemicals, and adherence to fair trade principles. This transparency fosters consumer trust, incentivises ethical producers, and mitigates the danger of food fraud, contamination, and adulteration. Food safety constitutes a significant pillar emphasised by Industry 5.0 (Singh et al., 2025).

The real-time surveillance using IoT sensors and AI-driven analytics facilitates the prompt identification of microbiological contamination, deterioration, or inadequate storage conditions. Sensors in cold storage units monitor temperature and humidity, issuing alerts when conditions deviate from safe parameters. This guarantees that perishable food items such as dairy, meat, and vegetables are managed with utmost diligence, hence minimising foodborne diseases, and waste. From an ethical perspective, Industry 5.0 prioritises equitable labour practices, environmental conservation, and animal welfare. Technologies are being developed to guarantee the absence of child labour in production, prevent animal mistreatment, and ensure farms adhere to sustainable principles (Hassoun et al., 2024; Jeyabalan et al., 2025). Drones and satellite imagery can track deforestation or illicit agricultural practices, while AI systems can evaluate compliance with ethical sourcing standards. This mandates corporate social responsibility throughout the agriculture supply chain. Furthermore, incorporating consumer feedback mechanisms into production systems enables farmers and food processors to enhance quality based on actual user experiences. This reciprocal engagement fosters a participatory food system, enabling consumers, producers, and policymakers to collaboratively establish ethical norms and behaviours (Šćepanović et al., 2025). Industry 5.0 improves ethical, secure, and transparent food systems by integrating responsibility, traceability, and equity throughout the whole food value chain. It revolutionises agricultural and food production into a framework where trust is established through data, safety is guaranteed through automation and oversight, and ethics direct innovation. This results in a future where individuals not only consume superior food but also possess a greater sense of satisfaction regarding the origins and production methods of their sustenance (Sarkar et al., 2025).

CASE STUDIES ON THE IMPLEMENTATION OF INDUSTRY 5.0 IN AGREPRENEURSHIP

AeroFarms (USA): Vertical Farming and AI Collaboration

AeroFarms, based in Newark, New Jersey, is internationally acknowledged as a pioneer in vertical farming and exemplifies the use of Industry 5.0 principles in agripreneurship. The company employs aeroponics, artificial intelligence-driven sensors, robots, and data analytics to establish meticulously regulated indoor conditions for the cultivation of leafy greens and other crops in vertical layers. AeroFarms utilises aeroponics to decrease water usage by as much as 95% relative to traditional soil-based agriculture, whilst eliminating pesticide requirements (Despommier, 2020). The LED lighting systems and sophisticated monitoring technologies enable exact regulation of temperature, humidity, and nutrient distribution, therefore optimising yields and enhancing nutritional quality (Benke & Tomkins, 2017). AeroFarms' alignment with Industry 5.0 is characterised by its human-centric technological approach. Although automation and AI enhance growing conditions, human experience is crucial in customising "plant recipes" for flavour, texture, and nutritional results to satisfy consumer preferences (AeroFarms, 2021). Scientists, engineers, and farmers interact intimately to guarantee that the result is both efficient and sustainable, while also being consumer-oriented. The integration of human creativity and mechanical accuracy encapsulates the core of Industry 5.0. AeroFarms encounters hurdles notwithstanding its achievements. The system necessitates substantial initial financial expenditure, hindering small-scale agripreneurs from replication. The energy consumption associated with artificial lighting prompts environmental issues, and the problem of sustaining profitability while providing affordable products persists (Kalantari et al., 2017). Moreover, dependence on digital technologies presents problems with data security and operational resilience. AeroFarms exemplifies that Industry 5.0 in agripreneurship may enhance sustainability, diminish resource reliance, and establish consumer-oriented food systems. AeroFarms exemplifies a paradigm for future agripreneurs by integrating AI, robots, and human expertise to create creative, sustainable, and human-centered agricultural enterprises.

AgriDigital (Australia): Blockchain and Traceability

AgriDigital, an Australian agri-fintech business established in 2015, exemplifies the transformative potential of Industry 5.0 concepts in agripreneurship via blockchain-enabled supply chain traceability. The technology offers farmers, dealers, and consumers comprehensive transparency in the grain supply chain by automating transactions, safeguarding payments, and validating product provenance in real time. Historically, farmers frequently encountered payment delays and inefficiencies in verifying grain ownership, resulting in mistrust and financial hazards. AgriDigital tackled these difficulties by employing blockchain technology to document immutable, nonetheless, the integration of blockchain in agripreneurship poses difficulties. Significant digital infrastructure demands, internet connectivity challenges in rural regions, and inadequate digital literacy among smallholder farmers impede extensive adoption (Kamilaris et al., 2019). Furthermore, issues pertaining to scalability, transaction expenses, and interoperability among various blockchain platforms remain unaddressed. Notwithstanding these challenges, AgriDigital has illustrated that blockchain technology can mitigate inefficiencies, enhance trust, and generate value-added services in agriculture, offering a model for future agripreneurs aiming to integrate technological innovation with human-centered, transparent, and sustainable food systems. Transparent and tamper-resistant transactions, fostering confidence among all stakeholders (AgriDigital, 2020).

Fasal (India): Drone-Assisted Precision Farming

Fasal, an agritech firm established in India in 2018, exemplifies the influence of Industry 5.0 concepts on agripreneurship in India. The company offers a precision farming platform enhanced by AI and IoT, which merges drones, sensors, and meteorological data to furnish farmers with crop-specific, real-time information. Farmers obtain tailored advises on irrigation, pesticide usage, and fertiliser management in their native language via the mobile application, thereby decreasing input expenses and enhancing yields (Fasal, 2023). Fasal utilises drone technology to monitor extensive and fragmented landholdings, facilitate early identification of pest infestations, and execute precise agrochemical applications, thereby reducing resource waste and environmental impact (PwC India, 2020). Nevertheless, the implementation of drone-assisted precision agriculture in India encounters numerous obstacles. The prohibitive expense of drones and IoT devices restricts accessibility for smallholder farmers, who constitute the majority of India's agricultural labour force. Connectivity challenges in rural regions impede real-time data transmission, and inadequate digital literacy limits farmers' capacity to effectively employ these tools (NABARD, 2021). Moreover, legislative obstacles pertaining to drone utilisation in agriculture and apprehensions over data ownership and privacy continue to pose substantial impediments. Notwithstanding these challenges, Fasal's model exemplifies the promise of Industry 5.0 in agripreneurship by integrating sustainability, efficiency, and inclusivity with cutting-edge technologies, providing a repeatable framework for India's digital agricultural evolution.

DeHaat (India): Farmer Network & Input Supply

Established in 2012 and based in India, DeHaat is among India's rapidly expanding agritech companies and exemplifies the capacity of Industry 5.0 concepts to enhance agripreneurship on a large scale. The company functions as a comprehensive digital platform linking more than two million smallholder farmers in Bihar, Uttar Pradesh, Odisha, and other areas to quality inputs, financial services, crop advising, and market connections (DeHaat, 2023). DeHaat utilises AI-driven advisory tools and a digital marketplace to provide farmers with real-time, crop-specific assistance on pest management, soil health, and weather predictions, while facilitating direct contacts with buyers to ensure equitable pricing. The Industry 5.0 aspect of DeHaat is characterised by its human-machine collaboration. Although the platform automates transactions, predictive analytics, and supply chain logistics, the human component—local micro-entrepreneurs and farmer producer organisations (FPOs)—is essential to deployment. These community-based entrepreneurs serve as tangible interfaces for farmers, converting digital insights into accessible, trust-oriented services. This hybrid strategy promotes inclusion by integrating advanced technologies with conventional farming methods. Notwithstanding its success, DeHaat has hurdles typical of Industry 5.0 implementation in agripreneurship. Infrastructure deficiencies, including inadequate rural connectivity and transit logistics, impede efficient operations. A multitude of smallholders encounter difficulties with digital literacy, hindering their capacity to properly utilise the platform's functionalities (NABARD, 2021). Moreover, expanding operations while preserving affordability and inclusivity presents a significant problem, as does safeguarding data security and protecting farmers' rights to their agricultural information (PwC India, 2020). DeHaat exemplifies the potential evolution of agripreneurship in India through Industry 5.0 by promoting human-centered, technology-enabled ecosystems that incorporate sustainability, efficiency, and farmer empowerment.

CHALLENGES, RISKS AND FUTURE RECOMMEDATIONS

Industry 5.0 introduces a human-centric approach to precision agriculture, where technology and human intelligence work together to make farming more efficient, sustainable, and meaningful. Unlike Industry 4.0, which focused on automation and machine-to-machine communication, Industry 5.0 emphasizes collaboration between humans and machines, placing the farmer at the heart of innovation. This fusion of cutting-edge technology with human insight is what defines human-centric precision agriculture. In this model, advanced tools like AI, IoT sensors, robotics, and drones are used not to replace the farmer, but to empower them (Shabur et al., 2025). For example, IoT-based soil sensors provide real-time data on moisture, pH, and nutrient content, helping farmers understand exactly what their soil needs. AI systems analyze this data and recommend specific actions such as targeted irrigation, crop rotation, or fertilization. But the decision to act is not left to machines alone (Dhanaraju et al., 2022).

The farmer's local knowledge, experience, and judgment are essential in customizing and executing these decisions according to on-ground conditions like market demand, traditional practices, or unexpected weather changes. Drones are used for crop monitoring, detecting pests, and spraying with pinpoint accuracy, reducing chemical use, and protecting the environment. However, farmers still decide when and where to deploy these technologies based on their understanding of crop cycles and field conditions. This collaborative decision-making process preserves the farmer's agency and ensures that technology is used ethically, effectively, and in harmony with nature (Pathak et al., 2020; Hafeez et al., 2023). Moreover, Industry 5.0 supports the development of user-friendly platforms and interfaces in local languages, making advanced agricultural technologies accessible even to small and marginal farmers. These platforms provide customized insights, voice-based instructions, and visual dashboards, allowing farmers to understand and benefit from complex data without needing technical expertise (Haloui et al., 2024). In essence, Human-Centric Precision Agriculture in Industry 5.0 is about creating a balance between digital intelligence and human wisdom. It enhances productivity while protecting the environment, respects traditional knowledge while embracing innovation, and ensures that farmers are not left behind in the race toward modernization. This approach not only improves yield and efficiency but also restores dignity and autonomy to farming communities, making agriculture a smarter, more sustainable, and more inclusive profession in the 21st century. Also, the future research on Industry 5.0 in agripreneurship should transition from theoretical discourse to practical frameworks that incorporate technology, sustainability, and inclusion in agricultural operations. Researchers and professionals must investigate how human-machine collaboration can be customised for various farming sizes, particularly in resource-limited environments, to guarantee that small and marginal agripreneurs are not excluded from the digital divide. Research ought to investigate methods for the cost-effective implementation of new technologies, including AI, robots, blockchain, and IoT, in rural regions, focussing on scalability, affordability, and long-term sustainability. A broad area of research is examining the socio-economic effects of Industry 5.0-driven agripreneurship, including its capacity to empower women, tribal farmers, and youth, while also evaluating cultural obstacles that may hinder acceptance. It is essential to conduct policy-oriented studies to provide supportive frameworks, subsidies, and training programs that enhance digital literacy and foster inclusive adoption. Moreover, forthcoming research must tackle issues related to data ownership, privacy, and cybersecurity in agriculture, given the growing reliance on digital platforms. The environmental research must assess how Industry 5.0 technologies might improve climate resilience, foster circular bio-economy practices, and diminish carbon footprints in agricultural systems. Interdisciplinary research integrating agriculture, economics, engineering, and social sciences is advocated to develop comprehensive strategies that ensure Industry 5.0 in agripreneurship enhances productivity while promoting sustainability, equity, and resilience within the global food system.

CONCLUSION

Industry 5.0 empowers sustainable agripreneurship by harmonizing advanced technologies with human intelligence to create more resilient, inclusive, and eco-friendly agricultural systems. Unlike its predecessor, Industry 5.0 places people and the planet at the centre of innovation, enabling agripreneurs to use tools like AI, IoT, robotics, and blockchain not just for efficiency, but for long-term sustainability. It facilitates precision farming that minimizes resource wastage, promotes circular practices that reuse agricultural by-products, and ensures transparency in food production through traceability systems. Moreover, it empowers small and marginal farmers by making cutting-edge technology accessible, fostering local entrepreneurship, and encouraging ethical, inclusive practices. Through smart policies, education, and collaborative innovation, Industry 5.0 transforms agripreneurship into a force that balances economic growth with environmental care and social equity.

ACKNOWLEDGMENT

The author is thankful to Prof. Mamoni Banerjee, Indian Institute of Technology Kharagpur, Kharagpur, India for her valuable comments and suggestions during the preparation of the manuscript.

REFERENCES

Adel, A. (2022). Future of industry 5.0 in society: Human-centric solutions, challenges and prospective research areas. *Journal of Cloud Computing (Heidelberg, Germany)*, *11*(1), 40. DOI: 10.1186/s13677-022-00314-5 PMID: 36101900

AeroFarms. (2021). *AeroFarms: World leader in vertical farming*. Retrieved from https://www.aerofarms.com

AgriDigital. (2020). *AgriDigital: Blockchain for global agri-supply chains*. Retrieved from https://www.agridigital.io

Aheleroff, S., Huang, H., Xu, X., & Zhong, R. Y. (2022). Toward sustainability and resilience with Industry 4.0 and Industry 5.0. *Frontiers in Manufacturing Technology*, *2*, 951643.

Allioui, H., & Mourdi, Y. (2023). Exploring the full potentials of IoT for better financial growth and stability: A comprehensive survey. *Sensors (Basel)*, *23*(19), 8015. PMID: 37836845

Alojaiman, B. (2023). Technological modernizations in the industry 5.0 era: A descriptive analysis and future research directions. *Processes (Basel, Switzerland)*, *11*(5), 1318.

Atif, S. (2023). Analysing the alignment between circular economy and industry 4.0 nexus with industry 5.0 era: An integrative systematic literature review. *Sustainable Development*, *31*(4), 2155–2175.

Basulo-Ribeiro, J., & Teixeira, L. (2024). The future of healthcare with industry 5.0: Preliminary interview-based qualitative analysis. *Future Internet*, *16*(3), 68.

Benke, K., & Tomkins, B. (2017). Future food-production systems: Vertical farming and controlled-environment agriculture. *Sustainability: Science. Practice and Policy*, *13*(1), 13–26. DOI: 10.1080/15487733.2017.1394054

Bissadu, K. D., Sonko, S., & Hossain, G. (2025). Society 5.0 enabled agriculture: Drivers, enabling technologies, architectures, opportunities, and challenges. *Information Processing in Agriculture*, *12*(1), 112–124.

Carayannis, E. G., Dezi, L., Gregori, G., & Calo, E. (2022). Smart environments and techno-centric and human-centric innovations for Industry and Society 5.0: A quintuple helix innovation system view towards smart, sustainable, and inclusive solutions. *Journal of the Knowledge Economy*, *13*(2), 926–955. PMID: 40477337

Cheng, S., & Yahaya, M. F. B., bin Abd Rahman, A. R., & Tai, L. (2024). Scoping Review: Safety and Risk in Aesthetic Preference Determinants for Product Design. *Research Journal of Medical Sciences*, *20*, 1–17.

Czeczot, G., Rojek, I., Mikołajewski, D., & Sangho, B. (2023). AI in IIoT management of cybersecurity for industry 4.0 and industry 5.0 purposes. *Electronics (Basel)*, *12*(18), 3800.

DeHaat. (2023). *Empowering farmers through technology and services*. Retrieved from https://agrevolution.in

Despommier, D. (2020). *The vertical farm: Feeding the world in the 21st century*. Picador.

Dhanaraju, M., Chenniappan, P., Ramalingam, K., Pazhanivelan, S., & Kaliaperumal, R. (2022). Smart farming: Internet of Things (IoT)-based sustainable agriculture. *Agriculture*, *12*(10), 1745.

Erol, B. A., Majumdar, A., Benavidez, P., Rad, P., Choo, K. K. R., & Jamshidi, M. (2019). Toward artificial emotional intelligence for cooperative social human–machine interaction. *IEEE Transactions on Computational Social Systems*, *7*(1), 234–246.

Et-taibi, B., Abid, M. R., Boufounas, E. M., Morchid, A., Bourhnane, S., Hamed, T. A., & Benhaddou, D. (2024). Enhancing water management in smart agriculture: A cloud and IoT-Based smart irrigation system. *Results in Engineering*, *22*, 102283.

Fasal. (2023). *Transforming Indian agriculture with precision farming*. Retrieved from https://www.fasal.co

Fogaça, D. R., Grijalvo, M., & Sacomano Neto, M. (2025). What Are Industry 4.0 and Industry 5.0 All About? An Integrative Institutional Model for the New Industrial Paradigms. *Administrative Sciences*, *15*(4), 118.

Gamberini, L., & Pluchino, P. (2024). Industry 5.0: A comprehensive insight into the future of work, social sustainability, sustainable development, and career. *Australian Journal of Career Development*, *33*(1), 5–14.

Ghobakhloo, M., Iranmanesh, M., Tseng, M. L., Grybauskas, A., Stefanini, A., & Amran, A. (2023). Behind the definition of Industry 5.0: A systematic review of technologies, principles, components, and values. *Journal of Industrial and Production Engineering*, *40*(6), 432–447.

Gundeti, R., Vuppala, K., & Kasireddy, V. (2024). The future of AI and environmental sustainability: Challenges and opportunities. *Exploring Ethical Dimensions of Environmental Sustainability and Use of AI*, 346-371.

Habibi, F., Chakrabortty, R. K., & Abbasi, A. (2023). Evaluating supply chain network resilience considering disruption propagation. *Computers & Industrial Engineering*, *183*, 109531.

Hafeez, A., Husain, M. A., Singh, S. P., Chauhan, A., Khan, M. T., Kumar, N., & Soni, S. K. (2023). Implementation of drone technology for farm monitoring & pesticide spraying: A review. *Information Processing in Agriculture*, *10*(2), 192–203.

Haloui, D., Oufaska, K., Oudani, M., & El Yassini, K. (2024). Bridging industry 5.0 and agriculture 5.0: Historical perspectives, opportunities, and future perspectives. *Sustainability*, *16*(9), 3507.

Hassoun, A., Jagtap, S., Trollman, H., Garcia-Garcia, G., Duong, L. N., Saxena, P., & Aït-Kaddour, A. (2024). From Food Industry 4.0 to Food Industry 5.0: Identifying technological enablers and potential future applications in the food sector. *Comprehensive Reviews in Food Science and Food Safety*, *23*(6), e370040. PMID: 39437193

Holzinger, A., Fister, I., Kaul, H. P., & Asseng, S. (2024). Human-centered AI in smart farming: Toward agriculture 5.0. *IEEE Access : Practical Innovations, Open Solutions*, *12*, 62199–62214.

Hu, J. L., Li, Y., & Chew, J. C. (2025). Industry 5.0 and Human-Centered Energy System: A Comprehensive Review with Socio-Economic Viewpoints. *Energies*, *18*(9), 2345.

Islam, M. T., Sepanloo, K., Woo, S., Woo, S. H., & Son, Y. J. (2025). A review of the industry 4.0 to 5.0 transition: Exploring the intersection, challenges, and opportunities of technology and Human–Machine collaboration. *Machines (Basel)*, *13*(4), 267.

Ivanov, D. (2023). The Industry 5.0 framework: Viability-based integration of the resilience, sustainability, and human-centricity perspectives. *International Journal of Production Research*, *61*(5), 1683–1695.

Jäpel, N., Bielitz, P., & Reichelt, D. (2024). The Dresden Model of Adaptability: A Holistic Approach to Human-Centeredness, Resilience, Sustainability, and the Impact on the Sustainable Development Goals in the Era of Industry 5.0. *Digital*, *4*(3), 726–739.

Jeyabalan, J., Rohan, K., & Shanthalakshmi, M. (2025). Book: Food and Industry 5.0: Transforming the Food System for a Sustainable Future: Industry 5.0 Technologies for Sustainable Food Production. In *Food and Industry 5.0: Transforming the Food System for a Sustainable Future* (pp. 155–169). Springer Nature Switzerland.

Kalantari, F., Tahir, O. M., Joni, R. A., & Fatemi, E. (2017). Opportunities and challenges in sustainability of vertical farming: A review. *Journal of Landscape Ecology*, *10*(1), 35–60. DOI: 10.1515/jlecol-2017-0016

Kamilaris, A., Fonts, A., & Prenafeta-Boldú, F. X. (2019). The rise of blockchain technology in agriculture and food supply chains. *Trends in Food Science & Technology*, *91*, 640–652. DOI: 10.1016/j.tifs.2019.07.034

Kaur, A., Kukreja, V., Gopal, L., Verma, G., & Sharma, R. (2023, December). Cultivating Precision: A Multi-Layer Perceptron Approach for Accurate Classification of Maize Rust Disease Intensity in Precision Agriculture. In *2023 6th International Conference on Recent Trends in Advance Computing (ICRTAC)* (pp. 267-270). IEEE.

Kumar, A., Dhanka, S., Bansal, R., Sharma, A., Singh, J., Khan, A. A., & Maini, S. (2024). Agriculture in the Era of Industry 5.0. *Industry 5.0 and Emerging Technologies: Transformation Through. Technology and Innovation*, *565*, 111.

Leng, J., Zhong, Y., Lin, Z., Xu, K., Mourtzis, D., Zhou, X., & Shen, W. (2023). Towards resilience in Industry 5.0: A decentralized autonomous manufacturing paradigm. *Journal of Manufacturing Systems*, *71*, 95–114.

Majumdar, K., Verma, A. K., Kathpalia, K. V., Samajder, P., & Prabhakar, P. K. (2025). Utilizing Industry 5.0 Technologies to Improve Food Production and Promote Sustainability in Agriculture. In *Food and Industry 5.0: Transforming the Food System for a Sustainable Future* (pp. 143–153). Springer Nature Switzerland.

Mana, A. A., Allouhi, A., Hamrani, A., Rehman, S., El Jamaoui, I., & Jayachandran, K. (2024). Sustainable AI-based production agriculture: Exploring AI applications and implications in agricultural practices. *Smart Agricultural Technology*, *7*, 100416.

Matheson, E., Minto, R., Zampieri, E. G., Faccio, M., & Rosati, G. (2019). Human–robot collaboration in manufacturing applications: A review. *Robotics (Basel, Switzerland)*, *8*(4), 100.

Mihrete, T. B., & Mihretu, F. B. (2025). Crop Diversification for Ensuring Sustainable Agriculture, Risk Management and Food Security. *Global Challenges (Hoboken, NJ)*, •••, 2400267. PMID: 39925666

Muratovski, G. (2015). Paradigm shift: Report on the new role of design in business and society. *She Ji: The Journal of Design, Economics, and Innovation*, *1*(2), 118–139.

NABARD. (2021). *Digital agriculture: Enhancing farmer income through technology*. National Bank for Agriculture and Rural Development. Retrieved from https://www.nabard.org

Nahavandi, S. (2019). Industry 5.0—A human-centric solution. *Sustainability*, *11*(16), 4371.

Narkhede, G., Pasi, B., Rajhans, N., & Kulkarni, A. (2023). Industry 5.0 and the future of sustainable manufacturing: A systematic literature review. *Business Strategy & Development*, *6*(4), 704–723.

Narkhede, G. B., Pasi, B. N., Rajhans, N., & Kulkarni, A. (2025). Industry 5.0 and sustainable manufacturing: A systematic literature review. *Benchmarking*, *32*(2), 608–635.

Nishant, R., Kennedy, M., & Corbett, J. (2020). Artificial intelligence for sustainability: Challenges, opportunities, and a research agenda. *International Journal of Information Management*, *53*, 102104.

Oyekunle, D. O. T., Okwudili Matthew, U., Bakare, K. M., Fatai, L. O., & Asnui, O. (2024). *Industry 5.0: A Paradigm Shift Towards Sustainability, Adaptability and Human-Centeredness*. David Oyekunle, Ugochukwu Okwudili Matthew, Kafayat Motomori Bakare, Lateef Olawale Fatai, Olasubomi Asuni.

Pathak, H., Kumar, G., Mohapatra, S. D., Gaikwad, B. B., & Rane, J. (2020). Use of drones in agriculture: Potentials, Problems and Policy Needs. *ICAR-National Institute of Abiotic Stress Management*, *300*, 4–15.

Payer, R. C., Quelhas, O. L. G., & Bergiante, N. C. R. (2024). Framework to supporting monitoring the circular economy in the context of industry 5.0: A proposal considering circularity indicators, digital transformation, and sustainability. *Journal of Cleaner Production*, *466*, 142850.

Pietrantoni, L., Favilla, M., Fraboni, F., Mazzoni, E., Morandini, S., Benvenuti, M., & De Angelis, M. (2024). Integrating collaborative robots in manufacturing, logistics, and agriculture: Expert perspectives on technical, safety, and human factors. *Frontiers in Robotics and AI*, *11*, 1342130. PMID: 39687349

Prabhakar, P., Verma, D. K., & Banerjee, M. (2025). Safety and Toxicity of Nutraceuticals: Concerns, Challenges and Global Regulatory Aspects. In *Food Bioactives and Nutraceuticals: Dietary Medicine for Human Health and Well-Beings* (pp. 437–462). Springer Nature Singapore.

Prabhakar, S., & Nimesh, A. (2022). Skill development programmes for women in India: Current status and future perspectives. *World Journal of Advanced Engineering Technology and Sciences*, *7*(1), 128–136.

Prabhakar, S., Nimesh, A., & Prabhakar, P. (2023a). Assessment of Start-Up Ecosystems for Tribal Women Entrepreneurs in India. In *Diversity, Equity, and Inclusion Efforts of Businesses in Rural Areas* (pp. 1-22). IGI Global.

Prabhakar, S., Nimesh, A., & Prabhakar, P. (2023b). Startup ecosystem for rural development in India. In *Socio-Economic Disparities, Vulnerable Communities, and the Future of Work and Entrepreneurship* (pp. 26-50). IGI Global.

Prabhakar, S., Tiwari, T., Prabhakar, P., Banerjee, S., Pasayat, A. K., Gonela, S., . . . Nimesh, A. (2025). Frugal Innovation (FI): A Catalyst for Inclusive Economic Growth and Sustainable Entrepreneurship Development. In *Entrepreneurial Opportunities in Disadvantaged Rural Communities* (pp. 281-326). IGI Global Scientific Publishing.

PwC India. (2020). *Disrupting the Indian agriculture ecosystem: The role of agritech.* PricewaterhouseCoopers India. Retrieved from https://www.pwc.in

Raja Santhi, A., & Muthuswamy, P. (2023). Industry 5.0 or industry 4.0 S? Introduction to industry 4.0 and a peek into the prospective industry 5.0 technologies. [IJIDeM]. *International Journal on Interactive Design and Manufacturing*, *17*(2), 947–979. PMID: 40478102

Rame, R., Purwanto, P., & Sudarno, S. (2024). Industry 5.0 and sustainability: An overview of emerging trends and challenges for a green future. *Innovation and Green Development*, *3*(4), 100173.

Rani, S., Jining, D., Shoukat, K., Shoukat, M. U., & Nawaz, S. A. (2024). A human–machine interaction mechanism: Additive manufacturing for Industry 5.0—design and management. *Sustainability*, *16*(10), 4158.

Rashid, A. B., & Kausik, A. K. (2024). AI revolutionizing industries worldwide: A comprehensive overview of its diverse applications. *Hybrid Advances*, 100277.

Rejeb, A., Rejeb, K., Keogh, J. G., & Süle, E. (2025). When Industry 5.0 Meets the Circular Economy: A Systematic Literature Review. *Circular Economy and Sustainability*, •••, 1–32.

Santiago, B. D. S., Scavarda, L. F., Gusmão Caiado, R. G., Santos, R. S., & Mattos Nascimento, D. L. D. (2025). Corporate social responsibility and circular economy integration framework within sustainable supply chain management: Building blocks for industry 5.0. *Corporate Social Responsibility and Environmental Management*, *32*(1), 269–290.

Sarıoğlu, C. İ. (2023). Industry 5.0, digital society, and consumer 5.0. In *Handbook of Research on Perspectives on Society and Technology Addiction* (pp. 11-33). IGI Global.

Sarkar, B. D., Sharma, I., & Shardeo, V. (2025). A multi-method examination of barriers to traceability in Industry 5.0-enabled digital food supply chains. *International Journal of Logistics Management*, *36*(2), 354–380.

Šćepanović, S., Bogucka, E., & Quercia, D. (2025). AI in the city: Impact assessment of artificial intelligence uses in earth observation. *Urban Informatics*, *4*(1), 1–30. PMID: 39802502

Shabur, M. A., Shahriar, A., & Ara, M. (2025). From automation to collaboration: Exploring the impact of industry 5.0 on sustainable manufacturing. *Discover Sustainability*, *6*(1), 1–23.

Shahab, H., Iqbal, M., Sohaib, A., Khan, F. U., & Waqas, M. (2024). IoT-based agriculture management techniques for sustainable farming: A comprehensive review. *Computers and Electronics in Agriculture*, *220*, 108851.

Singh, K. A., Patra, F., Ghosh, T., Mahnot, N. K., Dutta, H., & Duary, R. K. (2025). Advancing food systems with industry 5.0: A systematic review of smart technologies, sustainability, and resource optimization. *Sustainable Futures : An Applied Journal of Technology, Environment and Society*, •••, 100694.

Singh, T., Singh, D., Singh, C. D., & Singh, K. (2023). Industry 5.0. *Factories of the Future: Technological Advancements in the Manufacturing Industry*, 21-45.

Tusquellas, N., Santiago, R., & Palau, R. (2025). Professional Development Analytics: A Smart Model for Industry 5.0. *Applied Sciences (Basel, Switzerland)*, *15*(4), 2057.

Victor, N., Maddikunta, P. K. R., Mary, D. R. K., Murugan, R., Chengoden, R., Gadekallu, T. R., & Paek, J. (2024). Remote Sensing for Agriculture in the Era of Industry 5.0–A survey. *IEEE Journal of Selected Topics in Applied Earth Observations and Remote Sensing*.

Chapter 6
Green and Circular Supply Chain Finance Supported by Carbon-Twin Accounting

Hamed Nozari
https://orcid.org/0000-0002-6500-6708
Azad University of the UAE, Dubai, UAE

Zornitsa Yordanova
https://orcid.org/0000-0002-6056-8445
University of National and World Economy, Sofia, Bulgaria

ABSTRACT

This research presents a novel framework for green and circular finance supply chains, which is designed based on carbon twin accounting in the context of Industry 5.0. By integrating real-time environmental data, financial indicators, and digital twin technology, the proposed model enables sustainable, transparent, and adaptive decision-making. This framework not only helps reduce carbon emissions and optimize financial resources, but also provides a basis for data-driven policymaking and the formation of a cognitive carbon-finance ecosystem in the future. The research results show that Industry 5.0 can become the driving force of the green economy and intergenerational justice.

DOI: 10.4018/979-8-3693-4525-2.ch006

1- INTRODUCTION

Growing environmental pressures, regulatory requirements related to carbon neutrality, and the need to redesign financial flows in global supply chains have led to the transformation of supply chain finance from a purely cash-based mechanism to a smart, data-driven, and sustainability-oriented system. In the meantime, the transition from a linear economy to a circular economy is not possible by modifying the production or recycling process alone, but requires changes in the logic of capital flows, valuation, and risk models at the inter-firm level. The main challenge is the lack of real-time transparency about the carbon footprint and environmental performance of production units throughout the product life cycle; an issue that not only hinders the optimal allocation of credit, but also perpetuates the phenomenon of "greenwashing" in global financial chains (Intonti et al., 2025). In such a situation, Industry 5.0, with its human-centered, resilient, and sustainability-oriented approach, provides a platform for financing, real-world data, and environmental operations to be managed in an integrated and interactive manner.

Despite the development of green financing tools such as green bonds, ESG-based loans, and carbon credits, the main problem remains in the assessment, compliance, and validation layer of environmental data. The traditional accounting system is unable to measure carbon emissions at the nodal, process, and inter-organizational levels in real time, which causes a gap between financial commitments and operational reality (Lai et al., 2025a). For this reason, the idea of "Carbon-Twin Accounting" is proposed as a new generation of environmental accounting; a mechanism that uses a digital twin to record, model, and validate the carbon footprint of products, machinery, logistics, and the recycling cycle in real time (Sun et al., 2025). This approach not only enables data-driven allocation of credit, interest rates, and risk ratings, but can also be the basis for designing novel circular finance mechanisms, where capital flows are driven by recycling efficiency and carbon intensity rather than resource consumption rates.

So far, the application of digital twins in supply chains has been mainly in the areas of simulation, capacity planning, predictive maintenance, and production control, but its integration with finance is a trans-industrial step towards the convergence of commodity, data, and money flows (Jiang et al., 2025a). With this integration, a "financial asset" is no longer simply an invoice or inventory, but a dynamic indicator that includes carbon content, recyclability, and compliance with green standards (Negash et al., 2025). This approach can be the basis for the transition from traditional balance sheet-based credit models to "Carbon-Backed Finance" models, where the collateral is not just the physical asset, but also the valid data of the digital twin.

From a macroeconomic perspective, such a shift will have a profound impact on pricing systems. In a context where carbon taxes and carbon border adjustment mechanisms are in place, companies that have access to real, quantitative data on their carbon performance can experience a lower cost of capital, as their environmental risk is lower (Nozari, 2026). This is especially important in chains that depend on exports to regulated markets. On the other hand, the digital twin link with distributed ledger or smart contract technologies allows for the automated execution of financing mechanisms such as Dynamic Green Loan, Sustainability-Linked Credit Line or Carbon Token Collateral (Ezeudu & Bristow, 2025). In this way, the financial flow is not only freed from administrative delays, but also from dependence on periodic reports, paper certificates or human audits.

Despite these opportunities, challenges remain, such as standardization of carbon data, interoperability between industrial and financial systems, supply chain data security, and how to convert environmental indicators into financially acceptable metrics (Nozari & Nassar, 2025). Also, although life cycle analysis and simulation tools exist in the environmental field, little research has translated their results into interest rates, credit models, or liquidity allocation (Asante Boakye et al., 2025). This research gap is precisely where the present topic addresses: designing a framework based on Carbon-Twin Accounting that acts as a link between the circular economy, financial management, and real-time data.

As a result, a completely new conceptual and methodological framework is needed; one in which financial resources are allocated to the circular flow of value, material recovery, and carbon reduction, rather than feeding linear consumption. With the aim of introducing such a framework, this chapter first explains the theoretical foundations related to green finance and digital twinning, then describes the conceptual model of "Green & Circular Supply Chain Finance Supported by Carbon-Twin Accounting", and then identifies possible research and industrial directions.

2- LITERATURE REVIEW

New trends in supply chain finance demonstrate that the transition from traditional models based on paper documents, static credit ratings and collateral to intelligent, data-driven and dynamic financial mechanisms is a structural necessity in today's industrial and digital economy. Early literature on supply chain finance focused more on facilitating liquidity, reducing the cost of capital and managing credit risk between suppliers and buyers (Nozari et al., 2024). However, the introduction of sustainability requirements, carbon neutrality targets and ESG indicators has led to finance being seen as more than a purely economic issue and becoming a tool for changing environmental behaviour and circular development (Kumar et al., 2024). Gradually, the concept of "Green Supply Chain Finance" was introduced, which attempted to link capital allocation with environmental performance, but these efforts were largely dependent on periodic reports, manual certifications and static assessments, and lacked real-time transparency (Nozari, 2025a).

In the circular economy literature, recycling, material recovery, design for remanufacturing and product life extension have been proposed as new value creation axes in supply chains. However, the link between these physical flows and financial flows has rarely been studied in a structural way (Judijanto et al., 2024). Most theoretical frameworks of the circular economy have modeled the flow of materials and energy, but how to translate the "level of circularity" into interest rates, credit levels or financial risk factors remains neglected (Nozari, Abdi, et al., 2025). This research gap becomes even more apparent when the concept of "Circular Supply Chain Finance" is introduced: that is, the allocation of capital based on the recovery capacity, recyclability and recyclability of materials. Although some studies have addressed the link between recycling and economic value, there is little evidence of the actual integration of these data into financing decisions (Gao et al., 2024).

In the field of digital twin, the main focus has so far been on simulation, process control, maintenance planning, operational risk management and resource optimization (Nozari, Szmelter-Jarosz, & Weiland, 2025). The use of digital twins in finance is still at a conceptual stage and most studies have been limited to industrial sectors. Some research has suggested the possibility of connecting industrial sensor data to financial systems, but there is still no comprehensive framework for translating real-time carbon emission data into financial metrics (Lai et al., 2025b). In recent years, the concept of "Carbon Digital Twin" has been proposed in a limited way, but mostly with the aim of monitoring emissions rather than linking them to supply chain financial decisions (Nozari, Nassar, & Szmelter-Jarosz, 2025).

On the other hand, the literature on "Green Finance" and "Sustainability-Linked Loans" shows that banks and financial institutions are moving towards models in which interest rates or access to credit change based on the sustainable performance of companies (Singh, 2025). However, the fundamental problem in this area is the lack of reliable, real-time, and operationally based data, with many green finance contracts still relying on self-declarations, annual audits, or unreliable certifications (Nozari & Samadi, 2025). This has led to the proliferation of financial greenwashing, i.e. the apparent use of green titles without any real change in operational performance (Jiang et al., 2025b).

The literature on new financial technologies, particularly smart contracts and distributed ledgers, has highlighted the potential for automating financing mechanisms, automated enforcement of guarantees, event-based settlement, and tokenization of assets (Nozari & Yordanova, 2025). However, the main challenge is that collateral is often limited to physical goods, invoices, or assets, and the environmental performance of the chain is not defined as a "financial asset" (Liu et al., 2024). The idea of "Carbon-Backed Collateral" is not yet well established in the literature and requires an interdisciplinary framework between finance, digital twin and carbon accounting (Nozari et al., 2025).

In another part of the research, life cycle analysis (LCA) has been proposed as the main tool for measuring carbon emissions at the product level, but this method has usually remained static, expensive and without the ability to connect to the financial flow of the supply chain (Ju et al., 2024). LCA can provide accurate environmental data, but without connecting to the digital twin, it cannot be updated in real time and interact with financial systems. This limitation means that the outcome of the life cycle analysis does not play a structural role in pricing, credit decisions or capital allocation (Alora & Gupta, 2024).

Therefore, the existing literature reveals three major gaps: first, the lack of a transparent and real-time mechanism to link carbon performance to financial credit; Second, the absence of an operational data-based accounting system that replaces the estimated carbon footprint calculations; and third, the lack of a framework that can represent financial flows, material flows, and digital data flows in a single model. These three gaps provide the basis for the development of the "Green & Circular Supply Chain Finance Supported by Carbon-Twin Accounting" framework, which can enable a new generation of sustainable finance by connecting the digital twin to credit allocation models, adaptive interest rates, and tokenization of revolving assets.

3- CONCEPTUAL FRAMEWORK

The proposed conceptual framework is based on a three-layer architecture that explains the simultaneous interaction between the physical supply chain, the data-driven layer based on the digital twin, and green financial mechanisms in the context of Industry 5.0. Instead of focusing solely on the physical flow of goods or traditional financial calculations, this structure creates an integrated system in which the actual environmental behavior of processes is directly reflected in financial decisions. As a result, economic efficiency, environmental sustainability, and data transparency are simultaneously enhanced. Figure 1, presented in this section, shows the conceptual architecture of this framework.

Figure 1. Conceptual Framework of Green and Circular Supply Chain Finance Supported by Carbon-Twin Accounting in Industry 5.0

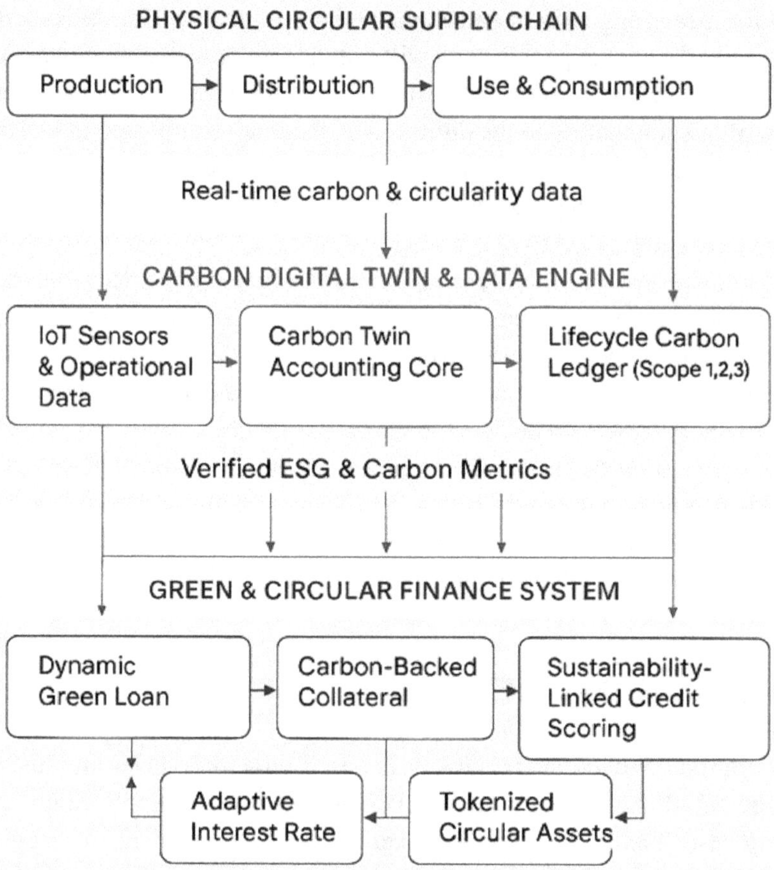

In the first layer, the supply chain is considered as a closed cycle that starts from production and continues with distribution, consumption, reverse logistics, and recycling or remanufacturing. This cycle is not limited to the mere transfer of products, but is based on the concept of a "perpetual circulation of value"; in such a way that materials and energy, after consumption, re-enter the system and return to the production axis. In this architecture, sustainability becomes an intrinsic and structural feature rather than an external goal.

The second layer acts as a bridge between physical reality and data-driven analytics. This layer includes a digital twin-based core that captures, classifies, and models real-time sensor data, carbon footprints, material flows, and circularity indicators. In this architecture, carbon accounting is not an ex post report, but a real-time process that is integrated with time-based validation, life cycle ledgers (including direct, indirect, and supply chain emissions), and distributed ledger technology-based tracking. In this way, environmental data is elevated from a descriptive state to an analytical and decision-making state.

The third layer is dedicated to the financial system and shows how information from the digital twin is directly connected to capital flows, risk pricing, and the design of smart financial instruments. In this layer, concepts such as dynamic green loans, carbon collateral, adaptive interest rates, sustainability-based credit scoring, and tokenized revolving assets are defined. Valuation in this system is based on the actual performance of operations against environmental indicators, not just on alleged documents; in other words, each unit of capital responds to the carbon and cyclical behavior of the supply chain.

The interaction of these three layers leads to the formation of a feedback system. Real data is transferred from the physical layer to the digital layer, where it is validated and standardized, and then sent to the financial layer. In turn, financial decisions based on this data return to the physical layer and are translated into capital incentives, carbon penalties, or capital absorption rates. In this way, the operational behavior of organizations is modified not by coercion but by economic logic, as "cost-effectiveness" and "environmental friendliness" are linked together.

This framework has two key advantages over classical approaches:

First, the supply chain is not seen as a linear process, but as a loop system based on the return of value. Second, instead of having a reporting role, environmental data becomes a financial variable that directly affects access to capital and its conditions. As a result, the link between digitalization, sustainability and financialization becomes not a slogan, but a structural and implementable mechanism.

This model is theoretically connected to the literature on circular supply chains, digital twins, and sustainable finance, but its main innovation is that instead of looking at these three areas separately, it connects them in the form of an operational hierarchy that can be implemented. Hence, the proposed framework not only enables modeling and simulation of supply chain behavior at a technical level, but also lays the groundwork for standardizing carbon reporting, automating monitoring, and accelerating sustainable investment at an industrial scale.

In this model, the output of the deep learning (DL) network is directly used as input for risk parameters in the optimization section. In other words, after training on historical and real-time supply chain data, the deep learning model predicts the probability of occurrence of various risks such as credit default, payment delay, and liquidity fluctuation for each supplier-buyer pair in each time interval. These predicted values are dynamically transferred to the optimization model to be embedded in the form of risk parameters and directly affect capital allocation decisions, credit levels, and financial relationship selection.

In this way, the multi-objective optimization model operates not on static assumptions, but on live data and deep learning-based predictions. This integration ensures that decisions are data-driven, adaptive, and sensitive to real market changes, and the system can adjust its credit allocation and risk management policies intelligently and in real time when financial fluctuations occur.

4- METHODOLOGICAL APPROACH

The methodological approach of this research is based on a systematic combination of conceptual modeling, digital twin-based data analysis, and multi-criteria assessment of financial sustainability. The aim of this approach is to transfer the theory of "green and circular financial supply chain" from the conceptual level to the operational and simulable level. For this purpose, three complementary methodological axes are designed, which include: (1) modeling of physical processes of the supply chain, (2) development of digital twin and carbon data structure, and (3) integration of the results with sustainable financial decision-making models.

In the first step, the flow of materials and energy in the supply chain is modeled based on the principles of the circular economy. This physical model includes the stages of production, distribution, consumption, reverse logistics, and recycling and is calibrated through input parameters such as recycling rate, energy intensity, and process losses. The aim of this step is to create a basis for assessing environmental performance at different levels of the supply chain. The data from this stage serves as input to the digital twin layer to establish a direct connection between the actual behavior of the system and the virtual model.

In the second step, the digital twin is built as a multi-level architecture. This architecture receives real-time data from IoT sensors, logistics information, and carbon emission indicators and organizes them into a "carbon lifecycle ledger". This ledger consists of three emission areas (Scope 1, 2, 3) and each event is stored in it with a time stamp and automatic validation. Using data flow analysis algorithms, the trend of changes in emissions and energy consumption throughout the product life cycle is identified and transferred to the financial model. In this step, sensitivity analysis is also performed to measure the stability of the model with respect to changes in key parameters (such as recycling efficiency or energy intensity).

In the third step, the results from the digital twin are integrated with the financial decision-making system. In this step, multi-criteria decision-making and multi-objective optimization approaches are used to balance economic interests with environmental goals. Decision variables include green interest rates, carbon collateral levels, and reward policies based on environmental performance. The combined objective function is defined in such a way that minimizing total cost, minimizing carbon footprint, and maximizing social return are pursued simultaneously. Meta-heuristic algorithms such as NSGA-II, MOPSO, or reinforcement learning-based algorithms can be used to generate the Pareto front and analyze trade-offs between objectives.

The decision-making process in this framework is designed based on a feedback loop. Real-time data from the digital twin is transmitted to the financial model, and then the decision results (such as changes in investment rates or credit policy) are sent back to the physical layer to implement operational changes. This feedback loop not only allows for continuous optimization, but also allows the model to learn from the system behavior and increase its prediction accuracy over time. At this stage, the use of adaptive learning models is recommended to automatically adjust the weights of the objectives and decision intervals.

At the implementation level, the proposed framework has the ability to connect to real industrial data. Data on production, energy consumption, logistics, and environmental indicators can be collected through ERP or IoT systems and fed into the digital twin module. The output of this module is also presented in the form of measurable indicators (such as "green financial score" or "carbon return on investment") through a financial decision engine. For the final evaluation, key performance indicators (KPIs) including energy savings, emission reductions, green return on investment, and recycling rates are measured at the system level.

Overall, the methodological approach of this research, combining process modeling tools, real-time data analysis, and multi-objective financial decision-making, enables the implementation of the proposed framework in real industrial environments. Its main advantage is that financial decisions are no longer made based on historical or estimated data, but are directly based on real and up-to-date digital twin data; thus, financial, environmental, and operational sustainability are achieved simultaneously and dynamically.

5- TRANSFORMATIVE INTEGRATION AND POLICY PERSPECTIVE

The digital transformation in Industry 5.0 is no longer based solely on technology, but rather on the convergence of technical, environmental and financial systems. In this regard, the concept of a "green and circular supply chain supported by the carbon twin" is considered one of the most comprehensive models of this transition, as it has been able to integrate three fundamental dimensions (data, value and sustainability) into a common architecture. This model is a bridge between producers, consumers, financial institutions and regulators that operates on the basis of a real-time flow of environmental and financial data. In such a structure, policy-making is not based on historical data, but on "instantaneous knowledge" of the carbon, economic and social situation.

The integration of a transformation makes sense when the physical chain, the digital twin and the financial mechanism are placed in a feedback loop. In this cycle, data extracted from IoT sensors, carbon reports, and environmental performance indicators automatically flow into financial and credit systems. This data becomes the basis for determining green interest rates, tax breaks, or even the level of access to credit resources. In other words, economic value in this new system is a function of environmental performance. This approach could transform the traditional concept of "financial credit" and lead to a kind of sustainable data-driven capitalism, where carbon twins are not just reporting tools, but real financial assets.

From a policy perspective, such a model provides unprecedented transparency by creating a national "carbon ledger." Every industrial unit, organization, or business can record the exact amount of carbon it emits, absorbs, or offsets in real time and send it to regulatory bodies. Governments will also be able to design tax and credit policies based on real data rather than estimates. For example, central banks could introduce a "carbon risk" indicator into the financial system as a component of corporate credit assessments, thereby optimizing capital allocation for sustainable development goals.

Transformational integration also requires a rethinking of the data governance structure. The digital twin transforms the nature of supply chain data from "static reports" to "dynamic and trusted streams." This requires new frameworks for data ownership, privacy, and inter-organizational exchange. Policymakers must develop standards for the accuracy, traceability, and consistency of environmental and financial data to ensure that the carbon-finance ecosystem functions in a coherent and trustworthy manner. Without such standards, the digital twin could create data fragmentation and undermine trust in green markets rather than transparency.

From an industrial transformation perspective, implementing such a framework means the emergence of a kind of cognitive infrastructure in the economy. This infrastructure can use machine learning and adaptive intelligence to identify supply chain behavior patterns and adjust financial policies based on real environmental changes. For example, if digital twin data shows that a factory has been able to consistently reduce its carbon emissions over a certain period, the system can automatically upgrade its green loan rate or credit score. This data-driven self-regulation not only increases economic efficiency, but also creates an incentive for sustainability internally in the system.

The policy vision of Industry 5.0 is also moving from "top-down monitoring" to "participatory data-driven governance." In this model, governments play the role of ecosystem regulators rather than direct controllers. Instead of fixed guidelines, policymaking is based on learning algorithms that respond to environmental, social, and economic changes. Such a model requires close collaboration between the finance, technology, energy, and environmental sectors, as decisions made in each area directly affect the others.

The key point in this vision is the integration of intergenerational justice and economic logic. A green finance supply chain with carbon twin support not only helps reduce emissions, but also allows for a more equitable distribution of resources. In this framework, investing in low-carbon projects means ensuring the well-being of future generations, and economic decisions at the micro and macro levels are redefined in the framework of a data-driven ethical system.

Finally, the transformational and policy integration proposed in this research could be the starting point for the formation of a Cognitive Carbon-Finance Ecosystem; An ecosystem in which digital twin technologies, smart data analytics, and adaptive financial policies work synergistically. This approach paves the way for a shift from "sustainability as a goal" to "sustainability as an inherent feature of the system." In this view, Industry 5.0 is not just a stage of technological progress, but also a step towards redefining the relationship between the economy, the environment, and humans a relationship based on awareness, transparency, and shared value.

6- FUTURE RESEARCH DIRECTIONS

The growing growth of smart and data-driven technologies in Industry 5.0 has provided unprecedented opportunities to redefine the concept of supply chain finance and sustainability assessment. However, future research directions in the field of green and circular supply chain finance supported by carbon twin accounting have not yet been fully mapped out. The field is at a stage that requires theory development, empirical testing, and the development of multi-layer decision-making models to reach scientific and industrial maturity.

One of the important future directions is the development of cognitive digital twin models that are able to learn system behavior at different levels and adapt to changing environmental and economic conditions. While current twin models mainly focus on reflecting physical data, the next generation can discover hidden patterns between financial, environmental, and behavioral data by leveraging deep learning, fuzzy logic, and reinforcement learning. Future research should explore how these capabilities can be used to create self-regulating mechanisms in the supply chain, especially for financial decisions made under uncertainty and market volatility.

A second research path is to develop data standards and open architecture for carbon ledgers. One of the key challenges in the practical implementation of the proposed model is the lack of international mechanisms for exchanging carbon and financial data in a secure and reliable manner. Future research could design protocols that are on par with blockchain technology to maintain transparency and traceability throughout the supply chain. In this regard, questions such as data ownership, ethical responsibility in environmental information disclosure, and the design of green validation algorithms should be explored in an interdisciplinary manner.

At a broader level, future research should integrate financial, industrial, and environmental policies into adaptive frameworks. Given that traditional policy models are usually static and based on historical averages, researchers can develop policy learning algorithms to automatically adjust financial and environmental parameters. For example, carbon tax rates or green subsidies can be updated in real time based on digital twin data. Such a system requires collaboration between academia, government, and industry to leverage data, algorithms, and indicators in a shared ecosystem.

Another direction is to focus on systems and dynamics analyses. Many of the relationships in the financial-carbon ecosystem are nonlinear and feedback-driven, especially when financial decisions affect production or consumption behavior. Future research could use dynamical system simulation, agent-based modeling, or complexity theory to analyze these interactions. The use of these tools will help to gain a deeper understanding of the long-term sustainability of the system and its critical points in the face of economic or environmental shocks.

On the other hand, an important research direction lies in the area of green financial behavior and human motivations. Although digital twin technology provides accurate and real-time data, the acceptance and effectiveness of these systems ultimately depend on human behavior and decisions. Future research should explore how motivational, cognitive, and cultural mechanisms can be integrated into carbon-finance models. In this context, the concept of "human-machine symbiosis" plays a crucial role in Industry 5.0, because sustainable decision-making only makes sense when humans are actively involved in the learning and control process as part of an intelligent system.

Another research horizon is Eco-Financial Life Cycle Assessment. So far, many studies have focused on physical LCA of products, but linking it to real financial flows is still rare. Future research could define new composite indicators that simultaneously measure financial, energy, and carbon impacts over the product life cycle. These indicators could be the basis for decisions on green investments or resource allocation in the supply chain.

There is also an important direction in the development of testbeds for the financial-carbon digital twin. These platforms could be simulated environments in which economic models, sensor data, and financial policies are tested in an integrated manner. Creating such infrastructures allows researchers to test their theoretical hypotheses in near-real-world conditions and predict the impact of policies or parameter changes before they are implemented in the real world.

Finally, future research directions should move towards institutionalizing collective intelligence and sustainability ethics in decision-making models. Industry 5.0 can only become a sustainable paradigm if it combines data science, artificial intelligence, and human values. Future research should develop frameworks for ethical evaluation of algorithms, transparency in automated decision-making, and ensuring intergenerational justice. This is especially important in financial systems based on environmental data, as automated decisions may have indirect social or geographical consequences.

Overall, the future of research in the field of carbon twin-based green finance supply chains is a data-driven, learning, and human-centered future. Focusing on the integration of cognitive technologies, data standards, and adaptive governance mechanisms can pave the way for the transition from traditional financial systems to self-learning, transparent, and sustainable ecosystems. In such a future, data will not only reflect reality, but also be a tool for shaping it a reality that connects the economy, the environment, and society in a sustainable and intelligent cycle.

7- CONCLUSION

The technological and environmental developments of the 21st century have brought economic systems and supply chains to a point where financial value and environmental sustainability can no longer be separated. The framework presented in this chapter, entitled "Green and Circular Finance Supply Chain Supported by Carbon Twin Accounting," is an attempt to redefine the relationship between data, value, and decision in the era of Industry 5.0; an era in which the boundary between physical and digital reality is blurred and real-time data becomes the backbone of a sustainable economy.

The theoretical findings of this study suggest that the combination of three key axes—circular economy, digital twin accounting, and green finance—can provide a coherent framework for guiding industrial and financial transition. As a data-driven infrastructure, the carbon twin enables the real-time recording, tracking, and analysis of carbon emissions and sequestration throughout the supply chain. When this information is transferred to the financial layer, the credit decision-making system can be based on actual environmental performance and no longer rely solely on self-reports or average estimates. This data-finance connection paves the way for the formation of transparent and learning financial ecosystems.

From a policy and governance perspective, the proposed framework can be a foundation for designing adaptive and data-driven financial systems. Governments and central banks can use digital twin data to dynamically adjust tax, subsidy, or credit policies based on the actual performance of industries. For example, if twin data shows that an industrial unit has succeeded in reducing carbon emissions during the year, the system can automatically reduce its carbon tax rate or financing cost. This type of adaptive policymaking not only increases economic productivity, but also makes environmental sustainability an intrinsic part of the economic decision-making system.

From an application perspective, the proposed model can be implemented at three levels. At the micro level, companies can simultaneously monitor environmental and financial performance indicators by connecting their ERP and IoT systems to the digital twin and make investment or production decisions based on up-to-date data. At the meso level, financial and banking institutions will be able to use twin data to more accurately assess credit risk, allocate green loans, and design sustainable financial products. And at the macro level, governments can increase economic and environmental transparency by developing national "National Carbon Ledger" platforms, while introducing new financial instruments such as "smart carbon bonds" or "environmental performance-based investing."

One of the conceptual achievements of this research is the introduction of the idea of a Cognitive Carbon-Finance Ecosystem, which is an evolved stage of the digital twin. In this ecosystem, financial and operational decisions operate in a self-learning and adaptive manner. The system can learn from past data, recognize sustainable patterns, and make optimal suggestions for resource allocation. This feature provides a path from reactive control to predictive management, allowing organizations to make corrective decisions before environmental or financial crises occur.

From a theoretical perspective, this framework helps to enrich the Industry 5.0 discourse, as Industry 4.0 focused mainly on automation and intelligence, while Industry 5.0 emphasizes human-centeredness, sustainability, and human-machine coexistence. In this framework, the digital twin is not simply a technological tool, but rather a "cognitive interface" between data, humans, and decisions. This new perspective will pave the way for new theories in the fields of sustainable financial intelligence, data-driven economics, and digital ethical governance.

Despite its vast potential, it must be acknowledged that the practical implementation of such a model also faces challenges. Issues such as data ownership, standardization of carbon information exchange, cybersecurity, and social trust in decision-making algorithms are among those that require precise legal and technical frameworks. In this direction, collaboration between universities, governments, and industries is crucial to form global standards for the carbon-financial digital twin.

At the strategic level, the practical implications of this research can be summarized in three axes: first, changing the decision-making paradigm from traditional approaches based on historical data to real-time predictive approaches; second, creating economic incentives for sustainability through smart and performance-based financial instruments; and third, empowering organizations and governments to simultaneously analyze financial, social, and environmental consequences. These three axes can provide the basis for the formation of a resilient, learning, and humane economy, an economy in which sustainability is not an external requirement, but part of the internal logic of the system.

Finally, the present research attempts to present a forward-looking picture of the nexus between technology, finance, and the environment; a nexus that makes sense in the context of Industry 5.0. The "carbon twin-supported green finance supply chain" is not only a technical or economic model, but also a civilizational vision; A vision in which the value created in the supply chain is no longer limited to financial profit, but also includes the health of the planet, social well-being and intergenerational sustainability. Realizing this vision requires the convergence of thought, technology and ethics, and it is precisely in this convergence that the future of the green and cognitive economy of Industry 5.0 will be shaped.

REFERENCES

Alora, A., & Gupta, H. (2024). Supplier selection among manufacturing companies based on their MSME partners' supply chain finance adoption capability using BWM and VIKOR. *Journal of Business and Industrial Marketing*, *39*(6), 1337–1351.

Asante Boakye, E., Zhao, H., Kwame Ahia, B. N., & Adu-Damoah, M. (2025). Modeling the adoption enablers of blockchain technology–based supply chain financing: an integrative dual DOI–TOE analysis. Journal of the International Council for Small Business, 1-22.

Ezeudu, O. B., & Bristow, D. (2025). Financing methods for solid waste management: A review of typology, classifications, and circular economy implications. *Sustainable Development*, *33*(2), 3062–3085.

Gao, J., Hua, G., & Huo, B. (2024). Green finance policies, financing constraints and corporate ESG performance: insights from supply chain management. Operations Management Research, 1-15.

Intonti, M., Mola, D., De Leonardis, M., & Starace, G. (2025). Enhancing Circular Practices in Olive Oil Production: The Role of Green Finance. *Sustainability*, *17*(1), 294.

Jiang, L., Cao, X., Wang, Z., Zhan, Y., Zhang, J., & Chen, S. (2025). Promoting energy saving and emission reduction benefits in small and medium-sized enterprises supply chains through green finance-Evidence based on artificial intelligence intervention. *International Review of Financial Analysis*, •••, 104112.

Jiang, L., Cao, X., Wang, Z., Zhan, Y., Zhang, J., & Chen, S. (2025). Promoting energy saving and emission reduction benefits in small and medium-sized enterprises supply chains through green finance-Evidence based on artificial intelligence intervention. *International Review of Financial Analysis*, •••, 104112.

Ju, Y., Hou, H., Cheng, Y., & Feng, Y. (2024). Assessing the impact of government-led green supply chain demonstration on firms' financial distress: The role of environmental information disclosure quality and supply chain concentration. *Journal of Cleaner Production*, *440*, 140786.

Judijanto, L., Utami, E. Y., & Harsono, I. (2024). Green supply chain finance: A bibliometric review of financing instruments, challenges, and opportunities. *West Science Interdisciplinary Studies*, *2*(03), 647–655.

Kumar, B., Kumar, L., Kumar, A., Kumari, R., Tagar, U., & Sassanelli, C. (2024). Green finance in circular economy: A literature review. *Environment, Development and Sustainability, 26*(7), 16419–16459. PMID: 37362997

Lai, Z., Lou, G., Yin, L., Ma, H., & Tu, X. (2025). Supply chain green strategy considering manufacturers' financial constraints: How to manage the risk of green supply chain financing. *Annals of Operations Research, 348*(2), 1037–1068.

Lai, Z., Lou, G., Yin, L., Ma, H., & Tu, X. (2025). Supply chain green strategy considering manufacturers' financial constraints: How to manage the risk of green supply chain financing. *Annals of Operations Research, 348*(2), 1037–1068.

Liu, T., Guan, X., Wang, Z., Qin, T., Sun, R., & Wang, Y. (2024). Optimizing green supply chain circular economy in smart cities with integrated machine learning technology. *Heliyon, 10*(9). PMID: 38726132

Negash, Y. T., Hassan, A. M., Lim, M. K., & Tseng, M. L. (2025). Sustainable supply chain finance enablers under disruption: The causal effect of collaboration value innovation on sustainability performance. *International Journal of Logistics Research and Applications, 28*(4), 449–473.

Nozari, H. (2025). Integrating Neuromorphic Intelligence with Fuzzy Multi-Objective Models in Resilient Green Supply Chain Design. Process Integration and Optimization for Sustainability, 1-14.

Nozari, H. (2026). Analyzing and Optimizing Customer Interactions in Smart Cities Using IoT Data Synchronization and Temporal Neural Networks (RNN). In Improving Consumer Engagement in Digital Marketing Through Cognitive AI (pp. 211-224). IGI Global Scientific Publishing.

Nozari, H., Abdi, H., & Szmelter-Jarosz, A. (2025). A Neuromorphic and Bio-Inspired Framework for Optimization in Multi-Echelon Supply Networks. *Transformative Science, 1*(1), 9–17.

Nozari, H., Abdi, H., Szmelter-Jarosz, A., & Rahmaty, M. (2025). A digital twin-based neutrosophic multi-objective optimization model for smart supply chains in the food industry. *Journal of Intelligent Manufacturing*, •••, 1–15.

Nozari, H., Ghahremani-Nahr, J., & Szmelter-Jarosz, A. (2024). AI and machine learning for real-world problems. [). Elsevier.]. *Advances in Computers, 134*, 1–12.

Nozari, H., & Nassar, S. (2025). Real-time data-driven multi-objective optimization in B2B marketing using digital twins. OPSEARCH, 1-27.

Nozari, H., Nassar, S., & Szmelter-Jarosz, A. (2025). Fuzzy multi-objective optimization model for resilient supply chain financing based on blockchain and IoT. *Digital*, *5*(3), 32.

Nozari, H., & Samadi, S. (2025). AIoE-Powered Neuromarketing for Decoding the Consumer Brain. In *Artificial Intelligence of Everything and Sustainable Development* (pp. 39–53). Springer Nature Singapore.

Nozari, H., Szmelter-Jarosz, A., & Weiland, D. (2025). A Fuzzy Multi-Objective Sustainable and Agile Supply Chain Model Based on Digital Twin and Internet of Things with Adaptive Learning Under Environmental Uncertainty. *Applied Sciences (Basel, Switzerland)*, *15*(19), 10399.

Nozari, H., & Yordanova, Z. (2025). Hybrid digital twin and quantum AI with fuzzy multiobjective modeling in supply chain management. *Edelweiss Applied Science and Technology*, *9*(10), 609–628.

Singh, R. K. (2025). Exploring the impact of green supply chain strategies and sustainable practices on circular supply chains. *Benchmarking*, *32*(4), 1387–1409.

Sun, K., Ooi, K. B., Wei-Han Tan, G., & Lee, V. H. (2025). Small and medium-sized enterprises' path to sustainable supply chains: Exploring the role of supply chain finance and risk management. *Supply Chain Management*, *30*(1), 1–18.

Chapter 7
AI-Driven Economic Intelligence for Adaptive Supply Chain Ecosystems

Parvaneh Zeraati Fokolaei
https://orcid.org/0000-0003-2518-2982
Department of Management, Islamic Azad University, Juybar, Iran

ABSTRACT

This research presents a new framework for AI-based economic intelligence in adaptive supply chains. The proposed model, by utilizing machine learning, predictive analytics, and intelligent feedback, enhances economic decision-making ability from static to dynamic. The results show that using this model reduces costs, increases capital efficiency, and improves economic flexibility. By combining the concepts of adaptive economics, data analytics, and AI, the present research presents a practical model for intelligent supply chain management in the era of Industry 5.0.

1- INTRODUCTION

Rapid technological developments in the last decade have fundamentally transformed the face of economic systems and supply chains. The emergence of Industry 5.0, centered on artificial intelligence, big data, machine learning, and human-machine collaboration, has ushered in a new era of economic decision-making in which organizations are no longer simply seeking to reduce costs or increase productivity, but are instead seeking structures that can respond adaptively, dynamically, and intelligently to environmental changes. In such circumstances, "AI-based economic intelligence" is emerging as a new approach to supply chain management that aims

DOI: 10.4018/979-8-3693-4525-2.ch007

to create harmony between data analysis, economic decision-making, and organizational adaptability (Wu et al., 2025).

Today's supply chains operate in an environment characterized by instability and complexity. Sudden changes in customer demand, sharp fluctuations in raw material prices, environmental crises, and sanctions or trade restrictions have all made it impossible for economic decisions to be made based on static patterns or fixed assumptions. On the other hand, the huge volume of financial, logistical, and market data generated in real time has provided a new opportunity for scientific decision-making. But extracting meaning from this data is not possible with traditional tools alone; it requires systems that can learn from experience, recognize patterns, and adjust economic decisions adaptively and automatically. This is where the concept of "economic intelligence" comes into play in conjunction with artificial intelligence technologies (Nozari et al., 2021).

Economic intelligence essentially refers to the process of collecting, analyzing, and interpreting economic and market data to support strategic decisions. But in the context of Industry 5.0, this concept is upgraded to a more advanced level and redefined as "intelligent economic intelligence"; that is, a system that is able to transform supply chain data into decision-making economic knowledge and use past feedback to refine and optimize future decisions. In this way, AI-based systems act not only as computational tools, but also as "learning economic agents" that are able to analyze supply and demand patterns, consumer behavior, pricing, and risk with unprecedented accuracy (Belhadi et al., 2024).

In the context of such a transformation, the present study aims to provide a comprehensive framework for "AI-based economic intelligence in adaptive supply chains." This framework seeks to answer the key question of how AI capabilities can be used for economic decision-making in a way that the supply chain can remain resilient to environmental fluctuations while maintaining the most optimal level of financial performance. In this direction, the present research attempts to present a model that can represent the relationships between operational data, financial information, and economic decisions in a dynamic and learning format (Riad et al., 2024).

The role of artificial intelligence in this framework is not limited to data analysis, but also includes prediction, optimization, and decision-making. Machine learning and predictive analytics algorithms identify hidden patterns in supply chain data and simulate possible economic scenarios. On the other hand, multi-objective optimization algorithms can balance sometimes conflicting indicators such as cost, time, productivity, and customer satisfaction. These capabilities enable organizations to achieve predictive and adaptive decision-making instead of retrospective decision-making. This means that every economic decision is made not based on past data, but on intelligent predictions of the future (Nozari et al., 2024).

One of the key points of this research is the emphasis on the "learning" nature of economic systems. In the proposed model, the supply chain is conceived as a living organism that continuously adapts to new environmental conditions through intelligent feedback loops (Ivanov, 2025). New data is continuously entered into the system, analyzed, decisions are adjusted based on them, and the results of decisions are returned to the cycle as re-learning data. This process not only drives economic dynamism, but also transforms the supply chain from a passive system into a self-adaptive and crisis-resistant network (Thuraka, 2021).

From an economic perspective, such a model has several benefits for organizations. First, it reduces the costs of the entire supply chain by increasing forecast accuracy, reducing excess inventory, and optimizing cash flow. Second, it increases operational and financial efficiency by accelerating decision-making and shortening the time to respond to market changes. Third, by providing real-time analytical data, managers will be able to make decisions that directly lead to increased profit margins, capital efficiency, and economic sustainability. Finally, due to its learning nature, this model has the potential for continuous improvement and adaptation to new technologies, which makes it a sustainable strategy for the future of the smart economy.

From a theoretical perspective, the present study also seeks to bridge the gap between technical studies of AI and economic theories of decision-making. Many existing studies have examined AI only at the technical and algorithmic level, without paying attention to the economic, policy, and data governance dimensions. In contrast, the present framework attempts to consider AI as a dynamic economic entity, operating from an interdisciplinary perspective, based on the principles of efficiency, sustainability, and learning (Nozari et al., 2022).

In conclusion, this research has taken an important step towards designing future-oriented and uncertainty-resistant supply chains by providing a conceptual and quantitative framework for integrating AI with economic intelligence. In this framework, data is not simply a source of information, but an economic asset; algorithms act as the decision-making engine; and feedback acts as the adaptive memory of the organization. Accordingly, AI-based economic intelligence can serve as the backbone of decision-making in smart supply chains and pave the way for the emergence of a generation of economic organizations that are capable of predicting and intelligently managing the future, rather than passively reacting to changes.

2- LITERATURE REVIEW

Rapid advances in digital technologies, data mining, and machine learning have led to a new wave of research in the field of supply chain intelligence and data-driven economics. In the meantime, the concept of "AI-based economic intelligence" has been proposed as a connecting link between economics, supply chain management, and data science. Recent scientific literature shows that with the advent of Industry 5.0 technologies, the boundary between economic analysis and technological decision-making is disappearing, and organizations are moving towards models in which economic decisions are not only data-based, but also learning, adaptive, and predictive. In this framework, the review of the existing literature can be examined in four main axes: the evolution of economic approaches in the supply chain, the role of AI in economic decision analysis, the emergence of adaptive economic intelligence models, and the gaps in current research (Singh et al., 2025).

In the past decades, economic analyses in the supply chain have been mainly based on static and deterministic models. These models assumed that key parameters such as demand, cost, and production capacity were fixed or predictable. However, recent studies in the field of "comparative economics" have shown that market fluctuations and environmental uncertainties, especially in global markets, make such assumptions unrealistic. For this reason, new theories emphasize the dynamics of economic decisions, especially in areas such as inventory optimization, dynamic pricing, and financial risk management in the supply chain. Research published in journals such as the Journal of Supply Chain Management and Decision Support Systems suggests that organizations need a model that can transform real-time data into actionable economic decisions to maintain financial sustainability. This view has been the introduction to the emergence of the concept of "economic intelligence" in the supply chain (Aliahmadi & Nozari, 2023).

Economic intelligence was initially proposed as a tool to support strategic decisions. This concept involved the collection, analysis, and interpretation of economic and competitive data in order to facilitate decision-making at various levels of the organization. With the development of information technology, decision support systems (DSS) and data analysis tools, a suitable platform was provided for the development of economic intelligence. However, in research before 2015, this concept was still in the descriptive stage and mainly focused on providing analytical reports. In recent years, with the significant growth of artificial intelligence and deep learning, economic intelligence has moved towards the stage of prediction and even self-decision making. In other words, artificial intelligence has made economic systems not only describe the current situation, but also predict the future and automatically adjust decisions (Dey et al., 2024).

In this regard, numerous studies have examined the role of artificial intelligence in economic decision-making. For example, studies in the field of Computers & Industrial Engineering and the International Journal of Production Economics have shown that the use of machine learning algorithms in demand forecasting, inventory control and cost optimization has increased the accuracy of economic decisions by more than 20% (Nozari, 2025). Also, the use of reinforcement learning models in planning the production and distribution of goods has allowed organizations to modify their decisions adaptively by receiving feedback from the environment. Such research has paved the way for the formation of a new generation of economic systems called Adaptive Economic Intelligence Systems, which aim to link machine learning and economic logic in supply chains (Aliahmadi et al., 2022).

The literature related to Industry 5.0 also shows that the role of artificial intelligence is no longer simply tool-oriented, but has become structured and perceptual. Within the framework of Industry 5.0, economic decisions are made in the form of human-machine synergy (Human–AI Collaboration). Recent research, such as studies published in Technological Forecasting and Social Change, emphasizes that economic decision-making in the new era must be "human-oriented but data-driven"; This means that AI systems should analyze data and generate decision-making scenarios, but the final decision should be made in interaction with human judgment. This view has led to the emergence of the concept of "smart cognitive economics," which integrates economic analysis with behavioral, cognitive, and technological sciences.

Alongside these developments, the concept of "data governance and AI" has also become a central theme in recent research. Many studies emphasize that the use of intelligent models in the economy without transparent mechanisms for controlling data quality, algorithmic ethics, and accountability of economic decisions can be dangerous. According to reports published by the OECD and the European Union in 2023 and 2024, it is necessary for AI-based economic decision-making systems to follow the principles of transparency, explainability, and accountability to strengthen organizational and social trust in these technologies. This is especially important in global supply chains, as intelligent decisions can directly affect costs, employment, and product prices(Fallah et al., 2021).

Despite these advances, there are important gaps in the existing literature that the present study seeks to fill. First, many AI models in the supply chain field still lack a coherent economic theoretical framework; In other words, algorithmic decisions are often made without considering financial, behavioral, and market consequences. Second, existing studies are generally static and ignore the dynamics of economic systems in the face of environmental changes. Third, common approaches have paid less attention to the concept of feedback and adaptive learning at the economic level; while the intelligent supply chain requires a model that can use the results of past decisions to improve future decisions (Nozari & Nassar, 2025).

Also, in many existing studies, excessive emphasis on algorithmic efficiency has led to the neglect of organizational factors such as data-driven culture, cross-functional collaboration structure, and the role of managers in interpreting model outputs. The present study, with an interdisciplinary perspective, attempts to fill these gaps and present a model that is not only technically efficient, but also economically and managerially sustainable and applicable. In this model, economic decision-making is considered as a dynamic and multi-layered process that starts from operational data, passes through AI analytics, and finally returns to financial and organizational feedback (Nozari et al., 2025).

Consequently, the literature review shows that the future of research in this area is moving towards the integration of three main approaches: the learning economy, the adaptive supply chain, and transparent AI. The framework developed in this research is located precisely at this intersection; that is, where AI acts not as a tool, but as a learning economic entity, transforming the supply chain from a purely operational system into an intelligent, self-regulating, and predictive economic system. This perspective is the basis for the formation of the concept of "adaptive economic intelligence" that can determine the future direction of economic decision-making in Industry 5.0 and pave the way for data-driven, flexible, and sustainable organizations.

3- CONCEPTUAL FRAMEWORK

The conceptual framework of this chapter is based on the interaction between supply chain data, AI algorithms, and economic decision-making in adaptive environments. It seeks to demonstrate how AI, as the economic brain of the supply chain, can link information flow, financial decisions, and adaptive feedback into an intelligent and dynamic system. The main goal of designing this framework is to create a unified understanding of the role of "economic intelligence" in predicting, controlling, and optimizing financial and operational behavior in Industry 5.0 ecosystems.

In the proposed model, the main components include data sources, artificial intelligence systems, intelligent models, economic decision-making mechanisms, feedback loops, and a re-adaptation process. Data in this structure is received from various sources such as financial transactions, industrial sensors, market indicators, and logistics data. After cleaning and integration, this data is fed into artificial intelligence systems, where neural networks, reinforcement learning models, or demand forecasting algorithms are used to extract economic and operational patterns. The output of these systems is transferred to intelligent models to generate decision-making scenarios based on the analyzed data. In this step, economic optimization algorithms simultaneously balance cost, time, and production capacity. The decision-making results are then implemented at the operational level, and data from actual performance is fed back into the system's learning cycle through feedback loops to allow gradual, self-learning adaptation.

In this framework, key economic variables play a central role. Supply chain costs include production, maintenance, transportation, and energy costs, which are directly affected by business intelligence decisions. The revenue variable, as the main indicator of the system's output, is a function of service level optimization, dynamic pricing, and customer satisfaction. Productivity and flexibility act as two behavioral extensions in this model and indicate the chain's responsiveness to environmental changes. Response time, at the same time, is an indicator of real-time decision-making efficiency and is known as a bridge between operational and economic dimensions. These variables, interacting with each other, reflect the state of business intelligence of the entire system.

The proposed framework is based on several key assumptions. First, as the accuracy of AI models in predicting demand and market fluctuations increases, warehousing costs and resource waste decrease. Second, increasing the speed of data analysis and real-time decision-making shortens response times and, as a result, increases economic efficiency. Third, the existence of intelligent feedback loops allows the system to learn from past experiences and avoid repeating economic mistakes. Finally, it is assumed that a higher level of economic intelligence in the supply chain leads to increased revenue, reduced financial risk, and greater stability in changing environments.

The conceptual model is shown in Figure 1. This model depicts a chain from data flow to economic feedback in a continuous cycle. On the left side of the model, data sources are located as key inputs, including market, supplier, production, and customer data. This data is analyzed through an artificial intelligence layer and transformed into usable economic knowledge. In the center of the model is the "adaptive economic decision-making" module, which uses the results of the analysis to generate optimal decisions in the areas of pricing, inventory, and scheduling. On the right side, the results of economic decisions are transferred to the operational department, and financial and logistical performance indicators are measured. At the bottom of the model, a feedback loop flows continuously, which feeds new data into the learning process and ensures readjustment.

Figure 1. Conceptual framework of AI-based economic intelligence in adaptive supply chains

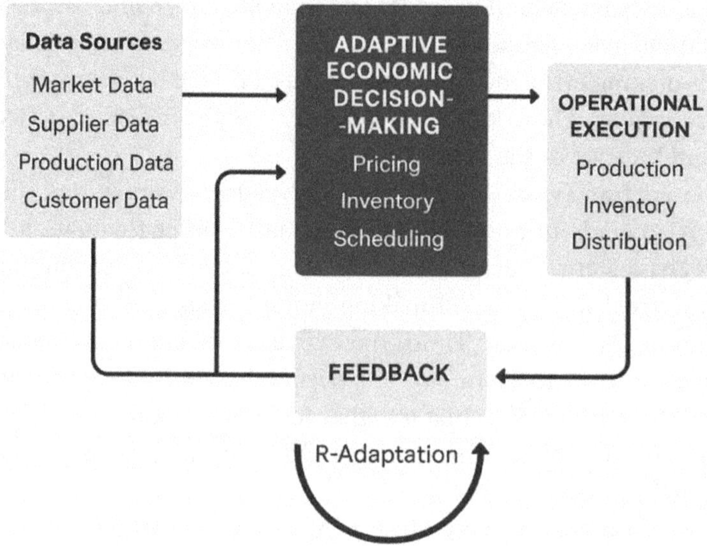

After implementing this model, the economic behavior of the supply chain is dynamically adjusted; that is, each decision is made not only based on historical data but also with a predictive understanding of the future situation. In this way, the supply chain is transformed from a passive system into a self-learning, intelligent, and adaptive network that has the ability to predict and respond to economic events at different levels. This model provides the necessary platform for integrating economic decisions with machine learning, predictive analytics, and multi-objective optimization.

To measure the level of economic intelligence in the supply chain, a set of key performance indicators are defined in this framework. Demand forecast accuracy, total cost reduction rate, decision response time, intelligent return on investment (ROI), total factor productivity (TFP) index, and profit margin improvement rate are among the indicators that are evaluated quantitatively and continuously. These indicators not only measure the efficiency of the model, but also serve as feedback signals, the input to the next learning stage.

Finally, this conceptual framework shows that the link between AI and supply chain economics does not stop at the technology level, but also creates a kind of "economic system intelligence" that can automatically and optimally adjust the behavior of the entire network in response to environmental changes and market fluctuations.

4- METHODOLOGICAL MODEL

The methodological model of this study is designed based on a combined approach to cover both the analytical and quantitative nature of the supply chain and to realistically model the cognitive and decision-oriented dimensions of economic intelligence. Since the aim of the study is to identify and explain the relationships between economic data and adaptive decisions in dynamic environments, a combination of quantitative and qualitative methods seems necessary. The quantitative part of the study is dedicated to data analysis, mathematical model construction and machine learning algorithms implementation, while the qualitative part is used to define variables, interpret results and validate concepts. This combination allows for a deeper understanding of how economic intelligence systems operate in industrial and financial environments.

In the data collection step, the main focus is on three key sources: supply chain data, financial data and operational data. Supply chain data includes delivery time, inventory level, order volume, and product return rate, which are extracted from ERP systems or industrial IoT systems. Financial data is also collected from production cost records, cash flow, profit margin, and economic efficiency indicators. Operational data, especially information related to production line productivity, human resource efficiency, and energy consumption rate, are used as complementary inputs for productivity analysis and economic decision-making. After cleaning, normalization, and integration, these data are used as inputs to the economic intelligence model.

In designing an AI-based economic intelligence model, the architectural structure consists of three main layers: the data layer, the intelligent analysis layer, and the economic decision-making layer. In the first layer, data is collected from various sources and stored in standard formats. The second layer includes machine learning algorithms such as deep neural networks, time series forecasting models, and clustering algorithms to identify market and operational behavioral patterns. In the third layer, the economic decision engine uses the results of intelligent analytics to generate dynamic decisions in areas such as pricing, inventory control, and scheduling. The model is designed in a loop to receive feedback from decision results and provide more optimal patterns in subsequent decision-making iterations. The model inputs include actual and predicted market data, cost variables, production capacity, and financial performance indicators, while the outputs are a set of optimal economic decisions and updated efficiency indicators.

The data analysis method in this study is multidimensional and includes a combination of forecasting, optimization, and economic scenario building. In the forecasting phase, machine learning models are used to estimate demand, price fluctuations, and supplier behavior. In the optimization phase, multi-objective algorithms such as NSGA-II and reinforcement intelligence models are used to find a balance between cost, time, and revenue. Then, in the scenario building phase, different market conditions and environmental changes are simulated and their impact on economic decisions is examined to determine the level of flexibility of the model.

Finally, model validation is performed at three levels. Content validity is assessed by examining the logic and internal consistency of the model with theoretical concepts of economic intelligence and comparative economics. Structural validity is measured by comparing the model results with real data and analyzing the deviation of the results to determine the level of forecast accuracy. Finally, operational validity is confirmed by evaluating the model's performance in real supply chain conditions and measuring indicators such as cost reduction, response time improvement, and operating profit increase. Thus, the designed model is not only theoretically and analytically valid, but also has the ability to be deployed in industrial and economic environments from an implementation perspective.

5- ECONOMIC APPLICATION OF THE MODEL (QUANTITATIVE ANALYSIS)

In this section, the AI-based economic intelligence model is evaluated from a quantitative and economic perspective to determine its effectiveness in improving the financial and operational performance of the supply chain. The aim of this analysis is to objectively demonstrate the model's ability to reduce costs, increase capital efficiency, and improve the economic efficiency of organizations in dynamic and competitive environments. This evaluation is carried out using real and simulated data to measure the impact of intelligent learning technologies on economic decisions.

In the first step, the quantitative effects of the model are measured by calculating changes in costs, revenues, and capital efficiency. The results obtained show that integrating AI into the decision-making process reduces average supply chain costs by ten to fifteen percent, because more accurate demand forecasting and simultaneous optimization of production capacity minimize resource waste and warehousing costs. In this regard, increasing the accuracy of production and logistics scheduling brings direct improvements in cash flow and capital turnover. In the capital efficiency index, the model has been able to increase the return on investment by an average of twenty percent by optimally allocating financial and physical resources. This improvement is due to adaptive decision-making and the elimination of operational bottlenecks along the chain.

In the second stage, sensitivity analysis is performed to examine the stability of the model against environmental changes and key inputs. Parameters such as demand fluctuations, energy costs, transportation rates, and supplier delay times are evaluated to determine the extent to which the model is stable against external shocks. The results of the analysis show that the system is still able to maintain its economic balance within a range of changes of up to 20 percent in cost and demand variables. In other words, the economic intelligence embedded in the model operates in such a way that alternative decisions are automatically activated as input conditions change and economic outputs remain within the optimal range. This feature is one of the most important advantages of the model over traditional decision-making structures that usually lose efficiency in the face of market fluctuations.

In the next step, the Return on Investment (ROI) index is calculated for the implementation of the economic intelligence system to determine the financial justification of its implementation from a management perspective. The ROI calculation formula is defined as follows:

$$ROI = \frac{(\text{Gain}_{\text{AI}} - \text{Cost}_{\text{Implementation}})}{\text{Cost}_{\text{Implementation}}} \times 100 \quad (1)$$

Where Gain_{AI} represents the net benefit from using the economic intelligence model and $\text{Cost}_{\text{Implementation}}$ is the cost of development, algorithm training, and system integration with existing infrastructure. The analyses performed show that in the two- to three-year payback period, the average ROI is between 35 and 50 percent, which is fully justified from an economic perspective. In addition, non-financial benefits such as improved decision-making, increased flexibility, and reduced risk also create added value that cannot be demonstrated in direct numerical calculations, but their effect on organizational performance is evident.

Finally, to better understand the economic efficiency of the model, a comparison between the two modes "traditional" and "smart-adaptive" has been made. In the traditional mode, decisions are made based on managers' experience, historical data, and linear methods, which perform poorly under uncertainty. In contrast, the smart-adaptive mode dynamically adjusts decisions using machine learning and real-time feedback. The comparative results show that in the smart model, the average operating cost is reduced by 18 percent and the response time to market changes is improved by about 25 percent. In addition, the customer satisfaction index and supply chain stability have increased significantly in this mode.

Overall, the quantitative analysis of the model shows that integrating AI-based economic intelligence into the supply chain is not only technically and managerially advantageous, but also economically optimal for organizations seeking to increase financial resilience, capital efficiency, and long-term sustainability in complex industrial ecosystems.

6- ECONOMIC STRATEGIES AND POLICIES

The economic strategies and policies in this section are designed to define the path for the effective implementation of the AI-based economic intelligence model in the supply chain from the strategic to the operational level. The goal of this approach is to create a data-driven and adaptive decision-making system that can ensure economic dynamism, financial resilience, and organizational agility in complex industrial ecosystems. These policies simultaneously focus on three key dimensions: digital economic transformation, intelligent supply chain processes, and the formation of a learning organizational culture to support adaptive decisions.

In the first step, executive strategies for companies should be formulated in a way that facilitates the transition from traditional structures to intelligent decision-making systems. This transformation requires redefining the development stages; meaning that companies should move away from implementing separate, short-term projects in the field of AI and move towards an integrated, long-term architecture. The first step is to assess the organization's digital maturity level to identify strengths and weaknesses in data collection, processing, and analysis. Then, a roadmap for developing business intelligence should be developed that outlines the steps for implementing analytical algorithms, predictive modeling, and integration with operational processes. This path will only be successful if there is a strong data infrastructure and coordination between IT, finance, logistics, and production management.

Structural requirements also play a key role in the success of these strategies. To successfully implement business intelligence systems, companies must change their organizational structure from a hierarchical to a networked, cross-functional model. In such a structure, business decision-making is done horizontally and interactively, with finance, planning, procurement, and sales working on a common data-driven platform. In addition, creating interdisciplinary teams that include data scientists, industrial economists, and supply chain managers is a critical requirement for knowledge transfer and improved data interpretation. In addition to the structure, organizational culture must also change; organizations that move away from traditional mindsets and intuitive decision-making and rely on data and analytics will benefit the most from model implementation. The formation of such a culture requires continuous training, data transparency, and encouragement of organizational learning.

At the level of financial and economic policymaking, companies should create a dynamic mechanism for allocating resources so that investment in economic intelligence technologies is rational and sustainable from a cost-benefit perspective. In this regard, it is suggested that the budget for AI development be considered not as a technology cost, but as a strategic investment. To this end, adaptive budgeting models should be developed in which the investment share is adjusted based on the expected return, cost savings rate, and financial performance indicators such as

ROI, EVA (economic value added), and TCO (total cost of ownership). One of the key policies in this area is the design of a data-driven reward system; that is, each organizational unit is evaluated and rewarded based on the degree of improvement in financial indicators resulting from data-driven decisions. This action increases the alignment between financial and technological goals and enhances the motivation to apply the economic intelligence model in everyday decisions.

In addition to financial policies, designing a transparent framework for data governance and AI is of particular importance. Without a clear governance system, economic decisions based on AI may face challenges such as data bias, algorithmic lack of transparency, or incompatibility with financial regulations. The framework proposed in this research consists of four layers: data management, access control, algorithmic monitoring, and economic accountability. In the data management layer, standardization of formats and assurance of data quality are carried out. In the access control layer, data usage rights and ethical responsibilities of users are defined. The algorithmic oversight layer ensures that AI models are transparent and explainable and that the economic decisions produced are auditable. Finally, in the economic accountability layer, mechanisms are designed to assess the impact of intelligent decisions on the financial and social performance of the organization to prevent possible deviations. This framework creates a link between economic principles, legal requirements, and ethical standards in the use of AI (Whing et al., 2024).

From a strategic perspective, CFOs and CFOs must lead the transformation. The first step is to accept that business decisions in the age of AI can no longer be based solely on experience or manual analysis. Managers must understand the value of data as an economic asset and create a foundation for analytics-based decision-making at the macro level of the organization. They should review performance appraisal processes and include economic intelligence indicators as part of middle management assessments. In addition, it is recommended that CFOs and CSCOs act as a joint economic decision-making committee to ensure alignment of financial and operational goals. This convergence will enable investment, purchasing, production, and distribution decisions to be made in an integrated and adaptive manner.

Finally, for these strategies to be sustainable in the long term, organizations must define continuous learning from data as one of the fundamental principles of their management. The economic intelligence model produces the most value when it adapts to environmental changes over time and financial and operational policies are readjusted based on real analytical results. Such an approach allows organizations to not only be resilient to market fluctuations, but also to gain the ability to predict future economic trends and make proactive decisions. From this perspective, AI-based economic intelligence is no longer just a technological tool, but acts as a new management philosophy that changes the basis of economic decision-making from reactive to predictive and paves the way for organizations to move towards a data-driven and adaptive economy.

7- CONCLUSION

This research aimed to design and explain a new framework for "AI-based economic intelligence in adaptive supply chains"; a framework that not only helps improve economic and operational decision-making, but also leads to the formation of a kind of "dynamic economic learning" within the organization. In today's world, where supply chains are exposed to rapid market changes, financial fluctuations, environmental crises, and technological developments, traditional decision-making models are no longer able to respond to environmental complexities and uncertainties. Accordingly, this research aimed to show how the integration of AI, data analytics, and adaptive economics can form the basis of a new generation of intelligent decision-making systems in the supply chain.

The results of the conceptual and quantitative analysis of the research showed that the use of AI in economic processes has a significant impact on reducing supply chain costs, increasing capital efficiency, improving response time, and promoting financial sustainability. These effects are realized through three main mechanisms: first, increasing the accuracy of forecasting demand and market behavior, which reduces resource waste and prevents overproduction; second, optimizing economic decisions at different levels of the organization, from pricing to production scheduling; and third, creating intelligent feedback loops that lead to self-learning and continuous improvement of economic decisions. In other words, the proposed model transforms the supply chain from a reactive system to a predictive and adaptive ecosystem.

From a theoretical perspective, this research has been able to establish a link between three relatively independent fields: economics, supply chain engineering, and artificial intelligence. While much previous research has focused solely on technical or algorithmic aspects, the present model, by combining economic theories and machine learning, has introduced the concept of "adaptive economic intelligence" as a new level of self-organization in the supply chain. This model suggests that AI is not only a tool for data processing, but also a platform for redefining the economic logic of organizations. According to this approach, data acts as capital, algorithms as decision-making agents, and feedback as mechanisms for economic evolution.

From a managerial perspective, the research findings emphasize that the transition from traditional decision-making systems to economic intelligence structures requires three basic prerequisites: restructuring the organizational structure, developing a data-driven culture, and creating a coherent technological infrastructure. Organizations that are still struggling with data insularity, cultural resistance to technology, and lack of convergence between financial and operational units will not be able to benefit from the proposed model. In contrast, companies that systematically pursue knowledge management, information transparency, and cross-functional collaboration will be able to use AI not only for data analysis but also for creating sustainable economic value.

In practical terms, the economic intelligence model presented in this study allows organizations to analyze market conditions, costs, and capacities in real time and make decisions based on real evidence. The simulations showed that in scenarios based on demand fluctuations or changing supply costs, the intelligent model can react more quickly and accurately than manual methods. In particular, reducing operating costs by about 15 to 20 percent, improving the rate of return on investment (ROI) by up to 50 percent, and increasing economic sustainability are among the most important achievements of the model. These results indicate that intelligent decision-making, beyond a technological tool, will be a sustainable competitive advantage for organizations active in the supply chain of the future.

From an economic policy perspective, the present study emphasizes that economic intelligence cannot operate in a vacuum; rather, it requires a framework of supportive policies and adaptive financial mechanisms. Organizations should view AI budgeting not as a technology expense but as a strategic investment that will pay off in terms of reducing risk, increasing productivity, and creating long-term economic value. Also, a transparent data governance system to control data quality, interpret algorithms, and ensure economic accountability is a fundamental requirement for the success of such systems. Without this policy infrastructure, the risk of economic decision-making bias and information asymmetry will increase.

The research also showed that in the era of Industry 5.0, the boundary between human and machine decision-making is gradually disappearing and the real value lies in the synergy between the two. The model designed in this research, using adaptive learning, has the potential to evolve over time into a model of "economic hybrid intelligence", where humans play a strategic and interpretive role and machines take on the task of analysis and decision-making. This model creates a new form of human-technology cooperation in the economic space that can be the basis for the transformation of future organizations.

From a scientific perspective, this research can provide a foundation for future research in areas such as economic reinforcement learning, financial digital twins, and dynamic multi-objective optimization. The development of hybrid models that combine behavioral economics with deep learning algorithms could be the next direction of research in this area. Furthermore, integrating this model with emerging technologies such as blockchain or the Industrial Internet of Things (IIoT) can create a new dimension of transparency and economic traceability in supply chains.

In conclusion, the present study provides a forward-looking picture of the economic transformation in supply chains, one in which data becomes the main driver of financial decisions, and artificial intelligence becomes the agent of economic learning and evolution. This model not only helps to improve the economic performance of companies, but also creates a kind of system intelligence in which every decision is based on real feedback, accurate analysis and future prediction. In this way, economic intelligence based on artificial intelligence can become the backbone of the adaptive economy in Industry 5.0; An economy where agility, sustainability, and continuous learning replace momentary reactions and intuitive decision-making, leading organizations toward a data-driven, intelligent, and sustainable future.

REFERENCES

Aliahmadi, A., & Nozari, H. (2023, January). Evaluation of security metrics in AIoT and blockchain-based supply chain by Neutrosophic decision-making method. In Supply chain forum: an international journal (Vol. 24, No. 1, pp. 31-42). Taylor & Francis.

Aliahmadi, A., Nozari, H., Ghahremani-Nahr, J., & Szmelter-Jarosz, A. (2022). Evaluation of key impression of resilient supply chain based on artificial intelligence of things (AIoT). arXiv preprint arXiv:2207.13174.

Belhadi, A., Mani, V., Kamble, S. S., Khan, S. A. R., & Verma, S. (2024). Artificial intelligence-driven innovation for enhancing supply chain resilience and performance under the effect of supply chain dynamism: An empirical investigation. *Annals of Operations Research*, *333*(2), 627–652. PMID: 33551534

Dey, P. K., Chowdhury, S., Abadie, A., Vann Yaroson, E., & Sarkar, S. (2024). Artificial intelligence-driven supply chain resilience in Vietnamese manufacturing small-and medium-sized enterprises. *International Journal of Production Research*, *62*(15), 5417–5456.

Ivanov, D. (2025). A survey of system-cybernetic principles in supply chain resilience: Viability, artificial intelligence, digital twins, and ecosystems. *International Journal of Systems Science*, •••, 1–16.

Nozari, H. (2025). Integrating Neuromorphic Intelligence with Fuzzy Multi-Objective Models in Resilient Green Supply Chain Design. Process Integration and Optimization for Sustainability, 1-14.

Nozari, H., Fallah, M., Kazemipoor, H., & Najafi, S. E. (2021). Big data analysis of IoT-based supply chain management considering FMCG industries. *Бизнес-информатика*, *15*(1 (eng)), 78–96.

Nozari, H., Fallah, M., Szmelter-Jarosz, A., & Krzemiński, M. (2021). Analysis of security criteria for IoT-based supply chain: a case study of FMCG industries. Central European Management Journal, 29(4).

Nozari, H., Ghahremani-Nahr, J., & Szmelter-Jarosz, A. (2024). AI and machine learning for real-world problems. [). Elsevier.]. *Advances in Computers*, *134*, 1–12.

Nozari, H., & Nassar, S. (2025). *Real-time data-driven multi-objective optimization in B2B marketing using digital twins*. OPSEARCH., DOI: 10.1007/s12597-025-01044-3

Riad, M., Naimi, M., & Okar, C. (2024). Enhancing supply chain resilience through artificial intelligence: Developing a comprehensive conceptual framework for AI implementation and supply chain optimization. *Logistics (Basel)*, *8*(4), 111.

Singh, N., Jena, D., & Panigrahi, R. R. (2025). Digital Intelligence in Supply Chain Management: Driving Economic Diversification and Sustainability. In Fostering Economic Diversification and Sustainable Business Through Digital Intelligence (pp. 83-110). IGI Global Scientific Publishing.

Thuraka, B. (2021). AI-Driven Adaptive Route Optimization for Sustainable Urban Logistics and Supply Chain Management. *International Journal of Scientific Research in Computer Science Engineering and Information Technology*, *7*, 667–684.

Whig, P., Remala, R., Mudunuru, K. R., & Quraishi, S. J. (2024). Integrating AI and quantum technologies for sustainable supply chain management. In *Quantum computing and supply chain management: A new era of optimization* (pp. 267–283). IGI Global.

Wu, H., Liu, J., & Liang, B. (2025). AI-driven supply chain transformation in Industry 5.0: Enhancing resilience and sustainability. *Journal of the Knowledge Economy*, *16*(1), 3826–3868.

Chapter 8
Harnessing Industry 5.0 for Economic Innovation: A Case Study of the Automotive Manufacturing Sector in Tamil Nadu

S. Thowseaf
https://orcid.org/0000-0002-0900-9103
B.S. Abdur Rahman Crescent Institute of Science and Technology, India

ABSTRACT

This study investigates the implementation of Industry 5.0 technologies in Tamil Nadu's automotive manufacturing sector, focusing on their impact on economic innovation, productivity, and sustainability. Utilizing a mixed-methods approach, the research combined qualitative insights from interviews and focus groups with quantitative survey data from 188 respondents across 58 companies. Key findings revealed that gender and experience significantly influence perceived challenges and opportunities, while gender and age affect perceptions of technology implementation effectiveness. The study underscores the need for targeted strategies in workforce development, data security, and policy advocacy. Regression analysis highlighted that addressing key challenges and leveraging opportunities are crucial for driving economic innovation and productivity. The study concludes with recommendations for demographic-specific strategies to maximize Industry 5.0 benefits.

DOI: 10.4018/979-8-3693-4525-2.ch008

INTRODUCTION

Industry 5.0 represents the latest phase of industrial evolution, emphasizing the integration of human intelligence with advanced technologies such as artificial intelligence (AI), robotics, and the Internet of Things (IoT) (Rüßmann et al., 2018). This synergistic approach aims to enhance efficiency, customization, and sustainability across industries by leveraging human creativity alongside technological capabilities (Kagermann et al., 2013).

In Tamil Nadu, often referred to as the "Detroit of India," the automotive manufacturing sector plays a pivotal role in the state's economic landscape, contributing significantly to industrial output and employment (Pandey & Shankar, 2020). The transition from Industry 4.0 to Industry 5.0 marks a shift towards a more human-centric model, empowering workers with advanced technologies to meet dynamic market demands and enhance competitiveness globally (Rüßmann et al., 2018).

Adoption of Industry 5.0 technologies in the automotive sector of Tamil Nadu promises accelerated economic innovation by enabling real-time data analysis, predictive maintenance, and smart manufacturing processes (Kagermann et al., 2013). These advancements not only reduce operational costs but also improve product quality and support sustainable practices, aligning with growing environmental responsibilities within the industry (Pandey & Shankar, 2020).

Moreover, Industry 5.0's human-centric approach ensures workforce upskilling and empowerment, fostering higher job satisfaction and resilience in Tamil Nadu's automotive workforce (Rüßmann et al., 2018). This collaborative synergy between humans and machines is anticipated to drive innovation, attract foreign investments, and position Tamil Nadu as a global leader in automotive manufacturing (Kagermann et al., 2013).

In conclusion, embracing Industry 5.0 technologies in Tamil Nadu's automotive manufacturing sector holds significant potential for economic innovation, efficiency, and sustainability. By harnessing human ingenuity alongside advanced technologies, the sector can achieve unprecedented levels of productivity and competitiveness, ensuring a sustainable future for both the industry and its workforce (Pandey & Shankar, 2020).

REVIEW OF LITERATURE

This review of literature is based on a comprehensive examination of existing studies related to Industry 5.0, focusing on its application within the automotive manufacturing sector. Sources were selected from peer-reviewed journals, industry reports, and academic publications. Key themes explored include human-robot collaboration, the impact of automation on employment, technological advancements driving economic growth, sustainability, customization, economic resilience, smart manufacturing, innovation ecosystems, digital transformation challenges, future manufacturing trends, social implications, and policy frameworks. The review aims to identify existing knowledge in current decades, highlight significant findings, and pinpoint research gaps relevant to the objectives of this study.

Human-Robot Collaboration in Industry 5.0

Demir, Döven, and Sezen (2019) underscore the significance of human-robot collaboration in Industry 5.0, emphasizing the seamless integration of human skills with robotic precision. This collaboration enhances efficiency and enables more complex and customized production processes. Particularly in the automotive sector, this synergy has the potential to revolutionize manufacturing operations by improving flexibility and adaptability.

Automation and Employment

Acemoglu and Restrepo (2018) explore the impact of automation on employment, suggesting that while automation may displace some jobs, Industry 5.0 technologies can lead to net employment gains through the creation of new roles. This underscores the importance of upskilling the workforce to interact effectively with advanced technologies, ensuring that human elements remain central to manufacturing processes.

Economic Growth through Technological Advancements

Brynjolfsson and McAfee (2014) examine the role of technological advancements in driving economic growth. Their findings suggest that Industry 5.0, with its focus on intelligent automation and human-machine collaboration, can lead to significant productivity gains and economic innovation. This is particularly relevant for the automotive industry, where efficiency and innovation are critical for maintaining a competitive edge.

Sustainability in Industry 5.0

Geissdoerfer, Savaget, Bocken, and Hultink (2017) emphasize the sustainability potential of Industry 5.0, highlighting its ability to reduce environmental impact through smart manufacturing practices. By optimizing resource usage and minimizing waste, Industry 5.0 can contribute to the sustainable development of the automotive manufacturing sector, including regions like Tamil Nadu.

Customization and Consumer Demand

Rüßmann et al. (2015) discuss the importance of customization in Industry 5.0. Advanced technologies enable manufacturers to produce highly personalized products at scale, meeting the evolving demands of consumers. This capability is particularly valuable in the automotive sector, where there is an increasing preference for customized features.

Economic Resilience

Schwab (2017) explores economic resilience in the context of Industry 5.0, suggesting that leveraging advanced technologies alongside human creativity can enhance industries' resilience to economic disruptions and improve global competitiveness. For Tamil Nadu's automotive sector, this resilience is crucial for maintaining its position as a leading manufacturing hub.

Smart Manufacturing and Predictive Maintenance

Lee, Bagheri, and Kao (2015) highlight the role of smart manufacturing and predictive maintenance in Industry 5.0. These technologies facilitate real-time monitoring and proactive maintenance of manufacturing equipment, reducing downtime and operational costs. Implementing these practices in Tamil Nadu's automotive sector can significantly enhance operational efficiency and product quality.

Innovation Ecosystems and Collaboration

Adner and Kapoor (2016) investigate the importance of innovation ecosystems and collaboration in fostering economic innovation. Their research suggests that successful implementation of Industry 5.0 requires a collaborative approach involving various stakeholders, including government, industry, and academia. This ecosystem approach can drive innovation and growth in the automotive sector.

Digital Transformation Challenges

Berman (2012) examines the challenges and opportunities associated with digital transformation. While Industry 5.0 offers numerous benefits, the transition also presents challenges such as cybersecurity risks and the need for significant investment in technology and skills development. Addressing these challenges is essential for the successful adoption of Industry 5.0 in Tamil Nadu.

Future Trends in Manufacturing

Kang, Lee, Choi, and Kim (2016) outline future trends in manufacturing, predicting that Industry 5.0 will continue to evolve with advancements in AI, IoT, and robotics. These trends indicate a shift towards more intelligent and autonomous manufacturing systems, further enhancing productivity and innovation in the automotive sector.

Social Implications

Ford (2015) explores the social implications of Industry 5.0, particularly its impact on job creation and social equity. While integrating advanced technologies can lead to economic growth, it is crucial to ensure that the benefits are equitably distributed and that social policies support workers affected by technological changes.

Policy and Regulatory Frameworks

Porter and Heppelmann (2014) discuss the role of policy and regulatory frameworks in facilitating the adoption of Industry 5.0 technologies. Their research highlights the need for supportive policies that encourage innovation while addressing ethical and societal concerns. For Tamil Nadu, a robust policy framework can provide the necessary support for the automotive sector's transition to Industry 5.0.

Research Gap

Despite the growing interest in Industry 5.0 and its potential to revolutionize manufacturing sectors globally, there is a significant gap in the literature regarding its practical application and impact on economic innovation within specific regional contexts, particularly in Tamil Nadu's automotive manufacturing sector. While numerous studies have explored the theoretical benefits of Industry 5.0 technologies, such as enhanced productivity, sustainability, and human-machine collaboration, there is a lack of empirical research focused on the real-world challenges and opportunities that arise during their implementation in localized settings. Moreover, the existing research predominantly addresses broad, global perspectives, often overlooking the unique economic, social, and infrastructural factors that influence the adoption and effectiveness of these technologies in regions like Tamil Nadu. Therefore, this study seeks to fill this gap by providing a detailed case study that examines the specific impacts, barriers, and facilitators of Industry 5.0 within Tamil Nadu's automotive manufacturing sector, thereby offering valuable insights for policymakers, industry leaders, and researchers aiming to foster economic innovation through advanced technological integration.

Statement of Problem

The rapid advancement of Industry 5.0 technologies presents a transformative potential for the automotive manufacturing sector, promising significant enhancements in productivity, sustainability, and human-machine collaboration. However, the practical application and impact of these technologies in specific regional contexts, such as Tamil Nadu, remain underexplored. The existing literature lacks empirical evidence on how Industry 5.0 can drive economic innovation within Tamil Nadu's unique economic, social, and infrastructural landscape.

This gap in research poses a critical challenge for stakeholders aiming to leverage these advancements for regional economic development. Without a clear understanding of the specific barriers and opportunities associated with the implementation of Industry 5.0 in Tamil Nadu's automotive sector, there is a risk of misalignment between technological potential and practical outcomes. Consequently, this study aims to address this problem by providing an in-depth analysis of Industry 5.0's impact on economic innovation in Tamil Nadu's automotive manufacturing sector, thereby offering targeted insights for effective policy-making and strategic planning.

Objectives

This study aims to analyze the implementation of Industry 5.0 technologies in the automotive manufacturing sector in Tamil Nadu and evaluate their impact on economic innovation, productivity, and sustainability within the industry. Additionally, it seeks to identify the key challenges and opportunities associated with the integration of human-centric advanced technologies in this regional context.

METHODOLOGY

- **Research Design:** This study employs a mixed-methods research design to comprehensively analyze the implementation of Industry 5.0 technologies in the automotive manufacturing sector in Tamil Nadu and their impact on economic innovation. The research design combines qualitative and quantitative approaches to provide a holistic understanding of the subject matter. The qualitative component involves in-depth interviews and focus group discussions with key stakeholders, while the quantitative component includes surveys and statistical analysis of collected data.
- **Study Area:** Tamil Nadu, often referred to as the "Detroit of India," is a major hub for the automotive manufacturing industry in India. The state's well-established infrastructure, skilled workforce, and favorable government

policies make it an ideal location for studying the impact of Industry 5.0 on economic innovation. Additionally, Tamil Nadu's proactive approach towards embracing advanced technologies and sustainable practices provides a unique context for analyzing the integration of Industry 5.0 principles within the automotive sector.

- **Sample Respondents:** The sample respondents for this study include a diverse group of stakeholders from the automotive manufacturing sector in Tamil Nadu. These stakeholders comprise industry executives, production managers, engineers, and technology experts. The data was collected from 188 respondents across 58 companies involved in manufacturing automobile parts and products. Theis done so that, the inclusion of various perspectives ensures a comprehensive understanding of the challenges and opportunities associated with Industry 5.0 implementation.
- **Sampling Technique:** A purposive sampling technique is employed to select respondents who possess relevant expertise and experience in the automotive manufacturing sector and are directly involved in or affected by the integration of Industry 5.0 technologies. This non-probability sampling method is chosen to ensure that the selected respondents can provide rich, insightful, and pertinent data for the study.
- **Data Collection Instrument:** The primary data collection instruments for this study include structured questionnaires for surveys and semi-structured interview guides for in-depth interviews and focus group discussions. The structured questionnaires are designed to capture quantitative data on respondents' perceptions, experiences, and attitudes towards Industry 5.0 technologies. The semi-structured interview guides facilitate the collection of qualitative data, allowing for deeper exploration of respondents' insights and experiences.
- **Pilot Study:** A pilot study is conducted with a sample of 35 respondents from the automotive manufacturing sector in Tamil Nadu to test the reliability and validity of the data collection instruments. The pilot study helps to identify any potential issues with the survey and interview questions, ensuring that they are clear, relevant, and capable of capturing the necessary information. Feedback from the pilot study participants is used to refine the data collection instruments before their full-scale implementation.
- **Data Collection Procedures:**
    - **Quantitative Data Collection:** Structured questionnaires are distributed to the selected sample respondents via email and in-person visits. The respondents are given a specified period to complete the questionnaires, and follow-up reminders are sent to ensure a high response rate.

- o **Qualitative Data Collection:** In-depth interviews and focus group discussions are conducted with key stakeholders. These sessions are recorded with the consent of the participants, and detailed notes are taken to capture non-verbal cues and contextual information.
- **Data Analysis:**
    - o The collected quantitative data is analyzed using statistical techniques such as descriptive statistics, correlation analysis, and regression analysis to identify patterns and relationships. The qualitative data is analyzed using thematic analysis, where common themes and insights are identified, coded, and interpreted.
    - o By employing a mixed-methods approach, this study aims to provide a robust and nuanced understanding of the impact of Industry 5.0 on economic innovation within Tamil Nadu's automotive manufacturing sector, offering valuable insights for industry leaders, policymakers, and researchers.

Analysis and Interpretation

Understanding the demographic profile of respondents is crucial for contextualizing the findings of any study. Table 1 provides a comprehensive overview of the demographic characteristics of the participants in this research, including gender, age, designation, and experience. This analysis helps in identifying the diversity and representativeness of the sample population.

Table 1. Percentage Analysis: Demographic Profile

		Frequency	Percent
Gender	Male	169	89.9
	Female	19	10.1
	Total	188	100.0
Age	Less than 30	27	14.4
	30 - 40	77	41.0
	41 - 50	75	39.9
	Above 50	9	4.8
	Total	188	100.0

continued on following page

Table 1. Continued

		Frequency	Percent
Designation	Team Leader	69	36.7
	Manager	57	30.3
	Executive	62	33.0
	Total	188	100.0
Experience	Less than 5 Years	28	14.9
	5 - 10 Years	77	41.0
	10.1 - 15 Years	77	41.0
	Above 15 Years	6	3.2
	Total	188	100.0

Source: (Primary data)

- **Gender:** The majority of the respondents are male, comprising 89.9% (169 out of 188), while females represent 10.1% (19 out of 188). This significant disparity suggests a male-dominated workforce in the automotive manufacturing sector in Tamil Nadu, which may reflect broader industry trends in this region.
- **Age:** The age distribution of the respondents indicates a balanced representation across different age groups. The largest age group is 30-40 years, accounting for 41.0% (77 out of 188) of the respondents. This is closely followed by those aged 41-50 years, who make up 39.9% (75 out of 188) of the sample. Respondents under 30 years constitute 14.4% (27 out of 188), while those above 50 years represent 4.8% (9 out of 188). The data suggests that the workforce is predominantly composed of individuals in their prime working years, which may influence the adoption and implementation of Industry 5.0 technologies.
- **Designation:** In terms of designation, the respondents are fairly evenly distributed. Team Leaders represent the largest group at 36.7% (69 out of 188), followed by Executives at 33.0% (62 out of 188), and Managers at 30.3% (57 out of 188). This distribution indicates a well-rounded representation from different levels of the organizational hierarchy, providing diverse perspectives on the implementation of Industry 5.0 technologies.
- **Experience:** The analysis of respondents' experience shows that those with 5-10 years and 10.1-15 years of experience each constitute 41.0% (77 out of 188) of the sample. This is followed by respondents with less than 5 years of experience at 14.9% (28 out of 188), and those with over 15 years of experience at 3.2% (6 out of 188). The predominance of respondents with mod-

erate levels of experience suggests that the insights provided are likely to be informed by substantial industry knowledge, yet not overly influenced by long-term incumbency.

The integration of human-centric advanced technologies in the automotive manufacturing sector presents several challenges that need to be addressed to ensure successful implementation. Table 2 provides a detailed multivariate analysis of these challenges, segmented by demographic factors such as gender, age, designation, and experience. The analysis includes both multivariate tests and tests of between-subjects effects, along with descriptive statistics for each challenge. This interpretation aims to provide a comprehensive understanding of how these demographic factors influence the perceived challenges of integrating human-centric advanced technologies.

Table 2. Multivariate Analysis: Key Challenges Associated with the Integration of Human-Centric Advanced Technologies

Effect		**Value**	**F**	**Hypothesis df**	**Error df**	**Sig.**
Multivariate Tests[a]						
Gender	Pillai's Trace	.178	4.621[b]	8.000	171.000	.000
Age	Pillai's Trace	.128	.964	24.000	519.000	.513
Designation	Pillai's Trace	.075	.835	16.000	344.000	.645
Experience	Pillai's Trace	.241	1.893	24.000	519.000	.007
Tests of Between-Subjects Effects						
Source		Type III Sum of Squares	df	Mean Square	F	Sig.

continued on following page

Table 2. Continued

Effect		Value	F	Hypothesis df	Error df	Sig.
Gender	The high cost of implementing human-centric advanced technologies is a significant challenge.	3.596	1	3.596	4.334	.039
	Lack of skilled workforce hinders the integration of advanced technologies.	5.922	1	5.922	8.008	.005
	Resistance to change from employees affects the adoption of new technologies.	1.532	1	1.532	2.158	.144
	Data security concerns are a major barrier to the implementation of human-centric technologies.	5.866	1	5.866	5.831	.017
	Technical complexity of Industry 5.0 technologies poses challenges for integration.	.191	1	.191	.245	.621
	Limited access to necessary technological infrastructure is a hindrance.	12.054	1	12.054	12.578	.000
	Insufficient government support affects the adoption of advanced technologies.	13.406	1	13.406	15.572	.000
	Lack of clear regulatory frameworks complicates the integration of new technologies.	10.332	1	10.332	10.633	.001

continued on following page

Table 2. Continued

Effect		Value	F	Hypothesis df	Error df	Sig.
Age	The high cost of implementing human-centric advanced technologies is a significant challenge.	5.082	3	1.694	2.041	.110
	Lack of skilled workforce hinders the integration of advanced technologies.	.730	3	.243	.329	.804
	Resistance to change from employees affects the adoption of new technologies.	4.394	3	1.465	2.063	.107
	Data security concerns are a major barrier to the implementation of human-centric technologies.	1.856	3	.619	.615	.606
	Technical complexity of Industry 5.0 technologies poses challenges for integration.	6.020	3	2.007	2.575	.055
	Limited access to necessary technological infrastructure is a hindrance.	.723	3	.241	.251	.860
	Insufficient government support affects the adoption of advanced technologies.	.482	3	.161	.187	.905
	Lack of clear regulatory frameworks complicates the integration of new technologies.	5.259	3	1.753	1.804	.148

continued on following page

Table 2. Continued

Effect		Value	F	Hypothesis df	Error df	Sig.
Designation	The high cost of implementing human-centric advanced technologies is a significant challenge.	.654	2	.327	.394	.675
	Lack of skilled workforce hinders the integration of advanced technologies.	.294	2	.147	.199	.820
	Resistance to change from employees affects the adoption of new technologies.	1.980	2	.990	1.394	.251
	Data security concerns are a major barrier to the implementation of human-centric technologies.	2.796	2	1.398	1.390	.252
	Technical complexity of Industry 5.0 technologies poses challenges for integration.	.017	2	.008	.011	.989
	Limited access to necessary technological infrastructure is a hindrance.	.286	2	.143	.149	.861
	Insufficient government support affects the adoption of advanced technologies.	3.878	2	1.939	2.252	.108
	Lack of clear regulatory frameworks complicates the integration of new technologies.	.187	2	.094	.096	.908

continued on following page

Table 2. Continued

Effect		Value	F	Hypothesis df	Error df	Sig.
Experience	The high cost of implementing human-centric advanced technologies is a significant challenge.	3.057	3	1.019	1.228	.301
	Lack of skilled workforce hinders the integration of advanced technologies.	23.689	3	7.896	10.679	.000
	Resistance to change from employees affects the adoption of new technologies.	.096	3	.032	.045	.987
	Data security concerns are a major barrier to the implementation of human-centric technologies.	2.314	3	.771	.767	.514
	Technical complexity of Industry 5.0 technologies poses challenges for integration.	1.119	3	.373	.479	.698
	Limited access to necessary technological infrastructure is a hindrance.	3.758	3	1.253	1.307	.274
	Insufficient government support affects the adoption of advanced technologies.	.715	3	.238	.277	.842
	Lack of clear regulatory frameworks complicates the integration of new technologies.	6.833	3	2.278	2.344	.075

Descriptive Statistics					
	N	Minimum	Maximum	Mean	Std. Deviation
The high cost of implementing human-centric advanced technologies is a significant challenge.	188	1.00	5.00	3.7606	.96525
Lack of skilled workforce hinders the integration of advanced technologies.	188	1.00	5.00	4.1862	.97696
Resistance to change from employees affects the adoption of new technologies.	188	1.00	5.00	4.1968	.87055
Data security concerns are a major barrier to the implementation of human-centric technologies.	188	1.00	5.00	3.8298	1.04076

continued on following page

Table 2. Continued

Effect	Value	F	Hypothesis df	Error df	Sig.
Technical complexity of Industry 5.0 technologies poses challenges for integration.	188	1.00	5.00	4.2606	.90816
Limited access to necessary technological infrastructure is a hindrance.	188	1.00	5.00	3.8351	1.02349
Insufficient government support affects the adoption of advanced technologies.	188	1.00	5.00	3.7553	.98313
Lack of clear regulatory frameworks complicates the integration of new technologies.	188	1.00	5.00	3.8085	1.08245

Source: (Primary data)

- **Multivariate Analysis:** The multivariate tests reveal significant differences based on gender and experience, but not for age and designation. The Pillai's Trace values indicate that gender (Pillai's Trace = .178, $p < .001$) and experience (Pillai's Trace = .241, $p < .01$) significantly affect perceptions of the challenges associated with integrating human-centric advanced technologies. This suggests that these factors play a crucial role in shaping how individuals perceive the barriers to technology adoption.
- **Gender:** Gender significantly influences perceptions of several key challenges. The high cost of implementation, lack of skilled workforce, data security concerns, limited access to technological infrastructure, insufficient government support, and lack of clear regulatory frameworks are all significantly perceived challenges ($p < .05$). Notably, the lack of skilled workforce ($F = 8.008$, $p < .01$), limited access to necessary technological infrastructure ($F = 12.578$, $p < .001$), insufficient government support ($F = 15.572$, $p < .001$), and lack of clear regulatory frameworks ($F = 10.633$, $p < .01$) are perceived as more significant challenges among different gender groups. These findings highlight the need for gender-sensitive strategies to address these barriers effectively.
- **Age:** Age does not significantly affect the perception of most challenges, as indicated by the Pillai's Trace value (.128, $p > .05$) and the lack of significant F-values in the tests of between-subjects effects. This suggests that perceptions of the high cost of implementation, lack of skilled workforce, resistance to change, data security concerns, and other challenges are relatively consistent across different age groups. The only marginally significant challenge is the technical complexity of Industry 5.0 technologies ($F = 2.575$, $p = .055$),

indicating that younger and older employees may have slightly different views on this issue.

- **Designation:** The designation of respondents does not significantly influence the perception of the challenges associated with integrating human-centric advanced technologies, as indicated by the Pillai's Trace value (.075, $p > .05$) and the lack of significant F-values. This uniformity across different designations (Team Leaders, Managers, and Executives) suggests that the challenges are perceived similarly regardless of one's position within the organization. This finding emphasizes the widespread nature of these barriers and the need for organization-wide strategies to address them.
- **Experience:** Experience significantly influences perceptions of specific challenges, particularly the lack of skilled workforce ($F = 10.679$, $p < .001$). Respondents with different levels of experience perceive the availability of skilled workforce differently, highlighting the critical need for continuous training and development programs. Although other challenges like the high cost of implementation, data security concerns, and limited access to necessary technological infrastructure are not significantly influenced by experience, there is a marginal significance for the lack of clear regulatory frameworks ($F = 2.344$, $p = .075$), indicating varied perceptions based on experience levels.
- **Descriptive Statistics:** The descriptive statistics provide additional insights into the perceived severity of each challenge. The challenges with the highest mean scores include the technical complexity of Industry 5.0 technologies (Mean = 4.2606) and resistance to change from employees (Mean = 4.1968), indicating that these are viewed as the most significant barriers. Conversely, the high cost of implementation (Mean = 3.7606) and insufficient government support (Mean = 3.7553) are perceived as moderately significant challenges.

Table 3 provides a comprehensive multivariate analysis of the key opportunities associated with the integration of human-centric advanced technologies in the automotive manufacturing sector. This analysis is segmented by demographic factors such as gender, age, designation, and experience. The results include multivariate tests, tests of between-subjects effects, and descriptive statistics for each identified opportunity. The aim is to understand how different demographic groups perceive the potential benefits of adopting Industry 5.0 technologies.

Table 3. Multivariate Analysis: Key Opportunities Associated with the Integration of Human-Centric Advanced Technologies

Effect		**Value**	**F**	**Hypothesis df**	**Error df**	**Sig.**
Multivariate Tests[a]						
Gender	Pillai's Trace	.428	16.002[b]	8.000	171.000	.000
Age	Pillai's Trace	.296	2.368	24.000	519.000	.000
Designation	Pillai's Trace	.102	1.155	16.000	344.000	.303
Experience	Pillai's Trace	.221	1.719	24.000	519.000	.019
Tests of Between-Subjects Effects						
Source		Type III Sum of Squares	df	Mean Square	F	Sig.
Gender	Human-centric advanced technologies can significantly improve operational efficiency.	4.480	1	4.480	5.623	.019
	Advanced technologies offer opportunities for enhanced product quality.	12.156	1	12.156	14.608	.000
	Integration of Industry 5.0 technologies enables greater customization capabilities.	33.278	1	33.278	61.330	.000
	Adoption of human-centric technologies increases competitiveness in the market.	11.626	1	11.626	13.322	.000
	Human-centric technologies provide opportunities for innovation and R&D advancements.	1.278	1	1.278	1.247	.266
	Advanced technologies enhance customer satisfaction through improved services.	16.958	1	16.958	20.473	.000
	Human-centric technologies facilitate better decision-making processes.	30.871	1	30.871	55.535	.000
	Integration of advanced technologies offers opportunities for workforce upskilling.	15.853	1	15.853	21.765	.000

continued on following page

Table 3. Continued

Effect		Value	F	Hypothesis df	Error df	Sig.
Age	Human-centric advanced technologies can significantly improve operational efficiency.	2.689	3	.896	1.125	.340
	Advanced technologies offer opportunities for enhanced product quality.	5.962	3	1.987	2.388	.070
	Integration of Industry 5.0 technologies enables greater customization capabilities.	3.200	3	1.067	1.966	.121
	Adoption of human-centric technologies increases competitiveness in the market.	4.108	3	1.369	1.569	.198
	Human-centric technologies provide opportunities for innovation and R&D advancements.	2.629	3	.876	.855	.466
	Advanced technologies enhance customer satisfaction through improved services.	12.165	3	4.055	4.895	.003
	Human-centric technologies facilitate better decision-making processes.	3.238	3	1.079	1.941	.125
	Integration of advanced technologies offers opportunities for workforce upskilling.	5.435	3	1.812	2.487	.062

continued on following page

Table 3. Continued

Effect		Value	F	Hypothesis df	Error df	Sig.
Designation	Human-centric advanced technologies can significantly improve operational efficiency.	.314	2	.157	.197	.821
	Advanced technologies offer opportunities for enhanced product quality.	2.100	2	1.050	1.262	.286
	Integration of Industry 5.0 technologies enables greater customization capabilities.	.173	2	.086	.159	.853
	Adoption of human-centric technologies increases competitiveness in the market.	1.999	2	.999	1.145	.320
	Human-centric technologies provide opportunities for innovation and R&D advancements.	1.228	2	.614	.599	.550
	Advanced technologies enhance customer satisfaction through improved services.	4.200	2	2.100	2.535	.082
	Human-centric technologies facilitate better decision-making processes.	1.724	2	.862	1.550	.215
	Integration of advanced technologies offers opportunities for workforce upskilling.	.346	2	.173	.238	.789

continued on following page

Table 3. Continued

Effect		Value	F	Hypothesis df	Error df	Sig.
Experience	Human-centric advanced technologies can significantly improve operational efficiency.	3.819	3	1.273	1.598	.192
	Advanced technologies offer opportunities for enhanced product quality.	.048	3	.016	.019	.996
	Integration of Industry 5.0 technologies enables greater customization capabilities.	6.636	3	2.212	4.077	.008
	Adoption of human-centric technologies increases competitiveness in the market.	2.314	3	.771	.884	.451
	Human-centric technologies provide opportunities for innovation and R&D advancements.	.480	3	.160	.156	.926
	Advanced technologies enhance customer satisfaction through improved services.	11.577	3	3.859	4.659	.004
	Human-centric technologies facilitate better decision-making processes.	8.375	3	2.792	5.022	.002
	Integration of advanced technologies offers opportunities for workforce upskilling.	3.579	3	1.193	1.638	.182
Descriptive Statistics						
		N	Minimum	Maximum	Mean	Std. Deviation
Human-centric advanced technologies can significantly improve operational efficiency.		188	1.00	5.00	4.2074	.93908
Advanced technologies offer opportunities for enhanced product quality.		188	1.00	5.00	4.2553	1.01261
Integration of Industry 5.0 technologies enables greater customization capabilities.		188	1.00	5.00	4.2074	.97813
Adoption of human-centric technologies increases competitiveness in the market.		188	1.00	5.00	4.2074	.99976
Human-centric technologies provide opportunities for innovation and R&D advancements.		188	1.00	5.00	3.8138	1.01456

continued on following page

Table 3. Continued

Effect	Value	F	Hypothesis df	Error df	Sig.
Advanced technologies enhance customer satisfaction through improved services.	188	1.00	5.00	3.8138	1.00927
Human-centric technologies facilitate better decision-making processes.	188	1.00	5.00	4.1489	1.00222
Integration of advanced technologies offers opportunities for workforce upskilling.	188	1.00	5.00	4.2394	.94283

Source: (Primary data)

- **Multivariate Analysis:** The multivariate tests reveal significant differences based on gender, age, and experience, but not for designation. The Pillai's Trace values indicate that gender (Pillai's Trace = .428, $p < .001$), age (Pillai's Trace = .296, $p < .001$), and experience (Pillai's Trace = .221, $p < .05$) significantly affect perceptions of the opportunities associated with the integration of human-centric advanced technologies. This suggests that these factors play a crucial role in shaping how individuals perceive the benefits of technology adoption.
- **Gender:** Gender significantly influences perceptions of various opportunities. The findings indicate that men and women perceive the benefits of advanced technologies differently, with significant differences observed for operational efficiency ($F = 5.623$, $p < .05$), product quality ($F = 14.608$, $p < .001$), customization capabilities ($F = 61.330$, $p < .001$), market competitiveness ($F = 13.322$, $p < .001$), customer satisfaction ($F = 20.473$, $p < .001$), decision-making processes ($F = 55.535$, $p < .001$), and workforce upskilling ($F = 21.765$, $p < .001$). These results highlight the need to consider gender-specific strategies when promoting the adoption of Industry 5.0 technologies.
- **Age:** Age also significantly affects the perception of opportunities, particularly for customer satisfaction ($F = 4.895$, $p < .01$). Although most other opportunities did not show significant differences based on age, the marginal significance for product quality ($F = 2.388$, $p = .070$) and workforce upskilling ($F = 2.487$, $p = .062$) suggests that different age groups may have varying views on these aspects. This highlights the importance of tailoring communication and training programs to cater to the diverse age groups within the workforce.
- **Designation:** Designation does not significantly influence the perception of most opportunities, as indicated by the Pillai's Trace value (.102, $p > .05$) and the lack of significant F-values. This uniformity across different designations (Team Leaders, Managers, and Executives) suggests that the perceived

benefits of human-centric advanced technologies are consistent regardless of one's position within the organization. This finding emphasizes the widespread recognition of these opportunities across different hierarchical levels.

- **Experience:** Experience significantly influences perceptions of specific opportunities, particularly for customization capabilities ($F = 4.077$, $p < .01$), customer satisfaction ($F = 4.659$, $p < .01$), and decision-making processes ($F = 5.022$, $p < .01$). Respondents with varying levels of experience perceive the benefits of advanced technologies differently, highlighting the critical need for continuous professional development and training programs. Although other opportunities like operational efficiency and product quality are not significantly influenced by experience, these findings underscore the importance of leveraging experienced employees' insights to enhance technology adoption.
- **Descriptive Statistics:** The descriptive statistics provide additional insights into the perceived significance of each opportunity. The opportunities with the highest mean scores include enhanced product quality (Mean = 4.2553), workforce upskilling (Mean = 4.2394), and operational efficiency (Mean = 4.2074). Conversely, opportunities for innovation and R&D advancements (Mean = 3.8138) and customer satisfaction (Mean = 3.8138) are perceived as moderately significant. These statistics indicate that while all opportunities are recognized, some are considered more critical than others.

Table 4 presents a detailed multivariate analysis examining the implementation of Industry 5.0 technologies within the automotive manufacturing sector. This analysis evaluates the effects of gender, age, designation, and experience on various aspects of Industry 5.0 implementation, including organizational investment, strategy clarity, employee training, resource allocation, collaboration, assessment processes, scaling roadmaps, and employee feedback. The table comprises multivariate tests, tests of between-subjects effects, and descriptive statistics to provide a comprehensive understanding of the factors influencing the successful implementation of these advanced technologies.

Table 4. Multivariate Analysis: Implementation of Industry 5.0 Technologies

Effect		Value	F	Hypothesis df	Error df	Sig.
Multivariate Tests[a]						
Gender	Pillai's Trace	.099	2.347[b]	8.000	171.000	.020
Age	Pillai's Trace	.228	1.774	24.000	519.000	.014

continued on following page

Table 4. Continued

Effect		**Value**	**F**	**Hypothesis df**	**Error df**	**Sig.**
Designation	Pillai's Trace	.072	.808	16.000	344.000	.676
Experience	Pillai's Trace	.175	1.340	24.000	519.000	.131
Tests of Between-Subjects Effects						
Source		Type III Sum of Squares	df	Mean Square	F	Sig.
Gender	The organization is actively investing in Industry 5.0 technologies.	.541	1	.541	.268	.605
	There is a clear strategy for implementing Industry 5.0 technologies in the organization.	.929	1	.929	.982	.323
	Employees are provided with adequate training for using Industry 5.0 technologies.	4.550	1	4.550	2.329	.129
	The organization has dedicated resources for the integration of advanced technologies.	9.086	1	9.086	9.027	.003
	Collaboration with technology partners is a key aspect of the implementation strategy.	.678	1	.678	.690	.407
	Regular assessments are conducted to evaluate the progress of Industry 5.0 implementation.	5.404	1	5.404	2.897	.090
	The organization has a roadmap for scaling up the use of Industry 5.0 technologies.	1.189	1	1.189	1.102	.295
	Feedback from employees is incorporated into the implementation process.	2.371	1	2.371	2.189	.141

continued on following page

Table 4. Continued

Effect		Value	F	Hypothesis df	Error df	Sig.
Age	The organization is actively investing in Industry 5.0 technologies.	1.150	3	.383	.190	.903
	There is a clear strategy for implementing Industry 5.0 technologies in the organization.	12.300	3	4.100	4.330	.006
	Employees are provided with adequate training for using Industry 5.0 technologies.	6.167	3	2.056	1.052	.371
	The organization has dedicated resources for the integration of advanced technologies.	13.562	3	4.521	4.491	.005
	Collaboration with technology partners is a key aspect of the implementation strategy.	1.648	3	.549	.559	.643
	Regular assessments are conducted to evaluate the progress of Industry 5.0 implementation.	15.242	3	5.081	2.723	.046
	The organization has a roadmap for scaling up the use of Industry 5.0 technologies.	4.636	3	1.545	1.431	.235
	Feedback from employees is incorporated into the implementation process.	.138	3	.046	.042	.988

continued on following page

Table 4. Continued

Effect		Value	F	Hypothesis df	Error df	Sig.
Designation	The organization is actively investing in Industry 5.0 technologies.	1.463	2	.732	.363	.696
	There is a clear strategy for implementing Industry 5.0 technologies in the organization.	1.326	2	.663	.700	.498
	Employees are provided with adequate training for using Industry 5.0 technologies.	.559	2	.280	.143	.867
	The organization has dedicated resources for the integration of advanced technologies.	.867	2	.433	.430	.651
	Collaboration with technology partners is a key aspect of the implementation strategy.	.824	2	.412	.419	.658
	Regular assessments are conducted to evaluate the progress of Industry 5.0 implementation.	13.591	2	6.796	3.643	.028
	The organization has a roadmap for scaling up the use of Industry 5.0 technologies.	.699	2	.350	.324	.724
	Feedback from employees is incorporated into the implementation process.	1.341	2	.671	.619	.540

continued on following page

Table 4. Continued

Effect		Value	F	Hypothesis df	Error df	Sig.
Experience	The organization is actively investing in Industry 5.0 technologies.	11.240	3	3.747	1.859	.138
	There is a clear strategy for implementing Industry 5.0 technologies in the organization.	5.273	3	1.758	1.856	.139
	Employees are provided with adequate training for using Industry 5.0 technologies.	3.498	3	1.166	.597	.618
	The organization has dedicated resources for the integration of advanced technologies.	2.053	3	.684	.680	.565
	Collaboration with technology partners is a key aspect of the implementation strategy.	4.403	3	1.468	1.493	.218
	Regular assessments are conducted to evaluate the progress of Industry 5.0 implementation.	6.218	3	2.073	1.111	.346
	The organization has a roadmap for scaling up the use of Industry 5.0 technologies.	3.844	3	1.281	1.187	.316
	Feedback from employees is incorporated into the implementation process.	7.588	3	2.529	2.335	.075

Descriptive Statistics

	N	Minimum	Maximum	Mean	Std. Deviation
The organization is actively investing in Industry 5.0 technologies.	188	1.00	5.00	2.9628	1.41561
There is a clear strategy for implementing Industry 5.0 technologies in the organization.	188	1.00	5.00	3.7979	1.03500
Employees are provided with adequate training for using Industry 5.0 technologies.	188	1.00	5.00	2.8617	1.39212
The organization has dedicated resources for the integration of advanced technologies.	188	1.00	5.00	3.9096	1.08825
Collaboration with technology partners is a key aspect of the implementation strategy.	188	1.00	5.00	3.9309	1.00294

continued on following page

Table 4. Continued

Effect	Value	F	Hypothesis df	Error df	Sig.
Regular assessments are conducted to evaluate the progress of Industry 5.0 implementation.	188	1.00	5.00	2.9521	1.40009
The organization has a roadmap for scaling up the use of Industry 5.0 technologies.	188	1.00	5.00	3.7234	1.04860
Feedback from employees is incorporated into the implementation process.	188	1.00	5.00	3.7553	1.05147

Source: (Primary data)

- **Multivariate Analysis:** The multivariate tests reveal significant differences based on gender and age, but not for designation and experience. Gender (Pillai's Trace = .099, $p < .05$) and age (Pillai's Trace = .228, $p < .05$) significantly influence perceptions of Industry 5.0 implementation. These findings indicate that both gender and age play crucial roles in shaping how employees perceive the organization's efforts and strategies related to Industry 5.0 technologies.
- **Gender:** The between-subjects effects show that gender significantly affects perceptions of resource allocation for advanced technologies ($F = 9.027$, $p < .01$). This suggests that men and women may have different views on how well the organization dedicates resources to the integration of these technologies. However, other aspects such as investment, strategy clarity, employee training, collaboration, assessments, scaling roadmaps, and employee feedback do not show significant gender differences, indicating a general consensus between genders on these issues.
- **Age:** Age significantly influences perceptions of strategy clarity ($F = 4.330$, $p < .01$), resource allocation ($F = 4.491$, $p < .01$), and regular assessments ($F = 2.723$, $p < .05$). These results suggest that different age groups may have varying opinions on how clearly the organization communicates its Industry 5.0 strategy, allocates resources, and conducts progress evaluations. This highlights the need for age-sensitive communication and implementation strategies to ensure all age groups are aligned with the organization's goals and practices.
- **Designation:** Designation does not significantly influence most aspects of Industry 5.0 implementation, as indicated by the lack of significant F-values across most variables. However, regular assessments ($F = 3.643$, $p < .05$) show some significance, suggesting that employees at different hierarchical levels may perceive the frequency and thoroughness of these evaluations dif-

ferently. This underscores the importance of consistent and transparent assessment practices across all organizational levels to maintain uniformity in implementation perceptions.

- **Experience:** Experience does not significantly affect perceptions of Industry 5.0 implementation, with no significant F-values across all examined aspects. This indicates that employees, regardless of their experience level, generally share similar views on the organization's investment, strategy, training, resource allocation, collaboration, assessment, scaling, and feedback processes related to Industry 5.0 technologies. This finding suggests that the organization's implementation strategies are perceived consistently across different experience levels, reflecting a uniform approach in communicating and executing these initiatives.
- **Descriptive Statistics:** The descriptive statistics provide further insights into the perceived effectiveness of Industry 5.0 implementation. The highest mean scores are observed for collaboration with technology partners (Mean = 3.9309) and resource allocation (Mean = 3.9096), indicating that these aspects are seen as well-handled by the organization. On the other hand, employee training (Mean = 2.8617) and investment in Industry 5.0 technologies (Mean = 2.9628) have lower mean scores, suggesting areas for improvement. These statistics highlight the organization's strengths in collaboration and resource allocation, while also pointing to the need for enhanced training and investment efforts.

Table 5 presents a univariate analysis examining the impact of implementing Industry 5.0 technologies on economic innovation, productivity, and sustainability within the automotive manufacturing sector. The analysis investigates the effects of gender, age, designation, and experience on these three dependent variables. The table includes tests of between-subjects effects and descriptive statistics to elucidate how different demographic factors influence perceptions of the impact of Industry 5.0 technologies.

Table 5. Univariate Analysis – Impact on Economic Innovation, Productivity, and Sustainability within the Industry

Tests of Between-Subjects Effects					
Dependent Variable:	**Implementation of Industry 5.0 technologies has led to significant economic innovation in the organization.**				
Source	**Type III Sum of Squares**	**df**	**Mean Square**	**F**	**Sig.**
Gender	5.242	1	5.242	5.239	.023
Age	4.137	3	1.379	1.378	.251
Designation	.390	2	.195	.195	.823
Experience	2.652	3	.884	.884	.451
Descriptive Statistics					
	N	Minimum	Maximum	Mean	Std. Deviation
Implementation of Industry 5.0 technologies has led to significant economic innovation in the organization.	188	1.00	5.00	3.9628	1.00464
Tests of Between-Subjects Effects					
Dependent Variable:	Productivity levels have improved with the adoption of Industry 5.0 technologies.				
Source	Type III Sum of Squares	df	Mean Square	F	Sig.
Gender	6.759	1	6.759	8.206	.005
Age	5.583	3	1.861	2.259	.083
Designation	.618	2	.309	.375	.688
Experience	3.890	3	1.297	1.574	.197
Descriptive Statistics					
	N	Minimum	Maximum	Mean	Std. Deviation
Productivity levels have improved with the adoption of Industry 5.0 technologies.	188	1.00	5.00	4.1702	.99880
Tests of Between-Subjects Effects					
Dependent Variable:	Industry 5.0 technologies have contributed to the sustainability practices of the organization.				
Source	Type III Sum of Squares	df	Mean Square	F	Sig.
Gender	.501	1	.501	.330	.566
Age	.406	3	.135	.089	.966

continued on following page

Table 5. Continued

Tests of Between-Subjects Effects					
Dependent Variable:	**Implementation of Industry 5.0 technologies has led to significant economic innovation in the organization.**				
Source	**Type III Sum of Squares**	**df**	**Mean Square**	**F**	**Sig.**
Designation	1.859	2	.930	.612	.543
Experience	6.738	3	2.246	1.479	.222
Descriptive Statistics					
	N	Minimum	Maximum	Mean	Std. Deviation
Industry 5.0 technologies have contributed to the sustainability practices of the organization.	188	1.00	5.00	3.2713	1.22620

Source: (Primary data)

- **Economic Innovation:** The implementation of Industry 5.0 technologies is perceived to lead to significant economic innovation within organizations. The between-subjects effects reveal that gender significantly influences this perception ($F = 5.239$, $p < .05$), while age, designation, and experience do not show significant effects. The descriptive statistics indicate that the mean score for economic innovation is 3.9628, with a standard deviation of 1.00464. This suggests that, on average, employees agree that Industry 5.0 technologies have positively impacted economic innovation, with gender differences playing a notable role in shaping this perception.
- **Productivity Improvement:** The analysis shows that productivity levels are perceived to have improved with the adoption of Industry 5.0 technologies. Gender again plays a significant role in this perception ($F = 8.206$, $p < .01$), indicating that men and women view the productivity gains from Industry 5.0 differently. Age shows a marginally non-significant effect ($F = 2.259$, $p = .083$), suggesting that age might also influence this perception to some extent. Designation and experience do not have significant effects on productivity perceptions. The mean score for productivity improvement is 4.1702, with a standard deviation of 0.99880, indicating a strong consensus among employees that Industry 5.0 technologies have enhanced productivity.
- **Sustainability Practices:** Regarding the contribution of Industry 5.0 technologies to sustainability practices, none of the demographic factors (gender, age, designation, experience) show significant effects. The descriptive statistics show a mean score of 3.2713 with a standard deviation of 1.22620, indi-

cating moderate agreement among employees that Industry 5.0 technologies have contributed to sustainability practices. The lack of significant differences across demographic factors suggests a uniform perception of the impact of these technologies on sustainability within the organization.

Table No. 6 presents the results of a correlation analysis examining the relationships between various factors within the context of the automobile industry's adoption of Industry 5.0 technologies. The factors analyzed include economic innovation, productivity levels, sustainability practices, key challenges, key opportunities, and the implementation of Industry 5.0 technologies. The Pearson correlation coefficients and their significance levels (2-tailed) are provided for each pair of variables, revealing the strength and direction of these relationships.

Table 6. Correlation Analysis – Relationship between Economic innovation, Productivity levels, Sustainability practices, Key Challenges, Key Opportunities, Implementation of Industry 5.0 in automobile Industry

Correlations							
		Economic innovation	**Productivity levels**	**Sustainability practices**	**Key Challenges**	**Key Opportunities**	**Implementation**
Economic innovation	Pearson Correlation	1	.257**	.060	.288**	.218**	.184*
	Sig. (2-tailed)		.000	.411	.000	.003	.011
	N	188	188	188	188	188	188
Productivity levels	Pearson Correlation	.257**	1	-.038	.385**	.384**	.017
	Sig. (2-tailed)	.000		.606	.000	.000	.812
	N	188	188	188	188	188	188
Sustainability practices	Pearson Correlation	.060	-.038	1	.135	.071	.087
	Sig. (2-tailed)	.411	.606		.064	.332	.233
	N	188	188	188	188	188	188
Key Challenges	Pearson Correlation	.288**	.385**	.135	1	.593**	.263**
	Sig. (2-tailed)	.000	.000	.064		.000	.000
	N	188	188	188	188	188	188

continued on following page

Table 6. Continued

Correlations								
		Economic innovation	Productivity levels	Sustainability practices	Key Challenges	Key Opportunities	Implementation
Key Opportunities	Pearson Correlation	.218**	.384**	.071	.593**	1	.309**
	Sig. (2-tailed)	.003	.000	.332	.000		.000
	N	188	188	188	188	188	188
Implementation	Pearson Correlation	.184*	.017	.087	.263**	.309**	1
	Sig. (2-tailed)	.011	.812	.233	.000	.000	
	N	188	188	188	188	188	188

Source: (Primary data)

- **Economic Innovation:** Economic innovation shows significant positive correlations with productivity levels ($r = .257$, $p < .01$), key challenges ($r = .288$, $p < .01$), key opportunities ($r = .218$, $p < .01$), and the implementation of Industry 5.0 technologies ($r = .184$, $p < .05$). These findings suggest that as organizations achieve higher levels of economic innovation, they also tend to experience improvements in productivity, recognize and address key challenges, identify and leverage key opportunities, and make significant strides in implementing Industry 5.0 technologies. However, the correlation between economic innovation and sustainability practices is not significant ($r = .060$, $p = .411$), indicating that economic innovation is not strongly associated with sustainability practices in this context.
- **Productivity Levels:** Productivity levels are significantly positively correlated with key challenges ($r = .385$, $p < .01$) and key opportunities ($r = .384$, $p < .01$). This indicates that higher productivity levels are associated with a greater recognition of key challenges and opportunities. Interestingly, there is no significant correlation between productivity levels and sustainability practices ($r = -.038$, $p = .606$) or the implementation of Industry 5.0 technologies ($r = .017$, $p = .812$). This suggests that while productivity is linked to challenges and opportunities, it does not have a strong direct relationship with sustainability practices or the overall implementation of Industry 5.0 technologies.
- **Sustainability Practices:** Sustainability practices do not show significant correlations with any of the other variables, including economic innovation ($r = .060$, $p = .411$), productivity levels ($r = -.038$, $p = .606$), key challenges ($r = .135$, $p = .064$), key opportunities ($r = .071$, $p = .332$), or the imple-

mentation of Industry 5.0 technologies ($r = .087$, $p = .233$). This suggests that sustainability practices are relatively independent of the other factors considered in this analysis within the context of Industry 5.0 adoption in the automobile industry.

- **Key Challenges:** Key challenges are significantly positively correlated with economic innovation ($r = .288$, $p < .01$), productivity levels ($r = .385$, $p < .01$), key opportunities ($r = .593$, $p < .01$), and the implementation of Industry 5.0 technologies ($r = .263$, $p < .01$). These strong correlations indicate that organizations facing more key challenges are also likely to experience higher levels of economic innovation and productivity, recognize key opportunities, and advance in their implementation of Industry 5.0 technologies.
- **Key Opportunities:** Key opportunities show significant positive correlations with economic innovation ($r = .218$, $p < .01$), productivity levels ($r = .384$, $p < .01$), key challenges ($r = .593$, $p < .01$), and the implementation of Industry 5.0 technologies ($r = .309$, $p < .01$). This implies that identifying and leveraging key opportunities is associated with greater economic innovation, improved productivity, a higher recognition of challenges, and more progress in implementing Industry 5.0 technologies.
- **Implementation of Industry 5.0 Technologies:** The implementation of Industry 5.0 technologies is significantly positively correlated with economic innovation ($r = .184$, $p < .05$), key challenges ($r = .263$, $p < .01$), and key opportunities ($r = .309$, $p < .01$). This suggests that organizations that are more advanced in their implementation of Industry 5.0 technologies are also likely to experience higher levels of economic innovation, recognize and address key challenges, and identify key opportunities. However, there is no significant correlation between the implementation of Industry 5.0 technologies and productivity levels ($r = .017$, $p = .812$) or sustainability practices ($r = .087$, $p = .233$).

The Table No. 7 presents the results of a regression analysis examining the impact of key challenges and key opportunities on economic innovation, productivity levels, and sustainability practices within the automobile industry, with the implementation of Industry 5.0 technologies serving as a mediating variable. The regression weights (estimates), standard errors (S.E.), critical ratios (C.R.), and significance levels (P) are provided for each relationship, offering insights into the direct and indirect effects of these factors.

Table 7. Regression Analysis –Impact of Key Challenges, Key Opportunities on Economic innovation, Productivity levels, Sustainability practices with Implementation of Industry 5.0 in automobile Industry as Mediating variables

Regression Weights						
			Estimate	**S.E.**	**C.R.**	**P**
Implementation	<	Opportunities	0.176	0.052	3.41	***
Implementation	<	Challenges	0.109	0.061	1.789	0.074
Sustainability	<	Opportunities	-0.047	0.125	-0.377	0.706
Productivity	<	Opportunities	0.371	0.092	4.048	***
Economic Innovation	<	Opportunities	0.064	0.098	0.649	0.516
Sustainability	<	Challenges	0.267	0.143	1.865	0.062
Productivity	<	Challenges	0.414	0.105	3.927	***
Economic Innovation	<	Challenges	0.374	0.113	3.312	***
Economic Innovation	<	Implementation	0.2	0.135	1.483	0.138
Productivity	<	Implementation	-0.246	0.126	-1.954	0.051
Sustainability	<	Implementation	0.135	0.171	0.788	0.431

Figure 1.

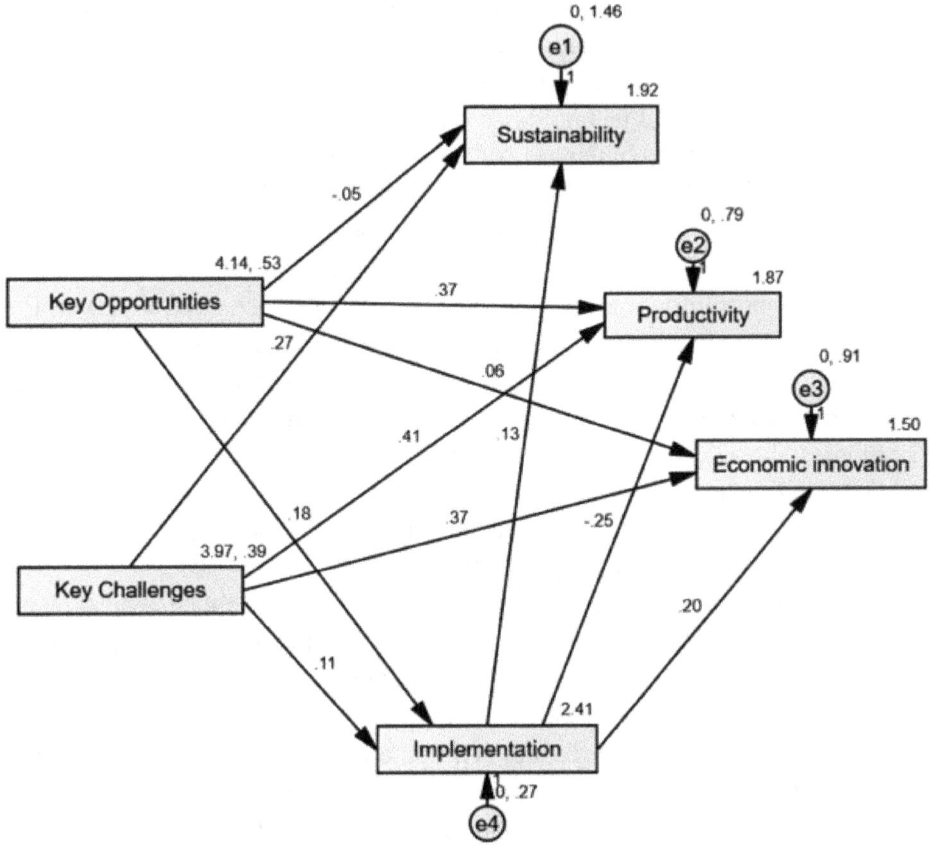

Source: (Primary data)

- **Implementation of Industry 5.0 Technologies:** The regression analysis reveals that key opportunities have a significant positive impact on the implementation of Industry 5.0 technologies (Estimate = 0.176, S.E. = 0.052, C.R. = 3.41, P < 0.001). This indicates that organizations that identify and leverage key opportunities are more likely to advance in their implementation of Industry 5.0 technologies. However, key challenges do not have a statistically significant impact on implementation (Estimate = 0.109, S.E. = 0.061, C.R. = 1.789, P = 0.074), although the effect is close to the threshold for significance.

- **Economic Innovation:** Economic innovation is significantly influenced by key challenges (Estimate = 0.374, S.E. = 0.113, C.R. = 3.312, $P < 0.001$), suggesting that organizations that recognize and address key challenges tend to experience higher levels of economic innovation. However, key opportunities do not have a significant direct effect on economic innovation (Estimate = 0.064, S.E. = 0.098, C.R. = 0.649, $P = 0.516$). Additionally, the implementation of Industry 5.0 technologies does not significantly mediate the relationship between key challenges, key opportunities, and economic innovation (Estimate = 0.2, S.E. = 0.135, C.R. = 1.483, $P = 0.138$).
- **Productivity Levels:** Productivity levels are significantly influenced by both key challenges (Estimate = 0.414, S.E. = 0.105, C.R. = 3.927, $P < 0.001$) and key opportunities (Estimate = 0.371, S.E. = 0.092, C.R. = 4.048, $P < 0.001$). This indicates that recognizing and addressing key challenges, as well as leveraging key opportunities, contribute to improved productivity levels within organizations. Interestingly, the implementation of Industry 5.0 technologies shows a negative but marginally significant effect on productivity levels (Estimate = -0.246, S.E. = 0.126, C.R. = -1.954, $P = 0.051$), suggesting a complex relationship where the implementation might initially pose challenges before leading to productivity gains.
- **Sustainability Practices:** The regression analysis indicates that sustainability practices are positively influenced by key challenges (Estimate = 0.267, S.E. = 0.143, C.R. = 1.865, $P = 0.062$), although the effect is not statistically significant at the 0.05 level. Key opportunities do not have a significant impact on sustainability practices (Estimate = -0.047, S.E. = 0.125, C.R. = -0.377, $P = 0.706$). Additionally, the implementation of Industry 5.0 technologies does not significantly mediate the relationship between key challenges, key opportunities, and sustainability practices (Estimate = 0.135, S.E. = 0.171, C.R. = 0.788, $P = 0.431$).

FINDINGS AND CONCLUSION

The demographic profile of the respondents in this study showcases a predominantly male, middle-aged workforce with a balanced distribution of roles across the organizational hierarchy and a significant representation of mid-level experience. These demographic characteristics provide a rich context for understanding the diverse perspectives on the integration and impact of Industry 5.0 technologies in Tamil Nadu's automotive manufacturing sector. The insights drawn from this varied sample are instrumental in comprehensively assessing the challenges and opportunities associated with advanced technological implementation in this industry.

The multivariate analysis reveals that gender and experience significantly influence the perception of key challenges associated with the integration of human-centric advanced technologies in the automotive manufacturing sector. Age and designation, however, do not have a significant impact. The findings underscore the importance of developing targeted strategies to address these challenges, particularly focusing on enhancing workforce skills, ensuring data security, improving access to technological infrastructure, and advocating for supportive government policies and clear regulatory frameworks. Addressing these issues will be crucial for successful Industry 5.0 implementation and driving economic innovation, productivity, and sustainability in the sector.

The multivariate analysis reveals that gender, age, and experience significantly influence the perception of key opportunities associated with the integration of human-centric advanced technologies in the automotive manufacturing sector. Designation, however, does not have a significant impact. The findings underscore the importance of developing targeted strategies to capitalize on these opportunities, particularly focusing on enhancing product quality, operational efficiency, customization capabilities, customer satisfaction, decision-making processes, and workforce upskilling. Addressing these opportunities will be crucial for driving economic innovation, productivity, and sustainability in the sector.

The multivariate analysis reveals that gender and age significantly influence perceptions of Industry 5.0 technology implementation, while designation and experience do not have a substantial impact. The findings emphasize the importance of considering demographic factors in developing and communicating implementation strategies. By addressing the specific needs and perceptions of different gender and age groups, organizations can enhance the effectiveness of their Industry 5.0 initiatives, leading to better alignment, improved employee satisfaction, and successful technology integration.

The univariate analysis highlights that gender significantly influences perceptions of economic innovation and productivity improvements resulting from Industry 5.0 technologies, while age, designation, and experience do not show substantial effects. The consistent perception across demographic factors regarding sustainability practices suggests a shared view of the benefits of Industry 5.0 technologies in this area. These findings emphasize the importance of considering gender differences when communicating and implementing Industry 5.0 technologies to ensure all employees recognize and benefit from their potential for economic innovation and productivity improvements.

The correlation analysis reveals important relationships between economic innovation, productivity levels, key challenges, key opportunities, and the implementation of Industry 5.0 technologies. Economic innovation is positively associated with productivity, challenges, opportunities, and implementation, highlighting the interconnected nature of these factors. While sustainability practices appear relatively independent, recognizing and addressing key challenges and opportunities plays a critical role in driving economic innovation and successful implementation of Industry 5.0 technologies within the automobile industry.

The regression analysis underscores the significant impact of key challenges and key opportunities on economic innovation and productivity levels within the automobile industry. Key challenges, in particular, drive economic innovation and productivity improvements. While the implementation of Industry 5.0 technologies is significantly influenced by key opportunities, its role as a mediating variable in this context is complex and warrants further investigation. The findings highlight the importance of addressing challenges and seizing opportunities to foster economic innovation and productivity in the era of Industry 5.0.

DISCUSSION

Our findings that gender and experience significantly affect key obstacle perceptions match with current work on demographic determinants in technology adoption. Venkatesh et al. (2003) observed that gender affects technology acceptability and use. Experience also affects technology adoption, as Igbaria and Iivari (1995) found that experienced users perceive and embrace new technologies differently than less experienced users. These similarities suggest that Industry 5.0 deployment must handle demographic differences.

Age and designation do not significantly affect views of critical problems, contrary to several studies that show a wider variety of demographic characteristics influence technology adoption. Morris and Venkatesh (2000) discovered that age and work function strongly influence technology acceptance. Our study's context-specific findings may represent Tamil Nadu's automobile industry's gender and experience-focused characteristics.

Our analysis of significant potential matches studies showing how sophisticated technologies improve product quality, operational efficiency, and customisation. Wamba et al. (2015) highlight similar prospects in Big Data analytics and organisational performance. Our findings support this literature, suggesting that Industry 5.0 technologies could improve car performance.

The consistent perception across demographic parameters of sustainability practices supports Hart (1995)'s natural-resource-based perspective of the enterprise and its implications for sustainable competitive advantage. Our findings indicate that

Industry 5.0 technologies are generally recognised for their sustainability benefits, highlighting their importance in achieving sustainable development goals.

The regression study shows that important challenges and opportunities affect automobile sector economic innovation and productivity. Porter and Heppelmann (2015) found that smart, connected devices can revolutionise economies and that tackling key concerns drives economic innovation and productivity.

Key opportunities drive Industry 5.0 technology implementation, but its position as a mediating variable is complex and requires further study. Kagermann et al. (2013) found Industry 4.0 complicated and required nuanced tactics to maximise its potential. Technology adoption and organisational change literature supports the necessity of overcoming barriers and embracing opportunities to boost economic innovation and productivity in Industry 5.0 (Rogers, 2003).

REFERENCES

Acemoglu, D., & Restrepo, P. (2018). The race between man and machine: Implications of technology for growth, factor shares, and employment. *The American Economic Review, 108*(6), 1488–1542.

Adner, R., & Kapoor, R. (2016). Innovation ecosystems and the pace of substitution: Re-examining technology S-curves. *Strategic Management Journal, 37*(4), 625–648.

Berman, S. J. (2012). Digital transformation: Opportunities to create new business models. *Strategy and Leadership, 40*(2), 16–24.

Brynjolfsson, E., & McAfee, A. (2014). *The Second Machine Age: Work, Progress, and Prosperity in a Time of Brilliant Technologies*. W.W. Norton & Company.

Demir, K. A., Döven, G., & Sezen, B. (2019). Industry 5.0 and human-robot co-working. *Procedia Computer Science, 158*, 688–695.

Ford, M. (2015). *Rise of the Robots: Technology and the Threat of a Jobless Future*. Basic Books.

Geissdoerfer, M., Savaget, P., Bocken, N. M. P., & Hultink, E. J. (2017). The Circular Economy – A new sustainability paradigm? *Journal of Cleaner Production, 143*, 757–768.

Hart, S. L. (1995). A natural-resource-based view of the firm. *Academy of Management Review, 20*(4), 986–1014.

Igbaria, M., & Iivari, J. (1995). The effects of self-efficacy on computer usage. *Omega, 23*(6), 587–605.

Kagermann, H., Wahlster, W., & Helbig, J. (2013). Recommendations for implementing the strategic initiative INDUSTRIE 4.0: Securing the future of German manufacturing industry. Final report of the Industrie 4.0 Working Group.

Kang, H. S., Lee, J. Y., Choi, S., & Kim, H. (2016). Smart manufacturing: Past research, present findings, and future directions. *International Journal of Precision Engineering and Manufacturing-Green Technology, 3*(1), 111–128.

Lee, J., Bagheri, B., & Kao, H. A. (2015). A cyber-physical systems architecture for industry 4.0-based manufacturing systems. *Manufacturing Letters, 3*, 18–23.

Morris, M. G., & Venkatesh, V. (2000). Age differences in technology adoption decisions: Implications for a changing work force. *Personnel Psychology, 53*(2), 375–403.

Pandey, A., & Shankar, R. (2020). Industry 4.0 and its applications in the automotive sector. In Kumar, N., Jha, A. N., & Singh, S. (Eds.), *Industry 4.0: Trends, technologies and impact* (pp. 149–161). Springer.

Porter, M. E., & Heppelmann, J. E. (2014). How smart, connected products are transforming competition. *Harvard Business Review*, *92*(11), 64–88.

Porter, M. E., & Heppelmann, J. E. (2015). How smart, connected products are transforming companies. *Harvard Business Review*, *93*(10), 96–114.

Rogers, E. M. (2003). *Diffusion of innovations* (5th ed.). Free Press.

Rüßmann, M., Lorenz, M., Gerbert, P., Waldner, M., Justus, J., Engel, P., & Harnisch, M. (2015). *Industry 4.0: The Future of Productivity and Growth in Manufacturing Industries*. Boston Consulting Group.

Rüßmann, M., Lorenz, M., Gerbert, P., Waldner, M., Justus, J., Engel, P., & Harnisch, M. (2018). *Industry 4.0: The future of productivity and growth in manufacturing industries*. Boston Consulting Group.

Schwab, K. (2017). *The Fourth Industrial Revolution*. Crown Business.

Venkatesh, V., Morris, M. G., Davis, G. B., & Davis, F. D. (2003). User acceptance of information technology: Toward a unified view. *Management Information Systems Quarterly*, *27*(3), 425–478.

Wamba, S. F., Akter, S., Edwards, A., Chopin, G., & Gnanzou, D. (2015). How 'big data' can make big impact: Findings from a systematic review and a longitudinal case study. *International Journal of Production Economics*, *165*, 234–246.

Chapter 9
Circular and Regenerative Economy in Industry 5.0: Human-Centric Innovation for Sustainable Industrial Transformation

Babak Jamshidi Naghani
https://orcid.org/0009-0006-5937-2230
Islamic Azad University, Tehran, Iran

ABSTRACT

This research examines the role of the circular and regenerative economy within the framework of Industry 5.0, and shows that the synergy between smart technologies, sustainable policymaking, and human values can form the foundation of the economy of the future. Relying on technologies such as digital twins, artificial intelligence, and blockchain, Industry 5.0 provides a platform in which economic growth, resource recovery, and social well-being can be realized simultaneously. The results show that the transition to a regenerative economy leads not only to environmental sustainability, but also to increased productivity and industrial innovation.

1- INTRODUCTION

Industrial developments over the past two centuries have always been based on increasing productivity, reducing costs, and improving the performance of production systems. From the era of steam engines to the digital revolution, the main goal of industry has been to optimize processes and expand markets through technological innovation. However, in the last decade, with the spread of environmental challeng-

DOI: 10.4018/979-8-3693-4525-2.ch009

es, the destruction of natural resources, and the crises caused by climate change, the traditional view of economic growth and industrialization has been faced with fundamental questions. In response to these challenges, the concept of Industry 5.0 has emerged as a new stage of industrial transformation; a stage that, unlike Industry 4.0's focus on digitalization and automation, emphasizes human-centeredness, sustainability, and resource regeneration (Rejeb et al., 2025).

In the framework of Industry 5.0, the economy is considered not as a purely production-oriented system, but as a dynamic network of interactions between technology, humans, and the environment. In the meantime, the concept of the Circular Economy is recognized as one of the key pillars of this transformation. Instead of the linear model of "produce-consume-dispose", the circular economy emphasizes the recovery of materials, the extension of product life and the reuse of resources. This approach reduces the pressure on natural resources, increases energy efficiency and creates new economic opportunities in the field of recycling, remanufacturing and sustainable design (Atif, 2023). But the approach that Industry 5.0 seeks goes beyond the mere circulation of resources; it moves towards a regenerative economy.

The regenerative economy seeks to create a system that not only reduces negative environmental impacts, but also actively contributes to the restoration of ecosystems, increasing social resilience and strengthening human capital. In such a model, the economy is considered as part of the living system of the planet and its role is to restore the balance between development and nature. This view is consistent with the principles of sustainability at a higher level, because instead of "reducing harm", the goal is to "create positive benefits for the whole system". In other words, in the regenerative economy, industries and organizations are considered "living systems" that evolve in continuous interaction with their surroundings (Lotfi et al., 2016).

Meanwhile, smart technologies in Industry 5.0 play a vital role in realizing the regenerative economy. Digital Twins, by enabling the modeling and simulation of the life cycle of products, allow companies to predict and modify the environmental impacts of their processes. Artificial intelligence and machine learning can analyze patterns of energy, waste and raw material consumption and guide economic decision-making towards the optimal use of resources. On the other hand, blockchain technology helps to provide transparency and traceability in circular supply chains, so that the path of each resource from production to recycling can be followed. These technologies are not only tools for increasing efficiency, but also the foundation of a data-driven and human-centered economy in which economic decisions are aligned with ethical and environmental criteria (Devender et al., 2025).

In the traditional approach of Industry 4.0, the main goal was to maximize efficiency through automation and reduce human costs. However, Industry 5.0 believes that technology should serve humans and the environment, not vice versa. For this reason, concepts such as Human–Robot Collaboration and Human-Centric Innovation are at the heart of this paradigm. This new economic approach does not see value only in financial profit, but defines it in the three dimensions of "economic value", "human value" and "ecological value". Therefore, the regenerative economy in Industry 5.0 emphasizes redefining the indicators of growth and success; Indicators in which social health, environmental quality, and ethical innovation are as important as profitability (Aliahmadi & Nozari, 2023).

From a policy perspective, the regenerative economy in Industry 5.0 offers an unprecedented opportunity to align economic and environmental goals. Governments and international organizations are developing policies that encourage investment in clean technologies, sustainable design, and smart supply chains. Initiatives such as the European Green Deal and the United Nations Sustainable Development Goals (UN SDGs) are in this direction, seeking to align future economic growth with the principles of regenerativeness and intergenerational justice. At the micro level, companies are also moving from linear to circular models and from a focus on ownership to a focus on "use," with services becoming the core of the business rather than products.

However, implementing the regenerative economy within the framework of Industry 5.0 also comes with challenges. The lack of coordination between technologies, the high cost of infrastructure transformation, and the cultural resistance of organizations to change are among the key obstacles. However, the future path shows that combining regenerative insight with the capabilities of smart technologies can lead to a self-healing, ethical, and efficient economy. Such an economy is not only able to reduce resource consumption, but can also create new capacities for innovation, sustainable employment, and human well-being.

Overall, Industry 5.0, relying on cognitive technologies and human values, provides the basis for the transition to an economy in which development, productivity, and sustainability are not in conflict with each other, but rather operate in a synergistic cycle. In this perspective, the circular and regenerative economy is not only an environmental strategy, but also a framework for redefining the meaning and purpose of the economy in the age of artificial intelligence and post-digitalization. This transition can be the basis for the formation of an industry that is beneficial to both people and the planet, and from which new models of sustainable growth and economic justice are born.

2- THEORETICAL BACKGROUND AND CONCEPTUAL FRAMEWORK

The circular and regenerative economy within the framework of Industry 5.0 is based on a rethinking of the concept of economic growth, productivity and value creation. Contrary to the traditional logic of the linear economy that emphasized extraction, production and uninterrupted consumption, this approach seeks to design a system that redefines the cycles of materials, energy and value and maintains the dynamics between humans, technology and nature in a synergistic structure (Aliahmadi et al., 2022). Relying on the principles of human-centeredness, resilience and sustainability, Industry 5.0 provides a platform for emerging technologies to act not only as means of production, but also as learning and adaptive agents in the service of recreating economic and environmental systems.

In the meantime, the concept of circular economy (Circular Economy) as the theoretical foundation of regenerative economy focuses on closing the loops of resource flows. Its main goal is to prevent waste and redesign products and processes in such a way that materials and energy remain in the production and consumption cycles. This approach is based on three fundamental principles: eliminating waste through smart design, reusing resources at different levels of the value chain, and restoring natural systems as part of economic performance (Manetti et al., 2025). However, the circular economy focuses mainly on efficiency and effectiveness, while the regenerative economy goes a step further and seeks to restore social and ecological systems. In this approach, economic value is created through processes that simultaneously lead to the growth of natural, human, and social capital, rather than simply reproducing materials or energy.

The regenerative economy, with its systemic and holistic perspective, is inspired by the theories of industrial ecology and bio-based economics. In this view, companies and industries are considered as living entities that are in constant interaction with their environment and must be able to learn, adapt and reinvent themselves in response to changes. This logic is consistent with the principles of Industry 5.0, as both emphasize the coexistence of humans and technology for long-term sustainability (Aliahmadi et al., 2023). As a result, the regenerative economy can be considered a more human and evolved dimension of the circular economy, which, instead of reducing negative impacts, aims to create positive impacts for the entire system.

From a theoretical perspective, Industry 5.0 provides an environment in which cognitive technologies, artificial intelligence and cyber-physical systems can shift economic performance from a linear logic to a circular and regenerative logic. In this framework, digital twins play the role of a bridge between the physical and digital worlds. By collecting real-time data from equipment, processes, and the environment, this technology enables the simulation and optimization of the entire value chain. As a result, economic decision-making is not based on static data, but on dynamic, learning feedback. This enables manufacturing systems to move towards "regenerative learning," that is, the ability to rebuild themselves in response to environmental pressures or market changes (Szmelter-Jarosz & Nozari, 2025).

On the other hand, artificial intelligence and machine learning act as the engine of analysis and prediction in this framework. By analyzing vast amounts of data, these technologies can identify points of waste, inefficiency, and resource degradation and provide suggestions for process redesign. For example, in regenerative economy models, deep learning algorithms can determine the optimal path for reusing materials or designing products with longer lifespans. In this way, smart technologies become not only production tools but also "decision-makers" in the direction of regeneration.

Blockchain technology is also considered as a factor of trust and transparency in this context. Using distributed ledgers, it is possible to record and track the path of materials, energy and products from origin to destination. This makes economic cycles more transparent, responsible and reliable. Also, 3D printing technology and additive manufacturing enable local and recycling-oriented production and reduce the consumption of new resources. Combining these technologies with green policies and collaborative business models paves the way for the realization of a regenerative economy in Industry 5.0.

In the theoretical dimension, the conceptual framework of this research (Figure 1) is based on the interaction of three main domains: smart technologies, humans, and the economic-environmental ecosystem. In this model, smart technologies including artificial intelligence, digital twins, and blockchain act as engines supporting regenerative decision-making. Humans are at the center of this system; not simply as labor, but as creative, ethical, and learning agents who guide technology towards social and environmental values. Ultimately, the economic-environmental ecosystem is the implementation platform for this interaction, in which policies, investments, and material flows are synergistically rearranged to lead to a dynamic balance between economic growth and sustainability (Narula et al., 2023).

Figure 1. Conceptual framework for circular and regenerative economy in Industry 5.0

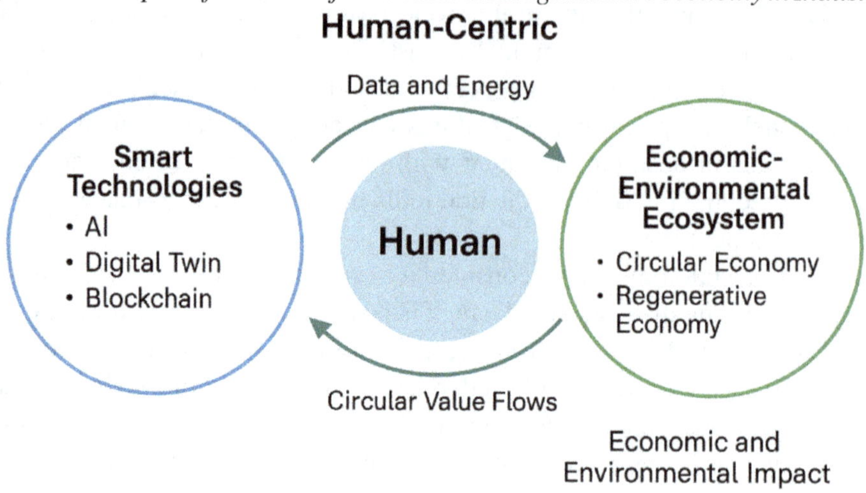

This conceptual framework shows that the regenerative economy in Industry 5.0 is not simply a sustainable production system, but a learning and self-healing ecosystem. The stronger the interaction between digital technologies, human values, and regenerative policies, the greater the system's capacity to innovate, reduce waste, and recover resources. Compared to previous approaches, this model emphasizes the combination of artificial intelligence and human ethics to guide economic decision-making. As a result, regeneration occurs not only at the resource level, but also at the level of mental, cultural, and organizational structures.

Ultimately, the theoretical foundations of the regenerative economy in Industry 5.0 seek to return to a balance between technology and nature. This view suggests that the future of the global economy depends on our ability to design systems that can be simultaneously creative, adaptable, and regenerative. If the circular economy is about closing the loop, the regenerative economy is about "bringing the loop back to life," and Industry 5.0 provides the platform for this idea to be realized by combining technological intelligence with human understanding.

3- KEY ENABLERS AND TECHNOLOGIES IN INDUSTRY 5.0

Achieving a circular and regenerative economy in Industry 5.0 is not possible without relying on smart technologies and digital infrastructure. In fact, technology in this framework is not seen as a mere tool, but as a factor of systemic transformation and a facilitator of the dynamics between humans, machines and the environment. The transition from Industry 4.0 to 5.0 represents a shift from a focus on technical efficiency to human-technological synergy and regenerative value creation, where cognitive technologies, machine learning, digital twins and blockchain-based supply chains provide new foundations for economic and environmental decision-making (Nozari & Samadi, 2025).

One of the most fundamental technologies of Industry 5.0 is Artificial Intelligence, which, by analyzing big data, plays the role of the decision-making brain in industrial systems. In the context of the regenerative economy, AI can build predictive models that help organizations predict the environmental impacts of production at different stages of design, production, and recycling. For example, deep learning algorithms can identify optimal material return paths in supply chains and minimize waste. In addition, AI in Industry 5.0 has been developed in the form of cognitive AI, a type of intelligence that not only analyzes data, but also understands the meaning, purpose, and human context of decisions. Such a capability strengthens the link between technology and human values, leading to the creation of ethical and sustainable decisions (Nozari et al., 2025).

Along with AI, the concept of the digital twin has become one of the main pillars of industrial transformation. Digital twins are virtual models of physical processes that simulate the behavior of real systems in real time. In the circular economy, this technology enables organizations to track and optimize the entire life cycle of products, from design to use and recycling, in a data-driven manner. Using digital twins, factories can calculate environmental impacts before they occur and implement corrective measures in real time. Furthermore, by connecting digital twins to artificial intelligence networks, a type of self-regenerative learning is formed, in which systems can automatically optimize, reduce energy and increase efficiency (Chaikovska et al., 2024).

Another key technology is blockchain, which brings transparency, trust and traceability to circular supply chains. In regenerative models, blockchain ensures that the path of every material and product from origin to destination can be tracked and validated. This transparency not only increases trust between economic actors, but also lays the foundation for new financial systems, such as regenerative tokens and digital carbon credits, that incentivize sustainable behavior. Blockchain can also be a tool for implementing smart contracts, contracts that are automatically activated only when certain environmental or social conditions are met. In this way, distributed ledger technology becomes a transparent and automated governance mechanism for the regenerative economy (Abdi & Nozari, 2025).

Cobot technology also plays a central role in Industry 5.0. Unlike traditional robots, these robots are designed to work safely with humans and work in shared environments. The presence of cobots in production processes increases flexibility and reduces human risks, while humans can focus on creative decisions, redesign, and innovation. This human-machine interaction results in a unique combination of technological productivity and human intelligence, a combination that forms the essence of Industry 5.0.

At the infrastructure level, the Industrial Internet of Things (IIoT) and Edge & Cloud Computing play a facilitating role in the communication between system components. Connected sensor networks collect environmental and operational data in real time and transmit it to analysis and control algorithms via cloud platforms. This chain of communication enables real-time management of production, consumption, and recycling cycles, transforming the system from a static state to a dynamic and learning state. Furthermore, combining IIoT with blockchain can ensure traceability and security of circular data, while combining it with artificial intelligence enables automated decision-making and continuous optimization (Nozari & Samadi, 2025).

Additive Manufacturing and Bio-Design technologies have also opened up new avenues for regenerative manufacturing. 3D printing enables the production of recyclable and personalized products using recycled materials and modular design. Bio-Design, on the other hand, focuses on drawing inspiration from natural patterns to produce products and structures that have the least destructive impact and the most environmental compatibility. In fact, rather than imitating linear industrial processes, these technologies follow the logic of living systems, a system in which each component serves the regeneration and sustainability of the whole.

Together, these technologies create a framework in which data, energy, and value move cyclically between humans, machines, and ecosystems. This technological synergy is the basis of the regenerative economy in Industry 5.0. Instead of being a tool for speeding up production, technology has now become a means of restoring the environment, enhancing collective intelligence, and creating sustainable value. As a result, the boundary between technology and the environment is blurring; factories are no longer mere places of production, but learning and regenerative organisms that transform data into value, and value into sustainability.

Ultimately, Industry 5.0 technologies provide the platform for a smart and regenerative economy in which every industrial process is not only more efficient but also more environmentally friendly. By creating transparency, continuous learning, and human-machine collaboration, these technologies create conditions where economic growth no longer means environmental degradation, but rather a sign of a balance between technological progress and planetary survival.

4- ECONOMIC AND POLICY DIMENSIONS

The circular and regenerative economy in Industry 5.0 is not just a technological transformation, but a structural shift in the logic of the global economy. This shift moves from models based on relentless extraction and consumption to models based on value regeneration, resource efficiency, and economic coexistence with the environment. From an economic perspective, this approach means a transition from quantitative to qualitative growth; growth in which the criterion for success is not an increase in GDP, but rather the promotion of resilience, social sustainability, and the restoration of natural capital (Nozari, Nassar, & Szmelter-Jarosz, 2025).

In this context, Industry 5.0 provides a platform for the formation of a new generation of economic models in which smart technologies, environmental data, and human values are simultaneously involved in economic decision-making. Among these models, one can mention the data-driven regenerative economy; a model in which data is considered the main source of value creation. In such a system, data from digital twins, sensors, and blockchain platforms are key tools for designing efficient policies and economic decision-making. This data increases transparency in the flow of materials and energy, allowing for optimal allocation of resources based on real-time analytics (Nozari, Szmelter-Jarosz, & Weiland, 2025).

At the macro level, the regenerative economy is related to the concept of "regenerative capitalism." This perspective sees the economy as part of a planetary ecosystem that should function not on destruction but on regeneration. In such a model, governments and policy-making institutions play a key role in designing incentives, standards, and financial mechanisms to facilitate the transition from a linear to a circular economy. Carbon credits and green taxes, which factor the environmental costs of production into economic decisions, are effective tools in this direction. Investment in clean technologies, renewable energy and sustainable design can also drive the growth of a regenerative economy (Rathi & Kathuria, 2025).

At the international policy level, the European Union has established a framework, with programmes such as the European Green Deal and the Circular Economy Action Plan, that aims not only to reduce greenhouse gas emissions but also to fundamentally change consumption and production patterns. These policies are aligned with Industry 5.0, as both seek to create a smart and human-centered system in which economic growth coexists with the conservation of natural resources. In industrialized countries, policymakers are looking for tools to measure new indicators of regenerative growth; indicators such as Regenerative GDP, Circular Resource Index and Human Value Contribution, which measure the ratio between economic efficiency and positive environmental impacts (Nozari, Abdi, et al., 2025).

Figure 2 illustrates this relationship in the form of a multi-level policy and economic model. In this model, the first level includes smart technologies and data infrastructure that provide the information necessary for economic and environmental analyses. The second level includes organizations and industries that use this data to develop circular and regenerative business models. The third level includes policymakers and governance institutions that make sustainability part of the economic system by developing regulations, creating financial incentives, and designing assessment systems. The two-way interaction between these three levels leads to the formation of a regenerative economy in the context of Industry 5.0.

Figure 2. Multilevel model of economic and policy dimensions of the regenerative economy in Industry 5.0

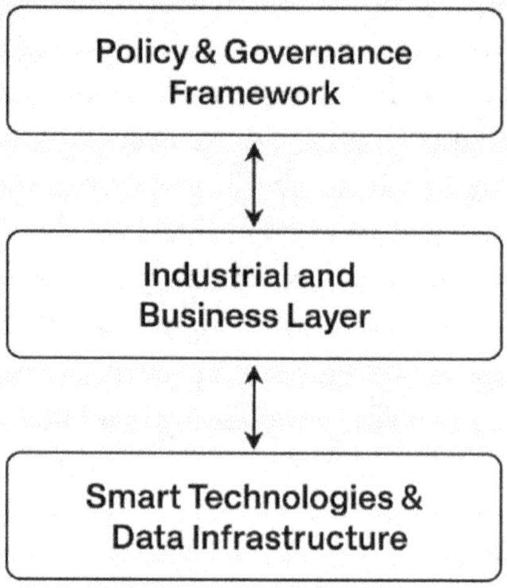

An important economic dimension in this framework is the cost-benefit analysis of the transition from a linear to a circular system. Although the implementation of regenerative policies initially requires significant investment in technology and human resource training, in the long run it leads to reduced production costs, increased productivity and strengthened economic resilience. Recent research has shown that countries that have institutionalized the circular economy approach in their industrial policies have saved up to 25% in raw material consumption and reduced energy costs by up to 15%. In addition, the creation of new markets for repair, recycling and redesign services creates diverse job opportunities that are in line with green employment policies (Nozari, 2025a).

From a social justice perspective, the regenerative economy seeks to democratize economic benefits. This means a more equitable distribution of resources and a redefinition of the concept of ownership. Models such as Product-as-a-Service and Collaborative Consumption are replacing individual ownership, and consumers are becoming active users in the value chain. This structural change requires institutional and cultural reforms to increase collaboration between the private sector, government and civil society.

In the policy dimension, the creation of coordinated mechanisms between national, regional and global levels is of particular importance. The regenerative economy is a borderless concept; for this reason, international cooperation in the areas of technology transfer, data standardization and carbon market regulation is essential. In this regard, global organizations such as UNEP, OECD and WEF are developing frameworks to support a just transition to a regenerative economy. These frameworks focus on aligning industrial policies with the Sustainable Development Goals, and creating new financial ecosystems for green investment.

Overall, the economic and political dimensions of Industry 5.0 show that the future of the global economy is moving towards participatory, ethical and intelligent models. This approach is based on the interaction between technology, people and politics and aims to create a balance between economic growth, environmental sustainability and social justice. The stronger the synergy between these three dimensions, the faster the regenerative economy will transform from a theoretical concept into an operational reality. In the meantime, the role of governments as designers of comprehensive policies and industrial institutions as implementers of change is decisive. The future of Industry 5.0 lies not in the accumulation of capital, but in the ability to regenerate human resources and values.

5- INDUSTRIAL APPLICATIONS

The circular and regenerative economy in Industry 5.0 is no longer just a theoretical concept, but is already being implemented in a significant way in various industrial sectors. Leading companies and industries have realized that combining smart technologies with sustainability principles not only reduces environmental impacts, but also increases efficiency, innovation and competitiveness in the global market. In this direction, key technologies such as artificial intelligence, digital twins, blockchain and additive manufacturing have provided the main platform for implementing regenerative solutions in various industries (Alaeddini et al., 2025).

In the field of advanced manufacturing, companies are moving from traditional mass production models to flexible and data-driven models. This transformation has led to factories becoming learning and self-regulating systems. For example, the use of digital twins in production lines allows factories to monitor and analyze the life cycle of materials, energy, and waste at any given moment. This information is used, with the help of artificial intelligence algorithms, to modify process design, reduce waste, and recycle materials in real time. As a result, energy efficiency is increased and operating costs are reduced, without compromising product quality (Nozari, 2026b).

In the chemical and advanced materials industries, the implementation of regenerative economy principles has revolutionized product design and supply chains. Many chemical companies are using blockchain technology to track chemical compounds throughout the value chain to ensure that recycled or bio-based materials are used in new processes. Also, the use of life cycle analysis and data-driven models in product design decisions has helped companies minimize their environmental impacts. By adopting regenerative models, these industries have not only achieved carbon and waste reduction, but also created new business opportunities through recycling and remanufacturing of materials.

In the automotive industry, the transition to sustainable production is accelerating. By combining digital technologies and artificial intelligence, car manufacturers have created models in which car parts are designed to be highly recyclable and remanufacturable. Digital twins in this sector serve as a key tool to track the condition of parts throughout the vehicle's life and predict the need for repair or replacement. As a result, cars not only last longer, but their components are also re-entered the production cycle after the end of their useful life. This is a clear example of the regenerative economy, in which no material is considered final waste (Aivazidou et al., 2025).

In the energy and industrial infrastructure sector, Industry 5.0 technologies have enabled the creation of regenerative energy systems. Smart Grids use machine learning algorithms to regulate supply and demand at the regional level and optimally use renewable energies such as solar and wind. Digital twins of power plants also play an important role in predicting system performance and reducing energy waste. In addition, the development of energy storage systems based on recyclable materials and the modular design of industrial equipment have ensured infrastructure sustainability at the infrastructure level. In this way, the energy industry is transforming from a mere consumer of natural resources to a regenerative actor that contributes to ecological balance.

The electronics and information technology industries are also among the most important areas for implementing the principles of the circular economy in the 5.0 era. These industries face a serious challenge of e-waste due to the high speed of innovation and the short life cycle of products. To address this challenge, manufacturers are using smart technologies to design circuits and devices that are easy to upgrade, repair, and recycle. In addition, blockchain-based platforms help companies track the path of rare materials such as lithium or cobalt throughout the supply chain and prevent irresponsible mining. As a result, the electronics industry is moving towards a model in which value lies not only in selling a new device, but also in continuing the life cycle of existing products.

In the agriculture and food industry, Industry 5.0 technologies are paving the way for regenerative agriculture. The use of smart sensors, drones, and data-driven predictive models has led to more accurate use of water, soil, and energy resources. Data collected from farms is analyzed with the help of digital twins, and management decisions about irrigation, fertilization, and harvesting are made optimally. Also, food supply chain systems using blockchain have full traceability from farm to consumer. This transparency has reduced food waste and increased consumer trust in sustainable products (Yin et al., 2024).

A regenerative economy is also emerging in the sustainable building and architecture industries. Smart buildings use real-time monitoring technologies to monitor energy consumption, air quality, and material sustainability. The use of recyclable materials, modular design, and 3D printing in construction allows for non-destructive renovation and redevelopment. In this area, urban digital twins are effective tools for simulating energy consumption, analyzing environmental flows, and optimizing urban infrastructure. This approach transforms cities into living, regenerative systems in which the economy, humans, and nature interact in a dynamic cycle.

Finally, a review of industrial applications shows that Industry 5.0 is not just a step towards automation, but a fundamental move towards reshaping the global production and consumption system. In this system, each industry becomes part of an intelligent, human-centered and sustainable ecosystem, rather than focusing on material outputs. Implementing a regenerative economy in different industries, especially with the support of national policies and technological innovation, can lead to a future in which economic growth is aligned with environmental protection and social well-being.

6- FUTURE RESEARCH DIRECTIONS

The transformation towards a circular and regenerative economy in Industry 5.0 is still in its infancy and requires extensive theoretical, applied and policy research to develop a sustainable and globally applicable framework. While key technologies such as digital twins, artificial intelligence and blockchain have shaped the foundation of this transformation, fundamental questions about the measurement, evaluation and governance of the regenerative economy remain unanswered. Future research in this area should seek models that place not only technological efficiency, but also human, ethical and environmental values at the center of industrial decision-making.

One of the most important future directions is the development of quantitative frameworks and analytical indicators to measure economic and environmental regeneration. Many existing models only assess mitigating impacts (such as carbon reduction or energy savings), while a regenerative economy requires measuring positive indicators such as "increased natural capital", "restored ecosystems" or "increased human well-being". The creation of indicators such as Regenerative GDP, Circular Impact Score or Human-Centric Value Index could provide new decision-making tools for governments and companies. Future research should focus on developing these metrics through real-time data from digital twins and AI analytics.

Another area of research is integrating machine learning with regenerative policymaking. Currently, most economic decisions rely on historical data, while adaptive learning algorithms can adjust policies based on environmental feedback in real time. Interdisciplinary research between data science, economics and public policy can lead to the development of "Smart Policy Systems" that propose dynamic adjustments to green taxes, renewable energy subsidies or carbon credits through automated data analysis. Such an approach means creating a system that learns, is flexible and relies on real-time evidence.

Another key future direction is the modeling of regenerative economies at the urban and regional scale. As major centers of resource consumption and waste generation, cities play a crucial role in achieving regenerative goals. The development of "urban digital twins" that simulate the interaction between energy, transport, buildings and consumption can help design urban policies based on the circulation of resources. This research path requires collaboration between the fields of urban engineering, environmental sciences and sustainable economics so that future cities can be self-healing from an economic, social and environmental perspective.

Another research horizon is to examine the role of humans and ethics in the regenerative economy. Although Industry 5.0 emphasizes human-centeredness, it is still unclear how to maintain the boundary between algorithmic decisions and human values. Research should seek to design algorithms that are not only efficient, but also ethical and incorporate principles such as justice, transparency, and social welfare into economic decision-making. Areas such as "algorithmic ethics," "human data sovereignty," and "social design of technology" are gaining increasing importance in this regard.

On the other hand, future research should focus on developing regenerative business models and innovative financial mechanisms. Models such as Product-as-a-Service, Regenerative Supply Contracts, and Circular Finance Platforms can form the foundation of a new economy in which profitability and sustainability are not in conflict. Exploring ways to finance regenerative projects through instruments such as "smart green bonds" or "impact investing" could open up new avenues in finance research. These studies could show how supportive policies and private sector investment can work synergistically to accelerate the transition to a regenerative economy.

Finally, the future of Industry 5.0 research requires a transdisciplinary and hybrid approach. The transition from a linear economy to a regenerative economy is possible not with a single technology, but with synergies between engineering sciences, behavioral economics, policy, system design, and data science. Future research should use hybrid models, including dynamic simulation, explainable artificial intelligence (XAI), and multi-factor analysis, to gain a deeper understanding of the dynamics of regenerative processes at different economic and industrial levels.

In general, futures research in this area should seek to answer the central question: How can we design a system that simultaneously fosters economic growth, resource regeneration, and human well-being? The answer to this question will determine not only the direction of academic research, but also the path of industrial development and global policymaking in the coming decades.

7- CONCLUSION

Industry 5.0 can be considered a turning point in the evolution of the world's industrial and economic systems; a stage that has crossed the boundary of automation and mere productivity and entered a realm where humans, technology and nature are in a regenerative and synergistic cycle. This research showed that the circular and regenerative economy is not only an environmental necessity, but also an economic and technological strategy that can redefine the path of future industrial development. By integrating smart technologies such as digital twins, cognitive artificial intelligence, blockchain and collaborative robots, Industry 5.0 has been able to provide a platform in which economic growth and environmental sustainability are not in conflict with each other, but are two complementary dimensions of a dynamic and self-healing system.

In this framework, the circular economy as a theoretical basis and the regenerative economy as its evolved form play an important role in redesigning the value creation system. In the linear economy, value was defined based on extraction, production and consumption; but in the regenerative economy, value is obtained from the restoration of resources, increasing resilience, and creating positive environmental and social impacts. This shift in economic logic has broad implications for policymaking, industrial design and consumption patterns. Industry 5.0, with its human-centered approach, emphasizes constructive interaction between humans and machines instead of eliminating human labor from the production process, and in this way, links technological productivity with human creativity.

The results of this research indicate that the key technologies of Industry 5.0, including digital twins, blockchain, industrial Internet of Things and artificial intelligence, constitute the main pillars of the realization of the regenerative economy. These technologies enable real-time monitoring of resources, analysis of life-cycle data, and prediction of the behavior of production systems. As a result, economic decision-making is based on accurate, transparent, and up-to-date data. Meanwhile, blockchain technology, by creating trust and traceability in supply chains, has paved the way for the transition to a transparent and ethical economy. This technological synergy not only leads to waste reduction and energy optimization, but also allows the design of new economic models in which profitability, responsibility, and sustainability are pursued simultaneously.

From a policy perspective, Industry 5.0 has provided a historic opportunity to redefine the relationship between the economy, technology, and governance. As noted in the previous sections, the transition from a linear economy to a regenerative economy requires multi-level policy frameworks in which technology, industry, and government are coordinated. The research showed that instruments such as green taxes, carbon credits, regenerative subsidies and new growth indicators can smooth the path of this transition. Future industrial policies must be based on data dynamics, scientific evidence and environmental feedback, so that they can be flexible in the face of rapid technological and climate change.

On the other hand, the industrial applications examined in this study show that the regenerative economy is being implemented widely in various fields; from advanced manufacturing and automotive to smart agriculture and sustainable architecture. In all of these cases, the common principle is that Industry 5.0 technologies allow industries to regenerate resources instead of just producing them. For example, digital twins in the manufacturing and energy industries act as a key tool for simulating and optimizing the resource cycle, while blockchain ensures supply chain transparency and artificial intelligence provides new paths to reduce waste and redesign processes. These findings show that implementing a regenerative economy in Industry 5.0 is not only environmentally necessary, but also economically sustainable, creating a competitive advantage.

The future research directions proposed in this study also show that there is still much work to be done in the field of regenerative economy in Industry 5.0. Developing new indicators to measure regenerativeness, designing data-driven decision-making models for dynamic policymaking, and integrating data science with human ethics are among the most important future research priorities. The focus of futures research will be on creating learning and self-organizing economies; systems that are able to adjust their performance through real-time feedback and achieve a balance between growth and sustainability.

Overall, it can be concluded that Industry 5.0 and the regenerative economy are a fundamental step towards a sustainable industrial civilization. In this new civilization, technology is not a means to dominate nature, but a means to harmonize and coexist with it. This research emphasizes that the future of the global economy depends on our ability to design systems that can simultaneously produce economic, social, and environmental value. If Industry 4.0 represented a revolution in efficiency, Industry 5.0 is the manifestation of technological humanism and ethical economics.

Ultimately, the success of this transition requires collaboration between three key areas: knowledge, technology, and governance. Universities must develop new theoretical frameworks for a regenerative economy; industries must integrate technological innovation with sustainability principles; and governments must design appropriate support policies and incentive systems. Only through this multilevel synergy can we build a future in which industrial growth is aligned with planetary regeneration and the promotion of human dignity. The regenerative economy in Industry 5.0 is a vision for a world where production does not mean destruction, but rather regeneration, learning, and excellence.

REFERENCES

Abdi, H., & Nozari, H. (2025). AIoE-Enhanced Multi-objective Optimization for Sustainable Bioprocesses in Smart Bioreactors. In *Artificial Intelligence of Everything and Sustainable Development* (pp. 19–38). Springer Nature Singapore.

[] Aivazidou, E., Tsolakis, N., & Mollona, E. (2025). Circular Economy 5.0 on Its Way: A Digital Sustainability Transition. Academy of Management Perspectives, (ja), amp-2023.

Alaeddini, M., Mallek, S., & Hönigsberg, S. (2025). Uncovering Research Trends: A Textual Analysis of AI Applications in Circular Economy under an Industry 5.0 Paradigm. *IFAC-PapersOnLine*, *59*(10), 214–219.

Aliahmadi, A., Ghahremani-Nahr, J., & Nozari, H. (2023). Pricing decisions in the closed-loop supply chain network, taking into account the queuing system in production centers. *Expert Systems with Applications*, *212*, 118741.

Aliahmadi, A., & Nozari, H. (2023, January). Evaluation of security metrics in AIoT and blockchain-based supply chain by Neutrosophic decision-making method. In Supply chain forum: an international journal (Vol. 24, No. 1, pp. 31-42). Taylor & Francis.

Aliahmadi, A., Nozari, H., Ghahremani-Nahr, J., & Szmelter-Jarosz, A. (2022). Evaluation of key impression of resilient supply chain based on artificial intelligence of things (AIoT). arXiv preprint arXiv:2207.13174.

Atif, S. (2023). Analysing the alignment between circular economy and industry 4.0 nexus with industry 5.0 era: An integrative systematic literature review. *Sustainable Development*, *31*(4), 2155–2175.

Chaikovska, I., Hryhoruk, P., Khrushch, N., Grygoruk, S., Tkach, T., & Chaikovskyi, M. (2024, September). Integration of Digital Economy, Knowledge Economy and Circular Economy in the Conditions of Industry 5.0. In 2024 14th International Conference on Advanced Computer Information Technologies (ACIT) (pp. 250-253). IEEE.

Devender, K. Kafila, Goli, G., & Shravan, M. (2025). Circular Economy Concept for Small Medium Enterprises Through Industry 5.0. In Sustainable Economy Models in the Age of Industry 5.0 (pp. 101-118). Singapore: Springer Nature Singapore.

Lotfi, F. H. Z., Najafi, S. E., & Nozari, H. (Eds.). (2016). *Data envelopment analysis and effective performance assessment*. IGI Global.

Manetti, S., Ni, M., Supino, S., & Troisi, O. (2025). Rethinking the circular economy in agri-food: Human-centred AI for a new circular economy 5.0 paradigm. *British Food Journal*, •••, 1–22.

Narula, S., Tamvada, J. P., Kumar, A., Puppala, H., & Gupta, N. (2023). Putting digital technologies at the forefront of Industry 5.0 for the implementation of a circular economy in manufacturing industries. *IEEE Transactions on Engineering Management*, *71*, 3363–3374.

[] Nozari, H. (2025). Integrating Neuromorphic Intelligence with Fuzzy Multi-Objective Models in Resilient Green Supply Chain Design. Process Integration and Optimization for Sustainability, 1-14.

Nozari, H. (2026). Combining Digital Twin and Metaverse for Immersive Marketing Experiences. In Improving Consumer Engagement in Digital Marketing Through Cognitive AI (pp. 289-310). IGI Global Scientific Publishing.

Nozari, H., Abdi, H., Szmelter-Jarosz, A., & Rahmaty, M. (2025). A digital twin-based neutrosophic multi-objective optimization model for smart supply chains in the food industry. *Journal of Intelligent Manufacturing*, •••, 1–15.

Nozari, H., Nassar, S., & Szmelter-Jarosz, A. (2025). Fuzzy multi-objective optimization model for resilient supply chain financing based on blockchain and IoT. *Digital*, *5*(3), 32.

Nozari, H., & Samadi, S. (2025). Digital Twin-Enhanced Sentiment Analysis for Targeted Marketing Optimization. In Dynamic and Safe Economy in the Age of Smart Technologies (pp. 121-138). IGI Global Scientific Publishing.

Nozari, H., & Samadi, S. (2025). AIoE-Powered Neuromarketing for Decoding the Consumer Brain. In *Artificial Intelligence of Everything and Sustainable Development* (pp. 39–53). Springer Nature Singapore.

Nozari, H., Szmelter-Jarosz, A., & Samadi, S. (2025). Machine Learning Models for Energy Optimization and Resource Consumption in Smart Factories. In *Artificial Intelligence of Everything and Sustainable Development* (pp. 175–189). Springer Nature Singapore.

Nozari, H., Szmelter-Jarosz, A., & Weiland, D. (2025). A Fuzzy Multi-Objective Sustainable and Agile Supply Chain Model Based on Digital Twin and Internet of Things with Adaptive Learning Under Environmental Uncertainty. *Applied Sciences (Basel, Switzerland)*, *15*(19), 10399.

Rathi, G., & Kathuria, S. (2025). Transforming Circular Economy Through Industry 5.0: A Deep Dive into Sustainable Innovations. In *Sustainable Economy Models in the Age of Industry 5.0* (pp. 253–274). Springer Nature Singapore.

Rejeb, A., Rejeb, K., Keogh, J. G., & Süle, E. (2025). When Industry 5.0 meets the circular economy: A systematic literature review. *Circular Economy and Sustainability*, •••, 1–32.

Szmelter-Jarosz, A., & Nozari, H. (2025). AI-Driven Decision Intelligence and Human-AI Collaboration in Economic Systems. In Dynamic and Safe Economy in the Age of Smart Technologies (pp. 171-190). IGI Global Scientific Publishing.

Yin, S., Liu, L., & Mahmood, T. (2024). New trends in sustainable development for industry 5.0: Digital green innovation economy. *Green and Low-Carbon Economy*, *2*(4), 269–276.

Chapter 10
Exploring the Dimensions and Indicators of the Digital Economy in the Age of Industry 5.0

Emil Joseph
https://orcid.org/0000-0002-0479-6929
St. Joseph's College of Commerce, Bengaluru, India

ABSTRACT

The 5th industrial revolution is a pioneer in the industry adjusting for both advanced technologies and human-centric-sustainable solutions, playing an important role that also brings us to a highly skilled workforce besides its adaptability. In this paper, the essence and its parts of the digital economy in Industry 5.0 have been analyzed. Besides, light is shed on important indicators that can lead industry to productivity improvement and enhance/GDP growth and economic development. These are all based around the three core pillars of sustainability, human-centricity, and resilience - demanding industrial progression to be more sustainable, being contextually matched with environmental responsibility, and valuing worker welfare. Capital investment in artificial intelligence (AI), the Internet of Things (IoT), robotics, additive manufacturing, and augmented reality (AR) can seem essential to this advancement. It utilizes AI and machine learning for real-time production, predictive maintenance, and quality control.

DOI: 10.4018/979-8-3693-4525-2.ch010

INTRODUCTION

Over time, the continuum of industrial paradigms has elevated us to the Industry 5.0 era — one that combines human-centric principles with emerging digital technologies, collectively catalyzing the development of sustainable and inclusive industry ecosystems. This paradigm shift is even more pronounced than the automation and digitalization pathway addressed in Industry 4.0, now with a focus on the symbiosis of human creativity, invention, and technical innovation for sustainable impacts both economically and socially (European Commission, 2021). Through the lens of Industry 5.0, this introduction investigates potential dimensions and components as well as key indicators in terms about innovation and digital economy by providing an overview on how that new industrial era intends to change our production processes & societal implications Industry 5.0 seeks to build on and augment the tenets of Industry 4.0, emphasizing across its planning three key dimensions: sustainability, human-centredness (tending back towards). In Industry 5.0, sustainability is a holistic term that extends beyond the elimination of waste and minimization of environmental footprint to a circular economy, where resources are utilized efficiently through low-waste production methodologies, recycling strategies, and other sustainable practices (Breque et al., 2021). In Industry 5.0, it is people who are the focus of production processes, which(Peltokorpi & Michel, 2021) Entails workplaces that allow for inclusive, flexible, and health-promoting work situations. It attempts to utilize human consciousness in its ability to address complex problem-solving engagements. At the same time, it introduces modern technologies, such as AI and robotics, to automate repetitive and hazardous jobs (Journal of Cloud Computing, 2021). The European Commission (2021) also emphasizes the importance of resilience in Industry 5.0, including resilient supply chains and production systems that can cope with, adapt to, or even benefit from disruptions such as the COVID-19 pandemic.

Let us understand the Components of the Digital Economy in Industry 5.0

In this context, the digital economy of Industry 5.0 is driven by several components that operate together to drive innovation and economic development. Leading-edge manufacturing capabilities, sophisticated data analytics, and an overarching vision for human-machine collaboration characterize these elements. Advanced Manufacturing Technologies: Industry 5.0 leverages the most advanced technologies, including AI, IoT, and robotics, to design production processes that incorporate a high level of automation at every stage. Such technologies allow both real-time and remote monitoring of manufacturing operations, which is extremely beneficial in terms of efficiency and productivity. For example, technology such as collaborative robots (cobots) helps human workers with tasks that require high skill levels and precision, while also reducing the risk of injury (European Commission, 2021).

Intelligent Input/Output: In Industry 5.0, the robust collection and analysis of quantities of data grows to constitute a foundation stone in how the digital economy functions on this level. With the help of advanced data analytics tools, companies can see inside their operations, discover trends, and make more fact-based decisions. This streamlined data approach enables organizations to fine-tune their supply chains, enhance product quality, and reduce operational costs (Journal of Cloud Computing, 2021). One main feature of Industry 5.0 is a focus on the collaboration between humans and machines. Rather than the fully automated systems of Industry 4.0, this fifth industrial revolution envisions a future where humans and machines collaborate seamlessly without interruption. Technologies like AR (Augmented Reality) and VR (Virtual Reality) enable more effective collaboration by providing workers with access to real-time information and guidance. Manufacturers are looking to Industry 5.0 as an opportunity for humans and machines to work together, encouraging manufacturers to facilitate a re-capture of the benefits that come with people joining forces alongside Industry 4.0 (Rastogi et al., 2019).

Digital Economy Industry 5.0 Key Performance Indicators

Several key indicators can be used to measure the progress and impact of Industry 5.0 as the digital economy evolves, including: These indicators are important to assess whether companies are performing well in the new industrial paradigm and whether economies will recover.(Benevene et al., 2022).

Digital Adoption Rate: It is one of the key indicators for calculating the maturity of a country's digital economy. Moreover, in this context, technologies such as AI, IoT, robotics, and other advanced technologies are also employed. In turn, the higher adoption rate signals a strong disposition for innovation and a willingness to change established behavior (European Commission, 2021).

Productivity and Efficiency Perks: The impact of Industry 5.0 on productivity and efficiency can be evaluated by monitoring specific key performance indicators (KPIs), including changes in production output, operating costs, and resource utilization. The results in these domains demonstrate evidence that companies are effectively utilizing digital technology to enhance their operations (Breque et al., 2021).

Employability & Skill Formation: Next, adaptability and skill formation among the workforce will be a stark indicator that demands attention. In other words, Industry 5.0 is about lifelong learning and upskilling to make it possible for workers to cooperate efficiently with technologies of the future. This can also be measured using training programs, certifications, and employee satisfaction surveys (Journal of Cloud Computing | Full Text).

Environmental Impact: One of the dimensions on which Industry 5.0 bases its model is sustainability, and monitoring environmental impact caused by manufacturing processes should be done in these settings(Obrenovic et al., 2020). These include reductions in waste, energy use, and carbon emissions. Organizations that have successfully implemented sustainable policies are contributing to a greener economy, and those that want to demonstrate their initiative towards the environment (European Commission, 2021).

Innovation and R&D Spend: It is the percentage of investment in research and development(R&D) that clearly shows how much an organization has invested to bring innovation. Industry 5.0 promotes the adoption of new technologies and solutions on a large scale, continually offering opportunities to explore and expand technological horizons, thereby facilitating further progress. A senior research manager said: “The higher R&D spend shows that EU firms are taking a proactive view, investing money into keeping pace in the tough global industrial landscape”.

Industry 5.0 denotes a drastic evolution of the industrial landscape, where advanced digital technologies are combined with human-centered methodologies like never before, in waves similar to those of Industry 4 and electromotive force driven by steam power engines. This new paradigm strives for sustainability, human-machine collaboration, and resilience towards a more inclusive and adaptive industrial domain. Industry 5.0 aims to foster innovation and boost the economy by focusing on critical enablers such as advanced manufacturing technologies, intelligent data analytics, and human-machine collaboration. Framed on a model for the digital economy, we expose five main indicators of Industry 5.0: not only you will hear about them but also learn how to measure and collect data from rates of adoption or productivity gains-to workforce adaptability (re-skilling) and environmental impact under R&D investment-and relating room solar radiation against outcoming PV power generation ratio which leads to ACP (All Collecting Power). This capability makes the dream of a more sustainable, resilient, and human-centric industrial future a reality as companies expand their footprint in Industry 5.0.

DIMENSIONS OF INDUSTRY 5.0

Moving from Industry 4.0 to Industry 5.0 signifies a substantial transformation in industry, not only accelerating technological development but also emphasizing the integration of human-focused principles and sustainability, along with keeping resilient focus areas within the new framework, future-proofing their role on stage, as well as endangering bees if they are nesting inside any hives (wherever that may be). Industry 5.0 builds upon Industry 4. This holistic approach is vital for addressing the complex issues of today and ensuring industrial advancement does not overshadow overarching societal aspirations.

Sustainability

Sustainability is one of the major pillars for Industry 5.0, where it goals to balance industrial developments with care and responsibility towards the environment Rather than just efficiency, which is the guiding principle behind almost all of Industry 4.0, Industry 5.0 goes a step further: sustainable production with waste reduction and an optimal use of resources even beyond sharing them between different components or workpieces. They argue for a shift towards circular economy principles for construction materials, emphasizing the reduction in environmental impact through reuse (upcycling/secondary use), remanufacturing, recycling when recovering products (loop 1), and disposal at the end of life (their own acronym). An example of this is the European Green Deal, which aims to achieve climate neutrality and reduce resource use in a manner that resembles Industry 5.0, showcasing more efficient processes that lead to environmental sustainability through the use of new technologies (European Commission, 2021). This is playing out in more practical ways, such as using renewable sources for energy (agriculture) to reduce emissions because of cleaner production technologies and a longer product cycle. A smart factory with sensors and AI can continuously monitor energy use within the manufacturing process to optimize in real-time, thus reducing emissions (Journal of Cloud Computing, 2021). With sustainability at the forefront of Industry 5.0, it is helping industrialists reduce environmental damage and sustain their businesses in the long run.

Human-Centricity

Human-centricity at the core of Industry 5.0 - human concerns are emphasized in a bottom-up manner, i.e., wellbeing and empowerment for workers come first before industrial development sections like assembly lines, etc. This dimension acknowledges that the purpose of technological advancements is not to replace human capabilities, but rather to supplement or enhance them. For example, Collaborative robots (cobots) assist in performing repetitive or dangerous tasks side-by-side with people, enabling employees to concentrate on more creative and strategic work (European Commission 2021). All set up within a symbiotic relationship to increase job satisfaction, safety, and productivity. Additionally, Industry 5.0 champions inclusive environments with configurations that allow their workspaces to cater to all needs and situations, as they are adaptable. For example, augmented reality (AR) and virtual reality (VR) provide real-time information feeds to workers, enabling them to perform complex jobs faster and more safely. It not only empowers the workforce to improve their skills and knowledge but also ensures that technological developments are accessible to all members of an organization (Journal of Cloud Computing, 2021). That means Industry 5.0 aims to create workplaces that are both more engaging, rewarding, and human-enriching through a Human-Centric Industrial ecosystem.

Resilience

Another critical aspect of Industry 5.0, resilience, which focuses on the ability to construct sturdy and flexible industrial systems that can withstand disruptions and bounce back from these disturbances, is also intertwined with this transformational wave across all levels, from institutional policymaking down through production methods up until resource usage as well as aid provision practices. The COVID-19 pandemic has drawn attention to the extreme importance of resilient supply chains and production processes that can adjust rapidly in such changing environments (European Commission, 2021). By utilizing high-end technologies such as AI, IoT, and predictive analytics, they become more informed about industry trends, enabling them to improve scalability in their operations. Predictive maintenance technologies that can forecast equipment failures, while simultaneously (and proactively) scheduling repairs long before breakdowns hit, help reduce downtime and contribute to keeping the product line flowing. Artificial intelligence-based supply chain management platforms that also dynamically rank inventory and warehouse size can help determine resource allocation in real-time, even during disturbances (Breque et al., 2021). By defining resilience in industrial operations, Industry 5.0 builds systems that are better equipped to handle unknown adversities and maintain business continuity.

Digital and Tangible Integration

One characteristic defining Industry 5.0 is the confluence of digital and physical systems that enable close interaction between humans and technology. This refers to the combination of high-level digital technologies, such as AI, IoT, and big data analytics, with physical manufacturing processes to create smart, interconnected factories or Cyber Physical Systems (CPS). They use real-time data to make decisions faster, expedite production processes, and improve productivity further (Journal of Cloud Computing 2021). This type of integration, between the digital and physical worlds, enables precision and flexibility in manufacturing that has never been possible before. AI algorithms can mine production data to find shortcomings and suggest improvements, while IoT sensors provide round-the-clock monitoring of equipment condition and environmental conditions. Overall, such a comprehensive effort can not only help improve operational efficiency but also enable increased customization and product personalization to specific clients (European Commission, 2021). Bioethics - Helping Needy but Intelligent People - Directing Science in Ethical Ways. Of course, some may argue that research to enhance the human brain is unjustifiably selfish. Industry 5.0 is very concerned with stewardship, and this technological progress needs to conform with national spirit values, ethical norms, etc... This entails preventing the substitution of jobs by new technologies with insufficient protection for those who are affected, ensuring both data security as well as privacy standards and fostering more inclusive practices that benefit a collective workforce (European Commission, 2021). This naturally includes the ethical implications of developing and deploying AI, as well as other advanced technologies. These technologies must be applied carefully and ethically; therefore, subjects such as algorithmic bias, transparency, and accountability must be carefully considered and addressed. Industry 5.0 is committed to enhancing ethical principles in order to promote a fairer and just industry, which favours all stakeholders (Breque et al., 2021).

Encouraging Innovation and Lifelong Learning

Research and development (R&D), as well as the continuous upskilling of workers for a state-of-the-art learning process, are crucial requirements in Industry 5.0. Achieving status accelerates industrial competition to remain ahead in the tech line while building a culture of innovation and creativity (Journal of Cloud Computing, 2021). To achieve this, companies should invest a larger share of their spending in research and development to explore new technologies and novel applications. This involves a combination of further research and the development (or reassessment) of skills to ensure that workers can collaborate on solutions that pair digital and human capabilities. That includes offering employees access to training programs, certifications, and other learning opportunities that help them stay current with the latest trends and practices in technology. - Breque et al., 2021

COMPONENTS OF THE DIGITAL ECONOMY IN INDUSTRY 5.0

Industry 5.0 ushers in a new era where the digital economy is not just powered by technology but is deeply rooted in human-centric, sustainable means. This paper examines the digitally enabled economy and highlights several key aspects of our digital future that, collectively, will shape the emergence of new forms of industrial production and economic growth. These include advanced manufacturing technologies, intelligent data analytics, human-machine collaboration, and innovative digital infrastructure, spanning the supply chain to the factory floor, which enables innovation ecosystems throughout the product life cycle.

Additive Manufacturing Technologies

The heart of the digital economy is Industry 5.0, which utilizes advanced manufacturing technologies to allow smarter and more efficient production processes. Mostly, artificial intelligence (AI) technologies and techniques play a significant role in such automation; another common factor is some form of Internet of Things, which can range from robotics to 3D printing or additive manufacturing. AI and machine learning algorithms can be trained on large datasets to gain a thorough understanding of production workflows, maintenance schedules, or quality issues (Breque et al., 2021). With the help of real-time access to machine condition monitoring and control through IoT, it is possible for manufacturing environments to respond more efficiently(Journal of Cloud Computing, 2021). Cobots, short for collaborative robots, are robots that work alongside humans to improve and fill gaps in human capabilities, as well as provide safer working environments. These robots can handle mature tasks or challenging chores, which frees up humans for other, more difficult and productive operations (European Commission, 2021). Additive manufacturing processes also contribute to more flexible and customized production, enhancing possibilities for waste reduction through the implementation of complex geometries and product personalization (Breque et al., 2021).

Intelligent Data Analytics

The digital economy of Industry 5.0 runs on data, plain and not so simple. A large amount of data with a latency of less than 0.1 ms will be essential for industrial process re-optimization and informed decision-making. Intelligent data analytics are data analytical solutions powered by Big Data technologies, cloud computing, and artificial intelligence to extract relevant insights on complex datasets (Journal of Cloud Computing 2021).

Such analytics can predict when maintenance is required, using data from sensors embedded in machinery to prevent unanticipated downtime and lengthen equipment life cycles (European Commission, 2021). Additionally, data analytics provides the capability to enhance supply chain management by enabling the tracking of inventory levels, demand forecasts, and logistics operations. This results in optimal resource utilization, reduced waste, and increased productivity (Breque et al., 2021).

Human-Machine Collaboration

Indeed, human-machine collaboration is one of the hallmarks of Industry 5.0. In contrast to the fully automatic systems of Industry 4.0, it is based on an image in which humans and machines interact smoothly: Industry 5. These technologies include augmented reality (AR) and virtual reality (VR), which facilitate real-time information and guidance for workers (Journal of Cloud Computing, 2021). For instance, AR superimposes digital information onto the physical world, meaning that workers can see instructions or data on top of machinery. It leads to significant productivity boosts and increases accuracy in tasks such as assembly, maintenance, or quality inspection (Breque et al., 2021). VR, conversely, may be used for guidance and demonstrative purposes that also allow workers to perform much more elaborate procedures through the virtual domain in advance of actually doing them practically(European Commission, 2021). Human-machine partnership includes creating intuitive systems and interfaces that allow employees to communicate with, control, or be guided by all things digital. Whether such an approach not only boosts productivity but also increases employee welfare and security has now been scientifically confirmed (Journal of Cloud Computing, 2021).

Digital Infrastructure

Industry 5.0 relies largely on robust digital infrastructure, necessarily to manage the schlub that otherwise populates Industry for Processes 1 through untold digits more than current numeration! This digital infrastructure comprises high-speed internet, robust cloud computing platforms, and trusted data storage solutions. 5G networks have an outsized impact on these uses, which require 5G's ultra-high bandwidth and low latency for live data transmission with proper integration of IoT devices (Breque et al.,2021).

The speed and efficiency with which this can happen through cloud computing platforms is allowing companies to scale their operations up, consuming the computational power, together with storage capacity, in order to process large datasets or run complex algorithms (European Commission, 2021). Cybersecurity tactics are also important to keep all the sensitive information safe and make sure that no system can be compromised. This includes actively using technologies related to encryption, access control, and threat detection to mitigate cyber threats (Journal of Cloud Computing 2021).

Innovation Ecosystems

Industry 5.0 digital economy also has dynamic innovation ecosystems that help in collaboration and knowledge sharing among various stakeholders. This is visible in emergent ecosystems aggregating a spectrum of entities, from more mature and established manufacturers to start-ups, the hottest technology advancement, alongside research institutions or universities.

To help organisations put theory into practice, innovation ecosystems encourage cultures of continuous learning and experimentation - where new (i.e., unproven) ideas can be tested quickly in the real world. This, coupled with the collaborative pipeline, is crucial for tackling grand challenges and creating novel yet applied responses (European Commission, 2021). Additionally, these ecosystems offer funding and resources that allow startups as well as small businesses to scale operations or release new products (Journal of Cloud Computing 2021).

ADVANCED MANUFACTURING TECHNOLOGIES

With Industry 5.0, manufacturing technologies have evolved to use more sophisticated tools and techniques, which impart better efficiency, sustainability, and human-centric design as well. Industry 5.0 is the digital economy, and foundational to it are those advanced manufacturing technologies that will enable smarter, more responsive, and adaptable production processes. The Key Advanced Manufacturing Technologies section provides a glimpse of how the top advanced manufacturing technologies (AI, IoT, robotics & automation, 3D printing, and AR) can revolutionize industrial operations.(Rahmat et al., 2021).

Artificial Intelligence (AI)

Industry 5.0 places a significant emphasis on the role of artificial intelligence in advanced manufacturing technologies. Certain jobs, such as decision-making, identifying patterns, and solving problems, have been traditionally carried out by humans due to ir complexity; now they can be done via AI algorithms. Artificial intelligence is used in manufacturing to reduce production costs, predict malfunctions, and optimize the quality of products. For instance, AI algorithms can process large data sets from shop floors to uncover inefficiencies and propose improvements (Breque et al., 2021). One of the most important AI applications in manufacturing is predictive maintenance. AI-enabled systems can also predict when a piece of machinery might fail by studying data from sensors installed on it, and scheduling maintenance before a failure happens. It also averts operational costs for long use of equipment, which further improves the performance efficiency and cost too (European Commission, 2021). Furthermore, machine learning can quickly catch more and better defects that human inspectors would perhaps miss. Machine learning Training Method: The procedure extracts the large-scale product image dataset and learns on different features of data to predict anomalous defects in products, which helps generate an overall depiction (Wang et al., 2021, Journal of Cloud Computing 2021). Artificial intelligence is simplifying quality control, which allows manufacturers to avoid post-due products and produce better goods(Nicklin et al., 2019).

Internet of Things (IoT)

IoT - The Internet of Things is all those devices that can be connected to each other and exchange data through the internet. IoT: In Industry 5.0, IoT has a vital role to manage smart factories where machines, sensors, and devices are communicable with each other in their production process for real-time monitoring and controlling (Breque et al., 2021).

Such devices gather information on different characteristics like temperature, humidity, vibration, and energy use, which is helpful in knowing the manufacturing environment. Data of this kind can be used to streamline operations, save energy, and improve security. The illustration shows that, for example, IoT-enabled energy management systems can track consumption of energy in real-time and thus allow for identifying options for reducing that, such as costs and environmental pollution (European Commission 2021). Moreover, IoT enables the deployment of digital twins, which are nothing but virtual counterparts for real-world entities. Manufacturers can then use these digital twins to simulate the performance of their machinery and production lines, test different scenarios for optimization purposes, or determine causes without stopping the actual manufacturing process. This feature improves the flexibility and adaptability of manufacturing systems, which becomes more resistant to disruptions (Journal of Cloud Computing, 2021).

Robotics

Collaborative robots or cobots are part of a paradigm shift in the manufacturing landscape, often referred to as Industry 5.0, and robotics takes centre stage! Traditional industrial robots, on the other hand, always work completely separately from any human interaction - cobots are made to interact with humans in an effort to augment (rather than replace) their jobs and provide enhanced safe working environments. The goal is that these will take care of repetitive, hazardous, or physically strenuous work so human workers can devote their attention to more diverse and meaningful activities (European Commission 2021b). Cobots are fitted with high-end sensors and AI-based algorithms that allow the cobot to safely work beside or near a human. They are capable of human-like movements, learning from interactions, and performing accurate tasks. Such a partnership of humans and robots is not only behind enhancement in productivity, but it also positively affects job satisfaction, workers' safety, and human-robot collaboration (S. I.Breque et al., 2021). Aside from cobots, autonomous mobile robots (AMRs) are also finding their way into manufacturing. The robots can work in a warehouse on their own, moving through difficult environments to convey materials and manage inventory. Using AMRs to automate these tasks in warehouses and production facilities will therefore lower labor costs as well as increase efficiency (Journal of Cloud Computing, 2021).

3D Printing (Additive Manufacturing)

3D printing, more commonly referred to as additive manufacturing, is a revolutionary development in engineering that enables the production of intricate geometries and bespoke products with minimal waste. Additive manufacturing produces parts by adding material layer upon the previous one (Breque et al., 2021), as opposed to traditional subtractive methods that machine a workpiece using tools until a desired shape is achieved.

It allows for the creation of complex shapes or forms that would be harder to manufacture using traditional methods. It is especially beneficial in sectors such as aerospace, automotive, and healthcare that often need components or prototypes to be tailor-made (European Commission DES).

Also, 3D printing adds the sustainability factor by functioning with no waste material and having the capability to produce locally. Whether it is being able to produce the parts on demand and close to where they need them, so there would be no transportation of these parts, or reducing their carbon miles. In addition, the possibility of recycling and reutilizing materials in AM values for principles aggregated by the circular economy (Journal of Cloud Computing 2021).

Augmented Reality (AR)

Augmented reality (AR): Aside from VR, AR is another innovative technology shaping the future of manufacturing by layering aetherial information on top of the physical realm. AR serves up real-time advice from the cloud to help workers craft, assemble, and otherwise master highly sophisticated tasks (Breque et al., 2021). Manufacturers can deploy AR for a number of applications: during the assembly process, but also while conducting maintenance or training (or learning on-the-job) to ensure better first-time fix rates and reduce time-to-competency. Examples of this include displaying step-by-step mechanized assembly guidance to reduce mistakes while directing your workers' hands and attention autonomously with AR glasses. AR is also used in maintenance so that the diagnostics show up on physical machinery itself, assisting technicians to spot and correct problems faster (European Commission, 2021). AR is also great for training, with workers able to mimic processes in a virtual area instead of the real world. This hands-on training technique both improves learning and makes workers learn new skills better (Journal of Cloud Computing, 2021).

CONCEPTUAL MODEL OF INDUSTRY 5.0: A SYNERGISTIC FRAMEWORK FOR VALUE CREATION

The shift from Industry 4.0 to Industry 5.0 is a massive philosophical and practical transformation between the structures of industry as we know them today. If Industry 4.0 is marked by its paradigm of automation, interconnectivity, and data-centric efficiency through Cyber-Physical Systems, then Industry 5.0 delivers a pivotal humanistic and more ecosophical counterpoint that cannot be ignored. The proposed C-Model suggests that Industry 5.0 is not a linear evolution but a holistic conception based on the three complementary and interconnected value pillars (Human-Centricity, Sustainability, and Resilience). These pillars are enabled and operationalized by an arsenal of Enabling Technologies and Strategic Components, which collectively underpin a multitude of Economic and Societal Outcomes. Performance and impact of the whole system are carefully measured by a multi-dimensional set of Key Performance Indicators (KPIs), to guarantee that technological development is always according to human flourishing and environmental sustainability.

The Foundational Value Pillars

At the heart of Industry 5.0 is its value logic of industrialization repositioning. Human-Centricity has two dimensions: a) first, it sets human needs, interests, and well-being as the center of production. And it goes way beyond human-in-the-loop towards human-in-command, where our tools are there to support and amplify our skills, creativity, and judgment, but not to replace them. This Pillar supports the creation of open, stimulating, and secure working environments that promote job satisfaction, lifelong learning, and professional/personal development. It knows that human intuition, moral reasoning, and creative thinking are unique treasures logically integrated in industrial value chains (Nahavandi, 2019; Leng et al., 2022). Second, Sustainability is moved from the periphery to the centre of operations. In the latter approach, sustainability is seen as an aspect of the circular economy, which requires a fundamental shift from linear "take-make-dispose" systems towards regenerative economies. This requires careful stewardship of resources, avoidance of waste at the design stage, utilization of renewable energy, and reduction in overall carbon footprint (end-to-end value chain) all along. It is to develop economic value and, at the same time, also creates value to society and the environment (Ghobakhloo et al., 2021; European Commission, 2021). Thirdly, Resilience is understood as the ability of industrial systems to sense, prepare for, and respond to incremental changes and sudden shocks. This involves investing in resilience in supply chains, production systems, and business models to better withstand shocks such as pandemics, geopolitical tensions, or climate-related disasters. A resilient system is dynamic, pliable, and has coping capabilities to sustain its operation and success amidst the diversity of change and unpredictability (Ivanov, 2021; Xu et al., 2021).

The Enabling Technologies and Strategic Components

The value pillars are playing out in combination with evolving technologies and methodologies. This layer of the model corresponds to Collaborative Robotics (Cobots) working with humans; they empower them and free them up from tedious or dangerous activities. AI(Artificial Intelligence) and big data analytics are the central nervous system, processing huge quantities of data to support predictive maintenance, logistics optimization, customized products, and intelligent decision making. The integration of the Internet of Things (IoT) and Digital Twins enables a continuous digital thread between the physical and virtual worlds, in order to facilitate monitoring, simulation, and optimization of products and production systems over time. AM (3DP) can contribute to sustainability and resilience through on-demand, localised production of intricate, lightweight parts and minimal material waste. This Extended Reality (XR) with virtual and augmented reality will, through its intuitive interface, revolutionize the way we work, improve human performance, and reduce errors in training, maintenance, and design. In the last place, a reliable Digital Infrastructure (e.g., 5G/6G connectivity, cloud-to-edge computing, and secure cybersecurity) is essential to enable real-time, safe, and trustworthy data flow both at small and medium levels as well as at large scale (Fraga-Lamas et al., 2021; Demir et al., 2022; Ozkeser, 2019).

Economic and Societal Outcomes

The synergetic impact of the value pillars and enabler technologies yields an impressive collection of end results. From an Economic point of view, this model leads to Enhanced Productivity and Innovation through optimized processes and collaboration between machine and worker. It enables new business models of Mass

Personalization and Servitization, where the value is not just derived from selling products but from providing customized solutions and services. At the societal level, it drives higher-quality employment through the creation of jobs that stress creativity and problem-solving over mindless repetition. It plays an active part in the Regeneration of the Environment, closure of Material cycling, and Reductions in Emissions. It also strengthens Societal Resilience by fostering local and flexible production networks that are better protected from global disruptions (Carayannis & Morawska-Jancelewicz, 2022; Javaid et al., 2021).

Measurement KPIs (Key Performance Indicators)

To make the step towards Industry 5.0 authentic and efficient, it should be assessed using a balanced set of KPIs that gives a complete picture of its different objectives. These include:

- Human-Centric KPIs: (Employee satisfaction and wellbeing indices), investment in upskilling/reskilling per employee, various workforce diversity metrics, and decline of workplace accidents.
- KPIs on sustainability: carbon footprint per product unit, percentage of energy consumed from renewable sources, circular material factor (ratio of recycled to virgin materials), and waste-to-landfill reduction rates.
- Resilience KPI's: Supply chain volatility index, time-to recover from a major disruption (e.g., supplier failure), overall equipment effectiveness (OEE) during demand shocks, and level of production flexibility (time to reconfigure a production line for a new product).
- Economic and Innovation KPIs: R&D investment as a % of revenue, speed of new product development, degree of customisation provided in products, and productivity growth (output per hour worked).

This holistic conceptual model demonstrates that Industry 5.0 represents a transformative journey to creating an industrial ecosystem that is not only smarter and more connected but equally inclusive, sustainable, and resilient for the betterment of our economy, society, and planet.

INTELLIGENT DATA ANALYTICS

Intelligent data analytics is a cornerstone of the digital economy in Industry 5.0, transforming vast amounts of raw data into actionable insights that drive decision-making and optimize industrial processes. This technology leverages advanced tools such as big data analytics, machine learning, and artificial intelligence (AI) to analyze complex datasets and uncover patterns, trends, and relationships that would be impossible to discern manually. The integration of intelligent data analytics into manufacturing processes offers numerous benefits, including enhanced productivity, predictive maintenance, and improved quality control.

Enhanced Productivity

One of the primary benefits of intelligent data analytics in Industry 5.0 is its ability to enhance productivity. By analyzing data collected from various stages of the production process, manufacturers can identify inefficiencies and bottlenecks that hinder performance. For example, data analytics can track machine performance and production outputs in real-time, allowing for immediate adjustments to improve efficiency. Advanced algorithms can optimize production schedules, manage inventory levels, and streamline supply chain operations, ensuring that resources are used effectively and reducing downtime (Breque, De Nul, & Petridis, 2021). In smart factories, data analytics tools can integrate data from sensors, machines, and human inputs to create a comprehensive view of the manufacturing environment. This holistic approach enables manufacturers to make data-driven decisions that enhance overall productivity and operational efficiency (European Commission, 2021).

Predictive Maintenance

Predictive maintenance is another critical application of intelligent data analytics in Industry 5.0. Traditional maintenance approaches often rely on scheduled checks or reactive repairs following a failure. Predictive maintenance, however, uses data analytics to predict when equipment is likely to fail and schedule maintenance activities before the failure happens. This approach minimizes unplanned downtime, reduces maintenance costs, and extends the lifespan of machinery.

By continuously monitoring data from IoT sensors embedded in equipment, predictive maintenance systems can detect anomalies and wear patterns that indicate potential issues. Machine learning algorithms analyze this data to predict future failures and optimize maintenance schedules accordingly (Journal of Cloud Computing, 2021). For example, sensors might detect slight increases in vibration or temperature in a motor, signaling that a component is wearing out. The system can then alert maintenance personnel to replace the part before it causes a breakdown.

Improved Quality Control

Intelligent data analytics also plays a vital role in improving quality control in manufacturing processes. Traditional quality control methods often involve manual inspections, which can be time-consuming and prone to human error. Data analytics, combined with AI, offers a more efficient and accurate alternative. Machine learning models can analyze data from production lines to identify defects and deviations from quality standards in real-time.

These systems can detect even subtle defects that might be missed by human inspectors, ensuring that only high-quality products reach the market. Additionally, data analytics can help identify the root causes of quality issues by correlating defects with specific stages of the production process or environmental conditions. This information allows manufacturers to implement corrective actions and process improvements to prevent future defects (European Commission, 2021).

HUMAN-MACHINE COLLABORATION

This is a core characteristic of Industry 5.0: human-machine collaboration in which the symbiotic relationship harnesses collaborative productivity, innovative capacity, and worker satisfaction. This goes beyond the traditional automation-oriented Industry 4.0 approach, highlighting a synergy between artificial and human intelligence as complementary technologies-working together. It is thus a form of collaboration that includes technologies and practices such as collaborative robots (cobots), augmented reality (AR), virtual reality, and human-machine interfaces.

Collaborative Robots (Cobots)

Cobots (collaborative robots) are state-of-the-art machines that work with humans, making them highly useful as they can assist in human activities and perform tasks that are traditionally done by humans. Unlike typical industrial robots that work in isolation, cobots are fitted with sensors and AI algorithms that allow them to detect people nearby and adjust their behavior accordingly. It largely increases productivity and safety in manufacturing environments (European Commission, 2021).

Cobots are especially advantageous in small and medium-sized enterprises (SMEs), which are typical of bringing flexibility to automation solutions where resources may be more limited. SMEs can achieve scale through the deployment of cobots without investing large sums into both infrastructure and labor. Additionally, cobots are flexible and quickly reprogrammable for various applications that make them agile to cater to the dynamic market requirements (Joseph & Dhanabhakyam, 2022; Baporikar, 2021).

AR/VR (Augmented Reality & Virtual Reality)

Augmented reality and virtual reality technologies are essential for improving human-machine collaboration through immersive and interactive experiences. Augmented reality (AR) is a technology that overlays digital information onto the physical world, providing real-time guidance and step-by-step instructions for workers. An example of this could be instructions for assembly being displayed to the worker through AR glasses, decreasing errors and increasing efficiency (Breque et al., 2021).

Workers can simulate-to-train using VR for complex workflows before they replicate in the real-world village. The method aids in upskilling workers while also making them ready for high-value responsibilities at low costs and risk of error (Dhanabhakyam & Joseph, 2022; Journal of Cloud Computing, 2021).

A treatise on advanced human-computer interfaces

An important part of human-machine cooperation in Industry 5.0 is also the development of sophisticated interfaces between man and computer. Given the complexity of machines and systems, these interfaces have to be user-friendly for workers so that they can use them confidently. Technologies like gesture recognition, voice command, or brain-computer interfaces (BCIs) are being introduced in industrial setups in order to improve the communication between human and machine bodies. Workers can control machines easily without the necessity to touch harmful equipment using gesture recognition systems, for example, making them efficient than ever. These voice command systems allow true hands-free operation, which is great in environments where manual dexterity may be needed. BCIs, although in the experimental stage, are capable of changing human-machine interaction forever by directly communicating between the brain and machines (Joseph et al., 2023).

The advantage of a man-machine team

Benefits of working with robots include boosted productivity, happier employees, and greater safety. If these human abilities are combined with the strengths of machines, companies end up having more efficient and flexible operations. Instances: Machines can be used for proprietary, scalable solutions that handle repeatable tasks to precision, while human brainpower is saved on creative solutioning and decision-making (Breque et al., 2021). The collaborative nature of the process also naturally increases worker morale, lessening their dependency on physical effort and permitting them to exercise their brain in more challenging work. More engaged workers are likely to be more satisfied in their jobs and, thus, stay because they feel valued in an empowered role (Joseph & Dhanabhakyam, 2022). Increased safety - When robots are able to perform unsafe, boring, and repetitive tasks, it becomes a great benefit, as with fewer people working in dangerous environments, there is a lower likelihood that someone would get harmed.

Challenges, Future Directions

Although there are many upsides of human-machine collaboration, it also comes with some challenges. This includes substantial technology and infrastructure investments required, which can pose a significant challenge for SMEs. Continuously training employees and developing skills on handling complex technologies-Coaching the workforce for tomorrow (Joseph,27/4/2023; Dhanabhakyam Joseph, 20th April 2022). Similarly, many other sources, Viz. Data Security and Confidentiality: The integration of AI with IoT devices creates additional threats to cybersecurity. Safeguarding organizations through effective cybersecurity is critical to securing data and the integrity of a business model (Journal of Cloud Computing, 2021). What will likely take place in Industry 5.0, then, with respect to the future of collaboration between humans and machines, is a further deepening of both AI and machine learning technologies, all leading toward more autonomous systems that are highly adaptive as well. AR and VR developments will further increase practical training opportunities, as well as improve operational efficiencies, while BCIs could help open the door to completely new possibilities in human-machine interaction. As these innovations progress, the spotlight is on how to find only a man and technological adjustments that can keep workers in line with new technologies of industrial growth without reducing the overarching objective for safety features.

CONCLUSION

By evaluating human and machine collaboration in the context of Industry 5.0, it is possible to identify a fundamental diversification from previous paradigms to one that highlights the interdependency between advanced solutions and continued exploration into what it means to be human will always remain pertinent in designing these relationships as well. The goal is to combine the best of both worlds - humans and machines, to create a more efficient, safe, and enjoyable industrial setting. This collaboration, underpinned by technologies such as collaborative robots (cobots), augmented reality (AR)/virtual reality (VR), and advanced human-computer interfaces, drives the best of both worlds between productivity/operational efficiency on one hand, and worker safety/satisfaction on the other. This is particularly beneficial to small and medium-sized enterprises (SMEs), allowing them a scalable automation solution that can mold around fluctuating market demands without the high-cost infrastructure plants of years gone by, in which businesses were restricted to consistent mass production forms:(Moitra, 2021; Joseph & Dhanabhakyam, Baporikar(Bhubaneswar) Jottey et al. AR and VR enable training using assistive technology frameworks, which guide workers in performing complex tasks more accurately and efficiently, as well as through the use of immersive simulations to prepare them for high-stakes scenarios (Breque et al., 2021; Dhanabhakyam & Joseph, 2022). This is the collaborative way, but it does not always come easily. Human-machine collaboration: Millions and millions of investment in technology, infrastructure, continuous training & upskilling workforce, and stringent security measures are required to get the complete benefits from human-machine collaboration(Joseph, 2023; Dhanabhakyam&Joseph, 2022). Aligned with broader societal goals, ethical considerations such as data privacy, job displacement, and inclusivity will also need to be tackled in the wake of rapid technology advances (European Commission 2021). Moving forward, the implementation of AI and IoT together with machine learning will allow for even more cohesion between humans and machines working in autonomous/adaptive systems. AR- and VR-leveraging advanced training procedures, as well as insights we have seen with brain-computer interfaces (BCI), can operate toward preparing the pinnacle of high-speed human-machine interface. It is therefore important that technologies are developed in a way that human capabilities are not substituted by technology and the industrial advancements contribute to sustainable economic growth, serving both employment and financial inclusion objectives. The human-machine collaboration paradigm envisioned in Industry 5.0 provides a glimpse of the promising new ways to approach the future industrial world, offering a more productive, sustainable, and humane outlook. Through the combined effort of advanced technologies to supplement human capabilities and create an atmosphere for collaboration, Industry 5.0 enhances operational efficiency as well as workforce satisfaction and safety. This introductory paragraph is followed by a thematic series concerning cloudonomics that indicates successful adoption of this paradigm will necessitate attending to the challenges associated with it and ensuring technologies are developed in alignment with societal well-being (Breque et al., 2021; Journal of Cloud Computing, 2021).

REFERENCES

Baporikar, N. (Ed.). (2021). *Handbook of research on sustaining SMEs and entrepreneurial innovation in the post-COVID-19 era*. IGI Global.

Benevene, P., Buonomo, I., & West, M. (2022). Editorial: Compassion and compassionate leadership in the workplace. *Frontiers in Psychology*, *13*, 1074068. DOI: 10.3389/fpsyg.2022.1074068 PMID: 36571014

Breque, M., De Nul, L., & Petridis, A. (2021). *Industry 5.0: Towards a sustainable, human-centric and resilient European industry*. Directorate-General for Research and Innovation, European Commission. https://research-and-innovation.ec.europa.eu/knowledge-publications-tools-and-data/publications/all-publications/industry-50-towards-sustainable-human-centric-and-resilient-european-industry_en

Carayannis, E. G., & Morawska-Jancelewicz, J. (2022). The futures of Europe: Society 5.0 and Industry 5.0 as driving forces of future universities. *Journal of the Knowledge Economy*, *13*(4), 3445–3471. DOI: 10.1007/s13132-021-00854-2 PMID: 40477679

Demir, K. A., Döven, G., & Sezen, B. (2022). Industry 5.0 and a critique of Industry 4.0. *Procedia Manufacturing*, *55*, 1–7. DOI: 10.1016/j.promfg.2022.10.001

Dhanabhakyam, M., & Joseph, E. (2022). Digital permissive management for aggregate and sustainable development of the employees. *International Journal of Health Sciences*, *6*(1).

Dhanabhakyam, M., & Joseph, E. (2022). *Digitalization and perception of employee satisfaction during pandemic with special reference to selected academic institutions in higher education. Mediterranean Journal of Basic and Applied Sciences*. MJBAS.

European Commission. (2021). *Industry 5.0: Towards a sustainable, human-centric and resilient European industry*. Publications Office of the European Union. https://op.europa.eu/en/publication-detail/-/publication/468a892a-5097-11eb-b59f-01aa75ed71a1

European Commission. (2021). *Industry 5.0: Towards more sustainable, resilient and human-centric industry*. https://research-and-innovation.ec.europa.eu/knowledge-publications-tools-and-data/publications/all-publications/industry-50-towards-sustainable-human-centric-and-resilient-european-industry_en

Fraga-Lamas, P., Lopes, S. I., & Fernández-Caramés, T. M. (2021). Green IoT and edge AI as key technological enablers for a sustainable digital transition towards a smart circular economy: An Industry 5.0 use case. *Sensors (Basel)*, *21*(17), 5745. DOI: 10.3390/s21175745 PMID: 34502637

Ghobakhloo, M., Iranmanesh, M., Grybauskas, A., Vilkas, M., & Petraite, M. (2021). Industry 4.0, innovation, and sustainable development: A systematic review and a roadmap to sustainable innovation. *Business Strategy and the Environment*, *30*(8), 4237–4257. DOI: 10.1002/bse.2867

Ivanov, D. (2021). Supply chain viability and the COVID-19 pandemic: A conceptual and formal generalisation of four major adaptation strategies. *International Journal of Production Research*, *59*(12), 3535–3552. DOI: 10.1080/00207543.2021.1890852

Javaid, M., Haleem, A., Singh, R. P., & Suman, R. (2021). Substantial capabilities of robotics in enhancing Industry 4.0 implementation. *Cognitive Robotics*, *1*, 58–75. DOI: 10.1016/j.cogr.2021.06.001

Joseph, E. (2023). Underlying Philosophies and Human Resource Management Role for Sustainable Development. In *Governance as a Catalyst for Public Sector Sustainability* (pp. 286–304). IGI Global.

Joseph, E. (2024). Evaluating the Effect of Future Workplace and Estimating the Interaction Effect of Remote Working on Job Stress. [MJBAS]. *Mediterranean Journal of Basic and Applied Sciences*, *8*(1), 57–77.

Joseph, E. (2024). Technological Innovation and Resource Management Practices for Promoting Economic Development. In *Innovation and Resource Management Strategies for Startups Development* (pp. 104–127). IGI Global.

Joseph, E. (2025). Impact of Hybrid Entrepreneurs on Economic Development and Job Creation. In *Applications of Career Transitions and Entrepreneurship* (pp. 61–82). IGI Global Scientific Publishing.

Joseph, E. (2025). Leveraging AI to Inspire Innovation in Traditional and Digital Business Ecosystems. [JBE]. *Journal of Business Ecosystems*, *6*(1), 1–18. DOI: 10.4018/JBE.383049

Joseph, E. (2025). Public-Private Partnerships for Revolutionizing Personalized Education Through AI-Powered Adaptive Learning Systems. In *Public Private Partnerships for Social Development and Impact* (pp. 265–290). IGI Global Scientific Publishing.

Joseph, E. (2025). Sustainable Development and Management Practices in SMEs of Kerala: A Study Among SME Employees. *Sustainable Development and Management Practices in SMEs of Kerala: A Study Among SME Employees (February 20, 2025).*

Joseph, E., & Dhanabhakyam, M. M. (2022). Role of Digitalization Post-Pandemic for Development of SMEs. In *Research anthology on business continuity and navigating times of crisis* (pp. 727–747). IGI Global.

Joseph, E., Koshy, N. A., & Manuel, A. (2025). Exploring the Evolution and Global Impact of Public-Private Partnerships.

Joseph, E., Shyamala, M., & Nadig, R. (2025). Understanding Public-Private Partnerships in the Modern Era. In Public Private Partnership Dynamics for Economic Development (pp. 1-26). IGI Global Scientific Publishing.

Journal of Cloud Computing. (2021). Future of Industry 5.0 in society: Human-centric solutions, challenges and prospective research areas. Journal of Cloud Computing. https://journalofcloudcomputing.springeropen.com/articles/10.1186/s13677-021-00279-4

Kumar, A., & Joseph, E. (2025). Examining the mediating role of workforce agility in the relationship between emotional intelligence and workforce performance in small entrepreneurial firms in India. [MJBAS]. *Mediterranean Journal of Basic and Applied Sciences*, *9*(3), 14–24.

Leng, J., Sha, W., Wang, B., Zheng, P., Zhuang, C., Liu, Q., & Wang, L. (2022). Industry 5.0: Prospect and retrospect. *Journal of Manufacturing Systems*, *65*, 279–295. DOI: 10.1016/j.jmsy.2022.09.017

Nahavandi, S. (2019). Industry 5.0—A human-centric solution. *Sustainability*, *11*(16), 4371. DOI: 10.3390/su11164371

Nicklin, J. M., Seguin, K., & Flaherty, S. (2019). Positive work-life outcomes: Exploring self-compassion and balance. *European Journal of Applied Positive Psychology*, *3*, 1–13. https://www.nationalwellbeingservice.com/journals

Obrenovic, B., Jianguo, D., Khudaykulov, A., & Khan, M. A. S. (2020). Work-family conflict impact on psychological safety and psychological well-being: A job performance model. *Frontiers in Psychology*, *11*, 475. DOI: 10.3389/fpsyg.2020.00475 PMID: 32296367

Ozkeser, B. (2019). Lean innovation approach in Industry 5.0. *The Eurasia Proceedings of Science, Technology. Engineering & Mathematics*, *5*, 422–428.

Peltokorpi, V., & Michel, J. (2021). The moderating effect of core self-evaluations between the relationships of work–family conflict and voluntary turnover, job promotions and physical health. *Stress and Health*, *37*(1), 162–174. DOI: 10.1002/smi.2982 PMID: 32926522

Rahmat, A., Asri, A., & Wulandari, R. M. (2021). Pengaruh self-compassion dan dukungan sosial terhadap work-family conflict pada wanita di Kota Makassar. *Jurnal Sosialisasi*, *2*(12), 84–97.

Rastogi, M., Karatepe, O. M., & Mehmetoglu, M. (2019). Linking resources to career satisfaction through work–family enrichment. *Service Industries Journal*, *39*(11–12), 855–876. DOI: 10.1080/02642069.2018.1449835

Wang, L., ... (2021). Future of Industry 5.0 in society: Human-centric solutions, challenges and prospective research areas. *Journal of Cloud Computing*. https://journalofcloudcomputing.springeropen.com/articles/10.1186/s13677-021-00279-4

Xu, X., Lu, Y., Vogel-Heuser, B., & Wang, L. (2021). Industry 4.0 and Industry 5.0—Inception, conception and perception. *Journal of Manufacturing Systems*, *61*, 530–535. DOI: 10.1016/j.jmsy.2021.10.006

Chapter 11
Future Trends in Apparel Consumption Through Collaborative Models:
A Systematic Literature Review and Bibliometric Framework

Abhishek Choudhary
https://orcid.org/0000-0001-7951-719X
Indian Institute of Crafts and Design, India

Amit Jain
https://orcid.org/0000-0001-7978-1556
Amity University, Jaipur, India

Tejas S. Shah
https://orcid.org/0000-0002-9840-8172
SVKM's NMIMS University, India

Toolika Gupta
Indian Institute of Crafts and Design, India

Sourabh Kumar
https://orcid.org/0000-0001-9040-2019
Anand International College of Engineering, India

ABSTRACT

Apparel waste has significantly increased, becoming a global issue amid concerns about landfills in many countries. The solution lies in collaborative apparel consumption, provided a suitable structure is established for its implementation. The research

DOI: 10.4018/979-8-3693-4525-2.ch011

investigates the correlation between apparel and collaborative consumption through comprehensive literature assessment, including bibliometric and text analysis, to identify shared characteristics and underlying theories. The resulting conceptual framework defines apparel consumption through collaborative practices. This study provides a solid basis for scholars and researchers exploring novel opportunities in fashion marketing via collaborative consumption. It examines the characteristics and relationships of publications in collaborative consumption during the study period, offering a comprehensive understanding. The study aims to guide industry players, policymakers, and scholars toward creative and sustainable cooperation models in the apparel sector.

1. INTRODUCTION

Collaborative consumption of goods and services has evolved as a new kind of consumption in areas such as transportation, hospitality, consumer goods, and textiles during the past decade or so. Collaborative Consumption (CC) has expanded from economically advanced countries to emerging markets with varying social and economic conditions (Hall *et al.*, 2012; Schor and Fitzmaurice, 2015). Collaborative economy or collaborative consumption (CC) takes place when consumers share and access belongings such as clothing, housing, vehicles, and other merchandise temporarily. Consumers gain from CC in terms of cost, time, waste reduction, and environmental benefits (Frenken and Schor, 2017). Apparel consumption through collaboration (ACC) is the result of increased environmental and sustainability concerns (Amasawa *et al.*, 2023; Arrigo, 2021; Cavalcante Costa *et al.*, 2024; Henninger *et al.*, 2021) ACC is slowly gaining popularity in the Apparel industry. Online marketplaces for the sale and exchange of goods, as well as garment rental services (like Rent the Runway), are instances of ACC in the apparel industry (Arrigo, 2022; Herold and Prokop, 2023; Lang *et al.*, 2020; Park and Armstrong, 2017)

The current study contributes to ACC by reviewing the literature on CC and the apparel industry. On collaborative fashion consumption, a literature review was undertaken (Arrigo, 2021; Becker-Leifhold and Iran, 2018; Henninger *et al.*, 2021; Wei *et al.*, 2021). Researchers have mentioned that ACC brings opportunities for the apparel industry regarding sustainable growth (Becker-Leifhold, 2018; Cavalcante Costa *et al.*, 2024), but a clear theoretical model of ACC in the apparel industry is still missing (Arrigo, 2021; Henninger *et al.*, 2019, 2021). Many previous studies have focused on customer intention or motivation to adopt CC (e.g., renting, exchanging, bartering, or sharing) or on individual enterprises (Becker-Leifhold and Iran, 2018; Iran and Schrader, 2017; Pedersen and Netter, 2015; Ramtiyal *et al.*, 2023; Wei *et al.*, 2021)/ As a result, existing academic literature needs to be categorised to better understand the key ACC methodologies utilised in the apparel sector, identify suitable study topics, and lay the foundation for future research. The customer orientation towards shopping belief is considered a significant predictor for ACC behaviour for both online and offline shopping. Quality, price, trend, and brand are the frameworks of shopping beliefs (Gopalakrishnan and Matthews, 2018; Herold and Prokop, 2023; Lang *et al.*, 2020). This study investigates the characteristics and connections in the field of ACC during a particular time frame to introduce a more substantial and coherent approach.

The main objective of the study is to identify key research publications, journals, and authors who have contributed to the development of ACC literature in the fields of business and management. This study also aims to develop a conceptual framework for apparel consumption from the perspective of collaboration consumption and suggest ACC guidelines for future research in the apparel context.

The following research questions were proposed based on prior discussion.

1. What are the most influential research and study themes in the ACC domain?
2. Analysis of authors, journals, disciplines, countries and institutions, that have worked on apparel consumption through collaboration?
3. What are the research gaps and areas for future investigations?

1.2 Collaborative Consumption

CC is founded on the principles of renting, swapping, sharing, and bartering, where products and services are used collaboratively rather than individually (Barbosa and Fonseca, 2019; Bardhi and Eckhardt, 2012; Iran and Schrader, 2017; Kim and Jin, 2020a, 2020b; Pfajfar *et al.*, 2022). The CC model was initially grasped by Botsman and Rogers, (2010). Later, Botsman, (2013) concentrated on three distinct characteristics of CC: paying for product utilization rather than owing it; redistribution of unattractive or underutilized products and trading of non-utilized resources.

Collaborative consumption and the sharing economy are linked to the circular economy since they aim to redirect unused resources (such as clothing, textiles, and accessories) away from being thrown away and instead prolong their overall usefulness (RSA, 2020; RSA and The Great Recovery Project, 2016). Collaborative consumption refers to a commercial exchange between two persons. It has gained significant attention in the last decade (Ormrod, 2020). Belk, (2014) concentrated on pecuniary and nonpecuniary consumption that involves consumers arranging the procurement and allocation of resources. According to Hamari *et al.*, (2016), the stimulation of CC with user-generated content, sharing, and collaboration has been proclaimed with the expansion of information and communication technology, such as web 2.0 and mobile applications (Abbes *et al.*, 2020). They further emphasize that CC includes "actions such as procurement, gifting, or sharing ownership of products and services that are coordinated via community-based online services." The focus of CC is on the two major components of utilization: - Utility-based non-ownership that provides products temporarily and paid-in advance rentals, in which the consumer can offer the goods by renting or swapping (Arrigo, 2021; Dreyer *et al.*, 2017; Park and Armstrong, 2017).

In the fashion retail sector, fast fashion has become a successful business strategy (Byun and Sternquist, 2011; Hayes and Jones, 2006; Hu *et al.*, 2014; Moore and Fernie, 2004). According to McKinsey, (2019), ACC is likely to spring up in fast fashion. ACC in fashion retail is eco-friendly, extending the life of clothing encouraging reuse and allowing them to become mainstream alternatives (Brownbridge *et al.*, 2018; Herold and Prokop, 2023; Iran and Schrader, 2017). According to Lang and Joyner Armstrong, (2018), ACC provides an opportunity to achieve sustainability goals (Cavalcante Costa *et al.*, 2024; Choudhary *et al.*, 2022; Ganak *et al.*, 2020; Henninger *et al.*, 2019). Customers may obtain fashionable and costly luxury apparel thanks to CC (Park and Joyner Armstrong, 2019b), which leads to improved consumer engagement and experience (Akbar and Hoffmann, 2023; Gopalakrishnan and Matthews, 2018; Henninger *et al.*, 2019).

Additional factors contributing to increased interest in the ACC include growth prospects, emerging markets, digital disruptions, and changes associated with Covid-19 (Akbar & Hoffmann, 2023; Anwar, 2023; de Medeiros et al., 2021; García-Rodríguez et al., 2022; Kim & Jin, 2020; Park & Lee, 2022). The advent of digitalization has significantly influenced the business models for ACC (Amit & Zott, 2012), encompassing both innovative and conventional sectors that are typically not associated with substantial technological investments(Arrigo, 2022;Warner & Wäger, 2019) The role of technology 4.0 in the future survival of ACC is crucial, particularly in terms of marketing (Amoozad Mahdiraji et al., 2023). This involves the implementation of new technologies and regulations, such as payments and insurance, to enhance the speed, efficiency, and profitability of ACC interactions for Consumers(Fraanje & Spaargaren, 2019). The capacity of digital platforms to surpass capitalist principles and dynamics, hence creating opportunities for more sustainable narratives that prioritize human existence (Schröder et al., 2019).

2.1. Methodology

The Systematic Literature Review (SLR) approach is employed to investigate current research and identify research gaps in the field of collaborative cosnumption (CC) and apparel consumption through collaboration (ACC), which will guide future research. The initial phase involves choosing pertinent keywords and doing a literature search and analysis to obtain answers to specific queries formulated by the author (Saunders et al., 2007). In this research, the authors conducted a literature search using specified combinations of keywords, namely "Collaborative consumption, Apparel, Clothing, Fashion, Garment." The articles were chosen from high-quality publications identified by criteria such as Scopus database, articles, journal publication house, and publication during the past 10 years.

The systematic review is directed by the well-defined research questions. In this paper, review questions were designed to investigate the phenomenon of collaborative consuming. The research questions are: "How can the CC contribute to environmental sustainability objectives?" and "How do parameters of customer behaviour influence the CC?" What corporate activities facilitate the implementation of the CC?

A conceptual framework was established for supporting the results and establishment a foundation for future research.

2.2 Bibliometric analysis

Bibliometrics is a widely employed method for examining the intellectual structure of a certain study domain (Li *et al.*, 2017). It is commonly utilized to investigate and analyse various research themes (Blanco-Mesa *et al.*, 2017). Bibliometrics was started around the 1960s and 1970s, and work like "Co-authorship, bibliographic coupling, and co-citation networks" were introduced (Kessler, 1963; Price, 1965; Small, 1973). Fahimnia *et al.*, (2015) supported "bibliometric analysis" as a useful tool for research. Bibliometric coupling networks can be formulated for multiple types of analysis, including journals, publications, and researchers. Bibliometric analysis serves as a valuable approach in generating a "scientific knowledge map," a visual depiction of the knowledge landscape within a specific research field that can be likened to a synthesis of "spectra" and "maps."(Cobo *et al.*, 2011) Citation and co-citation analysis are the prevailing bibliometric methodologies employed to demonstrate commonalities between the citing and cited documents (Small, 1973). The main advantage of bibliometric review is the capacity to discover interpretations about future research areas by doing citation analysis followed by content analysis of the major themes of previous and current research (Baker *et al.*, 2020, 1992; Rey-Martí *et al.*, 2016; Vallaster *et al.*, 2019).

2.3. Bibliometric Tools

In this analysis, two established tools were employed: the Bibliometrix R package and VOSviewer. Essential for this bibliometric study, these tools facilitated the creation of scientific knowledge maps by leveraging bibliographic data from the Scopus database to enrich scholarly understanding of the ACC topic. The Bibliometrix R package, accessible within the R programming environment, offers a comprehensive suite of tools for the analysis of bibliometric data, supporting the exploration and visual depiction of research trends and patterns ((Walsh and Rowe, 2023). Conversely, VOSviewer, a no-cost Java-based application, features an intuitive graphical interface that simplifies the examination of complex bibliometric networks, enhancing the understanding of scholarly relationships (Van Eck and Waltman, 2010; van Eck and Waltman, 2007; Shen *et al.*, 2023). These applications synergistically augment the analytical capabilities vital for academics, professionals, and policymakers

2.4. Data Collection

The first stage is to acquire relevant information to choose appropriate keywords to search for related publications, such as "collaborative consumption". Alternative keyword combinations include "collaborative consumption+ Apparel," "collaborative consumption+ Fashion," and "collaborative consumption+ Clothing", "collaborative consumption+ Garment". The required research papers were collected from Web of Science and Scopus databases. During the process, it was found that both databases covered similar data thus, Elsevier's Scopus database was used as the primary source of information. Initially, 772 papers were identified during the search. The English-language articles were downloaded that had been published between January 2014 and 2024. Stage two involved setting the inclusion and exclusion criteria for the final article selection from downloaded articles. (Table 1)

Table 1. Inclusion and Exclusion Criteria

Characteristics	Inclusion	Exclusion
Period	Between January 2014 to February 2024,	All articles published before January 2014
Type of Research	Empirical, Conceptual, Review	
Language	English	All other languages.
Publication	Academic Journals	Professional journals, Books, and Conference Proceedings
Subject Domain	Business, Management and Accounting and Social Science	All other subject areas.

During the screening stage, 347 articles were eliminated owing to incompatibility with the inclusion requirements, leaving 425 for the eligibility stage. The inclusion and exclusion criteria were used to select, identify, and critically analyse existing research that was specifically linked to the review objectives as they were predefined (Tranfield *et al.*, 2003). All the articles were screened based on abstracts and full-length papers to explore their relevance. After scrutiny of the data, 279 research publications out of 425 were taken into consideration for further analysis. After the initial stages, the cleaned data was exported to Microsoft Excel to perform the citation analysis.

This study employs a thorough literature evaluation and bibliometric analysis. A comprehensive literature review was conducted to synthesise the content of the literature, eliminate bias, and identify research gaps. Bibliometrics is the most widely used method for tracing the knowledge anatomy of a research area (Li *et al.*, 2017). The key study fields were identified using techniques such as citation analysis and bibliographic coupling, which are routinely utilised by researchers (Ekanayake *et al.*, 2019; Podsakoff *et al.*, 2008; Zupic and Čater, 2015).

The flowchart depicts the data retrieval methodology (Figure 1).

Figure 1. Flowchart Showing data retrieval process.

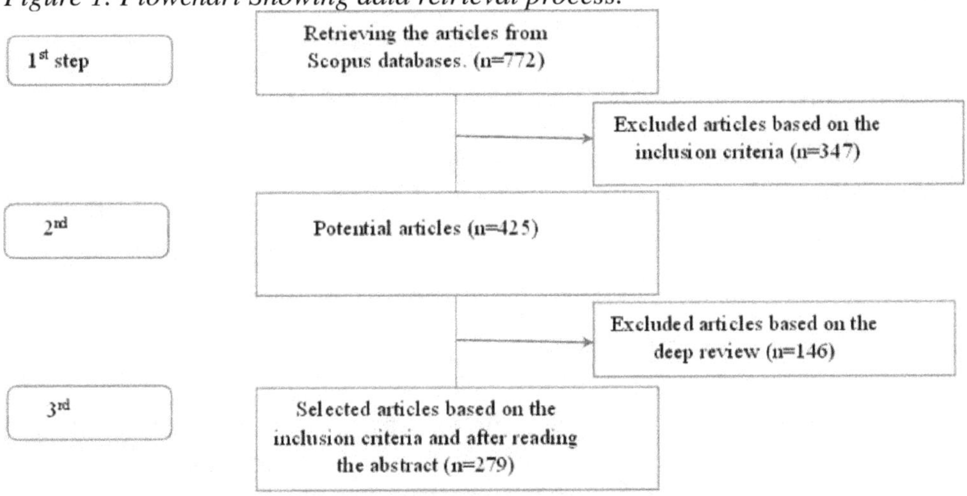

Based on the content analysis, obstacles and possibilities, CC model, and theories, which demonstrates how articles are categorised based on the following factors: author, journal, title of publication, year, objective, and findings. Highly cited and most relevant articles chronologically have been analyzed in detail.

3. ANALYSIS & FINDINGS

This research utilized the Bibliometrix R package to gather data from the SCOPUS core collection, focusing on extracting 279 articles pertinent to the theme of collaborative consumption in the apparel sector between 2014 and 2024. According to Table 2, these articles have been disseminated through 136 distinct sources, achieving an average citation rate of 64.08. The compilation consists of 259 original studies and 20 review papers. Additionally, the investigation into the collaborative consumption of apparel engaged 689 key keywords and was contributed to by 637 authors, highlighting the interdisciplinary nature and extensive academic interest in this area.

Table 2. Main Information about the Data

Description	Results
Timespan	2014 to 2024
Number of Sources	136
Average citations per research paper	64
Documents	279
Number of Authors	637
Keywords Plus (ID)	689
Number of original papers	259
Number of review papers	20
References	16573

3.1. Trend of Publications

Figure 2 illustrates a decade-long upward trajectory in publication volumes within this research domain, peaking in 2021 with over forty-three published works. This surge reflects an intensifying focus on collaborative research in apparel consumption post-2014. The citation dynamics, detailed in Figure 3, show fluctuations with notable peaks in 2014, 2016, 2017, and 2018, signifying heightened scholarly interest during these periods. A decline in citations since 2019 likely reflects the maturation time required for newer articles to accumulate citations and influence. The publication trend indicates that recent scholarly contributions are on the rise and are expected to garner increasing citations over time. Furthermore, Figure 4 highlights the interdisciplinary nature of this field, with "Business, Management, and Accounting" accounting for 29.1% of publications, contrasted by "Material Science" at 0.2%. underscoring the multidisciplinary integration in contemporary research. It is also worth noting that many of the studies are a part of more than one subject area which goes to shows that CC is multidisciplinary.

Figure 2. Contribution of Apparel Consumption through collaboration including total number of publications,

Figure 3. Mean total citations per year (MeanTCperYear).

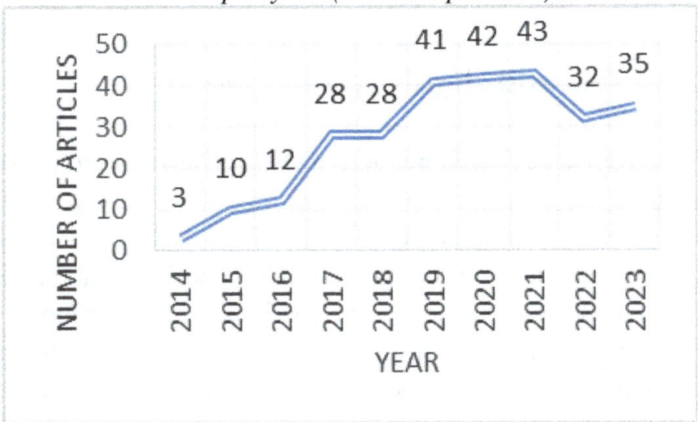

Figure 4.Subject-wise publication

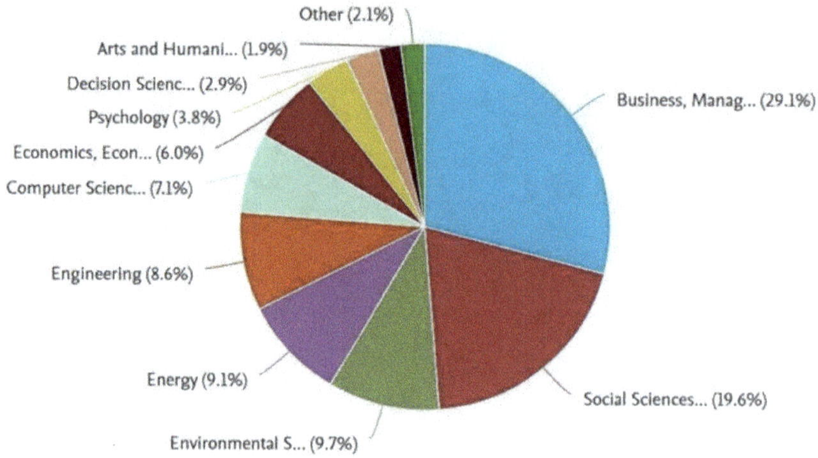

Source: - Scopus website (*https://www.scopus.com/term/analyzer.uri*)

3.2. Main Journals and Highly Cited Journals.

An in-depth review revealed a total of 279 research articles published in 136 different journals, indicating the widespread academic attention towards collaborative consumption in the apparel industry. Figure 5a illustrates the top 10 journals ranked by the number of publications on the subject. 'Sustainability' is at the forefront with 35 articles, closely followed by the 'Journal of Cleaner Production'. Furthermore, when evaluating the metric of total citation counts, the journal 'Journal of Business Research' stands out as the leader with 2,945 citations, followed by 'Journal of Cleaner Production' with 2,019 citations, as shown in Figure 5b. Furthermore, the 'Journal of Cleaner Production' holds the top position in terms of H-index, as indicated in Figure 4c. Moreover, figure 5d provides a clear representation of the top five journals ranked by the cumulative l number of publications. 'Sustainability' (35) and 'Journal of Cleaner Production' (22) stand out as the most significant in terms of cumulative occurrences, as specified in Table 3.

Figure 5. Most Relevant Sources from 2014 to 2024 (a), Most cited journals (b), H-Index (c), Most cumulative occurrence (d)

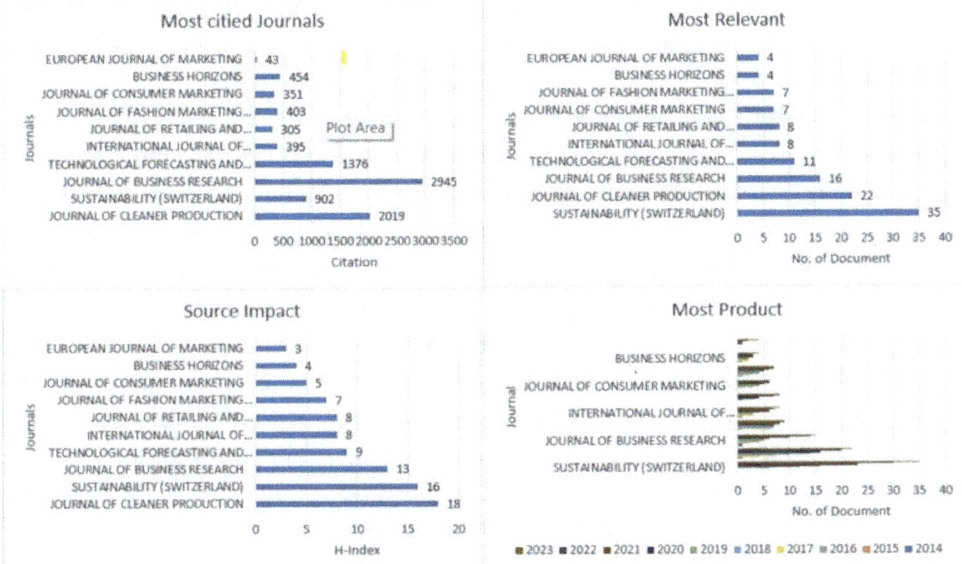

Table 3. Cumulative occurrence

Journal	2014	2015	2016	2017	2018	2019	2020	2021	2022	2023
SUSTAINABILITY (SWITZERLAND)	0	0	0	0	6	12	16	23	30	35
JOURNAL OF CLEANER PRODUCTION	0	1	4	7	10	14	16	20	20	22
JOURNAL OF BUSINESS RESEARCH	1	1	2	4	4	5	6	10	14	15
TECHNOLOGICAL FORECASTING AND SOCIAL CHANGE	0	0	1	6	7	7	7	8	8	9
INTERNATIONAL JOURNAL OF CONSUMER STUDIES	0	1	1	3	3	4	6	6	7	8
JOURNAL OF RETAILING AND CONSUMER SERVICES	0	0	0	0	0	1	3	4	7	8
JOURNAL OF CONSUMER MARKETING	0	0	0	0	1	3	4	5	6	6
JOURNAL OF FASHION MARKETING AND MANAGEMENT	0	0	1	2	3	4	5	5	6	7
BUSINESS HORIZONS	0	0	0	1	2	2	2	3	3	3
EUROPEAN JOURNAL OF MARKETING	0	0	0	0	0	0	0	1	1	2

3.3. Dominant authors and their affiliation

The dataset indicates that 637 authors are associated with 524 distinct institutions from 58 countries that have contributed to research on the topic of CC and the apparel sector. A substantial amount of these contributions comes from countries such as the United States, Germany, China, the United Kingdom, and Australia. The United States is at the forefront with 114 research publications, demonstrating a significant research focus in this field, but India is ranked eighth with 39 articles, highlighting the increasing research momentum in developing economies. Half of the top ten contributing countries, which jointly account for 50% of the research output, are located in Europe. On the other hand, the main contributions from North America come from the United States, while Asia is represented by both India and China. Table 4 reveals that Hyejune Park is a prominent researcher who primarily focuses on investigating consumer motives for engaging in collaborative consumption and the variations in these motivations among different consumption models. Washington State University is recognised as the most productive institution, with Oklahoma State University coming in a close second.

Table 4. Countries, Authors, Institution publication (P) and Citation (C) on Collaborative Consumption.

Top Countries			Top Authors			Top Institution		
Country	**P**	**C**	**Author**	**P**	**C**	**Institution**	**P**	**C**
USA	114	1507	Park H	5	229	Washington State University	15	387
GERMANY	52	697	Ertz M	4	175	Oklahoma State University	11	169
CHINA	46	187	Marimon F	4	118	University Of Potsdam	11	89
UK	46	1534	Chi T	3	34	The University Of Tokyo	9	2216
AUSTRALIA	44	1053	Joyner Armstrong Cm	3	135	Universitat Internacional De Catalunya	9	405
SPAIN	41	408	Mas-Machuca M	3	118	Kth Royal Institute Of Technology	8	352
FRANCE	40	1017	Abutaleb S	2	14	North Carolina State University	8	268
INDIA	39	78	Balderjahn I	2	97	German University In Cairo	7	185
SWEDEN	29	1280	Barnes Sj	2	467	Lund University	7	138
BRAZIL	22	79	Belk R	2	2330	Vilnius Gediminas Technical University	7	68

3.4. Research Methods used in previous studies

The authors used a variety of research methods to study CC. The researcher classified 279 publications into three different study approaches to investigate the various research methods used in the field, which are empirical, conceptual and review. Figure 6 represents different research methods used by authors in CC research. The authors used both qualitative and quantitative methods as well as a mixed methodology. The analysis also suggests that authors frequently studied consumer adoption of CC. Authors have commonly used case studies and interviews to demonstrate the right research technique for CC. The examination of the results provides evidence that scholars frequently research to investigate the extent to which customers adopt collaborative consumption patterns (Arrigo, 2021).

Figure 6. Research method based on 279 publications.

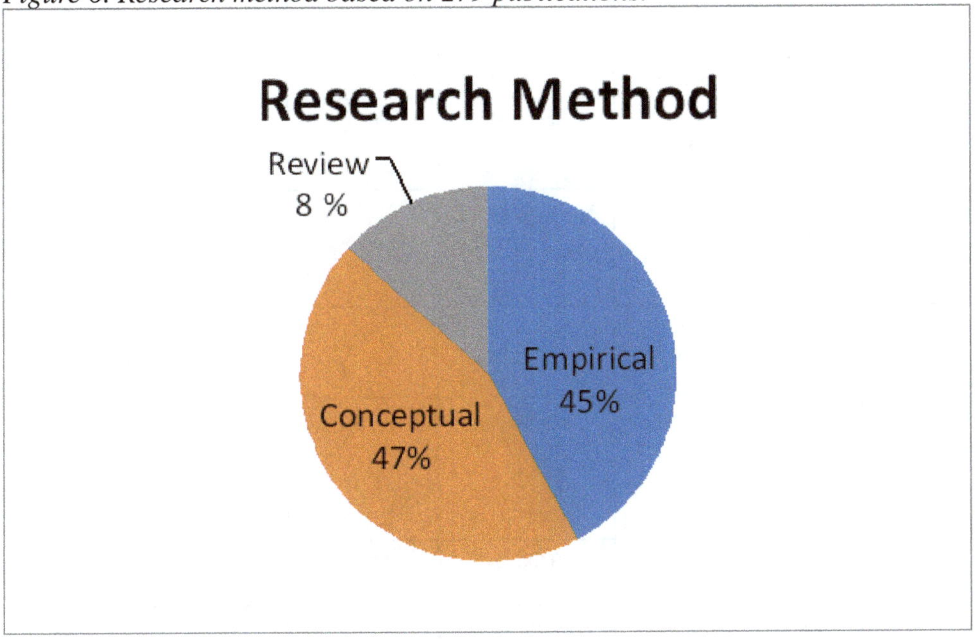

3.5 Most Cited Papers

The database reveals that papers on CC have been authored by a collective of 637 scholars. The recognition and influence of these papers are often assessed by their citation count within the specific area of research. Through an analysis of citations across 279 selected publications, we aimed to discern the level of scholarly acceptance each work has achieved. To identify the most influential papers in this domain from 2014 to 2024, we assembled a ranking of the top 10 most cited papers, as indicated in Table 5. This ranking showed that the articles authored by Hamari, J.; Sjöklint, M.; and Ukkonen, A. in 2016, along with the work of Belk, R. in 2014, received the highest number of citations, positioning them as leading contributions within the timeframe under consideration, as demonstrated in Table 5.

Table 5. Publication related to the topic.

S.no	Publication	Author	Total Citation	Local Citations	Year
1	"The sharing economy: Why people participate in collaborative consumption"	Hamari, J.; Sjöklint, M.; and Ukkonen, A.	2026	120	2016
2	"You are what you can access: Sharing and collaborative consumption online"	Belk, R.	1906	157	2014 (a)
3	"Sharing economy: A review and agenda for future research"	Cheng M.	614	32	2016
4	"Promises and paradoxes of the sharing economy: An organizing framework"	Acquire a.	501	34	2017
5	"Environmental impact of textile reuse and recycling – A review"	Sandin G.	487	38	2018
6	"Sharing for people, planet or profit? Analysing motivations for intended sharing economy participation"	Bãcker L	422	37	2017
7	"Sharing Versus Pseudo-Sharing in Web 2.0"	Belk, R.	416	37	2014
8	"The sharing economy and digital platforms: A review and research agenda"	Sutherland, W.	407	34	2018

S.no	Publication	Author	Total Citation	Local Citations	Year
9	"A triadic framework for collaborative consumption (CC): Motives, activities and resources & capabilities of actors"	Benoit s	394	34	2017
10	"Understanding current and future issues in collaborative consumption: A four-stage Delphi study"	Barnes SJ	266	32	2016

The reference of two or more publications coming together in other publications is considered as co-citation (Yu *et al.*, 2018). Three methods involved in co-citation are- multi-dimensional scaling, clustering, and factor analysis (Charvet *et al.*, 2008). VOS Viewer is used for multidimensional scaling and to construct the connectivity on co-citation in the research area of CC. From 16377 cited references, 20 references have met the threshold and have co-cited the publication more than 20 times. Figure 7 displays that Belk, (2014) is most often co-cited by the other researchers in CC. It is considered a pioneer and provided a significant contribution to the field of CC research.

Figure 7. Co-cited reference in the research area of collaborative consumption.

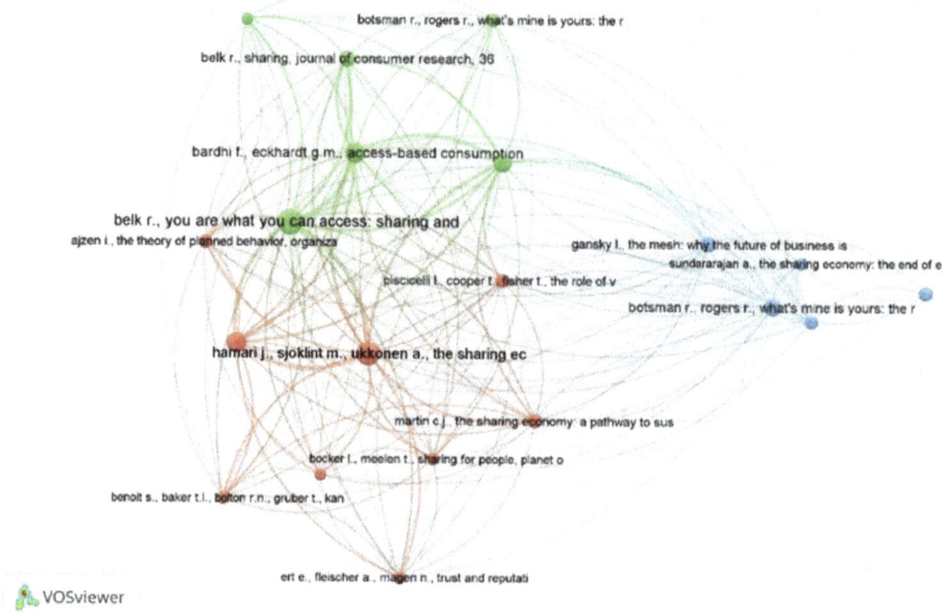

Figure 8 is a map that shows the major producing countries' national collaboration. There is a link-line between the two countries that shows how collaborative they are. The line thickness serves as a representation of the collaboration scale. Scholarly collaboration and exchange across nations increased in the USA, Germany, China, and the United Kingdom. According to (Bugge et al., 2016), several organizations—including research institutions and universities—were grouped together in a geographical area for collaborative efforts.

Figure 8. Country collaboration map.

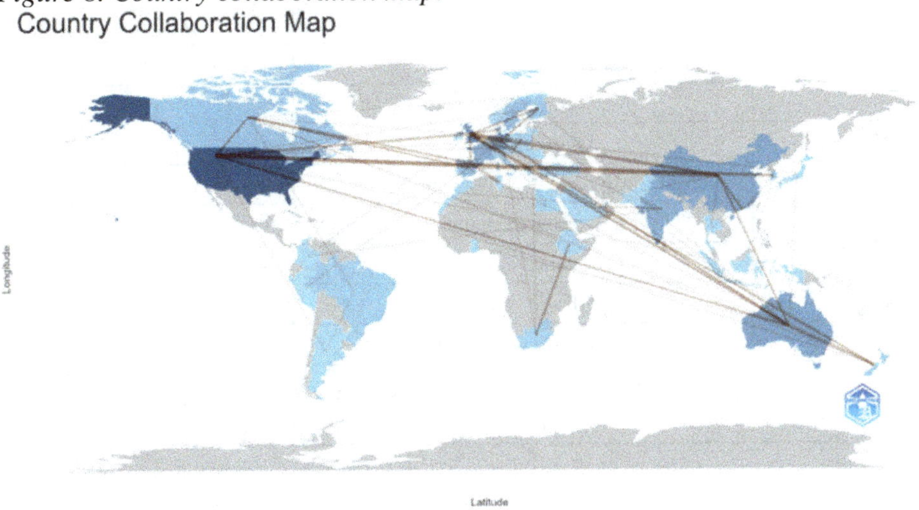

3.6. Keyword analysis

A comprehensive review of the trends and focal points in collaborative consumption research within the apparel industry can be achieved through an analysis of keywords. This investigation encompassed a collection of 840 author-specified keywords and 689 keywords Plus, derived from the Scopus database, which serves as a resource for scholars. Keywords provided by authors are selected to accurately reflect the essence of their work, whereas keywords plus is generated by Scopus and might not be directly linked to the paper's title or the author-selected keywords. Both categories of keywords are crucial for scholarly communication. By mining and evaluating these keywords from the literature, insights into the progression and emerging themes in the realm of research on apparel consumption through collaboration can be discerned (Table 6). By utilising Bibliometrix in R to construct the keyword frequency analysis, as illustrated in Figure 9, the current study has identified the most frequently occurring keywords.

Table 6. Keyword analysis

Sr. No.	Keyword	Occurrences
1	Collaborative consumption	248
2	Sharing economy	151
3	Sustainability	47
4	Consumption behaviour	36
5	Sustainable development	21
6	Collaborative economy	18
7	Acess-based consumption	16
8	Sustainable consumption	16
9	Trust	16
10	Innovation	15

Figure 9. Keywords frequency

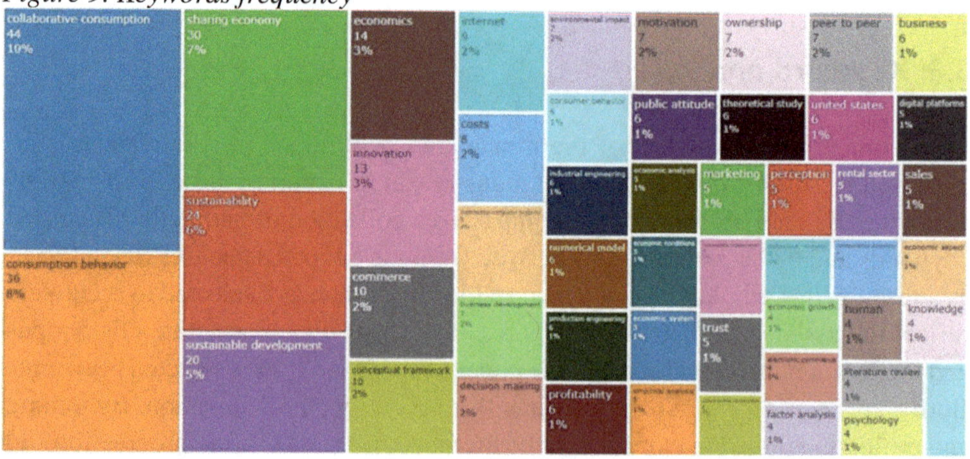

In Figure 10, we utilize VOS viewer to develop a keyword cluster map, aiming to scrutinize the overarching categorization of keywords, encompassing a total of 58 selected keywords across 7 clusters. The figure illustrates the relationship between the magnitude of each circle representing a keyword and its prevalence. The lines linking the circles signify the co-occurrence of two keywords across one or several papers. From this analysis, four principal clusters emerge. Cluster 1 encompasses the realm of the sharing economy and collaborative consumption, weaving together themes of the gig economy, collaborative economy, and economic systems. Examination of the articles' conceptual references reveals a propensity to merge Attitude, motivation, and trust frameworks in the context of Collaborative consumption within the apparel sector (Clube and Tennant, 2020; Kim and Yoon, 2021; McCoy *et al.*, 2021; Roos and Hahn, 2019).

Cluster 2 highlights the interplay between business development and consumer behaviour, shifting focus towards ownership perspectives. Here, conceptual frameworks and materialism serve as pivotal instruments for identifying trends within prevailing business models (Campos *et al.*, 2023; Ek Styvén and Mariani, 2020; Henninger *et al.*, 2019; McCoy *et al.*, 2021).

Cluster 3 is linked to economic advancement, emphasizing sustainable consumption and incorporating Industrial engineering and circular economy as pivotal keywords. The discourse on collaborative consumption in the business sector evolves towards Circular Economy paradigms and economic prerequisites for a sustainable circular economy, emphasizing product development with reuse in mind to maintain materials within the production cycle. This perspective is underscored as a vital alternative for the apparel industry by the reviewed authors (Geissdoerfer *et al.*, 2017; Mishra *et al.*, 2020; Möhlmann, 2015).

Lastly, Cluster 4 focuses on marketing, innovation, and environmental impacts related to sustainable development. Within this context, business model strategies are explored as researchers endeavour to identify, formulate, and implement methods and tools for generating, advancing, and delivering sustainable value in businesses (Guyader, 2018; Huang *et al.*, 2021; McCoy *et al.*, 2021; Roos and Hahn, 2019; Seo and Kim, 2019).

Figure 10. Network Visualization of the keywords

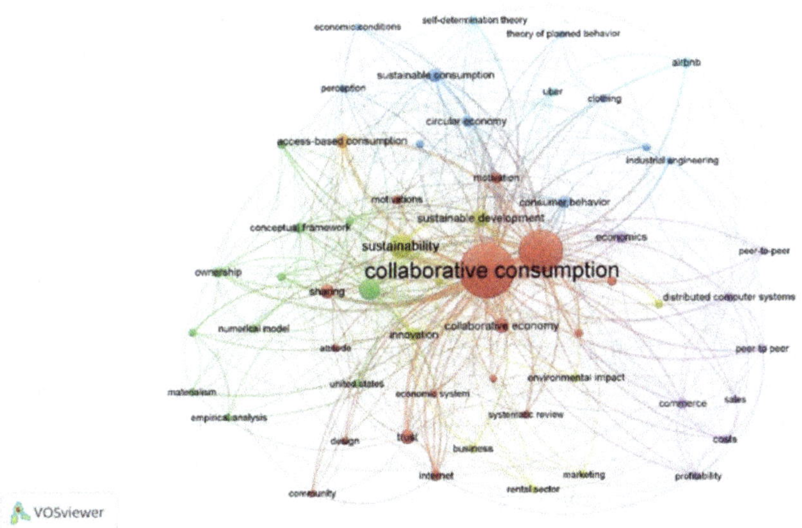

4. THEMATIC ANALYSIS

This section explores the two main clusters that were identified through analysis, review, and summary of study results. These clusters are closely related to research on apparel and collaborative consumption. Analysis was followed by a thorough study of 63 articles out of 279 articles mainly focused on fashion, apparel, clothing, and garments. The first theme focuses on the sharing economy and sustainability. The second theme explores ACC through consumer interaction. The third and final research theme focuses on business models and management perspectives.

4.1. Cluster 1: - Sustainability and the sharing economy

The first cluster discovered a positive correlation between ACC, sharing economy, and sustainability. Encourage people to rent the product instead of buying it (Iran and Schrader, 2017; Kim and Jin, 2020b; Zamani *et al.*, 2017). In terms of environmental benefits and drawbacks, customer involvement and business perspective have received the greatest attention. The researchers studied how ACC may be included in a new business plan (Becker-Leifhold, 2018). Further research focused on the sustainability goals that may motivate customers to participate in ACC (Becker-Leifhold and Iran, 2018; Hamari *et al.*, 2016; McNeill and Venter, 2019).

4.2. Cluster 2: Consumer Behaviour

This section investigates consumer satisfaction, consumer attitudes, consumer willingness and social interaction, which represent the consumer's consumption perception towards ACC mechanisms, based on the review's dominant theme.

a) Consumer satisfaction

According to researchers, consumer satisfaction is the key to uncovering the drivers in the CC for the apparel industry (Barnes and Mattsson, 2017; Clube and Tennant, 2020; Roos and Hahn, 2019; Testa *et al.*, 2020). The satisfaction of choosing CC consumers would be influenced by cost savings, utility, trust, cost savings, and familiarity with services (Möhlmann, 2015). Consumer satisfaction with collaborative consumption is positively influenced by platform reliability, platform responsiveness, vendor competence, vendor empathy, and co-sharer empathy (Abbes *et al.*, 2020; Lim *et al.*, 2021; Wicaksono *et al.*, 2023) and positively influences the continuance of collaborative consumption services (Lim *et al.*, 2021). Organizations adopting collaborative consumption as a form of innovation have the potential to elevate customer satisfaction by offering enhanced value. This is achieved by presenting an extensive and adaptable array of products and services, all while reducing costs for the consumer (Pfajfar *et al.*, 2022).

b) Consumer Attitude

The ACC has been proven to be substantially associated with both attitude and behavioural intention in previous studies (Johnson *et al.*, 2016). Consumer attitudes toward CC platforms were positively influenced by hedonic values and environmental concerns (Ek Styvén and Mariani, 2020; Gopalakrishnan and Matthews, 2018;Slaton and Pookulangara, 2022). Consumer attitude among the four sub-themes that focused on the collaborative consumption of apparel along with customer motivations, intentions, and adoption (Arrigo, 2021) and positively influence consumers' intentions to engage in CC (Guillen-Royo, 2023; Kong *et al.*, 2016; Lee and Chow, 2020; Lee and Huang, 2021). Significant customer attitudes toward CC differences were discovered across countries (Iran et al., 2019).

c) Consumer Willingness

Greater accessibility and visibility via rental services and the secondary market have been identified as factors contributing to increased involvement with ACC (Ek Styvén and Mariani, 2020; Gopalakrishnan and Matthews, 2018; Iran *et al.*, 2019; Lang *et al.*, 2020). Research examining the willingness of consumers concerning collaborative consumption (CC) has utilised consumer value theory in conjunction with the theory of planned behaviour to comprehend the underlying dynamics (Becker-Leifhold, 2018; Iran *et al.*, 2019; Lang *et al.*, 2020; Lang and Joyner Armstrong, 2018). Previous research has demonstrated that consumer receptiveness to ACC is notably influenced by brand consciousness (Gopalakrishnan and Matthews, 2018). Conversely, the adoption of CC has been largely driven by competitive pricing (Camacho-Otero *et al.*, 2019; Park and Joyner Armstrong, 2019b). The inclination to exchange personal clothing items highlights the reliance on apparel availability in the CC model on the preparedness of consumers to engage (Arrigo, 2021). Businesses are advised to prioritise the examination of consumer perceptions, pricing, and promotional strategies to cultivate a stronger propensity for CC participation (Ramtiyal *et al.*, 2023). Furthermore, a discernible change in consumer behaviour has been observed: an expanding inclination towards showcasing social status through CC engagements rather than acquiring expensive apparel; this trend serves to prolong the useful life of such products (Pantano and Stylos, 2020).

d) Social Interaction

Prior research (Belk, 2014a) has identified several key determinants of engagement within ACC, including economic benefits (McCoy *et al.*, 2021; Park and Joyner Armstrong, 2019a), societal factors (McNeill and Venter, 2019), consumer perceptions, and the ease of accessing services (Bhalla, 2021). The collaborative consumption (CC) framework encourages members to engage in communal, exploratory, and creative modes of consumption, including negotiating, leasing, and exchanging (Armstrong *et al.*, 2015). The utility aspect predominates in the decision-making process of prospective adopters, who prioritise practical benefits over delight or enjoyment. Previous research has demonstrated that the rate at which ACCs are accepted is significantly impacted by a variety of economic and demographic variables, such as income and age (Gopalakrishnan and Matthews, 2018; McNeill and Venter, 2019; Norum and Norton, 2017; Zaman *et al.*, 2019).

Furthermore, social interactions that occur within the CC ecosystem play a crucial role in increasing consciousness regarding sustainability and fostering a more dynamic atmosphere in these communities. These exchanges enable the identification and application of unused resources, which increases operational efficiency and cost-effectiveness (Kim and Yoon, 2021). Furthermore, they may potentially boost the self-esteem of individuals (Armstrong *et al.*, 2016). These interactions promote unique and authentic experiences, which encourages individuals to establish connections more often. The assessment of these exchanges between consumers and service providers as well as among CC participants is crucial for encouraging sustained engagement and a broader range of activities within the CC domain (Tussyadiah and Pesonen, 2016; Wicaksono *et al.*, 2023).

4.3. Cluster 3: - Business Practices.

Several studies have scrutinized methodologies and standards to enhance business practices within the ACC (Becker-Leifhold and Iran, 2018; Bodenheimer *et al.*, 2022; Dreyer *et al.*, 2017; Park and Armstrong, 2017). The primary hurdles faced by consumers in the ACC domain relate to inadequate infrastructure and knowledge for implementing recycling, repurposing, and redesign initiatives (Becker-Leifhold and Iran, 2018). It has been observed that businesses frequently venture into the second-hand marketplace by modifying their existing models, albeit without a definitive strategic plan (Abbes *et al.*, 2020). The role of ACC as a pivotal element of the collaborative economy has been acknowledged due to its environmental implications (Kim and Jin, 2020b). The research contrasts the ecological pros and cons of collaborative consumption (CC) against traditional business practices (Habibi *et al.*, 2017), focusing on the notions of efficiency, adequacy, and the rebound phenomenon (Arrigo, 2021)

Moreover, it suggests that devising marketing approaches that highlight creative problem-solving can lure consumers interested in novel experiences (Campos *et al.*, 2023). Every analyzed business model recognized financial profit as a primary advantage (Gopalakrishnan and Matthews, 2018), including models such as clothing libraries (Pedersen and Netter, 2015; Zamani *et al.*, 2017), second-hand outlets (Ek Styvén and Mariani, 2020; Gopalakrishnan and Matthews, 2018), rental services (Lang *et al.*, 2019, 2020; McCoy *et al.*, 2021), and exchange programs (Henninger *et al.*, 2019). A recurring challenge across these models is their operation at a minimal scale. Research by Becker-Leifhold and Iran, (2018) suggests a willingness among consumers to serve as product distributors, either by selling or lending their clothing (Gopalakrishnan and Matthews, 2018). However, the uncertainty surrounding product availability poses limitations to revenue generation (Pedersen and Netter, 2015) and the achievement of potential social advantages (Schor and Cansoy, 2019; Schor and Fitzmaurice, 2015).

5. CONCEPTUAL FRAMEWORK

Environmental issues have arisen in recent decades, prompting researchers to study the concept of sustainability and ACC. The term "sustainability" refers to the production of clothing as well as its use and post-usage (Iran and Schrader, 2017). A new conceptual framework has been developed based on the literature related to CC, to provide a systematisation of the ACC model in the apparel sector (Arrigo, 2021; Gopalakrishnan and Matthews, 2018; Henninger *et al.*, 2021; Iran and Schrader, 2017; Park and Armstrong, 2017; Pedersen and Netter, 2015). Figure 11 is based on the concept of sustainable fashion as presented by (Iran and Schrader, 2017).

Figure 11. Element of sustainable fashion (Adopted from Samira Iran and Ulf Schrader (2017).

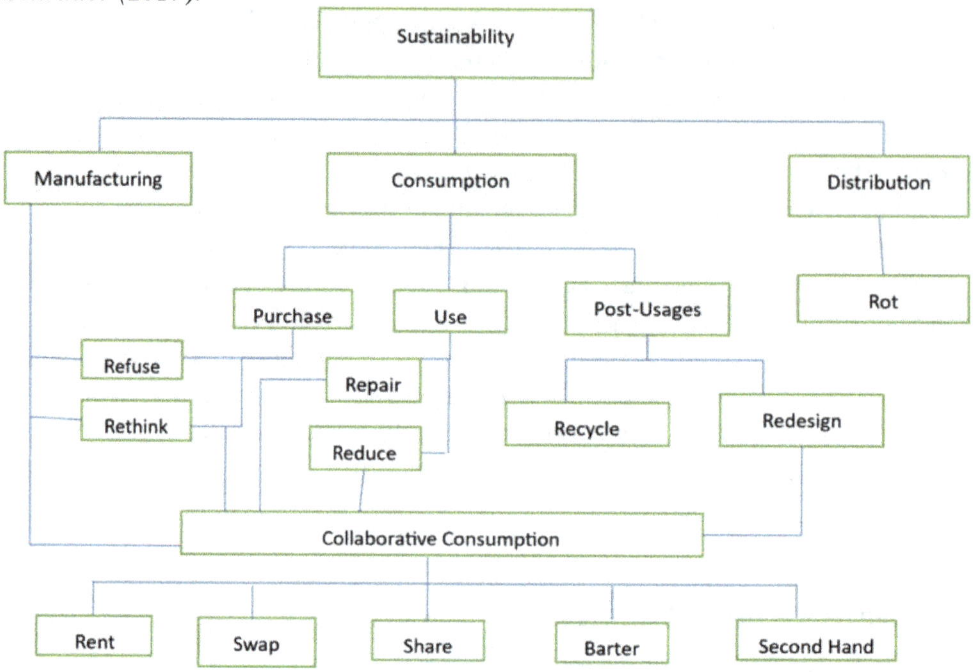

Based on a review of the literature, ACC can be divided into five basic behaviour types that all reflect the same foundational personality: rent, swap, share, barter, and second-hand (Belk, 2014a; Botsman and Rogers, 2011). Utility-based ownership (UO) and redistributed ownership (RO) (Arrigo, 2021; Park and Armstrong, 2017) are two ACC mechanisms established through a systematic literature review. However, all five behaviours involve consumer-organization partnerships. The concept takes a holistic perspective of remuneration, separating it into non-monetary and monetary components (Park and Armstrong, 2017), where sharing activities do not show any due on compensation (Botsman and Rogers, 2010). These sorts of behaviour can be seen in commercial market structures such as consumer-to-consumer (C2C) and business-to-consumer (B2C), as well as offline and online methods. Figure 12 depicts the categorization for collaborative apparel consumption adapted from (Arrigo, 2021; Park and Armstrong, 2017).

Figure 12. Categorization for sustainable apparel consumption (ACC)

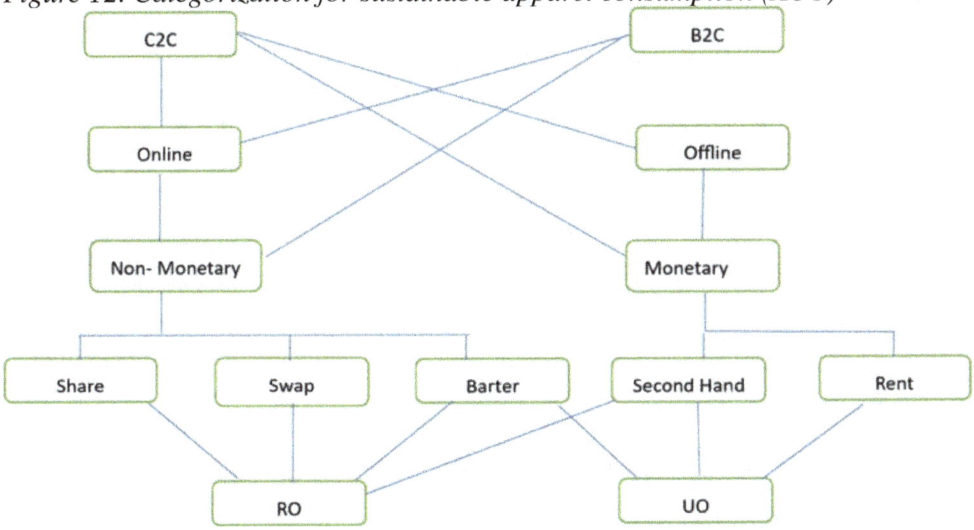

(Adapted from Arrigo, 2021; Park and Armstrong, 2017)

Figure 13 shows adopting a comprehensive view of ACC that includes the potential benefits to consumer gains from participation in ACC such as pleasure, social connection with a community of the same interest, and environmental issues. The literature identified four primary perspectives on consumer adoption and engagement with ACC: environmental concern, society belonging, product utility, and ownership (Botsman and Rogers, 2010b; Gopalakrishnan, 2018; Gopalakrishnan and Matthews, 2018; Hamari *et al.*, 2016). Monetary motivation is found to positively affect ACC (Baek and Oh, 2020; Möhlmann, 2015; Roos and Hahn, 2019). The function of consumer attitude and factors influencing their desire to engage in ACC is examined using the theory of planned behaviour (Brandão and Costa, 2021; Chang and Watchravesringkan, 2018; Chi *et al.*, 2019; Nekmahmud *et al.*, 2022; Ramtiyal *et al.*, 2023; Seo and Kim, 2019). Consumers' environmental beliefs and perceptions about ACC have influenced positive attitudes, which has the greatest influence on consumer purchase intention (Seo and Kim, 2019).

The customer orientation towards shopping belief is considered a significant predictor for ACC behaviour for both online and offline shopping. The research towards apparel shopping is identified as a psychological orientation for choosing apparel in the marketplace (Cho *et al.*, 2015). The framework represents the shopping beliefs in terms of Trait, Price, Trend and Brand (Gopalakrishnan and Matthews, 2018).

Figure 13. Conceptual Framework for Apparel Consumption Through Collaboration.

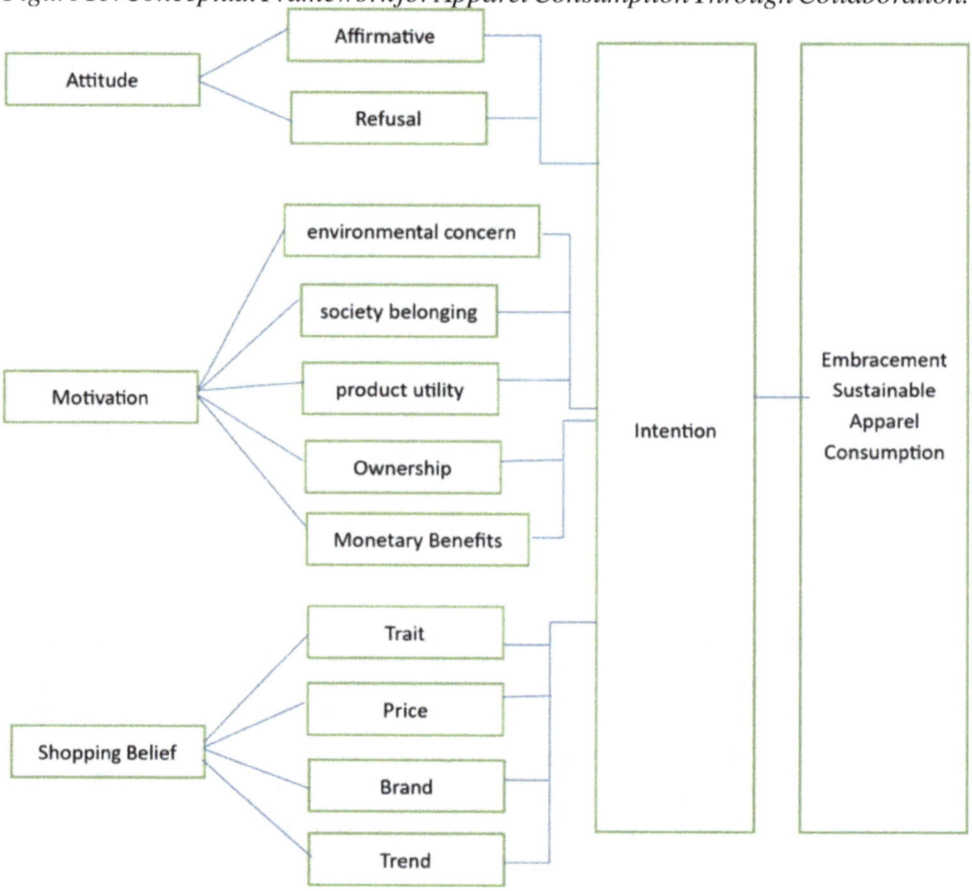

6. PRACTICAL IMPLICATIONS & CONCLUSION

The in-depth review and bibliometric analysis result significantly enhance the understanding of apparel consumption through collaboration in academic literature. subsequently the references influential works by researchers like (Belk, 2014b; Benoit *et al.*, 2017; Botsman and Rogers, 2010a; Ertz *et al.*, 2019; Fraanje and Spaargaren, 2019; Hamari *et al.*, 2016; Park and Armstrong, 2017). This highlights the critical matter of establishing a precise definition for ACC, which may spur normative debates concerning the criteria that qualify as or do not qualify various modalities of consumption. For companies seeking to establish their market differentiation and enhance the relationship between service providers and customers, it is critical to clearly define the scope of ACC. This study represents an attempt to compile major findings made in the field during the previous ten years, providing a thorough picture of the state of ACC-related research. The data suggest a pattern in which previous investigations have a greater impact.

The paper enhances the discussion on ACC by delineating three primary study dimensions identified i.e: Sustainability, consumption services, and business practices. Recent research has established that the theory of planned behaviour (TPB) and enhancement of TPB is primarily utilised to analyse consumer perceptions and experiences in various domains, including collaborative apparel consumption (Arrigo, 2022; Ashaduzzaman *et al.*, 2022; Iran *et al.*, 2019; Lang and Joyner Armstrong, 2018; McNeill and Venter, 2019; Ramtiyal *et al.*, 2023; Roos and Hahn, 2019; Seo and Kim, 2019).

This study establishes a foundation for a market-specific business model focused on ACC, thereby bridging the existing knowledge divide in the field. This study conducts a detailed analysis of the apparel industry, which is known for its significant economic impact and environmental footprint. The study highlights the potential of ACC frameworks to guide sustainability practices in many industries. This implies that gaining insight into these systems specifically within the apparel sector could function as an exemplar for more extensive implementation, thereby promoting the shift towards a circular economy. The increasing number of digital platforms that provide access to a wide range of clothing options highlights the growing academic interest in ACC. This indicates a potential path towards widespread acceptance through improved infrastructure support, such as swap shops, rental platforms, and secondhand stores (Henninger *et al.*, 2019).

This study provides practical and implementable insights for professionals. This framework offers a strategic approach for second-hand stores, rental services, and fashion entrepreneurs to differentiate their collaborative consumption activities, thus obtaining a competitive edge. Furthermore, fashion and luxury firms that are already well-established and are contemplating a transition to a circular economy model can greatly benefit from this research. It provides vital insights on how to effectively include collaborative consumption activities, such as rentals or resales, into their business operations. The thorough examination of current literature on motivations and obstacles in the field of apparel consumption through collaboration (ACC) provides valuable insights for the fashion industry, academia, and consumers who are interested in sustainable clothing choices. A legal and political debate has started, especially about how different rules and laws that encourage new ideas and competition might help or hurt the growth of the ACC (Benoit et al., 2017; Rojanakit et al., 2022). This research has the potential to inform policy-making and legislative initiatives aimed at promoting a more sustainable apparel industry. In summary, the results of this study enhance the discussion surrounding ACC and provide practical strategies for its application.

7. LIMITATIONS AND FUTURE RESEARCH

The research has certain limitations. The authors tried to include all relevant keywords in the search criteria, however, some studies may have been missed. Second, the author's study period is 2014-2024, resulting in the exclusion of a few studies. The search considered the most recent studies, however other databases may provide more results. These restrictions can be discussed in the future by scaling up the database and using equivalent keywords. Although ACC has been evolving, comprehensive work in developing countries is still missing that need to be explored further.

A detailed analysis reveals that innovative research on the ACC, the role of sustainability and the sharing economy, consumer intention, motivation, and the digital future can pave the way for future research. Future research could investigate other aspects of collaborative apparel consumption, such as how the customer-brand relationship can support or increase consumer engagement in ACC. A few studies have focused on Millennials, so future research can investigate the differences between consumer cohorts in terms of their involvement in the ACC. Future research can focus on Generation Z, which is recognised as one of the most environmentally mindful and sensitive to issues of sustainability (McCoy *et al.*, 2021). According to the findings, future research could take the form of multi/cross-country studies on customer motivation, attitude, intention, and acceptance of ACC to identify potential disparities, as there has been a limited amount of cross-nation research (Albinsson *et al.*, 2019; Botsman and Rogers, 2010a; Davidson *et al.*, 2018; Henninger *et al.*, 2019; Iran *et al.*, 2019; Kim and Jin, 2020a). As a result, future research can investigate how customers use clothing to express their values. Furthermore, the previous literature primarily focused on luxury consumption via the second-hand market, ignoring the link between the customer and the brand. (Pantano and Stylos, 2020). According to the research, ACC is a feasible area that could contribute to the reduction of textile waste. Future research could help to better understand the implications of the ACC model on minimizing the adverse sustainability impact of the apparel business.

New business models (emerging out of ACC) need to be tested in terms of acceptability, feasibility, viability and sustainable. Several studies have shown increased awareness and environmental consciousness post pandemic. The effects of COVID-19 have changed the ecosystem for the collaborative consumption as well as people's behaviour (Akan & Tepeler, 2022; Duan, 2023). Some longitudinal studies are required studies are required to analyse pre-& post pandemic impact on attitude, behaviour and values of consumers. Digital platforms provide a key channel to interact with customers for marketing purposes including sending personalized marketing communication, carrying out customer profiling and providing customer service(Arrigo, 2022). Although several studies explain the importance of technology in the context of ACC(Benoit et al., 2017; Fraanje & Spaargaren, 2019; Hamari et al., 2016; Paro et al., 2021). Advancement in technology and use of AI may lead to further disruption in the said domain not enough studies are available to check the impact. Future advances in technology, such as artificial intelligence, robotics and 3D printing, will become ever more present in the lives of users. Companies and suppliers that pay attention to this new market reality will be able to create strategies and aggregate value, together with their customers.

DECLARATION OF COMPETING INTEREST

The authors claim that they have no recognized competing personal or financial interests that could have impacted the results of this study.

REFERENCES

Abbes, I., Hallem, Y. and Taga, N. (2020), "Second-hand shopping and brand loyalty: The role of online collaborative redistribution platforms", *Journal of Retailing and Consumer Services*, Elsevier Ltd, Vol. 52 No. April 2019, p. 101885, doi: .DOI: 10.1016/j.jretconser.2019.101885

Akan, Y., & Tepeler, M. İ. (2022). Sharing Economy in the Dimension of Sustainability and Trust. *Sosyoekonomi, 30*(53), 447–464. DOI: 10.17233/sosyoekonomi.2022.03.22

Akbar, P., & Hoffmann, S. (2023). Collaborative space: Framework for collaborative consumption and the sharing economy. *Journal of Services Marketing, 37*(4), 496–509. DOI: 10.1108/JSM-03-2021-0078

Albinsson, P. A., Perera, B. Y., Nafees, L., & Burman, B. (2019). Collaborative Consumption Usage in the US and India: An Exploratory Study. *Journal of Marketing Theory and Practice, 27*(4), 390–412. DOI: 10.1080/10696679.2019.1644956

Amasawa, E., Brydges, T., Henninger, C. E., & Kimita, K. (2023). Can rental platforms contribute to more sustainable fashion consumption? Evidence from a mixed-method study. *Cleaner and Responsible Consumption, Elsevier Ltd, 8*(January), 100103. DOI: 10.1016/j.clrc.2023.100103

Amit, R., & Zott, C. (2012). Creating value through business model innovation. *MIT Sloan Management Review*.

Amoozad Mahdiraji, H., Sharifpour Arabi, H., Beheshti, M., & Vrontis, D. (2023). A mixed-method analysis of Industry 4.0 technologies in value generation for collaborative consumption companies. *Management Decision*.

Anwar, S. T. (2023). The sharing economy and collaborative consumption: Strategic issues and global entrepreneurial opportunities. *Journal of International Entrepreneurship, 21*(1), 60–88. DOI: 10.1007/s10843-022-00323-0

Armstrong, C. M., Niinimäki, K., Kujala, S., Karell, E., & Lang, C. (2015). Sustainable product-service systems for clothing: Exploring consumer perceptions of consumption alternatives in Finland. *Journal of Cleaner Production, Elsevier Ltd, 97*, 30–39. DOI: 10.1016/j.jclepro.2014.01.046

Armstrong, C. M., Niinimäki, K., Lang, C., & Kujala, S. (2016). A Use-Oriented Clothing Economy? Preliminary Affirmation for Sustainable Clothing Consumption Alternatives. *Sustainable Development*, *24*(1), 18–31. DOI: 10.1002/sd.1602

Arrigo, E. (2021). Collaborative consumption in the fashion industry: A systematic literature review and conceptual framework. *Journal of Cleaner Production, Elsevier Ltd*, *325*(September), 129261. DOI: 10.1016/j.jclepro.2021.129261

Arrigo, E. (2022). Digital platforms in fashion rental: A business model analysis. *Journal of Fashion Marketing and Management*, *26*(1), 1–20. DOI: 10.1108/JFMM-03-2020-0044

Ashaduzzaman, M., Jebarajakirthy, C., Weaven, S. K., Maseeh, H. I., Das, M., & Pentecost, R. (2022). Predicting Collaborative Consumption Behaviour: A Meta-Analytic Path Analysis on the Theory of Planned Behaviour. *European Journal of Marketing*, *56*. Advance online publication. DOI: 10.1108/EJM-07-2020-0563

Baek, E., & Oh, G. E. (2020). (Grace). (2021), "Diverse values of fashion rental service and contamination concern of consumers. *Journal of Business Research, Elsevier Inc.*, *123*(March), 165–175. DOI: 10.1016/j.jbusres.2020.09.061

Baker, H. K., Pandey, N., Kumar, S., & Haldar, A. (2020). A bibliometric analysis of board diversity: Current status, development, and future research directions. *Journal of Business Research, Elsevier*, *108*, 232–246.

Baker, J., Levy, M., & Grewal, D. (1992). An Experimental Approach to Making Retail Store Environment Decisions. *Journal of Retailing*, *68*(Winter), 445–460.

Barbosa, B., & Fonseca, I. (2019). A phenomenological approach to the collaborative consumer. *Journal of Consumer Marketing*, *36*(6), 705–714. DOI: 10.1108/JCM-11-2017-2468

Bardhi, F., & Eckhardt, G. M. (2012). Access-Based Consumption: The Case of Car Sharing. *The Journal of Consumer Research*, *39*(4), 881–898. DOI: 10.1086/666376

Barnes, S. J., & Mattsson, J. (2017). Understanding collaborative consumption: Test of a theoretical model. *Technological Forecasting and Social Change, Elsevier Inc.*, *118*, 281–292. DOI: 10.1016/j.techfore.2017.02.029

Becker-Leifhold, C., & Iran, S. (2018). Collaborative fashion consumption – drivers, barriers and future pathways. *Journal of Fashion Marketing and Management, 22*(2), 189–208. DOI: 10.1108/JFMM-10-2017-0109

Becker-Leifhold, C. V. (2018). "The role of values in collaborative fashion consumption - A critical investigation through the lenses of the theory of planned behavior", *Journal of Cleaner Production. Elsevier B.V., 199*, 781–791. DOI: 10.1016/j.jclepro.2018.06.296

Belk, R. (2014a). You are what you can access: Sharing and collaborative consumption online. *Journal of Business Research, Elsevier Inc., 67*(8), 1595–1600. DOI: 10.1016/j.jbusres.2013.10.001

Belk, R. (2014b). Sharing versus pseudo-sharing in web 2.0. *Anthropologist, 18*(1), 7–23. DOI: 10.1080/09720073.2014.11891518

Benoit, S., Baker, T. L., Bolton, R. N., Gruber, T., & Kandampully, J. (2017). A triadic framework for collaborative consumption (CC): Motives, activities and resources & capabilities of actors. *Journal of Business Research, Elsevier, 79*(May), 219–227. DOI: 10.1016/j.jbusres.2017.05.004

Bhalla, S. (2021). Testing the Motivations and Constraints of Collaborative Consumption: An Empirical Analysis of Disruptive Innovative Business Model. *FIIB Business Review, 10*(2), 146–157. DOI: 10.1177/23197145211007320

Blanco-Mesa, F., Merigó, J. M., & Gil-Lafuente, A. M. (2017). Fuzzy decision making: A bibliometric-based review. *Journal of Intelligent & Fuzzy Systems, 32*(3), 2033–2050. DOI: 10.3233/JIFS-161640

Bodenheimer, M., Schuler, J., & Wilkening, T. (2022). "Drivers and barriers to fashion rental for everyday garments: An empirical analysis of a former fashion-rental company", *Sustainability. Science, Practice, and Policy, Taylor & Francis, 18*(1), 344–356. DOI: 10.1080/15487733.2022.2065774

Botsman, R. (2013), "The Sharing Economy Lacks a Shared Definition. Fast Co", *Exist. URL* Http://Www. Fastcoexist. Com/3022028/the-Sharing-Economy-Lacks-a-Shared-Definition

Botsman, R. and Rogers, R. (2010a), "What's mine is yours", *The Rise of Collaborative Consumption.*

Botsman, R. and Rogers, R. (2010b), "What's Mine Is Yours: The Rise of Collaborative Consumption".

Botsman, R., & Rogers, R. (2011). *What's Mine Is Yours: How Collaborative Consumption Is Changing the Way We Live*. Collins.

Brandão, A., & da Costa, A. G. (2021). Extending the theory of planned behaviour to understand the effects of barriers towards sustainable fashion consumption. *European Business Review, 33*(5), 742–774. DOI: 10.1108/EBR-11-2020-0306

Brownbridge, K., Gill, S., Grogan, S., Kilgariff, S., & Whalley, A. (2018). Fashion misfit: Women's dissatisfaction and its implications. *Journal of Fashion Marketing and Management, 22*(3), 438–452. DOI: 10.1108/JFMM-05-2017-0050

Bugge, M. M., Hansen, T., & Klitkou, A. (2016). What is the bioeconomy? A review of the literature. *Sustainability (Switzerland), 8*(7). Advance online publication. DOI: 10.3390/su8070691

Bugge, M. M., Hansen, T., & Klitkou, A. (2016). What is the bioeconomy? A review of the literature. *Sustainability (Switzerland), 8*(7). Advance online publication. DOI: 10.3390/su8070691

Byun, S. E., & Sternquist, B. (2011). Fast fashion and in-store hoarding: The drivers, moderator, and consequences. *Clothing & Textiles Research Journal, 29*(3), 187–201. DOI: 10.1177/0887302X11411709

Camacho-Otero, J., Boks, C., & Pettersen, I. N. (2019). User acceptance and adoption of circular offerings in the fashion sector: Insights from user-generated online reviews. *Journal of Cleaner Production, Elsevier Ltd, 231*(June), 928–939. DOI: 10.1016/j.jclepro.2019.05.162

Campos, P. de O., Costa, C. S. R., & da Costa, M. F. (2023). Relationship between personality traits and consumer rationality regarding the intention to purchase collaborative fashion. *Journal of Fashion Marketing and Management, 27*(1), 42–60. DOI: 10.1108/JFMM-02-2021-0049

Cavalcante Costa, M.R., Silva, M.E., & Duarte, M. de F. (2024). Sustainable Consumption and Practice Theories: Connecting Elements of Clothing Sharing. *Brazilian Business Review, 21*(1). Advance online publication. DOI: 10.15728/bbr.2021.1182.en

Chang, H.J., & Watchravesringkan, K. (Tu). (2018). Who are sustainably minded apparel shoppers? An investigation to the influencing factors of sustainable apparel consumption. *International Journal of Retail & Distribution Management, 46*(2), 148–162. DOI: 10.1108/IJRDM-10-2016-0176

Charvet, F. F., Cooper, M. C., & Gardner, J. T. (2008). "The intellectual structure of supply chain management: A bibliometric approach", *Journal of Business Logistics. Wiley Online Library*, *29*(1), 47–73.

Chi, T., Gerard, J., Dephillips, A., Liu, H., & Sun, J. (2019). Why U.S. consumers buy sustainable cotton made collegiate apparel? A study of the key determinants. *Sustainability (Switzerland)*, *11*(11). Advance online publication. DOI: 10.3390/su11113126

Cho, E., Gupta, S., & Kim, Y. K. (2015). Style consumption: Its drivers and role in sustainable apparel consumption. *International Journal of Consumer Studies*, *39*(6), 661–669. DOI: 10.1111/ijcs.12185

Choudhary, A., Amity, A. J., Gupta, T., & Shah, T. R. (2022). A greener world through Collaborative Consumption of Apparel: An Exploratory Study of consumers' perception and preferences. *Electronic Green Journal*, *1*(47). Advance online publication. DOI: 10.5070/G314754088

Clube, R. K. M., & Tennant, M. (2020). Exploring garment rental as a sustainable business model in the fashion industry: Does contamination impact the consumption experience? *Journal of Consumer Behaviour*, *19*(4), 359–370. DOI: 10.1002/cb.1817

Cobo, M. J., López-Herrera, A. G., Herrera-Viedma, E., & Herrera, F. (2011). "Science mapping software tools: Review, analysis, and cooperative study among tools", *Journal of the American Society for Information Science and Technology*, John Wiley & Sons. *Ltd*, *62*(7), 1382–1402. DOI: 10.1002/asi.21525

Davidson, A., Habibi, M.R. and Laroche, M. (2018), "Materialism and the sharing economy: A cross-cultural study of American and Indian consumers", *Journal of Business Research*, Elsevier, Vol. 82 No. July 2015, pp. 364–372, doi: .DOI: 10.1016/j.jbusres.2015.07.045

de Medeiros, J. F., Marcon, A., Ribeiro, J. L. D., Quist, J., & D'Agostin, A. (2021). Consumer emotions and collaborative consumption: The effect of COVID-19 on the adoption of use-oriented product-service systems. *Sustainable Production and Consumption*, *27*, 1569–1588. DOI: 10.1016/j.spc.2021.03.010

Dreyer, B., Lüdeke-Freund, F., Hamann, R., & Faccer, K. (2017). Upsides and downsides of the sharing economy: Collaborative consumption business models' stakeholder value impacts and their relationship to context. *Technological Forecasting and Social Change, Elsevier Inc.*, *125*, 87–104. DOI: 10.1016/j.techfore.2017.03.036

Duan, C. (2023). Towards a comprehensive analytical framework and future research agenda for research on sharing economy business models: thematic analyses approach. In *Information Systems and e-Business Management* (Vol. 21, Issue 4). Springer Berlin Heidelberg. https://doi.org/DOI: 10.1007/s10257-023-00657-

Ek Styvén, M., & Mariani, M. M. (2020). Understanding the intention to buy secondhand clothing on sharing economy platforms: The influence of sustainability, distance from the consumption system, and economic motivations. *Psychology and Marketing*, *37*(5), 724–739. DOI: 10.1002/mar.21334

Ekanayake, E. M. A. C., Shen, G., & Kumaraswamy, M. M. (2019). Mapping the knowledge domains of value management: A bibliometric approach. *Engineering, Construction, and Architectural Management*, *26*(3), 499–514. DOI: 10.1108/ECAM-06-2018-0252

Ertz, M., Durif, F., & Arcand, M. (2019). A conceptual perspective on collaborative consumption. *AMS Review, Springer*, *9*(1), 27–41.

Fahimnia, B., Sarkis, J. and Davarzani, H. (2015), *Green Supply Chain Management: A Review and Bibliometric Analysis, International Journal of Production Economics*, Vol. 162, Elsevier, doi: .DOI: 10.1016/j.ijpe.2015.01.003

Fraanje, W., & Spaargaren, G. (2019). "What future for collaborative consumption? A practice theoretical account", *Journal of Cleaner Production. Elsevier B.V.*, *208*, 499–508. DOI: 10.1016/j.jclepro.2018.09.197

Frenken, K., & Schor, J. (2017). "Putting the sharing economy into perspective", *Environmental Innovation and Societal Transitions. Elsevier B.V.*, *23*, 3–10. DOI: 10.1016/j.eist.2017.01.003

Ganak, J., Chen, Y., Liang, D., Liu, H., & Chi, T. (2020). "Understanding US millennials' perceived values of denim apparel recycling: Insights for brands and retailers", *International Journal of Sustainable Society* [IEL]. *Inderscience Publishers*, *12*(4), 267–290.

García-Rodríguez, F. J., Gutiérrez-Taño, D., Ruiz-Rosa, I., & Baute-Díaz, N. (2022). New Models for Collaborative Consumption: The Role of Consumer Attitudes Among Millennials. *SAGE Open*, *12*(4), 1–14. DOI: 10.1177/21582440221140389

Geissdoerfer, M., Savaget, P., Bocken, N. M. P., & Hultink, E. J. (2017). The Circular Economy – A new sustainability paradigm? *Journal of Cleaner Production, Elsevier Ltd*, *143*, 757–768. DOI: 10.1016/j.jclepro.2016.12.048

Gopalakrishnan, S. (2018), "Motivations and Shopping Orientations for Engagement in Collaborative Consumption among Fashion Consumers", No. 1, p. 103.

Gopalakrishnan, S., & Matthews, D. (2018). Collaborative consumption: A business model analysis of second-hand fashion. *Journal of Fashion Marketing and Management, 22*(3), 354–368. DOI: 10.1108/JFMM-05-2017-0049

Guillen-Royo, M. (2023). 'I prefer to own what I use': Exploring the role of emotions in upscaling collaborative consumption through libraries in Norway. *Cleaner and Responsible Consumption, 8*(December), 2022. DOI: 10.1016/j.clrc.2023.100108

Guyader, H. (2018). No one rides for free! Three styles of collaborative consumption. *Journal of Services Marketing, 32*(6), 692–714. DOI: 10.1108/JSM-11-2016-0402

Habibi, M. R., Davidson, A., & Laroche, M. (2017). What managers should know about the sharing economy. *Business Horizons, 60*(1), 113–121. DOI: 10.1016/j.bushor.2016.09.007

Hall, J., Matos, S., Sheehan, L., & Silvestre, B. (2012). Entrepreneurship and innovation at the base of the Pyramid: A recipe for inclusive growth or social exclusion? *Journal of Management Studies, 49*(4), 785–812. DOI: 10.1111/j.1467-6486.2012.01044.x

Hamari, J., Sjöklint, M., & Ukkonen, A. (2016). "The sharing economy: Why people participate in collaborative consumption", *Journal of the Association for Information Science and Technology*, John Wiley & Sons. *Ltd, 67*(9), 2047–2059. DOI: 10.1002/asi.23552

Hayes, S. G., & Jones, N. (2006). Fast fashion: A financial snapshot. *Journal of Fashion Marketing and Management, 10*(3), 282–300. DOI: 10.1108/13612020610679277

Henninger, C. E., Brydges, T., Iran, S., & Vladimirova, K. (2021). Collaborative fashion consumption – A synthesis and future research agenda. *Journal of Cleaner Production, Elsevier Ltd, 319*(August), 128648. DOI: 10.1016/j.jclepro.2021.128648

Henninger, C. E., Bürklin, N., & Niinimäki, K. (2019). The clothes swapping phenomenon – when consumers become suppliers. *Journal of Fashion Marketing and Management, 23*(3), 327–344. DOI: 10.1108/JFMM-04-2018-0057

Herold, P. I., & Prokop, D. (2023). Is fast fashion finally out of season? Rental clothing schemes as a sustainable and affordable alternative to fast fashion. *Geoforum, Elsevier Ltd, 146*(October), 103873. DOI: 10.1016/j.geoforum.2023.103873

Hu, Z. H., Li, Q., Chen, X. J., & Wang, Y. F. (2014). Sustainable rent-based closed-loop supply chain for fashion products. *Sustainability (Switzerland), 6*(10), 7063–7088. DOI: 10.3390/su6107063

Huang, L., Li, Y., Huang, X., & Zhou, L. (2021). How social distance affects the intention and behavior of collaborative consumption: A study based on online car-hailing service. *Journal of Retailing and Consumer Services, Elsevier Ltd, 61*(March), 102534. DOI: 10.1016/j.jretconser.2021.102534

Iran, S., Geiger, S. M., & Schrader, U. (2019). "Collaborative fashion consumption – A cross-cultural study between Tehran and Berlin", *Journal of Cleaner Production. Elsevier B.V., 212*, 313–323. DOI: 10.1016/j.jclepro.2018.11.163

Iran, S., & Schrader, U. (2017). Collaborative fashion consumption and its environmental effects. *Journal of Fashion Marketing and Management: An International Journal, Emerald Publishing Limited, 21*(4), 468–482. DOI: 10.1108/JFMM-09-2016-0086

Johnson, K. K. P., Mun, J. M., & Chae, Y. (2016). Antecedents to internet use to collaboratively consume apparel. *Journal of Fashion Marketing and Management, 20*(4), 370–382. DOI: 10.1108/JFMM-12-2015-0092

Kessler, M. M. (1963). "Bibliographic coupling between scientific papers", *American Documentation*, John Wiley & Sons. *Ltd, 14*(1), 10–25. DOI: 10.1002/asi.5090140103

Kim, E., & Yoon, S. (2021). Social capital, user motivation, and collaborative consumption of online platform services. *Journal of Retailing and Consumer Services, Elsevier Ltd, 62*(June), 102651. DOI: 10.1016/j.jretconser.2021.102651

Kim, N. L., & Jin, B. E. (2020a). Addressing the contamination issue in collaborative consumption of fashion: Does ownership type of shared goods matter? *Journal of Fashion Marketing and Management, 2026*. Advance online publication. DOI: 10.1108/JFMM-11-2019-0265

Kim, N. L., & Jin, B. E. (2020b). Why buy new when one can share? Exploring collaborative consumption motivations for consumer goods. *International Journal of Consumer Studies, 44*(2), 122–130. DOI: 10.1111/ijcs.12551

Kong, H. M., Ko, E., Chae, H., & Mattila, P. (2016). Understanding fashion consumers' attitude and behavioral intention toward sustainable fashion products: Focus on sustainable knowledge sources and knowledge types. *Journal of Global Fashion Marketing, 7*(2), 103–119. DOI: 10.1080/20932685.2015.1131435

Lang, C., & Joyner Armstrong, C. M. (2018). "Collaborative consumption: The influence of fashion leadership, need for uniqueness, and materialism on female consumers' adoption of clothing renting and swapping", *Sustainable Production and Consumption. Elsevier B.V., 13*, 37–47. DOI: 10.1016/j.spc.2017.11.005

Lang, C., Li, M., & Zhao, L. (2020). "Understanding consumers' online fashion renting experiences: A text-mining approach", *Sustainable Production and Consumption. Elsevier B.V., 21*, 132–144. DOI: 10.1016/j.spc.2019.12.003

Lang, C., Seo, S., & Liu, C. (2019). Motivations and obstacles for fashion renting: A cross-cultural comparison. *Journal of Fashion Marketing and Management, 23*(4), 519–536. DOI: 10.1108/JFMM-05-2019-0106

Lee, S. H., & Huang, R. (2021). Consumer responses to online fashion renting: Exploring the role of cultural differences. *International Journal of Retail & Distribution Management, 49*(2), 187–203. DOI: 10.1108/IJRDM-04-2020-0142

Li, C., Wu, K., & Wu, J. (2017). A bibliometric analysis of research on haze during 2000–2016. *Environmental Science and Pollution Research International, 24*(32), 24733–24742. DOI: 10.1007/s11356-017-0440-1

Lim, W. M., Gupta, G., Biswas, B., & Gupta, R. (2021). "Collaborative consumption continuance: A mixed-methods analysis of the service quality-loyalty relationship in ride-sharing services", *Electronic Markets. Springer Berlin Heidelberg*, (0123456789). Advance online publication. DOI: 10.1007/s12525-021-00486-z

McCoy, L., Wang, Y. T., & Chi, T. (2021). Why is collaborative apparel consumption gaining popularity? An empirical study of us gen z consumers. *Sustainability (Switzerland), 13*(15). Advance online publication. DOI: 10.3390/su13158360

McNeill, L., & Venter, B. (2019). Identity, self-concept and young women's engagement with collaborative, sustainable fashion consumption models. *International Journal of Consumer Studies, 43*(4), 368–378. DOI: 10.1111/ijcs.12516

Mishra, S., Jain, S., & Malhotra, G. (2020). The anatomy of circular economy transition in the fashion industry. *Social Responsibility Journal, 17*(4), 524–542. DOI: 10.1108/SRJ-06-2019-0216

Möhlmann, M. (2015). "Collaborative consumption: Determinants of satisfaction and the likelihood of using a sharing economy option again", *Journal of Consumer Behaviour*, John Wiley & Sons. *Ltd, 14*(3), 193–207. DOI: 10.1002/cb.1512

Moore, C. M., & Fernie, J. (2004). *"Retailing within an international context", International Retail Marketing: A Case Study Approach*. Elsevier Oxford.

Nekmahmud, M., Naz, F., Ramkissoon, H., & Fekete-Farkas, M. (2022). Transforming consumers' intention to purchase green products: Role of social media. *Technological Forecasting and Social Change, Elsevier Inc., 185*(March), 122067. DOI: 10.1016/j.techfore.2022.122067

Norum, P., & Norton, M. (2017). Factors affecting consumer acquisition of second-hand clothing in the USA. *Journal of Fashion Marketing and Management, 21*(2), 206–218. DOI: 10.1108/JFMM-10-2016-0090

Ormrod, J. S. (2020). *Changing Our*. No. June.

Pantano, E., & Stylos, N. (2020). The Cinderella moment: Exploring consumers' motivations to engage with renting as collaborative luxury consumption mode. *Psychology and Marketing*, *37*(5), 740–753. DOI: 10.1002/mar.21345

Park, H., & Armstrong, C. M. J. (2017). "Collaborative apparel consumption in the digital sharing economy: An agenda for academic inquiry", *International Journal of Consumer Studies*, John Wiley & Sons. *Ltd*, *41*(5), 465–474. DOI: 10.1111/ijcs.12354

Park, H., & Joyner Armstrong, C. M. (2019a). Is money the biggest driver? Uncovering motives for engaging in online collaborative consumption retail models for apparel. *Journal of Retailing and Consumer Services, Elsevier Ltd, 51*(April), 42–50. DOI: 10.1016/j.jretconser.2019.05.022

Park, H. and Joyner Armstrong, C.M. (2019b), "Will 'no-ownership' work for apparel?: Implications for apparel retailers", *Journal of Retailing and Consumer Services*, Elsevier Ltd, Vol. 47 No. July 2018, pp. 66–73, doi: .DOI: 10.1016/j.jretconser.2018.10.012

Park, H., & Lee, M. Y. (2022). The Two-Sided Effect of the COVID-19 Pandemic on Online Apparel Renting. *Sustainability (Switzerland)*, *14*(24). Advance online publication. DOI: 10.3390/su142416771

Paro, C. E., Ribeiro da Silva, H. M., Spers, E. E., Jugend, D., & Hamza, K. M. (2021). The technology effect, green consumption and age in propensity to collaborative consumption. *Cleaner and Responsible Consumption*, *2*(January). Advance online publication. DOI: 10.1016/j.clrc.2021.100008

Pedersen, E. R. G., & Netter, S. (2015). "Collaborative consumption: Business model opportunities and barriers for fashion libraries", *Journal of Fashion Marketing and Management. Emerald Group Publishing Limited, 19*(3), 258–273. DOI: 10.1108/JFMM-05-2013-0073

Pfajfar, G., Ma, A. and Mitr, M. (2022), "Adoption of collaborative consumption as sustainable social innovation : Sociability and novelty seeking perspective", Vol. 144 No. May 2021, pp. 163–179, doi: .DOI: 10.1016/j.jbusres.2022.01.062

Podsakoff, P. M., MacKenzie, S. B., Podsakoff, N. P., & Bachrach, D. G. (2008). Scholarly Influence in the Field of Management: A Bibliometric Analysis of the Determinants of University and Author Impact in the Management Literature in the Past Quarter Century. *Journal of Management, SAGE Publications Inc, 34*(4), 641–720. DOI: 10.1177/0149206308319533

Price, D. (1965), "Statistical studies of networks of scientific papers", *Statistical Association Methods for Mechanized Documentation: Symposium Proceedings*, Vol. 269, US Government Printing Office, p. 187.

Ramtiyal, B., Johari, S., Vijayvargy, L. and Prakash, S. (2023), "The impact of marketing mix on the adoption of clothes rental and swapping in collaborative consumption", *Journal of Global Operations and Strategic Sourcing*, doi: .DOI: 10.1108/JGOSS-04-2023-0027

Rey-Martí, A., Ribeiro-Soriano, D., & Palacios-Marqués, D. (2016). A bibliometric analysis of social entrepreneurship. *Journal of Business Research, 69*(5), 1651–1655. DOI: 10.1016/j.jbusres.2015.10.033

Rojanakit, P., de Oliveira, R. T., & Dulleck, U. (2022). The sharing economy: A critical review and research agenda. *Journal of Business Research, 139*, 1317–1334.

Roos, D., & Hahn, R. (2019). Understanding Collaborative Consumption: An Extension of the Theory of Planned Behavior with Value-Based Personal Norms. *Journal of Business Ethics, 158*(3), 679–697. DOI: 10.1007/s10551-017-3675-3

RSA. 2020. The Great Recovery. RSA: https://www.thersa.org/action-and-research/rsa-projects/economy-enterprise-manufacturing-folder/the-great-recovery/about, 08/03/2024.

RSA and The Great Recovery Project. (2016). Designing for a circular economy: Lessons from The Great Recovery 2012 – 2016. *RSA Action and Research Centre*, (March), 1–45.

Saunders, M., Lewis, P., & Thornhill, A. (2007). Research Methods for Buniess Students. In *Pearson*.https://www.researchgate.net/publication/330760964_Research_Methods_for_Business_Students_Chapter_4_Understanding_research_philosophy_and_approaches_to_theory_development

Schor, J. B., & Cansoy, M. (2019). *"The sharing economy", The Oxford Handbook of Consumption* (Vol. 51). Oxford University Press New York.

Schor, J. B., & Fitzmaurice, C. J. (2015), "Collaborating and connecting: The emergence of the sharing economy", *Handbook of Research on Sustainable Consumption*, pp. 410–425, doi: DOI: 10.4337/9781783471270.00039

Schröder, P., Bengtsson, M., Cohen, M., Dewick, P., Hoffstetter, J., & Sarkis, J. (2019). Degrowth within – Aligning circular economy and strong sustainability narratives. *Resources, Conservation and Recycling*, *146*(March), 190–191. DOI: 10.1016/j.resconrec.2019.03.038

Seo, M. J., & Kim, M. (2019). Understanding the purchasing behaviour of second-hand fashion shoppers in a non-profit thrift store context. *International Journal of Fashion Design, Technology and Education, Taylor & Francis*, *12*(3), 301–312. DOI: 10.1080/17543266.2019.1611945

Shen, Z., Ji, W., Yu, S., Cheng, G., Yuan, Q., Han, Z., & Liu, H.. (2023). Mapping the knowledge of traffic collision Reconstruction: A scientometric analysis in CiteSpace, VOSviewer, and SciMAT. *Science & Justice, Elsevier*, *63*(1), 19–37.

Slaton, K., & Pookulangara, S. (2022). The Secondary Luxury Consumer: An Investigation into Online Consumption. *Sustainability (Switzerland)*, *14*(21). Advance online publication. DOI: 10.3390/su142113744

Small, H. (1973). "Co-citation in the scientific literature: A new measure of the relationship between two documents", *Journal of the American Society for Information Science*, John Wiley & Sons. *Ltd*, *24*(4), 265–269. DOI: 10.1002/asi.4630240406

Testa, D. S., Bakhshian, S., & Eike, R. (2020). Engaging consumers with sustainable fashion on Instagram. *Journal of Fashion Marketing and Management*, *25*(4), 569–584. DOI: 10.1108/JFMM-11-2019-0266

Tranfield, D., Denyer, D., & Smart, P. (2003). "Towards a Methodology for Developing Evidence-Informed Management Knowledge by Means of Systematic Review", *British Journal of Management*, John Wiley & Sons. *Ltd*, *14*(3), 207–222. DOI: 10.1111/1467-8551.00375

Tussyadiah, I. P., & Pesonen, J. (2016). Impacts of Peer-to-Peer Accommodation Use on Travel Patterns. *Journal of Travel Research*, *55*(8), 1022–1040. DOI: 10.1177/0047287515608505

Vallaster, C., Kraus, S., Merigó Lindahl, J. M., & Nielsen, A. (2019). Ethics and entrepreneurship: A bibliometric study and literature review. *Journal of Business Research*, *99*, 226–237. DOI: 10.1016/j.jbusres.2019.02.050

Van Eck, N. and Waltman, L. (2010), "Software survey: VOSviewer, a computer program for bibliometric mapping", *Scientometrics*, Akadémiai Kiadó, co-published with Springer Science+ Business Media BV …, Vol. 84 No. 2, pp. 523–538.

van Eck, N. J., & Waltman, L. (2007). VOS: A New Method for Visualizing Similarities Between Objects BT - Advances in Data Analysis. In Decker, R., & Lenz, H.-J. (Eds.), *Springer Berlin Heidelberg, Berlin* (pp. 299–306).

Walsh, I., & Rowe, F. (2023). BIBGT: Combining bibliometrics and grounded theory to conduct a literature review. *European Journal of Information Systems, Taylor & Francis*, *32*(4), 653–674.

Warner, K. S. R., & Wäger, M. (2019). Building dynamic capabilities for digital transformation: An ongoing process of strategic renewal. *Long Range Planning*. https://api.semanticscholar.org/CorpusID:158197061

Wei, X., Lo, C. K. Y., Jung, S., & Choi, T. M. (2021). From co-consumption to co-production: A systematic review and research synthesis of collaborative consumption practices. *Journal of Business Research, Elsevier Inc.*, *129*(March), 282–294. DOI: 10.1016/j.jbusres.2021.02.027

Wicaksono, T., Illés, C. B., & Dunay, A. (2023). Enhancing collaborative apparel consumption model: Quality-driven insights from customers and industry professionals. *Journal of Open Innovation: Technology, Market, and Complexity, Elsevier*, *9*(2), 100077. DOI: 10.1016/j.joitmc.2023.100077

Yu, D., Xu, Z., & Wang, W. (2018). Bibliometric analysis of fuzzy theory research in China: A 30-year perspective. *Knowledge-Based Systems*, *141*, 188–199. DOI: 10.1016/j.knosys.2017.11.018

Zaman, M., Park, H., Kim, Y. K., & Park, S. H. (2019). Consumer orientations of second-hand clothing shoppers. *Journal of Global Fashion Marketing, Routledge*, *10*(2), 163–176. DOI: 10.1080/20932685.2019.1576060

Zamani, B., Sandin, G., & Peters, G. M. (2017). Life cycle assessment of clothing libraries: Can collaborative consumption reduce the environmental impact of fast fashion? *Journal of Cleaner Production, Elsevier Ltd*, *162*, 1368–1375. DOI: 10.1016/j.jclepro.2017.06.128

Zupic, I., & Čater, T. (2015). Bibliometric Methods in Management and Organization. *Organizational Research Methods*, *18*, 429–472. DOI: 10.1177/1094428114562629

Chapter 12
Human-Centric Business Models in Industry 5.0:
Redefining Economic Value Creation

Majid Toulabi
https://orcid.org/0000-0002-3867-8648
Allameh Tabatabai University, Iran

Ahmad Taherianfar
Allameh Tabatabai University, Iran

ABSTRACT

This research examines human-centric business models in the era of Industry 5.0, an era in which technology is put at the service of humans and economic value is redefined based on meaning, well-being, and sustainability. By combining human and artificial intelligence, Industry 5.0 offers a model of creative collaboration between humans and machines that leads to multidimensional value creation, ethical decision-making, and sustainable development. The conceptual framework presented introduces three key dimensions of human empowerment, intelligent human-machine interaction, and sustainable value systems as the foundation for future business transformation.

1- INTRODUCTION

In recent decades, the paradigm of the world's industrial systems has been transformed with the emergence of Industry 5.0. This transformation is not simply a continuation of Industry 4.0, but a profound redefinition of the relationship between

DOI: 10.4018/979-8-3693-4525-2.ch012

humans and technology; where humans are no longer simply users or observers of automated systems, but are at the center of decision-making, value creation, and innovation. With an emphasis on human-centeredness, sustainability, and resilience, Industry 5.0 is an attempt to restore the human dimension to the heart of the digital and technological economy. In this approach, advanced technologies such as artificial intelligence, digital twins, the Internet of Things, and collaborative robots are not considered to replace humans, but rather their partners in value creation (Ghahremani-Nahr et al., 2024).

While traditional business models focused mainly on productivity and profitability, Industry 5.0 emphasizes the development of models that define value based on human well-being, creativity, ethics, and sustainability. In other words, the goal of creating smart businesses in this era is not simply to increase economic efficiency, but to create a balance between profit, society and the environment. This change in attitude has led to a multidimensional redefinition of the concept of economic value; value is no longer limited to financial indicators or efficiency, but is tied to indicators such as human satisfaction, social justice and environmental sustainability (Aliahmadi et al, 2023).

From a theoretical perspective, Industry 5.0 can be seen as the intersection of cognitive technologies with human-centered principles. Within this framework, organizations seek to create business models that both take advantage of digital capabilities and maintain their human identity. Such a model emphasizes values such as trust, empathy, transparency and social responsibility. In fact, Industry 5.0 is based on the assumption that the future of business is not based on ruthless competition between humans and machines, but on creative cooperation between them. In this way, new models are formed in which human-machine interaction leads to the production of added value that exceeds the ability of each alone.

In this regard, the concept of Human-Centric Business Models has been proposed as one of the most fundamental axes of Industry 5.0. These models emphasize the active participation of humans in decision-making, service design, and the creation of personalized experiences. Humans are placed at the center of the value chain, not only as a labor force, but also as the main source of meaning, creativity, and moral judgment. In this model, organizations try to balance economic goals and social responsibilities and, by using cognitive technologies, combine the decision-making process with human perception. Such a model is based on the creation of shared values between the enterprise, society, and the environment.

On the other hand, changes caused by global crises such as pandemics, climate change and supply chain instability have made this approach even more important. Organizations have realized that long-term sustainability can only be achieved when people are at the center of digital transformation. Human-centricity has not only an ethical or social dimension, but also an efficiency benefit, as human decisions based on situational judgment and understanding of complexity can fill in the gaps that algorithms cannot. As a result, the combination of human intelligence with artificial intelligence is known as "hybrid intelligence" and forms the foundation of new generation business models (Nozari (a), 2026).

In addition, the concept of value creation in Industry 5.0 is strongly tied to the concepts of ethics, trust and social responsibility. Value is no longer limited to price or profit, but also includes the quality of human interactions and the degree of positive impact on society. As a result, Industry 5.0 organizations are forced to define new indicators for measuring value; indicators that take into account human and environmental criteria in addition to economic efficiency. In the meantime, B2H (Business-to-Human) models have replaced traditional B2B and B2C models to emphasize human experience and personalization of business interactions.

Technology plays a complementary role, not dominant. The goal of Industry 5.0 is to create an "intelligent symbiosis" between humans and technology; in such a way that machines perform repetitive and data-driven tasks and humans focus on creative, emotional and strategic aspects. In such a situation, the boundary between production and experience disappears and economic value is formed through the creation of meaning and a sense of belonging. This transformation affects not only organizations but also economic policies, educational systems and even governance practices.

In short, Industry 5.0 provides an opportunity to redefine the concept of "growth"; growth that is not only quantitative, but also qualitative and human. In this perspective, humans are the main focus of designing intelligent systems, and technology is a tool at the service of their flourishing. Therefore, rethinking business models and redefining economic value in this era is an inevitable necessity. This chapter seeks to provide a conceptual framework for designing human-centered business models that can simultaneously respond to economic, social, and ethical needs and shape a new paradigm of value creation in the digital economy by examining the theoretical and practical dimensions of Industry 5.0.

2- THEORETICAL BACKGROUND: FROM INDUSTRY 4.0 TO INDUSTRY 5.0

The transition from Industry 4.0 to Industry 5.0 can be considered not just a technological advancement, but a paradigm shift in the concept of production, work and economic value. Relying on digitalization, the Internet of Things, big data analytics and intelligent automation, Industry 4.0 was able to expand the boundaries of productivity and push industries towards widespread smartization. However, the extreme focus on technology and efficiency caused humans to gradually be marginalized in this process. In Industry 4.0, humans were often defined as part of the production chain or as agents monitoring automated systems, and their role in decision-making and value creation was given less attention. Industry 5.0 was formed precisely in response to this challenge; an attempt to restore the human to the center of the production and economic system with an emphasis on human-machine cooperation and the creation of sustainable and meaningful value (Nozari (b), 2026).

Industry 4.0 brought about a dramatic transformation in productivity and quality with the emergence of technologies such as advanced robotics, cyber-physical systems, artificial intelligence, and augmented reality. This era focused in particular on connectivity and data integration across the value chain, leading to the creation of smart factories and autonomous production networks. However, this focus on technology has sometimes led to a shift away from human and social goals. While Industry 4.0 sought to increase efficiency and reduce costs, Industry 5.0 seeks to put technology at the service of people and use it to improve well-being, creativity, and sustainability (Adel, 2022).

Conceptually, Industry 5.0 is based on three main pillars: human-centeredness, sustainability, and resilience. Together, these three axes provide a new theoretical framework for economic and industrial development. Human-centeredness means focusing on human needs, values, and capabilities in the design of intelligent systems. Sustainability ensures the coexistence of the economy with the environment and society, and resilience emphasizes resilience to crises. Industry 5.0 seeks to create synergies between human and artificial intelligence so that production systems can dynamically adapt to environmental changes and social needs. In this path, technology acts not as an end, but as a means to empower humans.

From a historical perspective, the transition from Industry 4.0 to 5.0 can be interpreted as a move from "automation" to "intelligent coexistence." In Industry 4.0, the main role was played by machines and algorithms, but Industry 5.0 focuses on human–machine collaboration. The goal of this collaboration is to take advantage of the strengths of both sides: machines with precision, speed and high processing power, and humans with creativity, moral judgment and understanding of the context of the situation. The result of this interaction is the emergence of a kind of "hybrid intelligence" that makes decisions based not only on data, but also on human judgment and ethical values (Nozari, 2025).

In Industry 4.0, the focus was on increasing productivity and reducing costs, while Industry 5.0 goes beyond that and seeks to create multidimensional value. This value is no longer just financial, but also includes human well-being, employee satisfaction, environmental sustainability and social growth. As a result, business models in Industry 5.0 move away from "shareholder value" approaches and towards "stakeholder value"; meaning that not only shareholders but also all stakeholders, including employees, customers and local communities, play a role in value creation.

Industry 5.0 also offers a new concept of human-technological innovation, in which human creativity is combined with the analytical power of new technologies. In this model, factories are no longer just production centers, but become learning ecosystems where humans and machines learn and adapt simultaneously. This model leads to the formation of adaptive organizations that are able to maintain their dynamism in the face of rapid economic and social changes (Nassar et al., 2025).

On the other hand, Industry 5.0 has enabled a deeper understanding of human and system behavior through the development of new technologies such as digital twins, blockchain, and the Internet of Things. As virtual versions of real processes and assets, digital twins play an important role in combining human and machine data. These technologies allow decisions to be made with a better understanding of the human context. For example, in Industry 5.0 factories, digital twins can analyze the behavioral patterns of employees interacting with robots to create safer and more efficient working conditions.

Another important point is the ethical and social dimension of Industry 5.0. With the increasing decision-making power of technologies, issues such as algorithmic transparency, data justice, and maintaining human dignity have gained special importance. Industry 5.0 seeks to apply advanced technologies within the framework of human ethics to prevent the formation of digital inequality and technological dominance. In other words, Industry 5.0 is not just about "technology for humans," but about "technology with humans," a two-way and reciprocal interaction that extracts value from the collaboration that lies within it.

Therefore, Industry 5.0 can be considered a stage of maturity of the digital industry in which technology and humans are not in opposition, but in the evolution of each other. This new approach proposes a concept of growth that goes beyond production and consumption indicators and thinks about improving the quality of life, social responsibility, and environmental sustainability. In this framework, the future industrial transformation will not only be about artificial intelligence and robotics, but also about human cognition, meaning, and ethics in the digital economy.

By emphasizing human values, Industry 5.0 paves the way for the formation of a human-smart economy; an economy in which the synergy between humans and technology will be the engine driving sustainable and justice-oriented development. This transformation necessitates a review of the principles of business design, industrial policymaking, and even human resource training, because success in the new era is not defined by the speed of technology, but by the depth of its connection with humans.

3- HUMAN–CENTRIC VALUE CREATION PARADIGM

In the era of Industry 5.0, the concept of value has undergone a fundamental transformation. Value is no longer limited to economic outputs or financial indicators, but also includes human, social, environmental and ethical dimensions. In this context, the Human–Centric Value Creation paradigm is proposed as a theoretical foundation for redefining the interaction between humans, technology and organizations. This paradigm emphasizes that real value is created when technology is put at the service of humans and at the same time leads to improved individual well-being, collective development and environmental sustainability. In other words, Industry 5.0 seeks to restore "meaning" to the heart of economic value, where innovation is not limited to financial profit alone, but is tied to human and social growth (Nozari & Nassar, 2025).

In traditional business models and even Industry 4.0, value creation was mainly defined in terms of efficiency, speed, and cost reduction. In this logic, humans were seen more as a source of production or final consumer and less as creative partners in the innovation process. However, Industry 5.0 has reversed this relationship by putting humans at the center. In the new paradigm, humans are not tools, but rather goals and creators of value. Smart technologies play a facilitating role, allowing humans to maximize their creative, cognitive, and ethical potential. Economic value is no longer achieved solely through productivity, but is produced through the creation of experience, meaning, trust, and human connections (Nozari, 2025).

This evolution in the definition of value is rooted in a new understanding of human nature in technological environments. In Industry 5.0, humans are seen not only as decision-makers but also as the center of systemic intelligence. In such a context, the concept of "value" is linked to a sense of belonging, creativity, and human empowerment. In fact, the more economic and production systems are able to inspire a sense of participation and meaning in humans, the more value is created. This view is the opposite of the mechanistic logic of Industry 4.0, in which technical efficiency was more important than human experience. By integrating technology and humans, Industry 5.0 attempts to simultaneously integrate productivity and meaning into the production of value.

One of the main features of the human-centered paradigm is the move from "value extraction" to "value co-creation." In the traditional logic, companies extracted value from resources—including human labor. But in Industry 5.0, value is formed through collaboration, co-creation, and mutual learning between humans, machines, and organizations. This co-creation process makes innovation no longer a one-way product, but the result of dynamic interactions between users, employees, and smart technologies. In this way, humans become the center of the value chain, not on its periphery.

From a philosophical perspective, this transformation means a transition from an "economy of performance" to an "economy of meaning." Value, in this view, cannot be measured only by measuring efficiency or output, but also depends on the quality of human experience, a sense of trust, moral satisfaction, and social impact. Such a change creates a new understanding of wealth and success, in which human well-being and environmental sustainability are integral parts of value creation models. In this paradigm, new criteria for measuring economic value are defined, which include indicators of human satisfaction, social justice, resource sustainability, and organizational responsibility (Nozari et al. (a), 2025).

From a practical perspective, this transformation is also reflected in the structure of Industry 5.0 business models. Companies are moving from B2B and B2C models to B2H (Business-to-Human) models, an approach in which the ultimate goal is not to interact with the market or the organization, but to create a meaningful human experience. This change in approach has forced organizations to focus on human emotions, needs and values from the perspective of design, communication and decision-making. New technologies such as emotional artificial intelligence, human digital twins and adaptive learning systems are serving this goal. By analyzing human behavior, emotions and preferences, these technologies pave the way for the creation of personalized values, which, as a result, naturally increase satisfaction and loyalty.

At a larger level, the human-centered value creation paradigm also emphasizes sustainability and resilience. In a post-industrial world, where climate, social and economic crises are rapidly affecting the performance of enterprises, only those organizations that can create value beyond economic profit will survive. Industry 5.0 sees this sustainability not as a constraint but as a source of innovation. By integrating human values into their strategies, organizations can create innovations that simultaneously lead to profitability and social responsibility. This nexus between technology, people and sustainability forms the foundation of future value creation (Nozari & Samadi, 2025).

On the other hand, the human-centered paradigm emphasizes that economic value will not be sustainable without trust and ethics. In a world where algorithms and data play a decisive role in decision-making, preserving human dignity, algorithmic transparency, and data justice are critical elements in creating value. Industry 5.0 is, in fact, a return to the fundamental principles of ethics in economics; principles that put technology at the service of people and society, not vice versa. This ethical aspect is the main difference between Industry 5.0 and previous industrial generations and will guarantee its sustainability in the long term.

In short, the human-centered value creation paradigm in Industry 5.0 is an attempt to redefine the relationship between humans, technology, and the economy. This paradigm believes that the successful future lies not in absolute automation, but in the intelligent coexistence of humans and machines. Value in this future does not come from mere efficiency, but from meaning, experience, trust, and human well-being. Industry 5.0 thus charts a new path for the global economy, in which technology is a tool for empowering humans and creating a more balanced, ethical, and humane world.

4- HUMAN–CENTRIC BUSINESS MODEL DESIGN

The design of human-centered business models in the era of Industry 5.0 marks a turning point in the evolution of economic and organizational systems; a point where technology, creativity, and human values combine in a synergistic way. In contrast to the approaches of previous generations of industry that focused primarily on efficiency, profit, and automation, Industry 5.0 seeks to create models that are centered on people, meaning, and experience. In this vision, organizations are viewed not simply as production units, but as living ecosystems in which people, technology, and values are in constant interaction. Such a shift in management thinking leads to a redefinition of the role of the organization, employees, and customers in the value creation process (Nozari et al.,(b) 2025).

In traditional business models, value was usually created through resource optimization, cost reduction, and scale expansion. But in the human-centered design of Industry 5.0, value comes from human interactions, experience, and co-creation. This transformation means moving from the logic of "value chain" to "value network," where different actors in an intelligent network create shared value through data, emotions, and multi-level collaboration. In such a model, technology is not just a tool, but a platform for creating a richer human experience and more informed decision-making. Artificial intelligence, digital twins, and cognitive systems serve to better understand human behavior and develop solutions that are aligned with human emotional, social, and ethical needs (Nozari, 2025).

One of the fundamental principles in the design of human-centered models is a focus on purpose. Organizations no longer pursue profit alone, but strive to define their social and spiritual role in society. This approach is in line with the concept of a "purpose-driven economy," an economy in which companies measure their value not just by financial indicators, but by the extent to which they positively impact people and the environment. In this framework, the organization's mission becomes a tool for inspiration, innovation, and trust. Designing such a model requires identifying deeper human needs, including meaning, justice, security, and self-actualization, which will ultimately lead to the organization's long-term sustainability.

On the other hand, designing human-centered models requires balancing technology with human experience. Industry 5.0 is built on intelligent human-machine collaboration; but this collaboration is only valuable when it empowers humans, not replaces them. For this reason, there is a special emphasis on the Human Experience (HX) in the design of these models. HX goes beyond user experience (UX) and encompasses all cognitive, emotional, cultural, and ethical dimensions of human interaction with the system. Human-centric business models, by understanding these dimensions, try to balance technical efficiency with human satisfaction.

In such a model, humans act as "creative partners" of technology. Robots and artificial intelligence take on repetitive and analytical tasks, while humans appear in the role of designers, decision-makers and innovators. This new role division pushes organizations towards creating open and collaborative structures; structures in which the boundary between producer and consumer disappears and each individual can participate in the value creation process. The result of this change is an increased sense of belonging and trust between individuals and organizations, which is one of the main foundations of sustainability in Industry 5.0 (Nozari et al.(c), 2025).

From an organizational architecture perspective, human-centric business models often move away from hierarchical structures and towards self-organizing and intelligent networks. In these structures, decision-making is based on real-time data and human feedback. Digital twins act as a bridge between the physical and virtual environments, enabling simulation, evaluation, and continuous improvement of processes. With the help of these tools, organizations can make decisions that are simultaneously consistent with economic logic and human values. In effect, technology becomes an "empathy accelerator"; a tool for better understanding human needs and emotions in the workplace and the marketplace.

Another characteristic of these models is the focus on the synergy between five key dimensions: Purpose, People, Platform, Partnership, and Planet. These dimensions show that Industry 5.0 business models pay attention not only to optimizing the internal performance of the organization, but also to its global responsibility. For example, data-driven platforms enable the creation of transparent and ethical networks, while collaboration with stakeholders in the form of cross-sector partnerships leads to the creation of shared value and the reduction of negative environmental impacts.

In practice, this approach has led to the emergence of new models of economic interaction such as B2H (Business-to-Human), in which the relationship between the organization and the human goes beyond a mere economic transaction and becomes a human and meaningful relationship. Industry 5.0 companies strive to create an emotional connection between themselves and their customers by creating a sense of belonging, personalized experiences, and transparency in communication. This shift has made "trust" a key value in human-centered models, as without trust, no sustainable relationship will survive in the digital world of the future (Abdi et al., 2025).

Ultimately, designing human-centered business models can be seen as an attempt to balance technological advancement with human authenticity. These models seek to create an economy that is both efficient and ethical by leveraging advanced technologies and ethical principles. Industry 5.0 teaches organizations that true success in the future depends on their ability to simultaneously integrate technology with empathy, data with understanding, and efficiency with meaning. Such a model will not only lead to improved economic performance, but also help rebuild the relationship between humans and work, society, and the environment.

5- REDEFINING ECONOMIC VALUE IN INDUSTRY 5.0

In the era of Industry 5.0, the concept of "economic value" has undergone a fundamental redefinition; a change that is not simply the result of technological advancements, but also the result of a philosophical shift in the way humans view growth, work, and development. In previous industrial paradigms, value was usually measured based on financial metrics such as profit, return on investment, and productivity. However, relying solely on quantitative and economic indicators has led to the human, social, and environmental dimensions of value being ignored. Industry 5.0 addresses this shortcoming and seeks to redefine the concept of value in a way that is aligned with the principles of human-centeredness, sustainability, and resilience (Yordanova & Nozari, 2025).

In this context, economic value is no longer simply defined as financial outputs, but is considered a multidimensional concept that also includes human well-being, quality of life, and social and environmental impacts. Industry 5.0 believes that economic and industrial systems must move beyond the logic of "efficiency" and move towards "meaningfulness". Value should be created not only through the production of goods and services, but also through improving people's lives and improving the sustainability of the planet. Thus, traditional measures of economic growth are being replaced by new indicators such as human satisfaction, social justice, ethical innovation and positive impact on society (Mourtzis, 2023).

In advanced economies, this change in perspective has led to the emergence of concepts such as the "Purpose Economy" and the "Wellbeing Economy". In these approaches, value depends on the extent to which organizations have a positive impact on society, the environment and future generations. Industry 5.0 extends these concepts to the industrial sphere and combines them with advanced technologies to create a system that is both productive and humane. For example, companies that use smart technologies to improve employee safety, reduce carbon emissions, and enhance human skills are actually creating economic value in a broader sense. Such value is reflected not only in the financial balance sheet, but also in social trust and moral capital (Li, 2025).

The redefinition of economic value in Industry 5.0 is also accompanied by a change in the role of technology. While in Industry 4.0 technology was a tool for automation and increased productivity, in Industry 5.0 technology becomes a factor of human empowerment. This change in attitude makes value not come from removing humans from the production process, but from enhancing their cognitive and creative capabilities. Machines take over repetitive tasks so that humans can focus on ethical decision-making, creative design, and innovation. In this new structure, economic value is created as a result of collaboration between human and artificial intelligence; Collaboration, referred to as "hybrid intelligence," is a key development in Industry 5.0.

One important consequence of this transformation is the expansion of the concept of capital. Economic value no longer comes only from financial capital, but also includes three other types of capital: human capital, data capital, and ethical capital. Human capital refers to the skills, creativity, and motivation of individuals; data capital is the result of transparent, secure, and ethical management of information; and ethical capital relates to the degree of trust and legitimacy that an organization generates among its stakeholders. The combination of these three types of capital creates a new framework for measuring value in Industry 5.0, in which trust and meaningfulness play key roles (Ghobakhloo et al., 2024).

On the other hand, Industry 5.0 attempts to create a deeper connection between economic value and social value. In this model, human well-being and environmental health are not obstacles to economic growth, but rather prerequisites for it. Companies that operate in line with the Sustainable Development Goals (SDGs) will not only fulfill their social responsibility, but will also be more sustainable and profitable from an economic perspective in the long term. Industry 5.0, in fact, outlines a model of the economy in which short-term financial interests are not sacrificed for long-term human goals, but the two are placed in a balanced framework.

In addition, the concept of redefining economic value in Industry 5.0 is also seriously related to technological ethics and data justice. With the spread of artificial intelligence and automated decision-making algorithms, the issue of transparency and justice in the value creation process has gained particular importance. Meanwhile, Industry 5.0, based on human-centered principles, emphasizes that value cannot be created without fairness, respect for privacy, and consideration of the social impacts of technological decisions. Therefore, organizations leading Industry 5.0 are increasingly using the principles of "ethical design" in their systems to ensure that technology remains at the service of humans, and not the other way around.

In practice, the redefinition of value in Industry 5.0 has led to the design of multifaceted economic models that, in addition to financial indicators, also include human and environmental criteria. For example, organizations now include indicators such as employee satisfaction index, carbon footprint, data transparency, and social participation rate in their performance evaluation. This transformation in measuring value is considered a kind of "metric revolution" in the new economy, in which qualitative and human criteria replace purely quantitative indicators.

Ultimately, Industry 5.0 redefines economic value, proposing a new paradigm of progress; one that sees growth not simply as capital accumulation, but as the harmonious advancement of humans, technology, and the environment. Value in this paradigm is the result of the intelligent coexistence of humans and machines, the balance between profit and meaning, and the convergence of ethics and innovation. In such a vision, the successful organizations of the future will be those that can create not only wealth, but also meaning and trust. This profound redefinition has transformed Industry 5.0 from a mere technological revolution into a human and ethical movement that is charting the future course of the global economy.

6- FRAMEWORK FOR HUMAN–CENTRIC BUSINESS TRANSFORMATION

The conceptual framework for human-centered business transformation in Industry 5.0 is a systematic response to the need for humans and technology to complement each other in creating sustainable value. This framework is based on three key dimensions that together constitute the foundation of new value creation systems in the human-technological economy: Human Empowerment, Collaborative Intelligence, and Sustainable Value Systems (Longo et al., 2020). These three axes interact not in isolation but in a dynamic, synergistic cycle, simultaneously ensuring human well-being, technological productivity, and economic sustainability.

In the first dimension, human empowerment means restoring the creative, decision-making, and ethically driven position of humans at the heart of industrial systems. Industry 5.0, with its emphasis on education, participation and trust, seeks to transform humans from mere observers into active and creative agents. In this regard, cognitive technologies and artificial intelligence should be tools for developing human thinking, judgment and innovation. True empowerment will be achieved when organizations redesign work structures in such a way that humans interact with technology, feel in control, grow and belong (Jourabchi Amirkhizi et al., 2025).

The second dimension, intelligent human-machine interaction, marks a stage of technological maturity in which cooperation replaces confrontation. By combining human and artificial intelligence, Industry 5.0 creates a model of "hybrid intelligence" in which decisions are the result of the interaction between data and human perception. At this level, humans and machines operate not in a linear manner, but in the form of a learning network; machines perform data-driven tasks and humans focus on creative and ethical dimensions. Tools such as Digital Twin, Explainable

AI and adaptive learning systems underpin this intelligent interaction and create an environment where technology helps to enhance human cognitive power (Ordieres-Meré et al., 2023).

In the third dimension, sustainable value systems, Industry 5.0 redefines the concept of "economic value". Value is no longer limited to financial indicators, but also includes social, ethical and environmental impacts. These systems strive to balance economic growth, social justice and environmental sustainability. Value in this approach is real time when it improves the quality of life and social health in the long term. Hence, Industry 5.0 organizations move towards models based on Shared Value and Purpose Economy, where the interests of the enterprise and society are aligned (Enose Kamalabai et al., 2025).

Figure 1. Human-Centric Business Transformation Framework in Industry 5.0

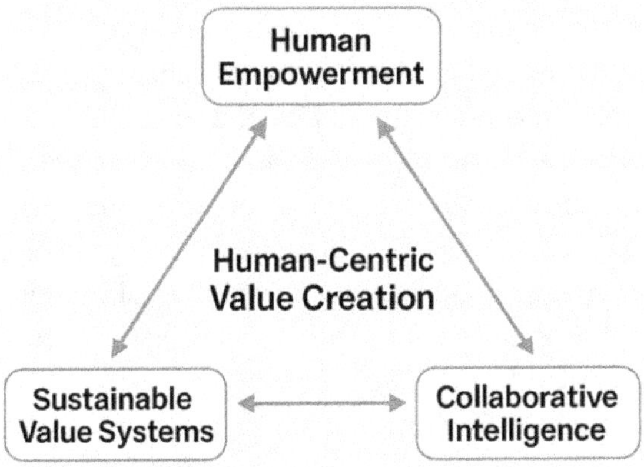

Figure 1 shows that the future of industrial transformation lies not in focusing on technology alone, but in the synergy between humans, machines, and ethical values. Each dimension is incomplete without the other; human empowerment remains ineffective without technological collaboration, and intelligent interaction without a sustainable value system leads to meaninglessness. As a result, Industry 5.0 offers a dynamic framework of "intelligent coexistence" in which economic growth, technological innovation, and human well-being move in a single direction. This conceptual model can be used as a roadmap for organizations seeking to redesign their future based on meaning, trust, and sustainability.

7- CONCLUSION

In conclusion, this research introduces Industry 5.0 as a fundamental transformation in the history of human industry, which aims to restore the centrality of humans in the age of technology. Unlike previous generations of industry, which focused on productivity, automation, and cost reduction, Industry 5.0 seeks to create a balance between artificial intelligence and human intelligence to form a system in which technology serves meaning, well-being, and human development.

This research showed that Industry 5.0 is more than just a technological stage, it is a transformation of ideas. In this model, humans are no longer simply the executors of machine processes, but are considered creative and decision-making partners alongside technology. For this reason, the concept of economic value is also redefined; value is no longer limited to profit and production, but is understood in satisfaction, trust, sustainability, and a positive impact on society. This approach is a kind of transition from a quantity-based economy to a quality-based economy, where human indicators replace purely financial criteria.

Analysis shows that three key dimensions of Industry 5.0 – human empowerment, intelligent human-machine interaction, and sustainable value systems – form the foundation of this transformation. Human empowerment enhances creativity, intellectual freedom, and ethical judgment in organizations. Intelligent interaction between humans and technology also increases the cognitive capacities of both, enabling more accurate and ethical decision-making. Ultimately, sustainable value systems ensure that these innovations serve social justice, environmental sustainability, and economic health.

In the new era, organizations must seek to create meaning rather than focus solely on efficiency. The successful companies of the future will be those that can balance technology with human emotion, data with ethics, and innovation with social responsibility. In such an environment, technology is not just a tool for automation, but a platform for human creativity and cultural development. Industry 5.0, relying on this logic, shows that real progress is sustainable only if humans remain at the center of design and decision-making.

This transformation is effective not only in the field of production, but also at the level of management philosophy and economic strategies. Industry 5.0 links the concept of competition to cooperation, and the concept of growth to sustainability. The future economy will be built on trust, empathy and meaning, and companies that institutionalize these values in their structure will move on the path of sustainable development and social legitimacy.

On the other hand, Industry 5.0 is a reminder of the fact that technology is meaningless without humans. It is humans who give meaning to data, guide decisions and instill ethics into intelligent systems. For this reason, future success lies not in the computational ability of machines, but in the quality of the relationship between humans and technology. The future that Industry 5.0 envisions is one in which the boundary between technology and humans is blurred, and both create new values in a mutual interaction.

Ultimately, Industry 5.0 can be said to be a kind of "quiet revolution"; a revolution that, instead of removing humans from the equation of progress, places them back at the center of it. This approach teaches us that real economic growth is only sustainable when it is accompanied by moral, social, and cultural growth. Industry 5.0 is, in fact, a return to the principle that technology should serve humans, not the other way around. The future of the global economy will be shaped based on this principle; a future in which meaning, empathy, and sustainability replace blind competition and endless consumption.

Therefore, Industry 5.0 is not the end of technology, but the beginning of a new era of "technological humanization"; an era in which humans and machines walk together on a common path to create an intelligent, ethical, and balanced world.

REFERENCES

Abdi, H., Jahanian, A., & Nozari, H. (2025). Digital Twin-Enabled Bioreactors: Transforming Industrial Biotechnology in Smart Economies. In Dynamic and Safe Economy in the Age of Smart Technologies (pp. 105-120). IGI Global Scientific Publishing.

Adel, A. (2022). Future of industry 5.0 in society: Human-centric solutions, challenges and prospective research areas. *Journal of Cloud Computing (Heidelberg, Germany)*, *11*(1), 40. PMID: 36101900

Aliahmadi, A., & Nozari, H. (2023, January). Evaluation of security metrics in AIoT and blockchain-based supply chain by Neutrosophic decision-making method. In Supply chain forum: an international journal (Vol. 24, No. 1, pp. 31-42). Taylor & Francis.

Ghahremani-Nahr, J., Nozari, H., & Szmelter-Jarosz, A. (2024). Designing a humanitarian relief logistics network considering the cost of deprivation using a robust-fuzzy-probabilistic planning method. *Journal of International Humanitarian Action*, *9*(1), 19.

Ghobakhloo, M., Mahdiraji, H. A., Iranmanesh, M., & Jafari-Sadeghi, V. (2024). From Industry 4.0 digital manufacturing to Industry 5.0 digital society: A roadmap toward human-centric, sustainable, and resilient production. *Information Systems Frontiers*, •••, 1–33.

Jourabchi Amirkhizi, P., Pedrammehr, S., & Pakzad, S. (2025). A system-based approach to value prioritization in industry 5.0 for sustainable value creation. *Discover Sustainability*, *6*(1), 364.

Kamalabai, N., Hannola, L., & Donoghue, I. (2025). Role of Industrial Artificial Intelligence in Advancing Human-Centric Sustainable Development of Industry 5.0.[eu2.1] In Contemporary Issues in Industry 5.0: Towards an AI Integrated Society (pp. 325–371). Springer Nature Switzerland.

Longo, F., Padovano, A., & Umbrello, S. (2020). Value-oriented and ethical technology engineering in industry 5.0: A human-centric perspective for the design of the factory of the future. *Applied Sciences (Basel, Switzerland)*, *10*(12), 4182.

Mourtzis, D. (2023). The Metaverse in industry 5.0: A human-centric approach towards personalized value creation. *Encyclopedia*, *3*(3), 1105–1120.

Nassar, S., Nozari, H., & Samadi, S. (2025). AIoE-Based Multi-objective Optimization for Smart and Sustainable Warehouse Management. In *Artificial Intelligence of Everything and Sustainable Development* (pp. 241–255). Springer Nature Singapore.

Nozari, H. (2025). Integrating Neuromorphic Intelligence with Fuzzy Multi-Objective Models in Resilient Green Supply Chain Design. Process Integration and Optimization for Sustainability, 1-14.

Nozari, H. (Ed.). (2025). *Dynamic and Safe Economy in the Age of Smart Technologies*. IGI Global.

Nozari, H. (a) (2026). Combining Digital Twin and Metaverse for Immersive Marketing Experiences. In Improving Consumer Engagement in Digital Marketing Through Cognitive AI (pp. 289-310). IGI Global Scientific Publishing.

Nozari, H. (b) (2026). Neuromorphic Models for Dynamic Customer Segmentation in Digital Marketing. In Improving Consumer Engagement in Digital Marketing Through Cognitive AI (pp. 311-326). IGI Global Scientific Publishing.

Nozari, H., Abdi, H., Szmelter-Jarosz, A., & Rahmaty, M. (a). (2025). A digital twin-based neutrosophic multi-objective optimization model for smart supply chains in the food industry. *Journal of Intelligent Manufacturing*, •••, 1–15.

Nozari, H., & Nassar, S. (2025). Real-time data-driven multi-objective optimization in B2B marketing using digital twins. OPSEARCH, 1-27.

Nozari, H., & Samadi, S. (2025). Digital Twin-Enhanced Sentiment Analysis for Targeted Marketing Optimization. In Dynamic and Safe Economy in the Age of Smart Technologies (pp. 121-138). IGI Global Scientific Publishing.

Nozari, H., Szmelter-Jarosz, A., & Samadi, S. (c)(2025). Machine Learning Models for Energy Optimization and Resource Consumption in Smart Factories. In Artificial Intelligence of Everything and Sustainable Development (pp. 175-189). Singapore: Springer Nature Singapore.

Nozari, H., Szmelter-Jarosz, A., & Weiland, D. (b). (2025). A Fuzzy Multi-Objective Sustainable and Agile Supply Chain Model Based on Digital Twin and Internet of Things with Adaptive Learning Under Environmental Uncertainty. *Applied Sciences (Basel, Switzerland)*, *15*(19), 10399.

Ordieres-Meré, J., Gutierrez, M., & Villalba-Díez, J. (2023). Toward the industry 5.0 paradigm: Increasing value creation through the robust integration of humans and machines. *Computers in Industry*, *150*, 103947.

Yordanova, Z., & Nozari, H. (2025). Harnessing Cyber-Physical Systems and Digital Twins for Industrial Innovation and Economic Resilience. In Dynamic and Safe Economy in the Age of Smart Technologies (pp. 33-48). IGI Global Scientific Publishing

Chapter 13

Revolutionizing Work from Home and Technological Transformation in the Age of Industry 5.0

Ridhima Goel
https://orcid.org/0000-0002-0505-9218
Institute of Management Studies and Research, Maharshi Dayanand University, Rohtak, India

Jagdeep Singla
https://orcid.org/0000-0001-8628-9244
Institute of Management Studies and Research, Maharshi Dayanand University, Rohtak, India

ABSTRACT

This study explores the transformative impact of Industry 5.0 on business operations, emphasizing how this new industrial era is redefining traditional business models, and the global economic landscape. By examining the confluence of advanced technologies and human creativity, the study illustrates how Industry 5.0 promotes sustainable and localized production, thereby fostering a more resilient and adaptable economy. The research methodology includes a historical review of the industrial revolution from Industry 1.0 to Industry 5.0, highlighting the critical developments that have shaped modern manufacturing and business practices. Additionally, it delves into the principles of human-machine collaboration and the growing emphasis on sustainability. The study reveals that the integration of human

DOI: 10.4018/979-8-3693-4525-2.ch013

skills with advanced technologies leads to more innovative and efficient production processes This briefing offers a novel perspective on the synergistic relationship between WFH and Industry 5.0.

1. INTRODUCTION

The business landscape stands at a crossroads, on the precipice of a transformative evolution fueled by the convergence of cutting-edge technological innovations and the principles of Industry 4.0 (Ji et al., 2024; Formica, 2023). This evolution heralds the emergent era of Industry 5.0, which is characterized by a profound integration of human creativity and advanced technology (Murphy et al., 2023; Budhwar et al., 2023). This monumental shift is not merely a modification of conventional business operations; it represents a seismic reconfiguration of how companies function, how employees interact with their work, and the global economic landscape (Zekhnini et al., 2024; Leng et al., 2023; Kolade and Owoseni, 2022).

Industry 5.0 builds upon the foundations laid by Industry 4.0, enhancing the capabilities of cyber-physical systems, the Internet of Things (IoT), and artificial intelligence (AI) with a renewed focus on human-machine collaboration. This new industrial era emphasizes the importance of human-centric approaches, ensuring that technological advancements are used to augment human skills rather than replace them (Ji et al., 2024). The integration of human intuition, creativity, and adaptability with automated systems results in more customized and sustainable production methods, transforming traditional business models into more resilient and adaptive structures (Formica, 2023).

As companies navigate this transition, remote work emerges as a pivotal component, reshaping how businesses operate and employees perform their tasks. The rise of work-from-home (WFH) practices complements the Industry 5.0 paradigm by empowering employees to harness their creativity and collaborate globally without being confined to physical office spaces (Murphy et al., 2023). This flexibility not only enhances productivity but also supports localized manufacturing practices, aligning with the sustainability goals of Industry 5.0 (Budhwar et al., 2023). The shift towards remote work and the decentralization of business operations contribute to a more dynamic and resilient global economy, capable of withstanding disruptions and adapting to changing market demands (Zekhnini et al., 2024). Moreover, the integration of remote work into business strategies fosters a more inclusive and diverse workforce, as companies can tap into a global talent pool without geographical limitations (Leng et al., 2023). This inclusivity drives innovation and broadens perspectives, leading to more comprehensive solutions to complex business challenges (Kolade and Owoseni, 2022). As businesses continue to embrace the principles of

Industry 5.0, the synergistic relationship between technological advancements and human capabilities will be crucial in achieving sustainable growth and redefining the future of work.

Therefore, this chapter explores the fascinating world of business transformation, delving into the impact of remote work on companies, employees, and the global economy. By examining the interplay between technological innovation and human-centric approaches, it provides insights into how businesses can successfully navigate the transition to Industry 5.0 and harness its potential to drive sustainable and inclusive economic growth.

1.2 Research Objectives and Significance of Study

This chapter aims to provide a comprehensive exploration of how Industry 5.0 technologies are reshaping the concept of remote work and vice versa. The integration of advanced technologies, such as artificial intelligence (AI), the Internet of Things (IoT), and augmented reality (AR), in Industry 5.0 offers new opportunities to enhance productivity, foster sustainability, and support employee well-being within remote work frameworks. Understanding these impacts is crucial as businesses worldwide adapt to a more dynamic, resilient, and inclusive industrial era.

1.2.1 Research Objectives:

1. Examine how Industry 5.0 technologies transform remote work.
2. Assess the impact on productivity, sustainability, and employee well-being.
3. Identify practical applications for overcoming remote work challenges.

2. BACKGROUND OF INDUSTRY 5.0

2.1 The Dawn of a New Industrial Era: A Game-Changer

The evolution of industrial revolutions has fundamentally shaped modern production and work practices. Industry 1.0, emerging in the late 18th century, introduced mechanized production through water and steam power, which shifted manufacturing away from manual labor (Loy et al., 2021). This foundation was further advanced with Industry 2.0, when electricity and assembly lines enabled mass production, making goods more widely accessible (Yin et al., 2017; Kurt, 2019; Sutthiphisal, 2006). By the late 20th century, Industry 3.0 revolutionized production with electronics, automation, and the integration of information technology, setting the stage for interconnected, partially automated manufacturing (Babel, 2022; Kennedy, 2017).

Industry 4.0, emerging in the 21st century, propelled these advancements into a digital age, incorporating IoT, artificial intelligence, and advanced data analytics to create smart, interconnected production systems (Echchakoui & Barka, 2020; Kagermann et al., 2013; Gholami et al., 2021). Yet, while Industry 4.0 centered on automation and digital integration, Industry 5.0 represents a transformative shift toward a human-centered approach, where the focus is on blending human creativity, problem-solving, and decision-making with advanced technology (Longo et al., 2020).

Unlike its predecessors, Industry 5.0 prioritizes sustainable, customized, and local production processes. The integration of green technologies and renewable energy sources aligns industrial activities with ecological preservation, promoting sustainable practices to reduce waste and carbon emissions (Adel, 2022; Nahavandi, 2019). This shift also reflects growing consumer demand for personalized products, which Industry 5.0 supports by allowing companies to tailor their offerings to meet specific customer preferences (Maddikunta et al., 2022). Additionally, Industry 5.0 embraces decentralized manufacturing, where local production can meet regional needs, thus supporting resilience and reducing supply chain dependencies (Golovianko et al., 2023).

Remote work, a byproduct of recent technological advancements, seamlessly integrates into the Industry 5.0 framework by enabling companies to access a diverse talent pool while fostering flexibility, inclusivity, and operational resilience (Goel et al., 2024b). This flexibility enhances employee satisfaction and productivity while decentralizing operations to mitigate disruptions during events such as pandemics or natural disasters (Groysberg et al., 2018). Furthermore, Industry 5.0 envisions a collaborative partnership between humans and machines, where technologies like AI, machine learning, and robotics handle data-intensive tasks, allowing humans to focus on creativity, ethics, and strategic planning (Vrontis et al., 2023; Soori et al., 2023). This synergy encourages innovation, enabling industries to address complex challenges through human insight supported by technological precision (Longo et al., 2020).

Therefore, it is clearly evident that Industry 5.0 is not merely a continuation but a reimagination of industrial practices, placing human skills and sustainable principles at the core. By valuing customization, sustainability, and local production, Industry 5.0 provides a path to a resilient and inclusive economy empowered by the strengths of both human talent and advanced technology.

2.2 Key Features of Industry 5.0

Industry 5.0 redefines the concept of work by fostering a collaborative environment between humans and machines, empowering employees to work remotely while enhancing productivity, sustainability, and customization. This human-centric approach prioritizes technology as a tool to augment rather than replace human capabilities, allowing remote workers to access resources and collaborate efficiently across diverse locations (Kagermann et al., 2013; Budhwar et al., 2023).

- **Human-Machine Collaboration: A** hallmark of Industry 5.0 is the seamless integration of human creativity with machine precision, fostering a collaborative environment that enhances productivity across sectors. Machines equipped with AI and advanced robotics are adept at performing repetitive, hazardous, and data-intensive tasks, allowing humans to focus on higher-order activities such as strategic thinking, innovation, and problem-solving (Ortiz et al., 2020). For instance, AI algorithms can process vast amounts of data to uncover patterns and insights beyond human capability (Wang et al., 2019). Human workers, in turn, leverage these insights to make informed decisions and drive creativity in ways machines cannot replicate. This collaboration optimizes efficiency and productivity in various industries. In manufacturing, collaborative robots (cobots) assist human operators on assembly lines, performing tasks like welding, painting, and quality inspection with remarkable precision, reducing errors and accelerating production (Liu et al., 2022; Segura et al., 2021). In healthcare, AI-driven diagnostic tools support medical professionals in identifying conditions and recommending treatments, improving patient care while alleviating the pressure on healthcare workers (Kalra et al., 2024). Creative fields also benefit from this synergy: in fashion, AI tools analyze consumer trends and preferences to generate design ideas, which designers then refine and personalize (Shi et al., 2021). Similarly, in entertainment, AI aids in scriptwriting, music composition, and video editing, offering creators novel ways to enhance their artistic endeavors (Anantrasirichai & Bull, 2021). In essence, human-machine collaboration in Industry 5.0 empowers both humans and machines to excel in their respective strengths, driving innovation and efficiency across diverse industries.
- **Customization and Personalization**: Industry 5.0 emphasizes customization and personalization, marking a significant departure from mass production toward tailored solutions that meet the specific needs and desires of individual consumers. This shift is fueled by the integration of human creativity with cutting-edge technologies, enabling businesses to offer products and services that align with customers' unique tastes, lifestyles, and values (Tian et al., 2021).

Traditionally, industrial production focused on standardized products to achieve economies of scale. However, evolving consumer expectations now demand personalized experiences that reflect individuality. Technologies such as 3D printing, AI, and IoT are central to enabling this customization (Maddikunta et al., 2022). 3D printing, or additive manufacturing, allows for the creation of intricate and personalized products by layering material based on digital designs (Prashar et al., 2022). This process not only enables the production of complex shapes that traditional methods cannot achieve but also reduces waste and shortens production cycles, making it ideal for bespoke manufacturing (Prashar et al., 2022). AI and IoT further enhance personalization by enabling the collection and analysis of real-time consumer data. Through connected devices and sensors, companies can gather insights on consumer preferences, behaviors, and feedback, which are then used to create more tailored products and services. In the automotive industry, for example, AI algorithms can analyze a driver's habits and preferences to customize vehicle features such as seating, climate control, and infotainment systems (Murali et al., 2021). Retailers also use AI to recommend products based on browsing history and purchase behavior, enhancing the shopping experience and boosting customer loyalty (Pereira et al., 2022; Bag et al., 2021). In healthcare, personalized medicine leverages genetic and lifestyle data to provide tailored treatments, improving outcomes and minimizing side effects (Kalra et al., 2024). This focus on customization extends beyond product manufacturing into services. In hospitality, AI-driven concierge services offer personalized recommendations for activities and dining based on individual guest preferences (Goel et al., 2024a). Similarly, in education, adaptive learning platforms use AI to customize curricula, enhancing student engagement and academic performance (Rane et al., 2023). In summary, Industry 5.0's emphasis on customization and personalization is transforming how businesses interact with consumers, offering more tailored, efficient, and innovative solutions across various sectors.

- **Local and Sustainable Production:** Sustainability is a cornerstone of Industry 5.0, which emphasizes local and environmentally friendly production practices. This shift addresses the growing concern over the environmental impact of industrial activities and the need for sustainable growth (Gholami et al., 2021). Local production reduces the carbon footprint associated with transportation and logistics. By producing goods closer to where they are consumed, companies can minimize the environmental impact of shipping products across long distances (Dekker et al., 2012). This also supports local economies by creating jobs and fostering innovation within communities. Industry 5.0 promotes sustainable production by encouraging the use of renewable energy sources—such as solar, wind, and hydroelectric power—to reduce dependence on fossil fuels (Sreelatha et al., 2023). Companies are increasingly adopting green technologies to minimize waste, conserve resources, and lower emissions. Advanced recycling processes and circular economy models, for example, allow materials to be reclaimed and products to be repurposed, thus reducing waste and preserving natural resources (Ahmad et al., 2021). Additionally, IoT and AI play pivotal roles in advancing sustainability. IoT sensors enable real-time monitoring of energy consumption, emissions, and waste, providing actionable data to optimize operations and reduce environmental impact (Sreelatha et al., 2023). AI algorithms further enhance this by analyzing the data to identify inefficiencies and suggest improvements. In agriculture, for instance, precision farming technologies use IoT and AI to optimize irrigation, fertilization, and pest control, reducing resource usage and minimizing the ecological footprint while boosting crop yields (Elijah et al., 2018). Sustainable production also entails designing products that last longer and are easier to recycle (Dekker et al., 2012). This approach reduces the need for frequent replacements and helps minimize waste. Eco-design principles are being adopted, including the use of biodegradable materials, reducing packaging, and designing products for easy disassembly and recycling (Lewis, 2008). Industry 5.0 also embraces the circular economy, a model that prioritizes the reuse, refurbishment, and recycling of products over the traditional linear model of production, use, and disposal (De Boer et al., 2021). This circular approach helps conserve resources, reduces waste, and creates new economic opportunities by extending the life cycle of materials and products (Genovese et al., 2017).

Therefore, Industry 5.0's focus on local and sustainable production—alongside human-machine collaboration and customization—marks a transformative shift in the industrial landscape. This new paradigm aims to foster innovation, efficiency, and sustainability by harnessing advanced technologies and emphasizing human creativity and responsibility. Companies that adopt these principles will be well-positioned to meet the growing demands for sustainability and contribute to a more equitable and environmentally conscious global economy.

3. THE ROLE OF REMOTE WORK IN SHAPING THE INDUSTRY 5.0

The rise of remote work in the context of Industry 5.0 offers an innovative approach to business operations, aligning with the core principles of creativity, collaboration, and sustainability. The seamless integration of remote work into this new industrial era creates a unique synergy, enhancing the flexibility of work environments while enabling businesses to become more agile, sustainable, and human-centric. This section explores how remote work plays a transformative role in driving creativity, facilitating global collaboration, and supporting local and sustainable manufacturing practices within the Industry 5.0 framework.

3.1 Empowering Creativity through Flexible Work Environments

Remote work empowers individuals by offering greater control over their workspaces, enabling them to create environments that stimulate creativity and innovation. The ability to tailor one's workspace to personal preferences fosters a sense of autonomy, which is a critical driver of job satisfaction and productivity (Tagliaro & Migliore, 2021). In the context of Industry 5.0, this flexibility allows employees to tap into their creative potential, think innovatively, and contribute to the development of cutting-edge solutions (Perry-Smith & Mannucci, 2017). Furthermore, the shift to remote work offers employees the opportunity to better balance their work and personal lives, which can reduce stress and improve overall well-being (Davidescu et al., 2020). This environment encourages employees to think outside the box, experiment with new ideas, and approach problems from diverse perspectives. Companies that embrace remote work provide workers with the autonomy to optimize their workdays and environments, directly fostering creative problem-solving, essential for navigating the challenges of Industry 5.0 (Kathleen et al., 2021). The role of digital technologies in remote work further supports creativity by enhancing access to collaborative tools and information. Cloud-based platforms and AI-driven tools enable employees to work seamlessly across projects, analyze data efficiently, and collaborate with others to generate and refine ideas (Dwivedi et al., 2021). This technological infrastructure not only facilitates creativity but also accelerates the pace at which new solutions can be developed and implemented (De Assis Dornelles et al., 2022).

3.2 Enhancing Global Collaboration through Remote Work

Remote work transcends geographical confines, enabling global collaboration and bringing together diverse perspectives and expertise. This aspect of remote work is integral to Industry 5.0, which aims to integrate diverse viewpoints and foster inclusive innovation (Paauwe & Boon, 2009). By breaking down geographical barriers, remote work allows organizations to build teams with members from different cultural, educational, and professional backgrounds, enriching the collaborative process (Afflerbach, 2020). Global collaboration in a remote work environment enables companies to tap into a broader talent pool, attracting top talent from around the world (Gordon, 2009). This diversity of thought and experience can lead to more innovative and effective solutions, as team members bring different perspectives and approaches to problem-solving (Post et al., 2009). Additionally, remote work facilitates the inclusion of individuals who may face barriers to traditional office-based employment, such as those with disabilities or caregiving responsibilities, further enhancing diversity and inclusion within the organization (Shirmohammadi et al., 2022). Advanced communication and collaboration technologies are pivotal in enabling global collaboration (Gordon, 2009). Tools such as video conferencing, instant messaging, and collaborative project management platforms allow team members to work together in real-time, regardless of their physical locations (Karis et al., 2014). These technologies support synchronous and asynchronous communication, ensuring that teams can collaborate effectively across different time zones (De Assis Dornelles et al., 2022). Moreover, global collaboration in a remote work setting encourages cross-functional and interdisciplinary teamwork (Kathleen et al., 2021). By bringing together experts from various fields, organizations can foster a holistic approach to innovation, addressing complex challenges with comprehensive and multifaceted solutions (Gorla et al., 2023). This interdisciplinary collaboration is particularly valuable in Industry 5.0, where the integration of digital, physical, and biological systems requires a broad range of expertise and perspectives.

3.3 Revolutionizing Manufacturing through Remote Work and Digital Technologies

Industry 5.0's emphasis on local and sustainable production practices is complemented by the rise of remote manufacturing. Remote work enables a decentralized approach to manufacturing, where digital blueprints and design files are shared globally, facilitating local production and minimizing environmental impact (Hossen et al., 2021). Through technologies such as 3D printing, IoT, and cloud computing, companies can produce customized products closer to the point of consumption, reducing transportation costs and minimizing the carbon footprint of manufacturing processes (Soori et al., 2024). Employees working remotely can oversee and manage manufacturing operations in real-time, ensuring quality control, optimizing production processes, and coordinating logistics from virtually anywhere (Butt, 2020). This flexibility allows businesses to be more responsive to customer demands, adapting quickly to market changes and enhancing operational efficiency. Additionally, remote manufacturing supports Industry 5.0's circular economy by promoting the reuse, refurbishment, and recycling of products, reducing waste, and conserving resources (Kühl et al., 2018).

Incorporating advanced technologies such as AI and machine learning into remote manufacturing further enhances sustainability. AI algorithms can analyze production data, predict maintenance needs, and optimize workflows, which helps reduce downtime and improves overall efficiency (Shahin et al., 2023). By integrating AI-driven tools into manufacturing, companies can ensure more sustainable and cost-effective production while maintaining high standards of quality and precision (Evans et al., 2007).

3.4 Conclusion: A New Era of Remote Work and Industry 5.0 Integration

The integration of remote work into Industry 5.0 creates a powerful combination that accelerates creativity, enables global collaboration, and supports local and sustainable manufacturing. Organizations can drive innovation, optimize business processes, and reduce their environmental impact by leveraging digital tools, flexible work environments, and advanced technologies. Remote work not only enhances the efficiency and sustainability of manufacturing operations but also aligns with the human-centric and inclusive goals of Industry 5.0, ultimately transforming the way we think about work and production. As businesses embrace this new paradigm, they will be better equipped to navigate the future of industrial growth—creating more resilient, inclusive, and sustainable operations in the process. Thereby, the chapter suggests the role of work-from-home in Industry 5.0 is multifaceted, enhancing creativity, fostering global collaboration, and supporting local and sustainable manufacturing practices. By leveraging the principles of remote work, organizations can optimize their operations, drive innovation, and achieve the human-centric and sustainable goals of Industry 5.0. This complementary relationship between remote work and Industry 5.0 is poised to redefine business operations, creating a more resilient, inclusive, and environmentally conscious industrial landscape.

4. CHALLENGES AND CONSIDERATIONS IN INDUSTRY 5.0

As Industry 5.0 ushers in a new era of industrial innovation and transformation, it brings with it a host of challenges and considerations that organizations must address to fully realize its potential. This chapter explores the key challenges of data security and privacy, upskilling and training, balancing automation and the human touch, and sustainability, especially in the context of a work-from-home environment.

4.1 Data Security and Privacy

The integration of human and machine capabilities in Industry 5.0 significantly increases the complexity of data security and privacy issues (Madhav & Tyagi,

2021). The widespread adoption of remote work further amplifies these concerns, as sensitive data is often transmitted and accessed over various networks and devices (Sicari et al., 2015). Ensuring the protection of this data is paramount to maintaining trust and compliance with regulatory standards (Condado & Lobo, 2023).

In a remote work environment, employees frequently use personal devices and home networks, which may not have the same level of security as corporate infrastructure (Posey & Shoss, 2023). This makes them more vulnerable to cyber-attacks, data breaches, and unauthorized access. Companies must implement robust cybersecurity measures to protect sensitive information (Madhav & Tyagi, 2021). This includes using encrypted communication channels, multi-factor authentication, and comprehensive monitoring systems to detect and respond to potential threats in real time. Moreover, organizations must educate their employees about best practices in data security and privacy . Regular training sessions on recognizing phishing attempts, securing personal devices, and safely handling confidential information are essential. Employees should also be encouraged to report suspicious activities promptly, enabling a swift and effective response to potential security incidents (Obada-Obieh et al., 2021).

Another critical aspect is the management of data privacy. With increasing amounts of personal data being collected and processed, organizations must ensure compliance with data protection regulations such as the General Data Protection Regulation (GDPR) in Europe or the California Consumer Privacy Act (CCPA) in the United States (Bakare et al., 2024). This involves not only securing data but also being transparent about data collection practices and providing individuals with control over their personal information.

4.2 Upskilling and Training

Industry 5.0 places a significant emphasis on human skills, as the synergy between humans and machines becomes a cornerstone of industrial processes. To thrive in this evolving landscape, companies must invest in upskilling and training programs to equip their workforce with the necessary competencies (Bessen, 2018). The rapid advancement of technologies such as AI, robotics, and IoT necessitates continuous learning and adaptation (Ahmad et al., 2021). Employees need to develop new technical skills to effectively collaborate with advanced machines and utilize emerging technologies. For instance, proficiency in data analysis, machine learning, and digital tools will be crucial for many roles (Hashish & Alnajjar, 2024).

Furthermore, soft skills such as critical thinking, creativity, and emotional intelligence will become increasingly important. As automation takes over routine tasks, human workers will be required to focus on more complex and strategic activities that demand innovative problem-solving and interpersonal skills (Gajdzik &

Wolniak, 2022). Training programs should therefore encompass both technical and soft skills to ensure a well-rounded and capable workforce. Organizations can adopt various approaches to upskilling and training. Online courses, workshops, and certifications provide flexible learning opportunities for employees to enhance their skills. Additionally, partnerships with educational institutions and industry experts can offer specialized training tailored to specific needs. Mentorship programs and cross-functional projects can also foster continuous learning and knowledge sharing within the organization.

4.3 Balancing Automation and Human Touch

One of the defining challenges of Industry 5.0 is achieving a delicate equilibrium between automation and the human touch. While automation and AI can significantly enhance efficiency and productivity, the human element remains indispensable for providing customized and personalized experiences (Groysberg et al., 2018). Organizations must carefully consider which tasks are best suited for automation and which require human intervention. Routine, repetitive, and data-intensive tasks are ideal candidates for automation, freeing up human workers to focus on more strategic, creative, and customer-centric activities (Huang & Rust, 2018). For example, chatbots and virtual assistants can handle basic customer inquiries, while human agents can address complex issues that require empathy and nuanced understanding (Budhwar et al., 2023). Maintaining this balance also involves integrating AI and automation in ways that augment human capabilities rather than replace them. Collaborative robots (cobots), for instance, can work alongside human employees, enhancing their productivity and reducing physical strain (Villani et al., 2018). AI tools can provide insights and recommendations based on data analysis, supporting human decision-making processes.

Additionally, organizations must ensure that the adoption of automation does not lead to a loss of personal connection with customers. Personalization technologies can help maintain this connection by tailoring products, services, and interactions to individual preferences (Fan & Poole, 2006). AI-driven analytics can provide valuable insights into customer behavior, enabling businesses to deliver more relevant and personalized experiences (Chandra et al., 2022). However, the human touch is essential in building and sustaining customer relationships, particularly in areas such as customer service, sales, and product development (Villani et al., 2018).

4.4 Sustainability

The sustainable production model advocated by Industry 5.0 has profound implications for remote work. As organizations strive to reduce their environmental impact, the carbon footprint of remote work practices becomes a critical consideration for environmentally-conscious businesses (Nahavandi, 2019). Remote work offers several sustainability benefits, such as reducing the need for commuting, which lowers greenhouse gas emissions and decreases traffic congestion (Lachapelle et al., 2017). Additionally, it reduces the energy consumption associated with maintaining large office spaces. However, it also presents new challenges, such as increased energy use in home offices and the environmental impact of digital infrastructure (Morley et al., 2018). To address these challenges, organizations can implement strategies to promote sustainable remote work practices (Gajdzik & Wolniak, 2022). This includes encouraging employees to use energy-efficient devices and renewable energy sources, providing guidelines for reducing energy consumption at home, and supporting sustainable digital practices, such as minimizing data storage and optimizing cloud usage. Moreover, companies can invest in green technologies and infrastructure to support remote work (Lachapelle et al., 2017). For instance, adopting energy-efficient data centers and cloud services can reduce the environmental impact of digital operations. Encouraging the use of virtual collaboration tools can minimize the need for business travel, further reducing carbon emissions (Shi et al., 2023).

This section of the chapter, thereby navigating the challenges and considerations of Industry 5.0, requires a comprehensive and strategic approach. Ensuring data security and privacy, investing in upskilling and training, balancing automation with the human touch, and promoting sustainability are essential to leveraging the full potential of this new industrial era (Sharma et al., 2024). By addressing these challenges thoughtfully and proactively, organizations can create a resilient, innovative, and sustainable future in Industry 5.0.

5. OPPORTUNITIES OF REMOTE WORK IN THE NEW ERA

The advent of Industry 5.0 is not only revolutionizing how businesses operate but also reshaping economic models and paradigms. One of the most significant shifts has been the rise of remote work, which has accelerated due to global disruptions and advancements in digital technology. This chapter explores the new opportunities that remote work brings within the context of Industry 5.0, focusing on its impact on productivity, cost structures, labor markets, and overall economic resilience. As a key component of Industry 5.0, remote work leverages advanced technologies to facilitate a decentralized workforce (Bedon et al., 2024). This shift has profound implications for economic structures and organizational strategies. Unlike traditional models, where economic activity is concentrated in specific geographic locations, remote work distributes economic activity across a broader spectrum, allowing for greater flexibility and efficiency (Tóth et al., 2023).

5.1 *Enhancing Productivity through Remote Work*

One of the primary economic opportunities of remote work is the potential for increased productivity. Studies have shown that remote workers often experience fewer interruptions, have more flexible schedules, and can create work environments tailored to their preferences (Bloom et al., 2015). The flexibility to work during peak productivity periods and the reduction in commuting time contribute to higher overall efficiency (Choudhury et al., 2019). In the context of Industry 5.0, productivity is further enhanced by the integration of AI and machine learning tools that support remote work (Bedon et al., 2024). These technologies automate routine tasks, analyze data for insights, and facilitate decision-making processes, allowing human workers to focus on higher-value activities. For example, AI-driven project management tools can track progress, identify bottlenecks, and suggest improvements, optimizing workflow and enhancing output.

5.2 Cost Structures and Financial Savings

Remote work also offers significant cost savings for both employers and employees. For businesses, the reduction in physical office space requirements leads to lower real estate costs, utility bills, and maintenance expenses (Naor et al., 2021). Additionally, remote work can reduce expenditures related to office supplies, equipment, and on-site amenities (Tanpipat et al., 2021). Employees benefit financially from reduced commuting costs, lower spending on work attire, and the potential for better work-life balance, which can lead to savings in areas such as childcare and healthcare (Cauthen, 2007). These financial savings contribute to higher disposable income and overall economic well-being, which can positively impact consumer spending and economic growth (Mahmood et al., 2022). From a broader economic perspective, the shift toward remote work leads to a more efficient allocation of resources. By reducing the need for large urban office spaces, resources can be redirected toward enhancing digital infrastructure and other areas that support remote work, stimulating innovation and investment in technology, and driving economic development (Zhou et al., 2020).

5.3 Expanding Job Opportunities and Workforce Distribution

Remote work is creating new opportunities in labor markets by expanding the geographic reach of job opportunities (Barrero et al., 2020). In traditional models, employment opportunities are often concentrated in urban centers, leading to regional disparities in economic activity. Remote work breaks down these geographic barriers, enabling companies to access a global talent pool and individuals to seek employment opportunities beyond their immediate vicinity (Soroui, 2021). This shift promotes more equitable economic development, allowing individuals in rural or underserved areas access to high-quality job opportunities (Choudhury, 2022). Businesses also benefit from diverse perspectives and skills by hiring talent from various regions and backgrounds, fostering innovation and creativity, which drives competitive advantage and economic growth. The decentralized nature of remote work allows for more flexible labor market participation (Ferreira et al., 2020). Individuals who may have been excluded from the traditional workforce due to caregiving responsibilities, disabilities, or other constraints can now engage in meaningful employment, enhancing overall workforce participation rates and contributing to a more resilient and adaptable economy (Sondermann, 2018).

5.4 *Strengthening Economic Resilience and Crisis Response*

The economic disruptions caused by global events such as the COVID-19 pandemic have underscored the importance of resilience and adaptability in business operations. Remote work has proven to be a critical component of economic resilience, allowing businesses to maintain continuity and productivity in the face of physical disruptions (Ambrogio et al., 2022). Industry 5.0's emphasis on remote work and digital integration enables organizations to quickly adapt to changing circumstances. For example, businesses can implement remote work policies, leverage digital communication tools, and ensure data security through cloud-based solutions (Ben-Zvi & Luftman, 2022). This adaptability not only mitigates the impact of crises but also positions businesses to seize new opportunities in a rapidly evolving market landscape. Furthermore, remote work supports economic resilience by reducing dependence on specific geographic locations and physical infrastructure (Abrardi & Sabatino, 2023). This decentralization can minimize the economic impact of localized disruptions, such as natural disasters or infrastructure failures, by ensuring that work can continue uninterrupted from various locations.

6.INNOVATIONS IN REMOTE WORK: ADVANCING BUSINESS TRANSFORMATION IN INDUSTRY 5.0

The economic innovations driving remote work within Industry 5.0 are central to fostering resilient, efficient, and flexible business environments. By leveraging cutting-edge technologies, organizations are transforming remote work from a temporary solution into a powerful tool for sustainable and scalable growth.

6.1 Advanced Communication and Collaboration Tools

Effective communication and collaboration are essential for successful remote work. Industry 5.0 leverages advanced tools such as video conferencing platforms, instant messaging applications, and collaborative project management software to facilitate seamless interaction among remote teams (Ortiz et al., 2020). These tools ensure that employees can communicate in real-time, share information, and collaborate on projects regardless of their physical location. Virtual reality (VR) and augmented reality (AR) technologies are also emerging as powerful tools for remote collaboration (Pidel & Ackermann, 2020). VR and AR can create immersive environments for meetings, training sessions, and collaborative work, providing a sense of presence and interaction similar to in-person experiences (Dwivedi et al., 2022). These technologies enhance engagement and productivity, making remote work more effective and enjoyable.

6.2 Cloud Computing and Data Security

Cloud computing is a cornerstone of remote work, enabling employees to access data, applications, and resources from any location with an internet connection. Cloud-based solutions provide flexibility, scalability, and cost-efficiency, making them ideal for supporting remote work environments (Hasiwar et al., 2024). Businesses can store and manage data securely in the cloud, ensuring that employees have the information they need at their fingertips (Patel et al., 2021). Data security is a critical consideration in remote work, particularly as sensitive information is accessed and transmitted across various locations (Sicari et al., 2015). Industry 5.0 addresses this challenge through robust cybersecurity measures, including encryption, multi-factor authentication, and secure access protocols (Ahmed et al., 2024). By prioritizing data security, businesses can protect their assets and maintain the trust of their customers and stakeholders.

6.3 Artificial Intelligence and Automation

Artificial intelligence (AI) and automation play pivotal roles in enhancing the efficiency and productivity of remote work. AI-powered tools can automate routine tasks, such as data entry, scheduling, and customer support, freeing up employees to focus on more strategic and creative activities (Lo et al., 2024). Machine learning algorithms can analyze data to provide insights, identify trends, and support decision-making processes (Chen et al., 2012). Automation extends to various aspects of remote work, including workflow management, performance tracking, and employee engagement. For example, AI-driven performance analytics can monitor productivity metrics, provide feedback, and suggest improvements (Dwivedi et al., 2022). This level of automation ensures that remote work remains efficient and aligned with organizational goals.

6.4 Digital Transformation and Innovation

The digital transformation enabled by Industry 5.0 fosters a culture of innovation within remote work environments. Businesses are increasingly adopting digital tools and strategies to streamline processes, enhance customer experiences, and drive innovation. This transformation involves rethinking traditional business models and embracing new ways of operating in a digital-first world (Bakke & Barland, 2022). Innovation in remote work is also driven by the integration of emerging technologies such as blockchain, which can enhance transparency, security, and efficiency in various processes (Rane & Narvel, 2021). For example, blockchain can be used to verify digital identities, secure transactions, and manage supply chains, providing a robust foundation for remote work operations (Aoun et al., 2021). The economic innovations brought about by remote work within Industry 5.0 are reshaping the business landscape and creating new opportunities for growth and development (Elangovan, 2021). Remote work is positioned as a key driver of economic progress in the digital age by enhancing productivity, optimizing cost structures, transforming labor markets, and bolstering economic resilience (Sturgeon, 2019).

As businesses continue to navigate the evolving landscape of Industry 5.0, the integration of remote work with advanced technologies and sustainable practices will be crucial. By embracing these economic innovations, organizations can build more agile, inclusive, and resilient operations, paving the way for a promising future of synergy and success in the era of Industry 5.0.

7. SUSTAINABILITY AND THE FUTURE OF WORK IN INDUSTRY 5.0

The convergence of Industry 5.0, remote work, and principles from Industry 4.0 heralds a new era of business transformation characterized by enhanced human-machine collaboration, sustainability, and a shift towards localized production. This evolution promises revolutionary improvements in customer experiences, fosters innovative problem-solving, and creates more adaptable business environments. The essence of Industry 5.0 lies in offering highly personalized products and services that enhance the customer experience through a synergy of advanced technology and human creativity.

Enhanced Customer Experiences

In Industry 5.0, businesses will use data analytics, AI, and machine learning to gain deeper insights into customer preferences and needs, allowing for highly tailored offerings (Lahteenmaki et al., 2021). Companies can create detailed customer profiles and personalize products and services, which boosts customer satisfaction and loyalty. This era also emphasizes unique products where AI designs based on specifications, and human creativity refines these products to ensure distinctiveness. Immersive technologies like AR and VR allow customers to visualize products in their environment before purchasing, enhancing decision-making (Agrawal et al., 2023). The combination of AI-powered support and human interaction further optimizes customer service, allowing brands to offer efficient and personalized assistance (Tóth et al., 2023).

Fostering Innovative Problem-Solving

Industry 5.0 emphasizes the creative potential of the workforce to solve complex problems through innovation. Human creativity, critical thinking, and emotional intelligence complement data-driven, machine efficiency (Adel, 2022). Remote work plays a pivotal role by allowing businesses to tap into a diverse global talent pool, enhancing creative problem-solving (Lindegaard & Kawasaki, 2010). Advanced collaboration tools, online brainstorming sessions, and AI-powered idea generation enable remote teams to work effectively despite geographic distances. Furthermore, continuous learning programs will equip employees with current skills and knowledge, helping them tackle new challenges and seize emerging opportunities (Borowski, 2021; Li, 2022).

Prioritizing Local and Sustainable Production

Sustainability and local production are central to Industry 5.0, aiming to reduce the environmental footprint of industrial activities. The integration of remote work supports these goals by enabling decentralized, localized production. Digital manufacturing technologies, like 3D printing and IoT, enable companies to produce goods closer to consumers, reducing transportation emissions and supporting circular economy initiatives (Ashima et al., 2022). Remote work further aids localized production by enabling employees to monitor and manage processes from anywhere using digital tools, creating a resilient and sustainable supply chain model (Srai et al., 2016).

Achieving Flexibility and Adaptability

Industry 5.0 emphasizes unprecedented flexibility and adaptability, supported by remote work. The ability to respond quickly to change is essential in today's volatile environment (Hommel et al., 2021). Remote work not only facilitates access to a global talent pool but also offers operational flexibility. Digital tools like cloud computing allow for seamless collaboration and data access, while AI and machine learning provide predictive insights for proactive decision-making (Attaran & Woods, 2018; Dwivedi et al., 2021). Additionally, a culture of trust and autonomy, fostered by remote work, empowers employees to make agile decisions, resulting in faster responses and enhanced innovation (Adana et al., 2023).

8. CONCLUSION: THE PATH FORWARD

Industry 5.0 represents a new frontier for business transformation, marked by a profound integration of advanced technology with human ingenuity. This evolution transcends traditional industrial boundaries, bringing forth enhanced customer experiences, innovative problem-solving, sustainable local production, and a new-found adaptability within organizations. By merging the principles of Industry 4.0's data-driven automation with the human-centric approach of Industry 5.0, businesses are creating resilient and agile models capable of thriving in the face of complexity and change.

Remote work plays a pivotal role within this landscape, not only as a mode of flexibility but as a strategic tool for leveraging global talent and driving efficiency. Leading companies such as Siemens and GitLab have already embraced remote work within Industry 5.0 frameworks, using advanced AI tools and smart devices to create seamless, optimized remote work environments. These organizations showcase how technology and human collaboration can harmonize to enhance productivity, foster creativity, and create flexible workspaces that adapt to both employee needs and organizational goals. Case studies demonstrate that the strategic use of AI, robotics, and smart devices is essential in creating work environments where employees, regardless of location, can collaborate as effectively as in traditional offices. For instance, AI-driven analytics help organizations customize workflows to improve individual performance, while robotics streamline complex operational tasks. Smart devices further connect teams, enabling real-time data sharing and decision-making that enhance project outcomes and speed.

Looking forward, Industry 5.0 will continue to foster a future where innovation is grounded in both technological progress and human values. This ongoing transformation offers companies not only the ability to respond dynamically to market demands but also to lead change, prioritizing sustainability and customer satisfaction. By adopting these principles, organizations can establish themselves as pioneers in an era where technology amplifies human potential, driving impactful, lasting progress in industries, workplaces, and communities worldwide.

REFERENCES

Abrardi, L., & Sabatino, L. (2023). Ultra-broadband investment and economic resilience: Evidence from the Covid-19 pandemic. *Telecommunications Policy*, *47*(2), 102480. DOI: 10.1016/j.telpol.2022.102480 PMID: 36467971

Adana, S., Manuj, I., Herburger, M., Cevikparmak, S., Celik, H., & Uvet, H. (2023). Linking decentralization in decision-making to resilience outcomes: A supply chain orientation perspective. *International Journal of Logistics Management*, *35*(1), 256–280. DOI: 10.1108/ijlm-07-2022-0308

Adel, A. (2022). Future of industry 5.0 in society: Human-centric solutions, challenges and prospective research areas. *Journal of Cloud Computing (Heidelberg, Germany)*, *11*(1). Advance online publication. DOI: 10.1186/s13677-022-00314-5 PMID: 36101900

Afflerbach, T. (2020). Hybrid Virtual Teams in Shared Services Organizations. In *Progress in IS*. https://doi.org/DOI: 10.1007/978-3-030-34300-2

Agrawal, P., Navgotri, S., & Nagesh, P. (2023). Impact of emerging technologies on digital manufacturing: Insights from literature review. *Materials Today: Proceedings*. Advance online publication. DOI: 10.1016/j.matpr.2023.03.187

Ahmad, T., Zhang, D., Huang, C., Zhang, H., Dai, N., Song, Y., & Chen, H. (2021). Artificial intelligence in sustainable energy industry: Status Quo, challenges and opportunities. *Journal of Cleaner Production*, *289*, 125834. DOI: 10.1016/j.jclepro.2021.125834

Ahmed, I., Hossain, N. U. I., Fazio, S. A., Lezzi, M., & Islam, M. S. (2024). A Decision Support Model for Assessing and Prioritization of Industry 5.0 Cybersecurity Challenges. *Sustainable Manufacturing and Service Economics*, *3*, 100018. DOI: 10.1016/j.smse.2024.100018

Ambrogio, G., Filice, L., Longo, F., & Padovano, A. (2022). Workforce and supply chain disruption as a digital and technological innovation opportunity for resilient manufacturing systems in the COVID-19 pandemic. *Computers & Industrial Engineering*, *169*, 108158. DOI: 10.1016/j.cie.2022.108158 PMID: 35431410

Anantrasirichai, N., & Bull, D. R. (2021). Artificial intelligence in the creative industries: A review. *Artificial Intelligence Review*, *55*(1), 589–656. DOI: 10.1007/s10462-021-10039-7

Aoun, A., Ilinca, A., Ghandour, M., & Ibrahim, H. (2021). A review of Industry 4.0 characteristics and challenges, with potential improvements using blockchain technology. *Computers & Industrial Engineering*, *162*, 107746. DOI: 10.1016/j.cie.2021.107746

Ashima, R., Haleem, A., Javaid, M., & Rab, S. (2022). Understanding the role and capabilities of Internet of Things-enabled Additive Manufacturing through its application areas. *Advanced Industrial and Engineering Polymer Research*, *5*(3), 137–142. DOI: 10.1016/j.aiepr.2021.12.001

Attaran, M., & Woods, J. (2018). Cloud computing technology: Improving small business performance using the Internet. *Journal of Small Business and Entrepreneurship*, *31*(6), 495–519. DOI: 10.1080/08276331.2018.1466850

Babel, W. (2022). Automation Pyramid and Solutions Business. In *Springer eBooks* (pp. 75–147). https://doi.org/DOI: 10.1007/978-3-658-37852-3_4

Bag, S., Srivastava, G., Bashir, M. A., Kumari, S., Giannakis, M., & Chowdhury, A. H. (2021). Journey of customers in this digital era: Understanding the role of artificial intelligence technologies in user engagement and conversion. *Benchmarking*, *29*(7), 2074–2098. DOI: 10.1108/bij-07-2021-0415

Bakare, N. S. S., Adeniyi, N. O., Akpuokwe, N. C. U., & Eneh, N. N. E. (2024). Data privacy laws and compliance: A comparative review of the eu gdpr and usa regulations. *Computer Science & IT Research Journal*, *5*(3), 528–543. DOI: 10.51594/csitrj.v5i3.859

Bakke, N. A., & Barland, J. (2022). Disruptive Innovations and Paradigm Shifts in Journalism as a Business: From Advertisers First to Readers First and Traditional Operational Models to the AI Factory. *SAGE Open*, *12*(2), 215824402210948. DOI: 10.1177/21582440221094819

Barrero, J. M., Bloom, N., & Davis, S. J. (2020). Why Working From Home Will Stick. SSRN *Electronic Journal*. https://doi.org/DOI: 10.2139/ssrn.3741644

Bedon, A., Pujol, F. A., & Ramirez, T. (2024). Examining Telework Adoption Through Cybersecurity and Industry 5.0. In *Communications in computer and information science* (pp. 379–388). https://doi.org/DOI: 10.1007/978-3-031-62843-6_36

Ben-Zvi, T., & Luftman, J. (2022). Post-Pandemic IT: Digital Transformation and Sustainability. *Sustainability*, *14*(22), 15275. DOI: 10.3390/su142215275

Bessen, J. E. (2018). Automation and Jobs: When Technology Boosts Employment. *Social Science Research Network*. https://doi.org/DOI: 10.2139/ssrn.2935003

Borowski, P. (2021). Digitization, Digital Twins, Blockchain, and Industry 4.0 as Elements of Management Process in Enterprises in the Energy Sector. *Energies, 14*(7), 1885. DOI: 10.3390/en14071885

Budhwar, P., Chowdhury, S., Wood, G., Aguinis, H., Bamber, G. J., Beltran, J. R., Boselie, P., Cooke, F. L., Decker, S., DeNisi, A., Dey, P. K., Guest, D., Knoblich, A. J., Malik, A., Paauwe, J., Papagiannidis, S., Patel, C., Pereira, V., Ren, S., & Varma, A. (2023). Human resource management in the age of generative artificial intelligence: Perspectives and research directions on ChatGPT. *Human Resource Management Journal, 33*(3), 606–659. DOI: 10.1111/1748-8583.12524

Budhwar, P., Chowdhury, S., Wood, G., Aguinis, H., Bamber, G. J., Beltran, J. R., Boselie, P., Cooke, F. L., Decker, S., DeNisi, A., Dey, P. K., Guest, D., Knoblich, A. J., Malik, A., Paauwe, J., Papagiannidis, S., Patel, C., Pereira, V., Ren, S., & Varma, A. (2023b). Human resource management in the age of generative artificial intelligence: Perspectives and research directions on ChatGPT. *Human Resource Management Journal, 33*(3), 606–659. DOI: 10.1111/1748-8583.12524

Butt, J. (2020). A Conceptual Framework to Support Digital Transformation in Manufacturing Using an Integrated Business Process Management Approach. *Designs, 4*(3), 17. DOI: 10.3390/designs4030017

Cauthen, N. K. (2007). *Improving Work Supports: Closing the Financial Gap for Low-wage Workers and Their Families*. https://doi.org/DOI: 10.7916/d8cr633w

Chandra, S., Verma, S., Lim, W. M., Kumar, S., & Donthu, N. (2022). Personalization in personalized marketing: Trends and ways forward. *Psychology and Marketing, 39*(8), 1529–1562. DOI: 10.1002/mar.21670

Chen, N., Chiang, N., & Storey, N. (2012). Business Intelligence and Analytics: From Big Data to Big Impact. *Management Information Systems Quarterly, 36*(4), 1165. DOI: 10.2307/41703503

Choudhury, P., Foroughi, C., & Larson, B. (2019). Work-from-anywhere: The Productivity Effects of Geographic Flexibility. SSRN *Electronic Journal*. https://doi.org/DOI: 10.2139/ssrn.3494473

Condado, P. A., & Lobo, F. G. (2023). Security and privacy concerns in assisted living environments. *Journal of Smart Cities and Society, 2*(2), 99–121. DOI: 10.3233/scs-230015

Davidescu, A. A., Apostu, S. A., Paul, A., & Casuneanu, I. (2020). Work Flexibility, Job Satisfaction, and Job Performance among Romanian Employees—Implications for Sustainable Human Resource Management. *Sustainability*, *12*(15), 6086. DOI: 10.3390/su12156086

De Assis Dornelles, J., Ayala, N. F., & Frank, A. G. (2022). Smart Working in Industry 4.0: How digital technologies enhance manufacturing workers' activities. *Computers & Industrial Engineering*, *163*, 107804. DOI: 10.1016/j.cie.2021.107804

De Boer, B. F., Rietveld, E., Rodrigues, J. F. D., & Tukker, A. (2021). Global environmental and socio-economic impacts of a transition to a circular economy in metal and electrical products: A Dutch case study. *Journal of Industrial Ecology*, *25*(5), 1264–1271. DOI: 10.1111/jiec.13133

Dekker, R., Bloemhof, J., & Mallidis, I. (2012). Operations Research for green logistics – An overview of aspects, issues, contributions and challenges. *European Journal of Operational Research*, *219*(3), 671–679. DOI: 10.1016/j.ejor.2011.11.010

Dwivedi, Y. K., Hughes, L., Ismagilova, E., Aarts, G., Coombs, C., Crick, T., Duan, Y., Dwivedi, R., Edwards, J., Eirug, A., Galanos, V., Ilavarasan, P. V., Janssen, M., Jones, P., Kar, A. K., Kizgin, H., Kronemann, B., Lal, B., Lucini, B., & Williams, M. D. (2021). Artificial Intelligence (AI): Multidisciplinary perspectives on emerging challenges, opportunities, and agenda for research, practice and policy. *International Journal of Information Management*, *57*, 101994. DOI: 10.1016/j.ijinfomgt.2019.08.002

Echchakoui, S., & Barka, N. (2020). Industry 4.0 and its impact in plastics industry: A literature review. *Journal of Industrial Information Integration*, *20*, 100172. DOI: 10.1016/j.jii.2020.100172

Elangovan, U. (2021). *Industry 5.0*. https://doi.org/DOI: 10.1201/9781003190677

Elijah, O., Rahman, T. A., Orikumhi, I., Leow, C. Y., & Hindia, M. N. (2018). An Overview of Internet of Things (IoT) and Data Analytics in Agriculture: Benefits and Challenges. *IEEE Internet of Things Journal*, *5*(5), 3758–3773. DOI: 10.1109/jiot.2018.2844296

Evans, S., Partidário, P. J., & Lambert, J. (2007). Industrialization as a key element of sustainable product-service solutions. *International Journal of Production Research*, *45*(18–19), 4225–4246. DOI: 10.1080/00207540701449999

Fan, H., & Poole, M. S. (2006). What Is Personalization? Perspectives on the Design and Implementation of Personalization in Information Systems. *Journal of Organizational Computing and Electronic Commerce, 16*(3–4), 179–202. DOI: 10.1080/10919392.2006.9681199

Ferreira, J., Coelho, A., & Moutinho, L. (2020). Dynamic capabilities, creativity and innovation capability and their impact on competitive advantage and firm performance: The moderating role of entrepreneurial orientation. *Technovation, 92–93*, 102061. DOI: 10.1016/j.technovation.2018.11.004

Formica, P. (2023). Carving the Transformative Enterprise Profile. In *Emerald Publishing Limited eBooks* (pp. 1–41). https://doi.org/DOI: 10.1108/978-1-80382-783-420231001

Gajdzik, B., & Wolniak, R. (2022). Smart Production Workers in Terms of Creativity and Innovation: The Implication for Open Innovation. *Journal of Open Innovation, 8*(2), 68. DOI: 10.3390/joitmc8020068

Genovese, A., Acquaye, A. A., Figueroa, A., & Koh, S. L. (2017). Sustainable supply chain management and the transition towards a circular economy: Evidence and some applications. *Omega, 66*, 344–357. DOI: 10.1016/j.omega.2015.05.015

Gholami, H., Abu, F., Lee, J. K. Y., Karganroudi, S. S., & Sharif, S. (2021). Sustainable Manufacturing 4.0—Pathways and Practices. *Sustainability, 13*(24), 13956. DOI: 10.3390/su132413956

Goel, R., Singla, J., Arora, M., & Mittal, A. (2024a). From stress to success: Role of green atmospherics on employee well-being in the Indian hotel and tourism industry. *Journal of Human Resources in Hospitality & Tourism. Journal of Human Resources in Hospitality & Tourism, 23*(3), 359–385. DOI: 10.1080/15332845.2024.2335091

Goel, R., Singla, J., Mittal, A., & Arora, M. (2024b). A decade analysis of employees' well-being and performance while working from home: A bibliometric approach. *Information Discovery and Delivery*. Advance online publication. DOI: 10.1108/idd-03-2023-0030

Golovianko, M., Terziyan, V., Branytskyi, V., & Malyk, D. (2023). Industry 4.0 vs. Industry 5.0: Co-existence, Transition, or a Hybrid. *Procedia Computer Science, 217*, 102–113. DOI: 10.1016/j.procs.2022.12.206

Gordon, E. E. (2009). *Winning the Global Talent Showdown: How Businesses and Communities Can Partner to Rebuild the Jobs Pipeline*. https://skills.scholarvox.com/catalog/book/docid/10294951

Gorla, F., Borojevic, A., Gibertoni, C., Landi, L., Storchi, M., Fontana, L., Regmi, J., Burmen, B., & Silenzi, A. (2023). The Hospital of Tomorrow Case Study: Multidisciplinarity, Inclusiveness and Holistic Approaches to Foster Innovation in Complex Organizations. *International Journal of Health Policy and Management*. Advance online publication. DOI: 10.34172/ijhpm.2023.7330 PMID: 37579430

Groysberg, B., Lee, J., Price, J., & Yo-Jud Cheng, J. (2018). The Leader's Guide to Corporate Culture: How to Manage the Eight Critical Elements of Organizational Life. *Harvard Business Review*, *96*(1), 44–52.

Hashish, E. A., & Alnajjar, H. (2024). Digital proficiency: Assessing knowledge, attitudes, and skills in digital transformation, health literacy, and artificial intelligence among university nursing students. *BMC Medical Education*, *24*(1). Advance online publication. DOI: 10.1186/s12909-024-05482-3 PMID: 38715005

Hasiwar, D., Gruber, A., Dragschitz, C., & Ivkić, I. (2024, March 27). *Towards a Cloud-based Smart Office Solution for Shared Workplace Individualization*. arXiv.org. https://arxiv.org/abs/2403.18883

Hommel, B. E., Ruppel, R., & Zacher, H. (2021). Assessment of cognitive flexibility in personnel selection: Validity and acceptance of a gamified version of the Wisconsin Card Sorting Test. *International Journal of Selection and Assessment*, *30*(1), 126–144. DOI: 10.1111/ijsa.12362

Hossen, B., Yabar, H., & Mizunoya, T. (2021). Land Suitability Assessment for Pulse (Green Gram) Production through Remote Sensing, GIS and Multicriteria Analysis in the Coastal Region of Bangladesh. *Sustainability*, *13*(22), 12360. DOI: 10.3390/su132212360

Huang, M. H., & Rust, R. T. (2018). Artificial Intelligence in Service. *Journal of Service Research*, *21*(2), 155–172. DOI: 10.1177/1094670517752459

Ji, F., Zhou, Y., Zhang, H., Cheng, G., & Luo, Q. (2024). Navigating the Digital Odyssey: AI-Driven Business Models in Industry 4.0. *Journal of the Knowledge Economy*. Advance online publication. DOI: 10.1007/s13132-024-02096-4

Kagermann, H., Wahlster W., Helbig, J. (2013). Recommendations for implementing the strategic initiative Industrie 4.0: Final report of the Industrie 4.0 Working Group.

Kalra, N., Verma, P., & Verma, S. (2024). Advancements in AI based healthcare techniques with FOCUS ON diagnostic techniques. *Computers in Biology and Medicine*, *179*, 108917. DOI: 10.1016/j.compbiomed.2024.108917 PMID: 39059212

Karis, D., Wildman, D., & Mané, A. (2014). Improving Remote Collaboration With Video Conferencing and Video Portals. *Human-Computer Interaction, 31*(1), 1–58. DOI: 10.1080/07370024.2014.921506

Kathleen, S., Sven, S., Claudia, N. B., & Frank, E. (2021). Fulfilling Remote Collaboration Needs for New Work. *Procedia Computer Science, 191*, 168–175. DOI: 10.1016/j.procs.2021.07.021

Kennedy, D. (2017). The machine in the market: Computers and the infrastructure of price at the New York Stock Exchange, 1965–1975. *Social Studies of Science, 47*(6), 888–917. DOI: 10.1177/0306312717739367 PMID: 29143591

Kolade, O., & Owoseni, A. (2022). Employment 5.0: The work of the future and the future of work. *Technology in Society, 71*, 102086. DOI: 10.1016/j.techsoc.2022.102086

Kühl, C., Tjahjono, B., Bourlakis, M., & Aktas, E. (2018). Implementation of Circular Economy principles in PSS operations. *Procedia CIRP, 73*, 124–129. DOI: 10.1016/j.procir.2018.03.303

Kurt, R. (2019). Industry 4.0 in Terms of Industrial Relations and Its Impacts on Labour Life. *Procedia Computer Science, 158*, 590–601. DOI: 10.1016/j.procs.2019.09.093

Lahteenmaki, I., Nätti, S., & Saraniemi, S. (2021). Digitalization-Enabled Evolution of Customer Value Creation: An Executive View in Financial Services. SSRN *Electronic Journal*. https://doi.org/DOI: 10.2139/ssrn.3887270

Leng, J., Zhong, Y., Lin, Z., Xu, K., Mourtzis, D., Zhou, X., Zheng, P., Liu, Q., Zhao, J. L., & Shen, W. (2023). Towards resilience in Industry 5.0: A decentralized autonomous manufacturing paradigm. *Journal of Manufacturing Systems, 71*, 95–114. DOI: 10.1016/j.jmsy.2023.08.023

Lewis, H. (2008). Eco-design of food packaging materials. In *Elsevier eBooks* (pp. 238–262). https://doi.org/DOI: 10.1533/9781845694784.2.238

Li, L. (2022). Reskilling and Upskilling the Future-ready Workforce for Industry 4.0 and Beyond. *Information Systems Frontiers*. Advance online publication. DOI: 10.1007/s10796-022-10308-y PMID: 35855776

Lindegaard, S., & Kawasaki, G. (2010). *The Open Innovation Revolution: Essentials, Roadblocks, and Leadership Skills*. https://ci.nii.ac.jp/ncid/BB0405033X

Liu, L., Guo, F., Zou, Z., & Duffy, V. G. (2022). Application, Development and Future Opportunities of Collaborative Robots (Cobots) in Manufacturing: A Literature Review. *International Journal of Human-Computer Interaction*, *40*(4), 915–932. DOI: 10.1080/10447318.2022.2041907

Lo, W., Yang, C. M., Zhang, Q., & Li, M. (2024). Increased Productivity and Reduced Waste with Robotic Process Automation and Generative AI-powered IoE Services. *Journal of Web Engineering*, •••, 53–88. DOI: 10.13052/jwe1540-9589.2313

Longo, F., Padovano, A., & Umbrello, S. (2020). Value-Oriented and Ethical Technology Engineering in Industry 5.0: A Human-Centric Perspective for the Design of the Factory of the Future. *Applied Sciences (Basel, Switzerland)*, *10*(12), 4182. DOI: 10.3390/app10124182

Loy, A. C. M., Chin, B. L. F., & Sankaran, R. (2021). Industrial Revolution 1.0 and 2.0. In *CRC Press eBooks* (pp. 1–14). https://doi.org/DOI: 10.1201/9781003080671-1-1

Maddikunta, P. K. R., & Pham, Q. V., B, P., Deepa, N., Dev, K., Gadekallu, T. R., Ruby, R., & Liyanage, M. (2022). Industry 5.0: A survey on enabling technologies and potential applications. *Journal of Industrial Information Integration*, *26*, 100257. DOI: 10.1016/j.jii.2021.100257

Maddikunta, P. K. R., & Pham, Q. V., B, P., Deepa, N., Dev, K., Gadekallu, T. R., Ruby, R., & Liyanage, M. (2022b). Industry 5.0: A survey on enabling technologies and potential applications. *Journal of Industrial Information Integration*, *26*, 100257. DOI: 10.1016/j.jii.2021.100257

Mahmood, S., Shuhui, W., Aslam, S., & Ahmed, T. (2022). The Financial Inclusion Development and Its Impacts on Disposable Income. *SAGE Open*, *12*(2), 215824402210933. DOI: 10.1177/21582440221093369

Morley, J., Widdicks, K., & Hazas, M. (2018). Digitalisation, energy and data demand: The impact of Internet traffic on overall and peak electricity consumption. *Energy Research & Social Science*, *38*, 128–137. DOI: 10.1016/j.erss.2018.01.018

Murali, P. K., Kaboli, M., & Dahiya, R. (2021). Intelligent In-Vehicle Interaction Technologies. *Advanced Intelligent Systems*, *4*(2). Advance online publication. DOI: 10.1002/aisy.202100122

Murphy, C., Carew, P. J., & Stapleton, L. (2023). A human-centred systems manifesto for smart digital immersion in Industry 5.0: A case study of cultural heritage. *AI & Society*. Advance online publication. DOI: 10.1007/s00146-023-01693-2

Nahavandi, S. (2019). Industry 5.0—A Human-Centric Solution. *Sustainability*, *11*(16), 4371. DOI: 10.3390/su11164371

Naor, M., Pinto, G. D., Hakakian, A. I., & Jacobs, A. (2021). The impact of COVID-19 on office space utilization and real-estate: A case study about teleworking in Israel as new normal. *Journal of Facilities Management, 20*(1), 32–58. DOI: 10.1108/jfm-12-2020-0096

Obada-Obieh, B., Huang, Y., & Beznosov, K. (2021). *Challenges and Threats of Mass Telecommuting: A Qualitative Study of Workers*. USENIX. https://www.usenix.org/conference/soups2021/presentation/obada-obieh

Ortiz, J., Gabriela, N., Carvalho, P., Cazarini, E., Gutierrez, W., Cifuentes, L., Claudia, A., Paula, A., Carvalho, A. P., Oztemel, E., Gursev, S., Spoettl, G., Chromjakova, F., Pandiyan, V., & Caesarendra, W. (2020). Industry 4.0 - Current Status and Future Trends. In *IntechOpen eBooks*. https://doi.org/DOI: 10.5772/intechopen.86000

Paauwe, J., & Boon, C. (2009). Strategic HRM : A critical review. *Human Resource Management, 2*, 49–73. DOI: 10.4324/9780203876336-11

Patel, V., Chesmore, A., Legner, C. M., & Pandey, S. (2021). Trends in Workplace Wearable Technologies and Connected-Worker Solutions for Next-Generation Occupational Safety, Health, and Productivity. *Advanced Intelligent Systems, 4*(1). Advance online publication. DOI: 10.1002/aisy.202100099

Pereira, A. M., Moura, J. a. B., & De, B Costa, E., Vieira, T., Landim, A. R., Bazaki, E., & Wanick, V. (2022). Customer models for artificial intelligence-based decision support in fashion online retail supply chains. *Decision Support Systems, 158*, 113795. DOI: 10.1016/j.dss.2022.113795

Perry-Smith, J. E., & Mannucci, P. V. (2017). From Creativity to Innovation: The Social Network Drivers of the Four Phases of the Idea Journey. *Academy of Management Review, 42*(1), 53–79. DOI: 10.5465/amr.2014.0462

Pidel, C., & Ackermann, P. (2020). Collaboration in Virtual and Augmented Reality: A Systematic Overview. In *Lecture notes in computer science* (pp. 141–156). https://doi.org/DOI: 10.1007/978-3-030-58465-8_10

Posey, C., & Shoss, M. (2023). Employees as a Source of Security Issues in Times of Change and Stress: A Longitudinal Examination of Employees' Security Violations during the COVID-19 Pandemic. *Journal of Business and Psychology*. Advance online publication. DOI: 10.1007/s10869-023-09917-4

Post, C., De Lia, E., DiTomaso, N., Tirpak, T. M., & Borwankar, R. (2009). Capitalizing on Thought Diversity for Innovation. *Research Technology Management, 52*(6), 14–25. DOI: 10.1080/08956308.2009.11657596

Prashar, G., Vasudev, H., & Bhuddhi, D. (2022). Additive manufacturing: Expanding 3D printing horizon in industry 4.0. [IJIDeM]. *International Journal on Interactive Design and Manufacturing*, *17*(5), 2221–2235. DOI: 10.1007/s12008-022-00956-4 PMID: 40479213

Rane, N., Choudhary, S., & Rane, J. (2023). Education 4.0 and 5.0: Integrating Artificial Intelligence (AI) for Personalized and Adaptive Learning. SSRN *Electronic Journal*. https://doi.org/DOI: 10.2139/ssrn.4638365

Rane, S. B., & Narvel, Y. M. (2021). Re-designing the business organization using disruptive innovations based on blockchain-IoT integrated architecture for improving agility in future Industry 4.0. *Benchmarking*, *28*(5), 1883–1908. DOI: 10.1108/bij-12-2018-0445

Segura, P., Lobato-Calleros, O., Ramírez-Serrano, A., & Soria, I. (2021). Human-robot collaborative systems: Structural components for current manufacturing applications. *Advances in Industrial and Manufacturing Engineering*, *3*, 100060. DOI: 10.1016/j.aime.2021.100060

Shahin, M., Chen, F. F., Hosseinzadeh, A., & Zand, N. (2023). Using machine learning and deep learning algorithms for downtime minimization in manufacturing systems: An early failure detection diagnostic service. *International Journal of Advanced Manufacturing Technology*, *128*(9–10), 3857–3883. DOI: 10.1007/s00170-023-12020-w

Sharma, M., Paliwal, T., & Baniwal, P. (2024). Challenges in Digital Transformation and Automation for Industry 4.0. In *CRC Press eBooks* (pp. 143–163). https://doi.org/DOI: 10.1201/9781003432319-9

Shi, M., Chussid, C., Yang, P., Jia, M., Lewis, V. D., & Cao, W. (2021). The exploration of artificial intelligence application in fashion trend forecasting. *Textile Research Journal*, *91*(19–20), 2357–2386. DOI: 10.1177/00405175211006212

Shi, Y., Sorrell, S., & Foxon, T. (2023). The impact of teleworking on domestic energy use and carbon emissions: An assessment for England. *Energy and Building*, *287*, 112996. DOI: 10.1016/j.enbuild.2023.112996

Shirmohammadi, M., Au, W. C., & Beigi, M. (2022). Remote work and work-life balance: Lessons learned from the covid-19 pandemic and suggestions for HRD practitioners. *Human Resource Development International*, *25*(2), 163–181. DOI: 10.1080/13678868.2022.2047380

Sicari, S., Rizzardi, A., Grieco, L., & Coen-Porisini, A. (2015). Security, privacy and trust in Internet of Things: The road ahead. *Computer Networks*, *76*, 146–164. DOI: 10.1016/j.comnet.2014.11.008

Sicari, S., Rizzardi, A., Grieco, L., & Coen-Porisini, A. (2015b). Security, privacy and trust in Internet of Things: The road ahead. *Computer Networks*, *76*, 146–164. DOI: 10.1016/j.comnet.2014.11.008

Sondermann, D. (2018). Towards more resilient economies: The role of well-functioning economic structures. *Journal of Policy Modeling*, *40*(1), 97–117. DOI: 10.1016/j.jpolmod.2018.01.002

Soori, M., Arezoo, B., & Dastres, R. (2023). Artificial intelligence, machine learning and deep learning in advanced robotics, a review. *Cognitive Robotics*, *3*, 54–70. DOI: 10.1016/j.cogr.2023.04.001

Soori, M., Arezoo, B., & Dastres, R. (2024). Virtual manufacturing in industry 4.0: A review. *Data Science and Management*, *7*(1), 47–63. DOI: 10.1016/j.dsm.2023.10.006

Soroui, S. T. (2021). Understanding the drivers and implications of remote work from the local perspective: An exploratory study into the dis/reembedding dynamics. *Technology in Society*, *64*, 101328. DOI: 10.1016/j.techsoc.2020.101328

Srai, J. S., Kumar, M., Graham, G., Phillips, W., Tooze, J., Ford, S., Beecher, P., Raj, B., Gregory, M., Tiwari, M. K., Ravi, B., Neely, A., Shankar, R., Charnley, F., & Tiwari, A. (2016). Distributed manufacturing: Scope, challenges and opportunities. *International Journal of Production Research*, *54*(23), 6917–6935. DOI: 10.1080/00207543.2016.1192302

Sreelatha, A. S., Pallavi, B., & Ajala, S. O. (2023). Energy Efficiency and Renewable Energy in Industry 5.0. In *CRC Press eBooks* (pp. 107–155). https://doi.org/DOI: 10.1201/9781032686363-6

Sturgeon, T. J. (2019). Upgrading strategies for the digital economy. *Global Strategy Journal*, *11*(1), 34–57. DOI: 10.1002/gsj.1364

Sutthiphisal, D. (2006). Learning-by-Producing and the Geographic Links Between Invention and Production: Experience from the Second Industrial Revolution. *The Journal of Economic History*, *66*(4), 992–1025. DOI: 10.1017/s0022050706000404

Tagliaro, C., & Migliore, A. (2021). "Covid-working": What to keep and what to leave? Evidence from an Italian company. *Journal of Corporate Real Estate*, *24*(2), 76–92. DOI: 10.1108/jcre-10-2020-0053

Tanpipat, W., Lim, H. W., & Deng, X. (2021). Implementing Remote Working Policy in Corporate Offices in Thailand: Strategic Facility Management Perspective. *Sustainability*, *13*(3), 1284. DOI: 10.3390/su13031284

Tian, J., Vanderstraeten, J., Matthyssens, P., & Shen, L. (2021). Developing and leveraging platforms in a traditional industry: An orchestration and co-creation perspective. *Industrial Marketing Management*, *92*, 14–33. DOI: 10.1016/j.indmarman.2020.10.007

Tóth, A., Nagy, L., Kennedy, R., Bohuš, B., Abonyi, J., & Ruppert, T. (2023). The human-centric Industry 5.0 collaboration architecture. *MethodsX*, *11*, 102260. DOI: 10.1016/j.mex.2023.102260 PMID: 37388166

Villani, V., Pini, F., Leali, F., & Secchi, C. (2018). Survey on human–robot collaboration in industrial settings: Safety, intuitive interfaces and applications. *Mechatronics*, *55*, 248–266. DOI: 10.1016/j.mechatronics.2018.02.009

Vrontis, D., Christofi, M., Pereira, V., Tarba, S., Makrides, A., & Trichina, E. (2023). Artificial intelligence, robotics, advanced technologies and human resource management: a systematic review. *Routledge eBooks*, 172–201. https://doi.org/DOI: 10.4324/9781003377085-7

Wang, D., Weisz, J. D., Muller, M., Ram, P., Geyer, W., Dugan, C., Tausczik, Y., Samulowitz, H., & Gray, A. (2019). Human-AI Collaboration in Data Science. *Proceedings of the ACM on Human-Computer Interaction*, *3*(CSCW), 1–24. https://doi.org/DOI: 10.1145/3359313

Yin, Y., Stecke, K. E., & Li, D. (2017). The evolution of production systems from Industry 2.0 through Industry 4.0. *International Journal of Production Research*, *56*(1–2), 848–861. DOI: 10.1080/00207543.2017.1403664

Zekhnini, K., Benabdellah, A. C., Bag, S., & Gupta, S. (2024). Supply chain 5.0 digitalization: An integrated approach for risk assessment. *Management Decision*. Advance online publication. DOI: 10.1108/md-12-2023-2329

Zhou, X., Song, M., & Cui, L. (2020). Driving force for China's economic development under Industry 4.0 and circular economy: Technological innovation or structural change? *Journal of Cleaner Production*, *271*, 122680. DOI: 10.1016/j.jclepro.2020.122680

Compilation of References

Abbes, I., Hallem, Y. and Taga, N. (2020), "Second-hand shopping and brand loyalty: The role of online collaborative redistribution platforms", *Journal of Retailing and Consumer Services*, Elsevier Ltd, Vol. 52 No. April 2019, p. 101885, doi: .DOI: 10.1016/j.jretconser.2019.101885

Abdi, H., Jahanian, A., & Nozari, H. (2025). Digital Twin-Enabled Bioreactors: Transforming Industrial Biotechnology in Smart Economies. In Dynamic and Safe Economy in the Age of Smart Technologies (pp. 105-120). IGI Global Scientific Publishing.

Abrardi, L., & Sabatino, L. (2023). Ultra-broadband investment and economic resilience: Evidence from the Covid-19 pandemic. *Telecommunications Policy*, *47*(2), 102480. DOI: 10.1016/j.telpol.2022.102480 PMID: 36467971

Acemoglu, D., & Restrepo, P. (2018). The race between man and machine: Implications of technology for growth, factor shares, and employment. *The American Economic Review*, *108*(6), 1488–1542.

Adana, S., Manuj, I., Herburger, M., Cevikparmak, S., Celik, H., & Uvet, H. (2023). Linking decentralization in decision-making to resilience outcomes: A supply chain orientation perspective. *International Journal of Logistics Management*, *35*(1), 256–280. DOI: 10.1108/ijlm-07-2022-0308

Adel, A. (2022). Future of industry 5.0 in society: Human-centric solutions, challenges and prospective research areas. *J Cloud Comp*, *11*, 40. DOI: 10.1186/s13677-022-00314-5

Adel, A. (2022). Future of industry 5.0 in society: Human-centric solutions, challenges and prospective research areas. *Journal of Cloud Computing (Heidelberg, Germany)*, *11*(1), 40. PMID: 36101900

Adner, R., & Kapoor, R. (2016). Innovation ecosystems and the pace of substitution: Re-examining technology S-curves. *Strategic Management Journal*, *37*(4), 625–648.

AeroFarms. (2021). *AeroFarms: World leader in vertical farming*. Retrieved from https://www.aerofarms.com

Afflerbach, T. (2020). Hybrid Virtual Teams in Shared Services Organizations. In *Progress in IS*. https://doi.org/DOI: 10.1007/978-3-030-34300-2

Agrawal, P., Navgotri, S., & Nagesh, P. (2023). Impact of emerging technologies on digital manufacturing: Insights from literature review. *Materials Today: Proceedings*. Advance online publication. DOI: 10.1016/j.matpr.2023.03.187

AgriDigital. (2020). *AgriDigital: Blockchain for global agri-supply chains*. Retrieved from https://www.agridigital.io

Aheleroff, S., Huang, H., Xu, X., & Zhong, R. Y. (2022). Toward sustainability and resilience with Industry 4.0 and Industry 5.0. *Frontiers in Manufacturing Technology*, *2*, 951643.

Ahmad, T., Zhang, D., Huang, C., Zhang, H., Dai, N., Song, Y., & Chen, H. (2021). Artificial intelligence in sustainable energy industry: Status Quo, challenges and opportunities. *Journal of Cleaner Production*, *289*, 125834. DOI: 10.1016/j.jclepro.2021.125834

Ahmed, I., Hossain, N. U. I., Fazio, S. A., Lezzi, M., & Islam, M. S. (2024). A Decision Support Model for Assessing and Prioritization of Industry 5.0 Cybersecurity Challenges. *Sustainable Manufacturing and Service Economics*, *3*, 100018. DOI: 10.1016/j.smse.2024.100018

Akan, Y., & Tepeler, M. İ. (2022). Sharing Economy in the Dimension of Sustainability and Trust. *Sosyoekonomi*, *30*(53), 447–464. DOI: 10.17233/sosyoekonomi.2022.03.22

Akbar, P., & Hoffmann, S. (2023). Collaborative space: Framework for collaborative consumption and the sharing economy. *Journal of Services Marketing*, *37*(4), 496–509. DOI: 10.1108/JSM-03-2021-0078

Alaeddini, M., Mallek, S., & Hönigsberg, S. (2025). Uncovering Research Trends: A Textual Analysis of AI Applications in Circular Economy under an Industry 5.0 Paradigm. *IFAC-PapersOnLine*, *59*(10), 214–219.

Albinsson, P. A., Perera, B. Y., Nafees, L., & Burman, B. (2019). Collaborative Consumption Usage in the US and India: An Exploratory Study. *Journal of Marketing Theory and Practice*, *27*(4), 390–412. DOI: 10.1080/10696679.2019.1644956

Aliahmadi, A., & Nozari, H. (2023, January). Evaluation of security metrics in AIoT and blockchain-based supply chain by Neutrosophic decision-making method. In Supply chain forum: an international journal (Vol. 24, No. 1, pp. 31-42). Taylor & Francis.

Aliahmadi, A., Nozari, H., Ghahremani-Nahr, J., & Szmelter-Jarosz, A. (2022). Evaluation of key impression of resilient supply chain based on artificial intelligence of things (AIoT). arXiv preprint arXiv:2207.13174.

Aliahmadi, A., Ghahremani-Nahr, J., & Nozari, H. (2023). Pricing decisions in the closed-loop supply chain network, taking into account the queuing system in production centers. *Expert Systems with Applications*, *212*, 118741.

Allioui, H., & Mourdi, Y. (2023). Exploring the full potentials of IoT for better financial growth and stability: A comprehensive survey. *Sensors (Basel)*, *23*(19), 8015. PMID: 37836845

Alojaiman, B. (2023). Technological modernizations in the industry 5.0 era: A descriptive analysis and future research directions. *Processes (Basel, Switzerland)*, *11*(5), 1318.

Alora, A., & Gupta, H. (2024). Supplier selection among manufacturing companies based on their MSME partners' supply chain finance adoption capability using BWM and VIKOR. *Journal of Business and Industrial Marketing*, *39*(6), 1337–1351.

Amasawa, E., Brydges, T., Henninger, C. E., & Kimita, K. (2023). Can rental platforms contribute to more sustainable fashion consumption? Evidence from a mixed-method study. *Cleaner and Responsible Consumption, Elsevier Ltd*, *8*(January), 100103. DOI: 10.1016/j.clrc.2023.100103

Ambrogio, G., Filice, L., Longo, F., & Padovano, A. (2022). Workforce and supply chain disruption as a digital and technological innovation opportunity for resilient manufacturing systems in the COVID-19 pandemic. *Computers & Industrial Engineering*, *169*, 108158. DOI: 10.1016/j.cie.2022.108158 PMID: 35431410

Amit, R., & Zott, C. (2012). Creating value through business model innovation. *MIT Sloan Management Review*.

Amoozad Mahdiraji, H., Sharifpour Arabi, H., Beheshti, M., & Vrontis, D. (2023). A mixed-method analysis of Industry 4.0 technologies in value generation for collaborative consumption companies. *Management Decision*.

Anantrasirichai, N., & Bull, D. R. (2021). Artificial intelligence in the creative industries: A review. *Artificial Intelligence Review*, *55*(1), 589–656. DOI: 10.1007/s10462-021-10039-7

Anwar, S. T. (2023). The sharing economy and collaborative consumption: Strategic issues and global entrepreneurial opportunities. *Journal of International Entrepreneurship, 21*(1), 60–88. DOI: 10.1007/s10843-022-00323-0

Aoun, A., Ilinca, A., Ghandour, M., & Ibrahim, H. (2021). A review of Industry 4.0 characteristics and challenges, with potential improvements using blockchain technology. *Computers & Industrial Engineering, 162*, 107746. DOI: 10.1016/j.cie.2021.107746

Ardanta, M. A., Fauzi, A., Patimah, P., Khadijah, F., Yunandi, S. R., & Ghowe, A. M. (2025). Human-AI Collaboration in Supply Chain Industry 5.0 to Build a Human-Centered Autonomous Ecosystem. [SIJDB]. *Siber International Journal of Digital Business, 2*(4), 357–368.

Armstrong, C. M., Niinimäki, K., Kujala, S., Karell, E., & Lang, C. (2015). Sustainable product-service systems for clothing: Exploring consumer perceptions of consumption alternatives in Finland. *Journal of Cleaner Production, Elsevier Ltd, 97*, 30–39. DOI: 10.1016/j.jclepro.2014.01.046

Armstrong, C. M., Niinimäki, K., Lang, C., & Kujala, S. (2016). A Use-Oriented Clothing Economy? Preliminary Affirmation for Sustainable Clothing Consumption Alternatives. *Sustainable Development, 24*(1), 18–31. DOI: 10.1002/sd.1602

Arrigo, E. (2021). Collaborative consumption in the fashion industry: A systematic literature review and conceptual framework. *Journal of Cleaner Production, Elsevier Ltd, 325*(September), 129261. DOI: 10.1016/j.jclepro.2021.129261

Arrigo, E. (2022). Digital platforms in fashion rental: A business model analysis. *Journal of Fashion Marketing and Management, 26*(1), 1–20. DOI: 10.1108/JFMM-03-2020-0044

Asante Boakye, E., Zhao, H., Kwame Ahia, B. N., & Adu-Damoah, M. (2025). Modeling the adoption enablers of blockchain technology–based supply chain financing: an integrative dual DOI–TOE analysis. Journal of the International Council for Small Business, 1-22.

Ashaduzzaman, M., Jebarajakirthy, C., Weaven, S. K., Maseeh, H. I., Das, M., & Pentecost, R. (2022). Predicting Collaborative Consumption Behaviour: A Meta-Analytic Path Analysis on the Theory of Planned Behaviour. *European Journal of Marketing, 56*. Advance online publication. DOI: 10.1108/EJM-07-2020-0563

Ashima, R., Haleem, A., Javaid, M., & Rab, S. (2022). Understanding the role and capabilities of Internet of Things-enabled Additive Manufacturing through its application areas. *Advanced Industrial and Engineering Polymer Research, 5*(3), 137–142. DOI: 10.1016/j.aiepr.2021.12.001

Atif, S. (2023). Analysing the alignment between circular economy and industry 4.0 nexus with industry 5.0 era: An integrative systematic literature review. *Sustainable Development, 31*(4), 2155–2175.

Attaran, M., & Woods, J. (2018). Cloud computing technology: Improving small business performance using the Internet. *Journal of Small Business and Entrepreneurship, 31*(6), 495–519. DOI: 10.1080/08276331.2018.1466850

Babel, W. (2022). Automation Pyramid and Solutions Business. In *Springer eBooks* (pp. 75–147). https://doi.org/DOI: 10.1007/978-3-658-37852-3_4

Babkin, A., Shkarupeta, E., Mamrayeva, D., Tashenova, L., Umarov, A., & Karimov, D. (2025). A Structural-Functional Model for Managing Digital Maturity in a Cluster-Based, Innovation-Active Industrial Ecosystem within Industry 5.0. *Int. J. Technol, 16*, 1209–1219.

Baek, E., & Oh, G. E. (2020). (Grace). (2021), "Diverse values of fashion rental service and contamination concern of consumers. *Journal of Business Research, Elsevier Inc., 123*(March), 165–175. DOI: 10.1016/j.jbusres.2020.09.061

Bag, S., Srivastava, G., Bashir, M. A., Kumari, S., Giannakis, M., & Chowdhury, A. H. (2021). Journey of customers in this digital era: Understanding the role of artificial intelligence technologies in user engagement and conversion. *Benchmarking, 29*(7), 2074–2098. DOI: 10.1108/bij-07-2021-0415

Bakare, N. S. S., Adeniyi, N. O., Akpuokwe, N. C. U., & Eneh, N. N. E. (2024). Data privacy laws and compliance: A comparative review of the eu gdpr and usa regulations. *Computer Science & IT Research Journal, 5*(3), 528–543. DOI: 10.51594/csitrj.v5i3.859

Bakator, M., Ćoćkalo, D., Ugrinov, S., & Premčevski, V. (2025). Industry 5.0 with AI Applications for Smart and Sustainable Production. In International Conference "New Technologies, Development and Applications" (pp. 56-63). Springer, Cham.

Baker, H. K., Pandey, N., Kumar, S., & Haldar, A. (2020). A bibliometric analysis of board diversity: Current status, development, and future research directions. *Journal of Business Research, Elsevier, 108*, 232–246.

Baker, J., Levy, M., & Grewal, D. (1992). An Experimental Approach to Making Retail Store Environment Decisions. *Journal of Retailing, 68*(Winter), 445–460.

Bakke, N. A., & Barland, J. (2022). Disruptive Innovations and Paradigm Shifts in Journalism as a Business: From Advertisers First to Readers First and Traditional Operational Models to the AI Factory. *SAGE Open*, *12*(2), 215824402210948. DOI: 10.1177/21582440221094819

Baporikar, N. (Ed.). (2021). *Handbook of research on sustaining SMEs and entrepreneurial innovation in the post-COVID-19 era*. IGI Global.

Barbosa, B., & Fonseca, I. (2019). A phenomenological approach to the collaborative consumer. *Journal of Consumer Marketing*, *36*(6), 705–714. DOI: 10.1108/JCM-11-2017-2468

Bardhi, F., & Eckhardt, G. M. (2012). Access-Based Consumption: The Case of Car Sharing. *The Journal of Consumer Research*, *39*(4), 881–898. DOI: 10.1086/666376

Barnes, S. J., & Mattsson, J. (2017). Understanding collaborative consumption: Test of a theoretical model. *Technological Forecasting and Social Change, Elsevier Inc.*, *118*, 281–292. DOI: 10.1016/j.techfore.2017.02.029

Barrero, J. M., Bloom, N., & Davis, S. J. (2020). Why Working From Home Will Stick. SSRN *Electronic Journal*. https://doi.org/DOI: 10.2139/ssrn.3741644

Basulo-Ribeiro, J., & Teixeira, L. (2024). The future of healthcare with industry 5.0: Preliminary interview-based qualitative analysis. *Future Internet*, *16*(3), 68.

Becker-Leifhold, C. V. (2018). "The role of values in collaborative fashion consumption - A critical investigation through the lenses of the theory of planned behavior", *Journal of Cleaner Production. Elsevier B.V.*, *199*, 781–791. DOI: 10.1016/j.jclepro.2018.06.296

Becker-Leifhold, C., & Iran, S. (2018). Collaborative fashion consumption – drivers, barriers and future pathways. *Journal of Fashion Marketing and Management*, *22*(2), 189–208. DOI: 10.1108/JFMM-10-2017-0109

Bedon, A., Pujol, F. A., & Ramirez, T. (2024). Examining Telework Adoption Through Cybersecurity and Industry 5.0. In *Communications in computer and information science* (pp. 379–388). https://doi.org/DOI: 10.1007/978-3-031-62843-6_36

Belhadi, A., Mani, V., Kamble, S. S., Khan, S. A. R., & Verma, S. (2024). Artificial intelligence-driven innovation for enhancing supply chain resilience and performance under the effect of supply chain dynamism: An empirical investigation. *Annals of Operations Research*, *333*(2), 627–652. PMID: 33551534

Belk, R. (2014a). You are what you can access: Sharing and collaborative consumption online. *Journal of Business Research, Elsevier Inc.*, *67*(8), 1595–1600. DOI: 10.1016/j.jbusres.2013.10.001

Belk, R. (2014b). Sharing versus pseudo-sharing in web 2.0. *Anthropologist*, *18*(1), 7–23. DOI: 10.1080/09720073.2014.11891518

Benevene, P., Buonomo, I., & West, M. (2022). Editorial: Compassion and compassionate leadership in the workplace. *Frontiers in Psychology*, *13*, 1074068. DOI: 10.3389/fpsyg.2022.1074068 PMID: 36571014

Benke, K., & Tomkins, B. (2017). Future food-production systems: Vertical farming and controlled-environment agriculture. *Sustainability: Science. Practice and Policy*, *13*(1), 13–26. DOI: 10.1080/15487733.2017.1394054

Benoit, S., Baker, T. L., Bolton, R. N., Gruber, T., & Kandampully, J. (2017). A triadic framework for collaborative consumption (CC): Motives, activities and resources & capabilities of actors. *Journal of Business Research, Elsevier*, *79*(May), 219–227. DOI: 10.1016/j.jbusres.2017.05.004

Ben-Zvi, T., & Luftman, J. (2022). Post-Pandemic IT: Digital Transformation and Sustainability. *Sustainability*, *14*(22), 15275. DOI: 10.3390/su142215275

Berman, S. J. (2012). Digital transformation: Opportunities to create new business models. *Strategy and Leadership*, *40*(2), 16–24.

Bessen, J. E. (2018). Automation and Jobs: When Technology Boosts Employment. *Social Science Research Network*. https://doi.org/DOI: 10.2139/ssrn.2935003

Bhalla, S. (2021). Testing the Motivations and Constraints of Collaborative Consumption: An Empirical Analysis of Disruptive Innovative Business Model. *FIIB Business Review*, *10*(2), 146–157. DOI: 10.1177/23197145211007320

Bhatia, M., & Kumar, V. (2026). The role of digital twin in urban infrastructure and building management: A global scientometric perspective. *Cluster Computing*, *29*(1), 38.

Bissadu, K. D., Sonko, S., & Hossain, G. (2025). Society 5.0 enabled agriculture: Drivers, enabling technologies, architectures, opportunities, and challenges. *Information Processing in Agriculture*, *12*(1), 112–124.

Blanco-Mesa, F., Merigó, J. M., & Gil-Lafuente, A. M. (2017). Fuzzy decision making: A bibliometric-based review. *Journal of Intelligent & Fuzzy Systems*, *32*(3), 2033–2050. DOI: 10.3233/JIFS-161640

Bodenheimer, M., Schuler, J., & Wilkening, T. (2022). "Drivers and barriers to fashion rental for everyday garments: An empirical analysis of a former fashion-rental company", *Sustainability. Science, Practice, and Policy, Taylor & Francis*, *18*(1), 344–356. DOI: 10.1080/15487733.2022.2065774

Borowski, P. (2021). Digitization, Digital Twins, Blockchain, and Industry 4.0 as Elements of Management Process in Enterprises in the Energy Sector. *Energies*, *14*(7), 1885. DOI: 10.3390/en14071885

Botsman, R. (2013), "The Sharing Economy Lacks a Shared Definition. Fast Co", *Exist. URL* Http://Www. Fastcoexist. Com/3022028/the-Sharing-Economy-Lacks-a-Shared-Definition

Botsman, R. and Rogers, R. (2010a), "What's mine is yours", *The Rise of Collaborative Consumption.*

Botsman, R. and Rogers, R. (2010b), "What's Mine Is Yours: The Rise of Collaborative Consumption".

Botsman, R., & Rogers, R. (2011). *What's Mine Is Yours: How Collaborative Consumption Is Changing the Way We Live*. Collins.

Brandão, A., & da Costa, A. G. (2021). Extending the theory of planned behaviour to understand the effects of barriers towards sustainable fashion consumption. *European Business Review*, *33*(5), 742–774. DOI: 10.1108/EBR-11-2020-0306

Breque, M., De Nul, L., & Petridis, A. (2021). *Industry 5.0: Towards a sustainable, human-centric and resilient European industry*. Directorate-General for Research and Innovation, European Commission. https://research-and-innovation.ec.europa.eu/knowledge-publications-tools-and-data/publications/all-publications/industry-50-towards-sustainable-human-centric-and-resilient-european-industry_en

Brownbridge, K., Gill, S., Grogan, S., Kilgariff, S., & Whalley, A. (2018). Fashion misfit: Women's dissatisfaction and its implications. *Journal of Fashion Marketing and Management*, *22*(3), 438–452. DOI: 10.1108/JFMM-05-2017-0050

Brynjolfsson, E., & McAfee, A. (2014). *The Second Machine Age: Work, Progress, and Prosperity in a Time of Brilliant Technologies*. W.W. Norton & Company.

Budhwar, P., Chowdhury, S., Wood, G., Aguinis, H., Bamber, G. J., Beltran, J. R., Boselie, P., Cooke, F. L., Decker, S., DeNisi, A., Dey, P. K., Guest, D., Knoblich, A. J., Malik, A., Paauwe, J., Papagiannidis, S., Patel, C., Pereira, V., Ren, S., & Varma, A. (2023). Human resource management in the age of generative artificial intelligence: Perspectives and research directions on ChatGPT. *Human Resource Management Journal*, *33*(3), 606–659. DOI: 10.1111/1748-8583.12524

Bugge, M. M., Hansen, T., & Klitkou, A. (2016). What is the bioeconomy? A review of the literature. *Sustainability (Switzerland), 8*(7). Advance online publication. DOI: 10.3390/su8070691

Butt, J. (2020). A Conceptual Framework to Support Digital Transformation in Manufacturing Using an Integrated Business Process Management Approach. *Designs, 4*(3), 17. DOI: 10.3390/designs4030017

Byun, S. E., & Sternquist, B. (2011). Fast fashion and in-store hoarding: The drivers, moderator, and consequences. *Clothing & Textiles Research Journal, 29*(3), 187–201. DOI: 10.1177/0887302X11411709

Camacho-Otero, J., Boks, C., & Pettersen, I. N. (2019). User acceptance and adoption of circular offerings in the fashion sector: Insights from user-generated online reviews. *Journal of Cleaner Production, Elsevier Ltd, 231*(June), 928–939. DOI: 10.1016/j.jclepro.2019.05.162

Campos, P. de O., Costa, C. S. R., & da Costa, M. F. (2023). Relationship between personality traits and consumer rationality regarding the intention to purchase collaborative fashion. *Journal of Fashion Marketing and Management, 27*(1), 42–60. DOI: 10.1108/JFMM-02-2021-0049

Carayannis, E. G., Dezi, L., Gregori, G., & Calo, E. (2022). Smart environments and techno-centric and human-centric innovations for Industry and Society 5.0: A quintuple helix innovation system view towards smart, sustainable, and inclusive solutions. *Journal of the Knowledge Economy, 13*(2), 926–955. PMID: 40477337

Carayannis, E. G., & Morawska-Jancelewicz, J. (2022). The futures of Europe: Society 5.0 and Industry 5.0 as driving forces of future universities. *Journal of the Knowledge Economy, 13*(4), 3445–3471. DOI: 10.1007/s13132-021-00854-2 PMID: 40477679

Cauthen, N. K. (2007). *Improving Work Supports: Closing the Financial Gap for Low-wage Workers and Their Families*. https://doi.org/DOI: 10.7916/d8cr633w

Cavalcante Costa, M.R., Silva, M.E., & Duarte, M. de F. (2024). Sustainable Consumption and Practice Theories: Connecting Elements of Clothing Sharing. *Brazilian Business Review, 21*(1). Advance online publication. DOI: 10.15728/bbr.2021.1182.en

Chaikovska, I., Hryhoruk, P., Khrushch, N., Grygoruk, S., Tkach, T., & Chaikovskyi, M. (2024, September). Integration of Digital Economy, Knowledge Economy and Circular Economy in the Conditions of Industry 5.0. In 2024 14th International Conference on Advanced Computer Information Technologies (ACIT) (pp. 250-253). IEEE.

Chandra, S., Verma, S., Lim, W. M., Kumar, S., & Donthu, N. (2022). Personalization in personalized marketing: Trends and ways forward. *Psychology and Marketing*, *39*(8), 1529–1562. DOI: 10.1002/mar.21670

Chang, H.J., & Watchravesringkan, K. (Tu). (2018). Who are sustainably minded apparel shoppers? An investigation to the influencing factors of sustainable apparel consumption. *International Journal of Retail & Distribution Management*, *46*(2), 148–162. DOI: 10.1108/IJRDM-10-2016-0176

Charvet, F. F., Cooper, M. C., & Gardner, J. T. (2008). "The intellectual structure of supply chain management: A bibliometric approach", *Journal of Business Logistics. Wiley Online Library*, *29*(1), 47–73.

Cheng, S., & Yahaya, M. F. B., bin Abd Rahman, A. R., & Tai, L. (2024). Scoping Review: Safety and Risk in Aesthetic Preference Determinants for Product Design. *Research Journal of Medical Sciences*, *20*, 1–17.

Chen, N., Chiang, N., & Storey, N. (2012). Business Intelligence and Analytics: From Big Data to Big Impact. *Management Information Systems Quarterly*, *36*(4), 1165. DOI: 10.2307/41703503

Chi, T., Gerard, J., Dephillips, A., Liu, H., & Sun, J. (2019). Why U.S. consumers buy sustainable cotton made collegiate apparel? A study of the key determinants. *Sustainability (Switzerland)*, *11*(11). Advance online publication. DOI: 10.3390/su11113126

Cho, E., Gupta, S., & Kim, Y. K. (2015). Style consumption: Its drivers and role in sustainable apparel consumption. *International Journal of Consumer Studies*, *39*(6), 661–669. DOI: 10.1111/ijcs.12185

Choudhary, A., Amity, A. J., Gupta, T., & Shah, T. R. (2022). A greener world through Collaborative Consumption of Apparel: An Exploratory Study of consumers' perception and preferences. *Electronic Green Journal*, *1*(47). Advance online publication. DOI: 10.5070/G314754088

Choudhury, P., Foroughi, C., & Larson, B. (2019). Work-from-anywhere: The Productivity Effects of Geographic Flexibility. SSRN *Electronic Journal*. https://doi.org/DOI: 10.2139/ssrn.3494473

Clube, R. K. M., & Tennant, M. (2020). Exploring garment rental as a sustainable business model in the fashion industry: Does contamination impact the consumption experience? *Journal of Consumer Behaviour*, *19*(4), 359–370. DOI: 10.1002/cb.1817

Cobo, M. J., López-Herrera, A. G., Herrera-Viedma, E., & Herrera, F. (2011). "Science mapping software tools: Review, analysis, and cooperative study among tools", *Journal of the American Society for Information Science and Technology*, John Wiley & Sons. *Ltd*, *62*(7), 1382–1402. DOI: 10.1002/asi.21525

Condado, P. A., & Lobo, F. G. (2023). Security and privacy concerns in assisted living environments. *Journal of Smart Cities and Society*, *2*(2), 99–121. DOI: 10.3233/scs-230015

Corsaro, D., Ramos, C., Henneberg, S. C., & Naudé, P. (2012). The impact of network configurations on value constellations in business markets—The case of an innovation network. *Industrial Marketing Management*, *41*(1), 54–67.

Czeczot, G., Rojek, I., Mikołajewski, D., & Sangho, B. (2023). AI in IIoT management of cybersecurity for industry 4.0 and industry 5.0 purposes. *Electronics (Basel)*, *12*(18), 3800.

Davidescu, A. A., Apostu, S. A., Paul, A., & Casuneanu, I. (2020). Work Flexibility, Job Satisfaction, and Job Performance among Romanian Employees—Implications for Sustainable Human Resource Management. *Sustainability*, *12*(15), 6086. DOI: 10.3390/su12156086

Davidson, A., Habibi, M.R. and Laroche, M. (2018), "Materialism and the sharing economy: A cross-cultural study of American and Indian consumers", *Journal of Business Research*, Elsevier, Vol. 82 No. July 2015, pp. 364–372, doi: .DOI: 10.1016/j.jbusres.2015.07.045

De Assis Dornelles, J., Ayala, N. F., & Frank, A. G. (2022). Smart Working in Industry 4.0: How digital technologies enhance manufacturing workers' activities. *Computers & Industrial Engineering*, *163*, 107804. DOI: 10.1016/j.cie.2021.107804

De Boer, B. F., Rietveld, E., Rodrigues, J. F. D., & Tukker, A. (2021). Global environmental and socio-economic impacts of a transition to a circular economy in metal and electrical products: A Dutch case study. *Journal of Industrial Ecology*, *25*(5), 1264–1271. DOI: 10.1111/jiec.13133

de Medeiros, J. F., Marcon, A., Ribeiro, J. L. D., Quist, J., & D'Agostin, A. (2021). Consumer emotions and collaborative consumption: The effect of COVID-19 on the adoption of use-oriented product-service systems. *Sustainable Production and Consumption*, *27*, 1569–1588. DOI: 10.1016/j.spc.2021.03.010

DeHaat. (2023). *Empowering farmers through technology and services*. Retrieved from https://agrevolution.in

Dekker, R., Bloemhof, J., & Mallidis, I. (2012). Operations Research for green logistics – An overview of aspects, issues, contributions and challenges. *European Journal of Operational Research, 219*(3), 671–679. DOI: 10.1016/j.ejor.2011.11.010

Demir, K. A., Döven, G., & Sezen, B. (2019). Industry 5.0 and human-robot co-working. *Procedia Computer Science, 158*, 688–695.

Demir, K. A., Döven, G., & Sezen, B. (2022). Industry 5.0 and a critique of Industry 4.0. *Procedia Manufacturing, 55*, 1–7. DOI: 10.1016/j.promfg.2022.10.001

Despommier, D. (2020). *The vertical farm: Feeding the world in the 21st century*. Picador.

Devender, K. Kafila, Goli, G., & Shravan, M. (2025). Circular Economy Concept for Small Medium Enterprises Through Industry 5.0. In Sustainable Economy Models in the Age of Industry 5.0 (pp. 101-118). Singapore: Springer Nature Singapore.

Dey, P. K., Chowdhury, S., Abadie, A., Vann Yaroson, E., & Sarkar, S. (2024). Artificial intelligence-driven supply chain resilience in Vietnamese manufacturing small-and medium-sized enterprises. *International Journal of Production Research, 62*(15), 5417–5456.

Dhanabhakyam, M., & Joseph, E. (2022). Digital permissive management for aggregate and sustainable development of the employees. *International Journal of Health Sciences, 6*(1).

Dhanabhakyam, M., & Joseph, E. (2022). *Digitalization and perception of employee satisfaction during pandemic with special reference to selected academic institutions in higher education. Mediterranean Journal of Basic and Applied Sciences*. MJBAS.

Dhanaraju, M., Chenniappan, P., Ramalingam, K., Pazhanivelan, S., & Kaliaperumal, R. (2022). Smart farming: Internet of Things (IoT)-based sustainable agriculture. *Agriculture, 12*(10), 1745.

Dmitrieva, E., Balmiki, V., Lakhanpal, S., Lavanya, G., & Bhandari, P. (2024). AI evolution in Industry 4.0 and Industry 5.0: an experimental comparative assessment. In BIO Web of Conferences (Vol. 86, p. 01069). EDP Sciences.

Dreyer, B., Lüdeke-Freund, F., Hamann, R., & Faccer, K. (2017). Upsides and downsides of the sharing economy: Collaborative consumption business models' stakeholder value impacts and their relationship to context. *Technological Forecasting and Social Change, Elsevier Inc., 125*, 87–104. DOI: 10.1016/j.techfore.2017.03.036

Duan, C. (2023). Towards a comprehensive analytical framework and future research agenda for research on sharing economy business models: thematic analyses approach. In *Information Systems and e-Business Management* (Vol. 21, Issue 4). Springer Berlin Heidelberg. https://doi.org/DOI: 10.1007/s10257-023-00657-

Dwivedi, Y. K., Hughes, L., Ismagilova, E., Aarts, G., Coombs, C., Crick, T., Duan, Y., Dwivedi, R., Edwards, J., Eirug, A., Galanos, V., Ilavarasan, P. V., Janssen, M., Jones, P., Kar, A. K., Kizgin, H., Kronemann, B., Lal, B., Lucini, B., & Williams, M. D. (2021). Artificial Intelligence (AI): Multidisciplinary perspectives on emerging challenges, opportunities, and agenda for research, practice and policy. *International Journal of Information Management*, *57*, 101994. DOI: 10.1016/j.ijinfomgt.2019.08.002

Echchakoui, S., & Barka, N. (2020). Industry 4.0 and its impact in plastics industry: A literature review. *Journal of Industrial Information Integration*, *20*, 100172. DOI: 10.1016/j.jii.2020.100172

Ek Styvén, M., & Mariani, M. M. (2020). Understanding the intention to buy secondhand clothing on sharing economy platforms: The influence of sustainability, distance from the consumption system, and economic motivations. *Psychology and Marketing*, *37*(5), 724–739. DOI: 10.1002/mar.21334

Ekanayake, E. M. A. C., Shen, G., & Kumaraswamy, M. M. (2019). Mapping the knowledge domains of value management: A bibliometric approach. *Engineering, Construction, and Architectural Management*, *26*(3), 499–514. DOI: 10.1108/ECAM-06-2018-0252

Elangovan, U. (2021). *Industry 5.0*. https://doi.org/DOI: 10.1201/9781003190677

Elijah, O., Rahman, T. A., Orikumhi, I., Leow, C. Y., & Hindia, M. N. (2018). An Overview of Internet of Things (IoT) and Data Analytics in Agriculture: Benefits and Challenges. *IEEE Internet of Things Journal*, *5*(5), 3758–3773. DOI: 10.1109/jiot.2018.2844296

Erol, B. A., Majumdar, A., Benavidez, P., Rad, P., Choo, K. K. R., & Jamshidi, M. (2019). Toward artificial emotional intelligence for cooperative social human–machine interaction. *IEEE Transactions on Computational Social Systems*, *7*(1), 234–246.

Ertz, M., Durif, F., & Arcand, M. (2019). A conceptual perspective on collaborative consumption. *AMS Review, Springer*, *9*(1), 27–41.

Et-taibi, B., Abid, M. R., Boufounas, E. M., Morchid, A., Bourhnane, S., Hamed, T. A., & Benhaddou, D. (2024). Enhancing water management in smart agriculture: A cloud and IoT-Based smart irrigation system. *Results in Engineering*, *22*, 102283.

European Commission. (2021). *Industry 5.0: Towards a sustainable, human-centric and resilient European industry*. Publications Office of the European Union. https://op.europa.eu/en/publication-detail/-/publication/468a892a-5097-11eb-b59f-01aa75ed71a1

European Commission. (2021). *Industry 5.0: Towards more sustainable, resilient and human-centric industry*. https://research-and-innovation.ec.europa.eu/knowledge-publications-tools-and-data/publications/all-publications/industry-50-towards-sustainable-human-centric-and-resilient-european-industry_en

Evans, S., Partidário, P. J., & Lambert, J. (2007). Industrialization as a key element of sustainable product-service solutions. *International Journal of Production Research, 45*(18–19), 4225–4246. DOI: 10.1080/00207540701449999

Ezeudu, O. B., & Bristow, D. (2025). Financing methods for solid waste management: A review of typology, classifications, and circular economy implications. *Sustainable Development, 33*(2), 3062–3085.

Fahimnia, B., Sarkis, J. and Davarzani, H. (2015), *Green Supply Chain Management: A Review and Bibliometric Analysis, International Journal of Production Economics*, Vol. 162, Elsevier, doi: .DOI: 10.1016/j.ijpe.2015.01.003

Fan, H., & Poole, M. S. (2006). What Is Personalization? Perspectives on the Design and Implementation of Personalization in Information Systems. *Journal of Organizational Computing and Electronic Commerce, 16*(3–4), 179–202. DOI: 10.1080/10919392.2006.9681199

Fasal. (2023). *Transforming Indian agriculture with precision farming*. Retrieved from https://www.fasal.co

Fernández-Miguel, A., García-Muiña, F. E., Ortíz-Marcos, S., Jiménez-Calzado, M., Fernández del Hoyo, A. P., & Settembre-Blundo, D. (2025). AI-Driven Transformations in Manufacturing: Bridging Industry 4.0, 5.0, and 6.0 in Sustainable Value Chains. *Future Internet, 17*(9), 430.

Ferreira, J., Coelho, A., & Moutinho, L. (2020). Dynamic capabilities, creativity and innovation capability and their impact on competitive advantage and firm performance: The moderating role of entrepreneurial orientation. *Technovation, 92–93*, 102061. DOI: 10.1016/j.technovation.2018.11.004

Fogaça, D. R., Grijalvo, M., & Sacomano Neto, M. (2025). What Are Industry 4.0 and Industry 5.0 All About? An Integrative Institutional Model for the New Industrial Paradigms. *Administrative Sciences, 15*(4), 118.

Ford, M. (2015). *Rise of the Robots: Technology and the Threat of a Jobless Future*. Basic Books.

Formica, P. (2023). Carving the Transformative Enterprise Profile. In *Emerald Publishing Limited eBooks* (pp. 1–41). https://doi.org/DOI: 10.1108/978-1-80382-783-420231001

Fraanje, W., & Spaargaren, G. (2019). "What future for collaborative consumption? A practice theoretical account", *Journal of Cleaner Production. Elsevier B.V.*, *208*, 499–508. DOI: 10.1016/j.jclepro.2018.09.197

Fraga-Lamas, P., Lopes, S. I., & Fernández-Caramés, T. M. (2021). Green IoT and edge AI as key technological enablers for a sustainable digital transition towards a smart circular economy: An Industry 5.0 use case. *Sensors (Basel)*, *21*(17), 5745. DOI: 10.3390/s21175745 PMID: 34502637

Frenken, K., & Schor, J. (2017). "Putting the sharing economy into perspective", *Environmental Innovation and Societal Transitions. Elsevier B.V.*, *23*, 3–10. DOI: 10.1016/j.eist.2017.01.003

Gajdzik, B., & Wolniak, R. (2022). Smart Production Workers in Terms of Creativity and Innovation: The Implication for Open Innovation. *Journal of Open Innovation*, *8*(2), 68. DOI: 10.3390/joitmc8020068

Gamberini, L., & Pluchino, P. (2024). Industry 5.0: A comprehensive insight into the future of work, social sustainability, sustainable development, and career. *Australian Journal of Career Development*, *33*(1), 5–14.

Ganak, J., Chen, Y., Liang, D., Liu, H., & Chi, T. (2020). "Understanding US millennials' perceived values of denim apparel recycling: Insights for brands and retailers", *International Journal of Sustainable Society* [IEL]. *Inderscience Publishers*, *12*(4), 267–290.

Gao, J., Hua, G., & Huo, B. (2024). Green finance policies, financing constraints and corporate ESG performance: insights from supply chain management. Operations Management Research, 1-15.

García-Rodríguez, F. J., Gutiérrez-Taño, D., Ruiz-Rosa, I., & Baute-Díaz, N. (2022). New Models for Collaborative Consumption: The Role of Consumer Attitudes Among Millennials. *SAGE Open*, *12*(4), 1–14. DOI: 10.1177/21582440221140389

Geissdoerfer, M., Savaget, P., Bocken, N. M. P., & Hultink, E. J. (2017). The Circular Economy – A new sustainability paradigm? *Journal of Cleaner Production*, *143*, 757–768.

Geissdoerfer, M., Savaget, P., Bocken, N. M. P., & Hultink, E. J. (2017). The Circular Economy – A new sustainability paradigm? *Journal of Cleaner Production, Elsevier Ltd*, *143*, 757–768. DOI: 10.1016/j.jclepro.2016.12.048

Genovese, A., Acquaye, A. A., Figueroa, A., & Koh, S. L. (2017). Sustainable supply chain management and the transition towards a circular economy: Evidence and some applications. *Omega*, *66*, 344–357. DOI: 10.1016/j.omega.2015.05.015

Ghahremani-Nahr, J., Nozari, H., & Szmelter-Jarosz, A. (2024). Designing a humanitarian relief logistics network considering the cost of deprivation using a robust-fuzzy-probabilistic planning method. *Journal of International Humanitarian Action*, *9*(1), 19.

Ghobakhloo, M., Iranmanesh, M., Grybauskas, A., Vilkas, M., & Petraite, M. (2021). Industry 4.0, innovation, and sustainable development: A systematic review and a roadmap to sustainable innovation. *Business Strategy and the Environment*, *30*(8), 4237–4257. DOI: 10.1002/bse.2867

Ghobakhloo, M., Iranmanesh, M., Tseng, M. L., Grybauskas, A., Stefanini, A., & Amran, A. (2023). Behind the definition of Industry 5.0: A systematic review of technologies, principles, components, and values. *Journal of Industrial and Production Engineering*, *40*(6), 432–447. DOI: 10.1080/21681015.2023.2216701

Ghobakhloo, M., Mahdiraji, H. A., Iranmanesh, M., & Jafari-Sadeghi, V. (2024). From Industry 4.0 digital manufacturing to Industry 5.0 digital society: A roadmap toward human-centric, sustainable, and resilient production. *Information Systems Frontiers*, •••, 1–33.

Gholami, H., Abu, F., Lee, J. K. Y., Karganroudi, S. S., & Sharif, S. (2021). Sustainable Manufacturing 4.0—Pathways and Practices. *Sustainability*, *13*(24), 13956. DOI: 10.3390/su132413956

Goel, R., Singla, J., Arora, M., & Mittal, A. (2024a). From stress to success: Role of green atmospherics on employee well-being in the Indian hotel and tourism industry. *Journal of Human Resources in Hospitality & Tourism. Journal of Human Resources in Hospitality & Tourism*, *23*(3), 359–385. DOI: 10.1080/15332845.2024.2335091

Goel, R., Singla, J., Mittal, A., & Arora, M. (2024b). A decade analysis of employees' well-being and performance while working from home: A bibliometric approach. *Information Discovery and Delivery*. Advance online publication. DOI: 10.1108/idd-03-2023-0030

Golovianko, M., Terziyan, V., Branytskyi, V., & Malyk, D. (2023). Industry 4.0 vs. Industry 5.0: Co-existence, Transition, or a Hybrid. *Procedia Computer Science, 217*, 102–113. DOI: 10.1016/j.procs.2022.12.206

Gopalakrishnan, S. (2018), "Motivations and Shopping Orientations for Engagement in Collaborative Consumption among Fashion Consumers", No. 1, p. 103.

Gopalakrishnan, S., & Matthews, D. (2018). Collaborative consumption: A business model analysis of second-hand fashion. *Journal of Fashion Marketing and Management, 22*(3), 354–368. DOI: 10.1108/JFMM-05-2017-0049

Gordon, E. E. (2009). *Winning the Global Talent Showdown: How Businesses and Communities Can Partner to Rebuild the Jobs Pipeline*. https://skills.scholarvox.com/catalog/book/docid/10294951

Gorla, F., Borojevic, A., Gibertoni, C., Landi, L., Storchi, M., Fontana, L., Regmi, J., Burmen, B., & Silenzi, A. (2023). The Hospital of Tomorrow Case Study: Multidisciplinarity, Inclusiveness and Holistic Approaches to Foster Innovation in Complex Organizations. *International Journal of Health Policy and Management*. Advance online publication. DOI: 10.34172/ijhpm.2023.7330 PMID: 37579430

Gorobynskaya, M., & Krivtsova, T. (2025). The Impact of Industry 5.0 on Enterprise Resilience in the Digital Environment. *FINANCIAL AND CREDIT SYSTEMS: PROSPECTS FOR DEVELOPMENT, 2*(17), 167–179.

Groysberg, B., Lee, J., Price, J., & Yo-Jud Cheng, J. (2018). The Leader's Guide to Corporate Culture: How to Manage the Eight Critical Elements of Organizational Life. *Harvard Business Review, 96*(1), 44–52.

Guillen-Royo, M. (2023). 'I prefer to own what I use': Exploring the role of emotions in upscaling collaborative consumption through libraries in Norway. *Cleaner and Responsible Consumption, 8*(December), 2022. DOI: 10.1016/j.clrc.2023.100108

Gundeti, R., Vuppala, K., & Kasireddy, V. (2024). The future of AI and environmental sustainability: Challenges and opportunities. *Exploring Ethical Dimensions of Environmental Sustainability and Use of AI*, 346-371.

Guyader, H. (2018). No one rides for free! Three styles of collaborative consumption. *Journal of Services Marketing, 32*(6), 692–714. DOI: 10.1108/JSM-11-2016-0402

Habibi, F., Chakrabortty, R. K., & Abbasi, A. (2023). Evaluating supply chain network resilience considering disruption propagation. *Computers & Industrial Engineering, 183*, 109531.

Habibi, M. R., Davidson, A., & Laroche, M. (2017). What managers should know about the sharing economy. *Business Horizons*, *60*(1), 113–121. DOI: 10.1016/j.bushor.2016.09.007

Hafeez, A., Husain, M. A., Singh, S. P., Chauhan, A., Khan, M. T., Kumar, N., & Soni, S. K. (2023). Implementation of drone technology for farm monitoring & pesticide spraying: A review. *Information Processing in Agriculture*, *10*(2), 192–203.

Hall, J., Matos, S., Sheehan, L., & Silvestre, B. (2012). Entrepreneurship and innovation at the base of the Pyramid: A recipe for inclusive growth or social exclusion? *Journal of Management Studies*, *49*(4), 785–812. DOI: 10.1111/j.1467-6486.2012.01044.x

Haloui, D., Oufaska, K., Oudani, M., & El Yassini, K. (2024). Bridging industry 5.0 and agriculture 5.0: Historical perspectives, opportunities, and future perspectives. *Sustainability*, *16*(9), 3507.

Hamari, J., Sjöklint, M., & Ukkonen, A. (2016). "The sharing economy: Why people participate in collaborative consumption", *Journal of the Association for Information Science and Technology*, John Wiley & Sons. *Ltd*, *67*(9), 2047–2059. DOI: 10.1002/asi.23552

Hammad, M. Y., Rahamaddulla, S. R., Muhamad Tamyez, P. F., & Fauzi, M. A. (2025). From Industry 4.0 to 5.0: leveraging AI and IoT for sustainable and human-centric operations. International Journal of Industrial Engineering and Operations Management, 1-19.

Hart, S. L. (1995). A natural-resource-based view of the firm. *Academy of Management Review*, *20*(4), 986–1014.

Hashish, E. A., & Alnajjar, H. (2024). Digital proficiency: Assessing knowledge, attitudes, and skills in digital transformation, health literacy, and artificial intelligence among university nursing students. *BMC Medical Education*, *24*(1). Advance online publication. DOI: 10.1186/s12909-024-05482-3 PMID: 38715005

Hasiwar, D., Gruber, A., Dragschitz, C., & Ivkić, I. (2024, March 27). *Towards a Cloud-based Smart Office Solution for Shared Workplace Individualization*. arXiv.org. https://arxiv.org/abs/2403.18883

Hassoun, A., Jagtap, S., Trollman, H., Garcia-Garcia, G., Duong, L. N., Saxena, P., & Aït-Kaddour, A. (2024). From Food Industry 4.0 to Food Industry 5.0: Identifying technological enablers and potential future applications in the food sector. *Comprehensive Reviews in Food Science and Food Safety*, *23*(6), e370040. PMID: 39437193

Hayes, S. G., & Jones, N. (2006). Fast fashion: A financial snapshot. *Journal of Fashion Marketing and Management, 10*(3), 282–300. DOI: 10.1108/13612020610679277

Henninger, C. E., Brydges, T., Iran, S., & Vladimirova, K. (2021). Collaborative fashion consumption – A synthesis and future research agenda. *Journal of Cleaner Production, Elsevier Ltd, 319*(August), 128648. DOI: 10.1016/j.jclepro.2021.128648

Henninger, C. E., Bürklin, N., & Niinimäki, K. (2019). The clothes swapping phenomenon – when consumers become suppliers. *Journal of Fashion Marketing and Management, 23*(3), 327–344. DOI: 10.1108/JFMM-04-2018-0057

Herold, P. I., & Prokop, D. (2023). Is fast fashion finally out of season? Rental clothing schemes as a sustainable and affordable alternative to fast fashion. *Geoforum, Elsevier Ltd, 146*(October), 103873. DOI: 10.1016/j.geoforum.2023.103873

Holzinger, A., Fister, I., Kaul, H. P., & Asseng, S. (2024). Human-centered AI in smart farming: Toward agriculture 5.0. *IEEE Access : Practical Innovations, Open Solutions, 12*, 62199–62214.

Hommel, B. E., Ruppel, R., & Zacher, H. (2021). Assessment of cognitive flexibility in personnel selection: Validity and acceptance of a gamified version of the Wisconsin Card Sorting Test. *International Journal of Selection and Assessment, 30*(1), 126–144. DOI: 10.1111/ijsa.12362

Hossen, B., Yabar, H., & Mizunoya, T. (2021). Land Suitability Assessment for Pulse (Green Gram) Production through Remote Sensing, GIS and Multicriteria Analysis in the Coastal Region of Bangladesh. *Sustainability, 13*(22), 12360. DOI: 10.3390/su132212360

Huang, L., Li, Y., Huang, X., & Zhou, L. (2021). How social distance affects the intention and behavior of collaborative consumption: A study based on online car-hailing service. *Journal of Retailing and Consumer Services, Elsevier Ltd, 61*(March), 102534. DOI: 10.1016/j.jretconser.2021.102534

Huang, M. H., & Rust, R. T. (2018). Artificial Intelligence in Service. *Journal of Service Research, 21*(2), 155–172. DOI: 10.1177/1094670517752459

Hu, J. L., Li, Y., & Chew, J. C. (2025). Industry 5.0 and Human-Centered Energy System: A Comprehensive Review with Socio-Economic Viewpoints. *Energies, 18*(9), 2345.

Hu, Z. H., Li, Q., Chen, X. J., & Wang, Y. F. (2014). Sustainable rent-based closed-loop supply chain for fashion products. *Sustainability (Switzerland), 6*(10), 7063–7088. DOI: 10.3390/su6107063

Igbaria, M., & Iivari, J. (1995). The effects of self-efficacy on computer usage. *Omega, 23*(6), 587–605.

Imandi, R., Chethana, B., Prasad, B. P., Sethi, K., & Kumar, B. P. (2025). Enhancing Data Management in Industry 5.0: The Role of Digital Twins in Optimizing Industrial Operations. In *Industry 5.0: Key Technologies and Drivers* (pp. 211–236). Springer Nature Switzerland.

Intonti, M., Mola, D., De Leonardis, M., & Starace, G. (2025). Enhancing Circular Practices in Olive Oil Production: The Role of Green Finance. *Sustainability, 17*(1), 294.

Iran, S., Geiger, S. M., & Schrader, U. (2019). "Collaborative fashion consumption – A cross-cultural study between Tehran and Berlin", *Journal of Cleaner Production. Elsevier B.V., 212*, 313–323. DOI: 10.1016/j.jclepro.2018.11.163

Iran, S., & Schrader, U. (2017). Collaborative fashion consumption and its environmental effects. *Journal of Fashion Marketing and Management: An International Journal, Emerald Publishing Limited, 21*(4), 468–482. DOI: 10.1108/JFMM-09-2016-0086

Islam, M. T., Sepanloo, K., Woo, S., Woo, S. H., & Son, Y. J. (2025). A review of the industry 4.0 to 5.0 transition: Exploring the intersection, challenges, and opportunities of technology and Human–Machine collaboration. *Machines (Basel), 13*(4), 267.

Ivanov, D. (2021). Supply chain viability and the COVID-19 pandemic: A conceptual and formal generalisation of four major adaptation strategies. *International Journal of Production Research, 59*(12), 3535–3552. DOI: 10.1080/00207543.2021.1890852

Ivanov, D. (2023). The Industry 5.0 framework: Viability-based integration of the resilience, sustainability, and human-centricity perspectives. *International Journal of Production Research, 61*(5), 1683–1695.

Ivanov, D. (2025). A survey of system-cybernetic principles in supply chain resilience: Viability, artificial intelligence, digital twins, and ecosystems. *International Journal of Systems Science*, •••, 1–16.

Jaeger, H. (2020). Exploring the landscapes of" computing": digital, neuromorphic, unconventional—and beyond. arXiv preprint arXiv:2011.12013.

Jäpel, N., Bielitz, P., & Reichelt, D. (2024). The Dresden Model of Adaptability: A Holistic Approach to Human-Centeredness, Resilience, Sustainability, and the Impact on the Sustainable Development Goals in the Era of Industry 5.0. *Digital, 4*(3), 726–739.

Javaid, M., Haleem, A., Singh, R. P., & Suman, R. (2021). Substantial capabilities of robotics in enhancing Industry 4.0 implementation. *Cognitive Robotics*, *1*, 58–75. DOI: 10.1016/j.cogr.2021.06.001

Jeyabalan, J., Rohan, K., & Shanthalakshmi, M. (2025). Book: Food and Industry 5.0: Transforming the Food System for a Sustainable Future: Industry 5.0 Technologies for Sustainable Food Production. In *Food and Industry 5.0: Transforming the Food System for a Sustainable Future* (pp. 155–169). Springer Nature Switzerland.

Jiang, L., Cao, X., Wang, Z., Zhan, Y., Zhang, J., & Chen, S. (2025). Promoting energy saving and emission reduction benefits in small and medium-sized enterprises supply chains through green finance-Evidence based on artificial intelligence intervention. *International Review of Financial Analysis*, •••, 104112.

Ji, F., Zhou, Y., Zhang, H., Cheng, G., & Luo, Q. (2024). Navigating the Digital Odyssey: AI-Driven Business Models in Industry 4.0. *Journal of the Knowledge Economy*. Advance online publication. DOI: 10.1007/s13132-024-02096-4

Johnson, K. K. P., Mun, J. M., & Chae, Y. (2016). Antecedents to internet use to collaboratively consume apparel. *Journal of Fashion Marketing and Management*, *20*(4), 370–382. DOI: 10.1108/JFMM-12-2015-0092

Joseph, E. (2025). Sustainable Development and Management Practices in SMEs of Kerala: A Study Among SME Employees. *Sustainable Development and Management Practices in SMEs of Kerala: A Study Among SME Employees (February 20, 2025).*

Joseph, E., Koshy, N. A., & Manuel, A. (2025). Exploring the Evolution and Global Impact of Public-Private Partnerships.

Joseph, E., Shyamala, M., & Nadig, R. (2025). Understanding Public-Private Partnerships in the Modern Era. In Public Private Partnership Dynamics for Economic Development (pp. 1-26). IGI Global Scientific Publishing.

Joseph, E. (2023). Underlying Philosophies and Human Resource Management Role for Sustainable Development. In *Governance as a Catalyst for Public Sector Sustainability* (pp. 286–304). IGI Global.

Joseph, E. (2024). Evaluating the Effect of Future Workplace and Estimating the Interaction Effect of Remote Working on Job Stress. [MJBAS]. *Mediterranean Journal of Basic and Applied Sciences*, *8*(1), 57–77.

Joseph, E. (2024). Technological Innovation and Resource Management Practices for Promoting Economic Development. In *Innovation and Resource Management Strategies for Startups Development* (pp. 104–127). IGI Global.

Joseph, E. (2025). Impact of Hybrid Entrepreneurs on Economic Development and Job Creation. In *Applications of Career Transitions and Entrepreneurship* (pp. 61–82). IGI Global Scientific Publishing.

Joseph, E. (2025). Leveraging AI to Inspire Innovation in Traditional and Digital Business Ecosystems. [JBE]. *Journal of Business Ecosystems*, *6*(1), 1–18. DOI: 10.4018/JBE.383049

Joseph, E. (2025). Public-Private Partnerships for Revolutionizing Personalized Education Through AI-Powered Adaptive Learning Systems. In *Public Private Partnerships for Social Development and Impact* (pp. 265–290). IGI Global Scientific Publishing.

Joseph, E., & Dhanabhakyam, M. M. (2022). Role of Digitalization Post-Pandemic for Development of SMEs. In *Research anthology on business continuity and navigating times of crisis* (pp. 727–747). IGI Global.

Jourabchi Amirkhizi, P., Pedrammehr, S., & Pakzad, S. (2025). A system-based approach to value prioritization in industry 5.0 for sustainable value creation. *Discover Sustainability*, *6*(1), 364.

Journal of Cloud Computing. (2021). Future of Industry 5.0 in society: Human-centric solutions, challenges and prospective research areas. Journal of Cloud Computing. https://journalofcloudcomputing.springeropen.com/articles/10.1186/s13677-021-00279-4

Judijanto, L., Utami, E. Y., & Harsono, I. (2024). Green supply chain finance: A bibliometric review of financing instruments, challenges, and opportunities. *West Science Interdisciplinary Studies*, *2*(03), 647–655.

Ju, Y., Hou, H., Cheng, Y., & Feng, Y. (2024). Assessing the impact of government-led green supply chain demonstration on firms' financial distress: The role of environmental information disclosure quality and supply chain concentration. *Journal of Cleaner Production*, *440*, 140786.

Kagermann, H., Wahlster W., Helbig, J. (2013). Recommendations for implementing the strategic initiative Industrie 4.0: Final report of the Industrie 4.0 Working Group.

Kagermann, H., Wahlster, W., & Helbig, J. (2013). Recommendations for implementing the strategic initiative INDUSTRIE 4.0: Securing the future of German manufacturing industry. Final report of the Industrie 4.0 Working Group.

Kalantari, F., Tahir, O. M., Joni, R. A., & Fatemi, E. (2017). Opportunities and challenges in sustainability of vertical farming: A review. *Journal of Landscape Ecology*, *10*(1), 35–60. DOI: 10.1515/jlecol-2017-0016

Kalra, N., Verma, P., & Verma, S. (2024). Advancements in AI based healthcare techniques with FOCUS ON diagnostic techniques. *Computers in Biology and Medicine, 179*, 108917. DOI: 10.1016/j.compbiomed.2024.108917 PMID: 39059212

Kamalabai, N., Hannola, L., & Donoghue, I. (2025). Role of Industrial Artificial Intelligence in Advancing Human-Centric Sustainable Development of Industry 5.0.[eu2.1] In Contemporary Issues in Industry 5.0: Towards an AI Integrated Society (pp. 325–371). Springer Nature Switzerland.

Kamilaris, A., Fonts, A., & Prenafeta-Boldú, F. X. (2019). The rise of blockchain technology in agriculture and food supply chains. *Trends in Food Science & Technology, 91*, 640–652. DOI: 10.1016/j.tifs.2019.07.034

Kang, H. S., Lee, J. Y., Choi, S., & Kim, H. (2016). Smart manufacturing: Past research, present findings, and future directions. *International Journal of Precision Engineering and Manufacturing-Green Technology, 3*(1), 111–128.

Karis, D., Wildman, D., & Mané, A. (2014). Improving Remote Collaboration With Video Conferencing and Video Portals. *Human-Computer Interaction, 31*(1), 1–58. DOI: 10.1080/07370024.2014.921506

Kathleen, S., Sven, S., Claudia, N. B., & Frank, E. (2021). Fulfilling Remote Collaboration Needs for New Work. *Procedia Computer Science, 191*, 168–175. DOI: 10.1016/j.procs.2021.07.021

Kaur, A., Kukreja, V., Gopal, L., Verma, G., & Sharma, R. (2023, December). Cultivating Precision: A Multi-Layer Perceptron Approach for Accurate Classification of Maize Rust Disease Intensity in Precision Agriculture. In *2023 6th International Conference on Recent Trends in Advance Computing (ICRTAC)* (pp. 267-270). IEEE.

Kennedy, D. (2017). The machine in the market: Computers and the infrastructure of price at the New York Stock Exchange, 1965–1975. *Social Studies of Science, 47*(6), 888–917. DOI: 10.1177/0306312717739367 PMID: 29143591

Kessler, M. M. (1963). "Bibliographic coupling between scientific papers", *American Documentation*, John Wiley & Sons. *Ltd, 14*(1), 10–25. DOI: 10.1002/asi.5090140103

Kim, E., & Yoon, S. (2021). Social capital, user motivation, and collaborative consumption of online platform services. *Journal of Retailing and Consumer Services, Elsevier Ltd, 62*(June), 102651. DOI: 10.1016/j.jretconser.2021.102651

Kim, N. L., & Jin, B. E. (2020a). Addressing the contamination issue in collaborative consumption of fashion: Does ownership type of shared goods matter? *Journal of Fashion Marketing and Management, 2026*. Advance online publication. DOI: 10.1108/JFMM-11-2019-0265

Kim, N. L., & Jin, B. E. (2020b). Why buy new when one can share? Exploring collaborative consumption motivations for consumer goods. *International Journal of Consumer Studies*, *44*(2), 122–130. DOI: 10.1111/ijcs.12551

Kolade, O., & Owoseni, A. (2022). Employment 5.0: The work of the future and the future of work. *Technology in Society*, *71*, 102086. DOI: 10.1016/j.techsoc.2022.102086

Kong, H. M., Ko, E., Chae, H., & Mattila, P. (2016). Understanding fashion consumers' attitude and behavioral intention toward sustainable fashion products: Focus on sustainable knowledge sources and knowledge types. *Journal of Global Fashion Marketing*, *7*(2), 103–119. DOI: 10.1080/20932685.2015.1131435

Kühl, C., Tjahjono, B., Bourlakis, M., & Aktas, E. (2018). Implementation of Circular Economy principles in PSS operations. *Procedia CIRP*, *73*, 124–129. DOI: 10.1016/j.procir.2018.03.303

Kumar, A., Dhanka, S., Bansal, R., Sharma, A., Singh, J., Khan, A. A., & Maini, S. (2024). Agriculture in the Era of Industry 5.0. *Industry 5.0 and Emerging Technologies: Transformation Through. Technology and Innovation*, *565*, 111.

Kumar, A., & Joseph, E. (2025). Examining the mediating role of workforce agility in the relationship between emotional intelligence and workforce performance in small entrepreneurial firms in India. [MJBAS]. *Mediterranean Journal of Basic and Applied Sciences*, *9*(3), 14–24.

Kumar, B., Kumar, L., Kumar, A., Kumari, R., Tagar, U., & Sassanelli, C. (2024). Green finance in circular economy: A literature review. *Environment, Development and Sustainability*, *26*(7), 16419–16459. PMID: 37362997

Kurt, R. (2019). Industry 4.0 in Terms of Industrial Relations and Its Impacts on Labour Life. *Procedia Computer Science*, *158*, 590–601. DOI: 10.1016/j.procs.2019.09.093

Lahteenmaki, I., Nätti, S., & Saraniemi, S. (2021). Digitalization-Enabled Evolution of Customer Value Creation: An Executive View in Financial Services. SSRN *Electronic Journal*. https://doi.org/DOI: 10.2139/ssrn.3887270

Lai, Z., Lou, G., Yin, L., Ma, H., & Tu, X. (2025). Supply chain green strategy considering manufacturers' financial constraints: How to manage the risk of green supply chain financing. *Annals of Operations Research*, *348*(2), 1037–1068.

Lang, C., & Joyner Armstrong, C. M. (2018). "Collaborative consumption: The influence of fashion leadership, need for uniqueness, and materialism on female consumers' adoption of clothing renting and swapping", *Sustainable Production and Consumption. Elsevier B.V.*, *13*, 37–47. DOI: 10.1016/j.spc.2017.11.005

Lang, C., Li, M., & Zhao, L. (2020). "Understanding consumers' online fashion renting experiences: A text-mining approach", *Sustainable Production and Consumption. Elsevier B.V., 21*, 132–144. DOI: 10.1016/j.spc.2019.12.003

Lang, C., Seo, S., & Liu, C. (2019). Motivations and obstacles for fashion renting: A cross-cultural comparison. *Journal of Fashion Marketing and Management, 23*(4), 519–536. DOI: 10.1108/JFMM-05-2019-0106

Lee, J., Bagheri, B., & Kao, H. A. (2015). A cyber-physical systems architecture for industry 4.0-based manufacturing systems. *Manufacturing Letters, 3*, 18–23.

Lee, S. H., & Huang, R. (2021). Consumer responses to online fashion renting: Exploring the role of cultural differences. *International Journal of Retail & Distribution Management, 49*(2), 187–203. DOI: 10.1108/IJRDM-04-2020-0142

Leng, J., Sha, W., Wang, B., Zheng, P., Zhuang, C., Liu, Q., & Wang, L. (2022). Industry 5.0: Prospect and retrospect. *Journal of Manufacturing Systems, 65*, 279–295. DOI: 10.1016/j.jmsy.2022.09.017

Leng, J., Zhong, Y., Lin, Z., Xu, K., Mourtzis, D., Zhou, X., & Shen, W. (2023). Towards resilience in Industry 5.0: A decentralized autonomous manufacturing paradigm. *Journal of Manufacturing Systems, 71*, 95–114.

Lewis, H. (2008). Eco-design of food packaging materials. In *Elsevier eBooks* (pp. 238–262). https://doi.org/DOI: 10.1533/9781845694784.2.238

Li, C., Wu, K., & Wu, J. (2017). A bibliometric analysis of research on haze during 2000–2016. *Environmental Science and Pollution Research International, 24*(32), 24733–24742. DOI: 10.1007/s11356-017-0440-1

Li, J., Sun, B., & Yu, B. (2024). Suitable innovation in Industry 5.0: The moderating mechanism of innovation transmission types in innovation ecosystem. *IEEE Transactions on Engineering Management, 71*, 6031–6043.

Li, L. (2022). Reskilling and Upskilling the Future-ready Workforce for Industry 4.0 and Beyond. *Information Systems Frontiers*. Advance online publication. DOI: 10.1007/s10796-022-10308-y PMID: 35855776

Lim, W. M., Gupta, G., Biswas, B., & Gupta, R. (2021). "Collaborative consumption continuance: A mixed-methods analysis of the service quality-loyalty relationship in ride-sharing services", *Electronic Markets. Springer Berlin Heidelberg*, (0123456789). Advance online publication. DOI: 10.1007/s12525-021-00486-z

Lindegaard, S., & Kawasaki, G. (2010). *The Open Innovation Revolution: Essentials, Roadblocks, and Leadership Skills*. https://ci.nii.ac.jp/ncid/BB0405033X

Liu, L., Guo, F., Zou, Z., & Duffy, V. G. (2022). Application, Development and Future Opportunities of Collaborative Robots (Cobots) in Manufacturing: A Literature Review. *International Journal of Human-Computer Interaction, 40*(4), 915–932. DOI: 10.1080/10447318.2022.2041907

Liu, T., Guan, X., Wang, Z., Qin, T., Sun, R., & Wang, Y. (2024). Optimizing green supply chain circular economy in smart cities with integrated machine learning technology. *Heliyon, 10*(9). PMID: 38726132

Li, Z., Ma, X., Li, J., Qiu, Q., & Wang, Y. (2019, June). Efficient cloud resource management using neuromorphic modeling and prediction for virtual machine resource utilization. In *2019 IEEE International Conference on Embedded Software and Systems (ICESS)* (pp. 1-8). IEEE.

Longo, F., Padovano, A., & Umbrello, S. (2020). Value-oriented and ethical technology engineering in industry 5.0: A human-centric perspective for the design of the factory of the future. *Applied Sciences (Basel, Switzerland), 10*(12), 4182.

Longo, F., Padovano, A., & Umbrello, S. (2020). Value-Oriented and Ethical Technology Engineering in Industry 5.0: A Human-Centric Perspective for the Design of the Factory of the Future. *Applied Sciences (Basel, Switzerland), 10*(12), 4182. DOI: 10.3390/app10124182

Lotfi, F. H. Z., Najafi, S. E., & Nozari, H. (Eds.). (2016). *Data envelopment analysis and effective performance assessment*. IGI Global.

Lo, W., Yang, C. M., Zhang, Q., & Li, M. (2024). Increased Productivity and Reduced Waste with Robotic Process Automation and Generative AI-powered IoE Services. *Journal of Web Engineering*, •••, 53–88. DOI: 10.13052/jwe1540-9589.2313

Loy, A. C. M., Chin, B. L. F., & Sankaran, R. (2021). Industrial Revolution 1.0 and 2.0. In *CRC Press eBooks* (pp. 1–14). https://doi.org/DOI: 10.1201/9781003080671-1-1

Maddikunta, P. K. R., & Pham, Q. V., B, P., Deepa, N., Dev, K., Gadekallu, T. R., Ruby, R., & Liyanage, M. (2022). Industry 5.0: A survey on enabling technologies and potential applications. *Journal of Industrial Information Integration, 26*, 100257. DOI: 10.1016/j.jii.2021.100257

Mahmood, S., Shuhui, W., Aslam, S., & Ahmed, T. (2022). The Financial Inclusion Development and Its Impacts on Disposable Income. *SAGE Open, 12*(2), 215824402210933. DOI: 10.1177/21582440221093369

Mana, A. A., Allouhi, A., Hamrani, A., Rehman, S., El Jamaoui, I., & Jayachandran, K. (2024). Sustainable AI-based production agriculture: Exploring AI applications and implications in agricultural practices. *Smart Agricultural Technology, 7*, 100416.

Manetti, S., Ni, M., Supino, S., & Troisi, O. (2025). Rethinking the circular economy in agri-food: Human-centred AI for a new circular economy 5.0 paradigm. *British Food Journal*, ●●●, 1–22.

Matheson, E., Minto, R., Zampieri, E. G., Faccio, M., & Rosati, G. (2019). Human–robot collaboration in manufacturing applications: A review. *Robotics (Basel, Switzerland)*, *8*(4), 100.

Mazzetto, S. (2024). A review of urban digital twins integration, challenges, and future directions in smart city development. *Sustainability*, *16*(19), 8337.

McCoy, L., Wang, Y. T., & Chi, T. (2021). Why is collaborative apparel consumption gaining popularity? An empirical study of us gen z consumers. *Sustainability (Switzerland)*, *13*(15). Advance online publication. DOI: 10.3390/su13158360

McNeill, L., & Venter, B. (2019). Identity, self-concept and young women's engagement with collaborative, sustainable fashion consumption models. *International Journal of Consumer Studies*, *43*(4), 368–378. DOI: 10.1111/ijcs.12516

Mihrete, T. B., & Mihretu, F. B. (2025). Crop Diversification for Ensuring Sustainable Agriculture, Risk Management and Food Security. *Global Challenges (Hoboken, NJ)*, ●●●, 2400267. PMID: 39925666

Mishra, S., Jain, S., & Malhotra, G. (2020). The anatomy of circular economy transition in the fashion industry. *Social Responsibility Journal*, *17*(4), 524–542. DOI: 10.1108/SRJ-06-2019-0216

Möhlmann, M. (2015). "Collaborative consumption: Determinants of satisfaction and the likelihood of using a sharing economy option again", *Journal of Consumer Behaviour*, John Wiley & Sons. *Ltd*, *14*(3), 193–207. DOI: 10.1002/cb.1512

Molina, R. I. R., Ruiz, M. J. S., Molina, R. J. R., Raby, N. D. L., & Severino-González, P. (2024). Innovation systems in industry 5.0: Theoretical and methodological bases. *Procedia Computer Science*, *231*, 595–600.

Moore, C. M., & Fernie, J. (2004). *"Retailing within an international context", International Retail Marketing: A Case Study Approach*. Elsevier Oxford.

Morley, J., Widdicks, K., & Hazas, M. (2018). Digitalisation, energy and data demand: The impact of Internet traffic on overall and peak electricity consumption. *Energy Research & Social Science*, *38*, 128–137. DOI: 10.1016/j.erss.2018.01.018

Morris, M. G., & Venkatesh, V. (2000). Age differences in technology adoption decisions: Implications for a changing work force. *Personnel Psychology*, *53*(2), 375–403.

Mourtzis, D. (2023). The Metaverse in industry 5.0: A human-centric approach towards personalized value creation. *Encyclopedia*, *3*(3), 1105–1120.

Murali, P. K., Kaboli, M., & Dahiya, R. (2021). Intelligent In-Vehicle Interaction Technologies. *Advanced Intelligent Systems*, *4*(2). Advance online publication. DOI: 10.1002/aisy.202100122

Muratovski, G. (2015). Paradigm shift: Report on the new role of design in business and society. *She Ji: The Journal of Design, Economics, and Innovation*, *1*(2), 118–139.

Murphy, C., Carew, P. J., & Stapleton, L. (2023). A human-centred systems manifesto for smart digital immersion in Industry 5.0: A case study of cultural heritage. *AI & Society*. Advance online publication. DOI: 10.1007/s00146-023-01693-2

Murthy, P., & Mehra, A. (2021). Exploring neuromorphic computing for ultra-low latency transaction processing in edge database architectures. *Journal of Emerging Technologies and Innovative Research*, *8*(1), 25–26.

NABARD. (2021). *Digital agriculture: Enhancing farmer income through technology*. National Bank for Agriculture and Rural Development. Retrieved from https://www.nabard.org

Nahavandi, S. (2019). Industry 5.0—A human-centric solution. *Sustainability*, *11*(16), 4371.

Nahavandi, S. (2019). Industry 5.0—A Human-Centric Solution. *Sustainability*, *11*(16), 4371. DOI: 10.3390/su11164371

Naor, M., Pinto, G. D., Hakakian, A. I., & Jacobs, A. (2021). The impact of COVID-19 on office space utilization and real-estate: A case study about teleworking in Israel as new normal. *Journal of Facilities Management*, *20*(1), 32–58. DOI: 10.1108/jfm-12-2020-0096

Narkhede, G. B., Pasi, B. N., Rajhans, N., & Kulkarni, A. (2025). Industry 5.0 and sustainable manufacturing: A systematic literature review. *Benchmarking*, *32*(2), 608–635.

Narkhede, G., Pasi, B., Rajhans, N., & Kulkarni, A. (2023). Industry 5.0 and the future of sustainable manufacturing: A systematic literature review. *Business Strategy & Development*, *6*(4), 704–723.

Narula, S., Tamvada, J. P., Kumar, A., Puppala, H., & Gupta, N. (2023). Putting digital technologies at the forefront of Industry 5.0 for the implementation of a circular economy in manufacturing industries. *IEEE Transactions on Engineering Management*, *71*, 3363–3374.

Negash, Y. T., Hassan, A. M., Lim, M. K., & Tseng, M. L. (2025). Sustainable supply chain finance enablers under disruption: The causal effect of collaboration value innovation on sustainability performance. *International Journal of Logistics Research and Applications*, *28*(4), 449–473.

Nekmahmud, M., Naz, F., Ramkissoon, H., & Fekete-Farkas, M. (2022). Transforming consumers' intention to purchase green products: Role of social media. *Technological Forecasting and Social Change, Elsevier Inc.*, *185*(March), 122067. DOI: 10.1016/j.techfore.2022.122067

Nicklin, J. M., Seguin, K., & Flaherty, S. (2019). Positive work-life outcomes: Exploring self-compassion and balance. *European Journal of Applied Positive Psychology*, *3*, 1–13. https://www.nationalwellbeingservice.com/journals

Nishant, R., Kennedy, M., & Corbett, J. (2020). Artificial intelligence for sustainability: Challenges, opportunities, and a research agenda. *International Journal of Information Management*, *53*, 102104.

Norum, P., & Norton, M. (2017). Factors affecting consumer acquisition of secondhand clothing in the USA. *Journal of Fashion Marketing and Management*, *21*(2), 206–218. DOI: 10.1108/JFMM-10-2016-0090

Nozari, H. (2025). Integrating Neuromorphic Intelligence with Fuzzy Multi-Objective Models in Resilient Green Supply Chain Design. Process Integration and Optimization for Sustainability, 1-14.

Nozari, H. (2026). Analyzing and Optimizing Customer Interactions in Smart Cities Using IoT Data Synchronization and Temporal Neural Networks (RNN). In Improving Consumer Engagement in Digital Marketing Through Cognitive AI (pp. 211-224). IGI Global Scientific Publishing.

Nozari, H. (2026). Combining Digital Twin and Metaverse for Immersive Marketing Experiences. In Improving Consumer Engagement in Digital Marketing Through Cognitive AI (pp. 289-310). IGI Global Scientific Publishing.

Nozari, H. (2026). Neuromorphic Models for Dynamic Customer Segmentation in Digital Marketing. In Improving Consumer Engagement in Digital Marketing Through Cognitive AI (pp. 311-326). IGI Global Scientific Publishing.

Nozari, H. (a) (2026). Combining Digital Twin and Metaverse for Immersive Marketing Experiences. In Improving Consumer Engagement in Digital Marketing Through Cognitive AI (pp. 289-310). IGI Global Scientific Publishing.

Nozari, H. (b) (2026). Neuromorphic Models for Dynamic Customer Segmentation in Digital Marketing. In Improving Consumer Engagement in Digital Marketing Through Cognitive AI (pp. 311-326). IGI Global Scientific Publishing.

Nozari, H., & Nassar, S. (2025). Real-time data-driven multi-objective optimization in B2B marketing using digital twins. OPSEARCH, 1-27.

Nozari, H., & Samadi, S. (2025). Digital Twin-Enhanced Sentiment Analysis for Targeted Marketing Optimization. In Dynamic and Safe Economy in the Age of Smart Technologies (pp. 121-138). IGI Global Scientific Publishing.

Nozari, H., & Yordanova, Z. (2025). An intelligent digital twin approach for optimizing multi-channel supply chains in uncertain environments. Green Technologies and Sustainability, 100309.

Nozari, H., Fallah, M., Szmelter-Jarosz, A., & Krzemiński, M. (2021). Analysis of security criteria for IoT-based supply chain: a case study of FMCG industries. Central European Management Journal, 29(4).

Nozari, H., Szmelter-Jarosz, A., & Samadi, S. (c)(2025). Machine Learning Models for Energy Optimization and Resource Consumption in Smart Factories. In Artificial Intelligence of Everything and Sustainable Development (pp. 175-189). Singapore: Springer Nature Singapore.

Nozari, H. (2024). Green supply chain management based on artificial intelligence of everything. *Journal of Economics and Management*, *46*, 171–188.

Nozari, H. (2026). Neuromorphic-driven energy optimization in smart urban logistics. In *Energy-Efficient Transformative Technologies for Data-Driven Smart Cities* (pp. 211–228). Elsevier.

Nozari, H. (Ed.). (2023). *Building Smart and Sustainable Businesses with Transformative Technologies*. IGI Global.

Nozari, H. (Ed.). (2025). *Dynamic and Safe Economy in the Age of Smart Technologies*. IGI Global.

Nozari, H., Abdi, H., & Szmelter-Jarosz, A. (2025). A Neuromorphic and Bio-Inspired Framework for Optimization in Multi-Echelon Supply Networks. *Transformative Science*, *1*(1), 9–17.

Nozari, H., Abdi, H., Szmelter-Jarosz, A., & Rahmaty, M. (2025). A digital twin-based neutrosophic multi-objective optimization model for smart supply chains in the food industry. *Journal of Intelligent Manufacturing*, •••, 1–15.

Nozari, H., Fallah, M., Kazemipoor, H., & Najafi, S. E. (2021). Big data analysis of IoT-based supply chain management considering FMCG industries. *Бизнес-информатика*, *15*(1 (eng)), 78–96.

Nozari, H., Ghahremani-Nahr, J., & Szmelter-Jarosz, A. (2024). AI and machine learning for real-world problems. [). Elsevier.]. *Advances in Computers*, *134*, 1–12.

Nozari, H., & Nassar, S. (2025). *Real-time data-driven multi-objective optimization in B2B marketing using digital twins*. OPSEARCH., DOI: 10.1007/s12597-025-01044-3

Nozari, H., Nassar, S., & Szmelter-Jarosz, A. (2025). Fuzzy multi-objective optimization model for resilient supply chain financing based on blockchain and IoT. *Digital*, *5*(3), 32.

Nozari, H., Szmelter-Jarosz, A., & Ghahremani-Nahr, J. (2022). Analysis of the challenges of artificial intelligence of things (AIoT) for the smart supply chain (case study: FMCG industries). *Sensors (Basel)*, *22*(8), 2931. PMID: 35458916

Nozari, H., Szmelter-Jarosz, A., & Samadi, S. (2025). Machine Learning Models for Energy Optimization and Resource Consumption in Smart Factories. In *Artificial Intelligence of Everything and Sustainable Development* (pp. 175–189). Springer Nature Singapore.

Nozari, H., Szmelter-Jarosz, A., & Weiland, D. (2025). A Fuzzy Multi-Objective Sustainable and Agile Supply Chain Model Based on Digital Twin and Internet of Things with Adaptive Learning Under Environmental Uncertainty. *Applied Sciences (Basel, Switzerland)*, *15*(19), 10399.

Nozari, H., & Yordanova, Z. (2025). Hybrid digital twin and quantum AI with fuzzy multiobjective modeling in supply chain management. *Edelweiss Applied Science and Technology*, *9*(10), 609–628.

Obada-Obieh, B., Huang, Y., & Beznosov, K. (2021). *Challenges and Threats of Mass Telecommuting: A Qualitative Study of Workers*. USENIX. https://www.usenix.org/conference/soups2021/presentation/obada-obieh

Obrenovic, B., Jianguo, D., Khudaykulov, A., & Khan, M. A. S. (2020). Work-family conflict impact on psychological safety and psychological well-being: A job performance model. *Frontiers in Psychology*, *11*, 475. DOI: 10.3389/fpsyg.2020.00475 PMID: 32296367

Omar, O. (2025). Digital twins for climate-responsive urban development: Integrating zero-energy buildings into smart city strategies. *Sustainability*, *17*(15), 6670.

Ordieres-Meré, J., Gutierrez, M., & Villalba-Díez, J. (2023). Toward the industry 5.0 paradigm: Increasing value creation through the robust integration of humans and machines. *Computers in Industry, 150*, 103947.

Ormrod, J. S. (2020). *Changing Our*. No. June.

Ortiz, J., Gabriela, N., Carvalho, P., Cazarini, E., Gutierrez, W., Cifuentes, L., Claudia, A., Paula, A., Carvalho, A. P., Oztemel, E., Gursev, S., Spoettl, G., Chromjakova, F., Pandiyan, V., & Caesarendra, W. (2020). Industry 4.0 - Current Status and Future Trends. In *IntechOpen eBooks*. https://doi.org/DOI: 10.5772/intechopen.86000

Oyekunle, D. O. T., Okwudili Matthew, U., Bakare, K. M., Fatai, L. O., & Asnui, O. (2024). *Industry 5.0: A Paradigm Shift Towards Sustainability, Adaptability and Human-Centeredness*. David Oyekunle, Ugochukwu Okwudili Matthew, Kafayat Motomori Bakare, Lateef Olawale Fatai, Olasubomi Asuni.

Ozkeser, B. (2019). Lean innovation approach in Industry 5.0. *The Eurasia Proceedings of Science, Technology. Engineering & Mathematics, 5*, 422–428.

Paauwe, J., & Boon, C. (2009). Strategic HRM : A critical review. *Human Resource Management, 2*, 49–73. DOI: 10.4324/9780203876336-11

Pandey, A., & Shankar, R. (2020). Industry 4.0 and its applications in the automotive sector. In Kumar, N., Jha, A. N., & Singh, S. (Eds.), *Industry 4.0: Trends, technologies and impact* (pp. 149–161). Springer.

Pantano, E., & Stylos, N. (2020). The Cinderella moment: Exploring consumers' motivations to engage with renting as collaborative luxury consumption mode. *Psychology and Marketing, 37*(5), 740–753. DOI: 10.1002/mar.21345

Park, H. and Joyner Armstrong, C.M. (2019b), "Will 'no-ownership' work for apparel?: Implications for apparel retailers", *Journal of Retailing and Consumer Services*, Elsevier Ltd, Vol. 47 No. July 2018, pp. 66–73, doi: .DOI: 10.1016/j.jretconser.2018.10.012

Park, H., & Armstrong, C. M. J. (2017). "Collaborative apparel consumption in the digital sharing economy: An agenda for academic inquiry", *International Journal of Consumer Studies*, John Wiley & Sons. *Ltd, 41*(5), 465–474. DOI: 10.1111/ijcs.12354

Park, H., & Joyner Armstrong, C. M. (2019a). Is money the biggest driver? Uncovering motives for engaging in online collaborative consumption retail models for apparel. *Journal of Retailing and Consumer Services, Elsevier Ltd, 51*(April), 42–50. DOI: 10.1016/j.jretconser.2019.05.022

Park, H., & Lee, M. Y. (2022). The Two-Sided Effect of the COVID-19 Pandemic on Online Apparel Renting. *Sustainability (Switzerland), 14*(24). Advance online publication. DOI: 10.3390/su142416771

Paro, C. E., Ribeiro da Silva, H. M., Spers, E. E., Jugend, D., & Hamza, K. M. (2021). The technology effect, green consumption and age in propensity to collaborative consumption. *Cleaner and Responsible Consumption, 2*(January). Advance online publication. DOI: 10.1016/j.clrc.2021.100008

Patel, V., Chesmore, A., Legner, C. M., & Pandey, S. (2021). Trends in Workplace Wearable Technologies and Connected-Worker Solutions for Next-Generation Occupational Safety, Health, and Productivity. *Advanced Intelligent Systems, 4*(1). Advance online publication. DOI: 10.1002/aisy.202100099

Pathak, H., Kumar, G., Mohapatra, S. D., Gaikwad, B. B., & Rane, J. (2020). Use of drones in agriculture: Potentials, Problems and Policy Needs. *ICAR-National Institute of Abiotic Stress Management, 300*, 4–15.

Payer, R. C., Quelhas, O. L. G., & Bergiante, N. C. R. (2024). Framework to supporting monitoring the circular economy in the context of industry 5.0: A proposal considering circularity indicators, digital transformation, and sustainability. *Journal of Cleaner Production, 466*, 142850.

Pedersen, E. R. G., & Netter, S. (2015). "Collaborative consumption: Business model opportunities and barriers for fashion libraries", *Journal of Fashion Marketing and Management. Emerald Group Publishing Limited, 19*(3), 258–273. DOI: 10.1108/JFMM-05-2013-0073

Peltokorpi, V., & Michel, J. (2021). The moderating effect of core self-evaluations between the relationships of work–family conflict and voluntary turnover, job promotions and physical health. *Stress and Health, 37*(1), 162–174. DOI: 10.1002/smi.2982 PMID: 32926522

Pereira, A. M., Moura, J. a. B., & De, B Costa, E., Vieira, T., Landim, A. R., Bazaki, E., & Wanick, V. (2022). Customer models for artificial intelligence-based decision support in fashion online retail supply chains. *Decision Support Systems, 158*, 113795. DOI: 10.1016/j.dss.2022.113795

Perry-Smith, J. E., & Mannucci, P. V. (2017). From Creativity to Innovation: The Social Network Drivers of the Four Phases of the Idea Journey. *Academy of Management Review, 42*(1), 53–79. DOI: 10.5465/amr.2014.0462

Pfajfar, G., Ma, A. and Mitr, M. (2022), "Adoption of collaborative consumption as sustainable social innovation : Sociability and novelty seeking perspective", Vol. 144 No. May 2021, pp. 163–179, doi: .DOI: 10.1016/j.jbusres.2022.01.062

Pidel, C., & Ackermann, P. (2020). Collaboration in Virtual and Augmented Reality: A Systematic Overview. In *Lecture notes in computer science* (pp. 141–156). https://doi.org/DOI: 10.1007/978-3-030-58465-8_10

Pietrantoni, L., Favilla, M., Fraboni, F., Mazzoni, E., Morandini, S., Benvenuti, M., & De Angelis, M. (2024). Integrating collaborative robots in manufacturing, logistics, and agriculture: Expert perspectives on technical, safety, and human factors. *Frontiers in Robotics and AI, 11*, 1342130. PMID: 39687349

Podsakoff, P. M., MacKenzie, S. B., Podsakoff, N. P., & Bachrach, D. G. (2008). Scholarly Influence in the Field of Management: A Bibliometric Analysis of the Determinants of University and Author Impact in the Management Literature in the Past Quarter Century. *Journal of Management, SAGE Publications Inc, 34*(4), 641–720. DOI: 10.1177/0149206308319533

Porter, M. E., & Heppelmann, J. E. (2014). How smart, connected products are transforming competition. *Harvard Business Review, 92*(11), 64–88.

Porter, M. E., & Heppelmann, J. E. (2015). How smart, connected products are transforming companies. *Harvard Business Review, 93*(10), 96–114.

Posey, C., & Shoss, M. (2023). Employees as a Source of Security Issues in Times of Change and Stress: A Longitudinal Examination of Employees' Security Violations during the COVID-19 Pandemic. *Journal of Business and Psychology*. Advance online publication. DOI: 10.1007/s10869-023-09917-4

Post, C., De Lia, E., DiTomaso, N., Tirpak, T. M., & Borwankar, R. (2009). Capitalizing on Thought Diversity for Innovation. *Research Technology Management, 52*(6), 14–25. DOI: 10.1080/08956308.2009.11657596

Prabhakar, S., Nimesh, A., & Prabhakar, P. (2023a). Assessment of Start-Up Ecosystems for Tribal Women Entrepreneurs in India. In *Diversity, Equity, and Inclusion Efforts of Businesses in Rural Areas* (pp. 1-22). IGI Global.

Prabhakar, S., Nimesh, A., & Prabhakar, P. (2023b). Startup ecosystem for rural development in India. In *Socio-Economic Disparities, Vulnerable Communities, and the Future of Work and Entrepreneurship* (pp. 26-50). IGI Global.

Prabhakar, S., Tiwari, T., Prabhakar, P., Banerjee, S., Pasayat, A. K., Gonela, S., . . . Nimesh, A. (2025). Frugal Innovation (FI): A Catalyst for Inclusive Economic Growth and Sustainable Entrepreneurship Development. In *Entrepreneurial Opportunities in Disadvantaged Rural Communities* (pp. 281-326). IGI Global Scientific Publishing.

Prabhakar, P., Verma, D. K., & Banerjee, M. (2025). Safety and Toxicity of Nutraceuticals: Concerns, Challenges and Global Regulatory Aspects. In *Food Bioactives and Nutraceuticals: Dietary Medicine for Human Health and Well-Beings* (pp. 437–462). Springer Nature Singapore.

Prabhakar, S., & Nimesh, A. (2022). Skill development programmes for women in India: Current status and future perspectives. *World Journal of Advanced Engineering Technology and Sciences*, *7*(1), 128–136.

Prashar, G., Vasudev, H., & Bhuddhi, D. (2022). Additive manufacturing: Expanding 3D printing horizon in industry 4.0. [IJIDeM]. *International Journal on Interactive Design and Manufacturing*, *17*(5), 2221–2235. DOI: 10.1007/s12008-022-00956-4 PMID: 40479213

Price, D. (1965), "Statistical studies of networks of scientific papers", *Statistical Association Methods for Mechanized Documentation: Symposium Proceedings*, Vol. 269, US Government Printing Office, p. 187.

PwC India. (2020). *Disrupting the Indian agriculture ecosystem: The role of agritech.* PricewaterhouseCoopers India. Retrieved from https://www.pwc.in

Rahmat, A., Asri, A., & Wulandari, R. M. (2021). Pengaruh self-compassion dan dukungan sosial terhadap work-family conflict pada wanita di Kota Makassar. *Jurnal Sosialisasi*, *2*(12), 84–97.

Raikar, A. S., Andrew, J., Dessai, P. P., Prabhu, S. M., Jathar, S., Prabhu, A., & Raikar, G. V. S. (2024). Neuromorphic computing for modeling neurological and psychiatric disorders: Implications for drug development. *Artificial Intelligence Review*, *57*(12), 318.

Raja Santhi, A., & Muthuswamy, P. (2023). Industry 5.0 or industry 4.0 S? Introduction to industry 4.0 and a peek into the prospective industry 5.0 technologies. [IJIDeM]. *International Journal on Interactive Design and Manufacturing*, *17*(2), 947–979. PMID: 40478102

Rajendran, B., & Alibart, F. (2016). Neuromorphic computing based on emerging memory technologies. *IEEE Journal on Emerging and Selected Topics in Circuits and Systems*, *6*(2), 198–211.

Rame, R., Purwanto, P., & Sudarno, S. (2024). Industry 5.0 and sustainability: An overview of emerging trends and challenges for a green future. *Innovation and Green Development*, *3*(4), 100173.

Ramtiyal, B., Johari, S., Vijayvargy, L. and Prakash, S. (2023), "The impact of marketing mix on the adoption of clothes rental and swapping in collaborative consumption", *Journal of Global Operations and Strategic Sourcing*, doi: .DOI: 10.1108/JGOSS-04-2023-0027

Rane, N., Choudhary, S., & Rane, J. (2023). Education 4.0 and 5.0: Integrating Artificial Intelligence (AI) for Personalized and Adaptive Learning. SSRN *Electronic Journal*. https://doi.org/DOI: 10.2139/ssrn.4638365

Rane, S. B., & Narvel, Y. M. (2021). Re-designing the business organization using disruptive innovations based on blockchain-IoT integrated architecture for improving agility in future Industry 4.0. *Benchmarking*, *28*(5), 1883–1908. DOI: 10.1108/bij-12-2018-0445

Rani, S., Jining, D., Shoukat, K., Shoukat, M. U., & Nawaz, S. A. (2024). A human–machine interaction mechanism: Additive manufacturing for Industry 5.0—design and management. *Sustainability*, *16*(10), 4158.

Rashid, A. B., & Kausik, A. K. (2024). AI revolutionizing industries worldwide: A comprehensive overview of its diverse applications. *Hybrid Advances*, 100277.

Rastogi, M., Karatepe, O. M., & Mehmetoglu, M. (2019). Linking resources to career satisfaction through work–family enrichment. *Service Industries Journal*, *39*(11–12), 855–876. DOI: 10.1080/02642069.2018.1449835

Rathi, G., & Kathuria, S. (2025). Transforming Circular Economy Through Industry 5.0: A Deep Dive into Sustainable Innovations. In *Sustainable Economy Models in the Age of Industry 5.0* (pp. 253–274). Springer Nature Singapore.

Rejeb, A., Rejeb, K., Keogh, J. G., & Süle, E. (2025). When Industry 5.0 meets the circular economy: A systematic literature review. *Circular Economy and Sustainability*, •••, 1–32.

Rejeb, A., Rejeb, K., Keogh, J. G., & Süle, E. (2025). When Industry 5.0 Meets the Circular Economy: A Systematic Literature Review. *Circular Economy and Sustainability*, •••, 1–32.

Rey-Martí, A., Ribeiro-Soriano, D., & Palacios-Marqués, D. (2016). A bibliometric analysis of social entrepreneurship. *Journal of Business Research*, *69*(5), 1651–1655. DOI: 10.1016/j.jbusres.2015.10.033

Riad, M., Naimi, M., & Okar, C. (2024). Enhancing supply chain resilience through artificial intelligence: Developing a comprehensive conceptual framework for AI implementation and supply chain optimization. *Logistics (Basel)*, *8*(4), 111.

Rogers, E. M. (2003). *Diffusion of innovations* (5th ed.). Free Press.

Rojanakit, P., de Oliveira, R. T., & Dulleck, U. (2022). The sharing economy: A critical review and research agenda. *Journal of Business Research*, *139*, 1317–1334.

Roos, D., & Hahn, R. (2019). Understanding Collaborative Consumption: An Extension of the Theory of Planned Behavior with Value-Based Personal Norms. *Journal of Business Ethics*, *158*(3), 679–697. DOI: 10.1007/s10551-017-3675-3

RSA and The Great Recovery Project. (2016). Designing for a circular economy: Lessons from The Great Recovery 2012 – 2016. *RSA Action and Research Centre*, (March), 1–45.

RSA. 2020. The Great Recovery. RSA: https://www.thersa.org/action-and-research /rsa-projects/economy-enterprise-manufacturing-folder/the-great-recovery/about, 08/03/2024.

Rüßmann, M., Lorenz, M., Gerbert, P., Waldner, M., Justus, J., Engel, P., & Harnisch, M. (2015). *Industry 4.0: The Future of Productivity and Growth in Manufacturing Industries*. Boston Consulting Group.

Rüßmann, M., Lorenz, M., Gerbert, P., Waldner, M., Justus, J., Engel, P., & Harnisch, M. (2018). *Industry 4.0: The future of productivity and growth in manufacturing industries*. Boston Consulting Group.

Santiago, B. D. S., Scavarda, L. F., Gusmão Caiado, R. G., Santos, R. S., & Mattos Nascimento, D. L. D. (2025). Corporate social responsibility and circular economy integration framework within sustainable supply chain management: Building blocks for industry 5.0. *Corporate Social Responsibility and Environmental Management*, *32*(1), 269–290.

Sarıoğlu, C. İ. (2023). Industry 5.0, digital society, and consumer 5.0. In *Handbook of Research on Perspectives on Society and Technology Addiction* (pp. 11-33). IGI Global.

Sarkar, B. D., Sharma, I., & Shardeo, V. (2025). A multi-method examination of barriers to traceability in Industry 5.0-enabled digital food supply chains. *International Journal of Logistics Management*, *36*(2), 354–380.

Saunders, M., Lewis, P., & Thornhill, A. (2007). Research Methods for Buniess Students. In *Pearson*.https://www.researchgate.net/publication/330760964_Research_Methods_for_Business_Students_Chapter_4_Understanding_research_philosophy_and_approaches_to_theory_development

Šćepanović, S., Bogucka, E., & Quercia, D. (2025). AI in the city: Impact assessment of artificial intelligence uses in earth observation. *Urban Informatics*, *4*(1), 1–30. PMID: 39802502

Schor, J. B., & Fitzmaurice, C. J. (2015), "Collaborating and connecting: The emergence of the sharing economy", *Handbook of Research on Sustainable Consumption*, pp. 410–425, doi: DOI: 10.4337/9781783471270.00039

Schor, J. B., & Cansoy, M. (2019). *"The sharing economy", The Oxford Handbook of Consumption* (Vol. 51). Oxford University Press New York.

Schröder, P., Bengtsson, M., Cohen, M., Dewick, P., Hoffstetter, J., & Sarkis, J. (2019). Degrowth within – Aligning circular economy and strong sustainability narratives. *Resources, Conservation and Recycling*, *146*(March), 190–191. DOI: 10.1016/j.resconrec.2019.03.038

Schwab, K. (2017). *The Fourth Industrial Revolution*. Crown Business.

Segura, P., Lobato-Calleros, O., Ramírez-Serrano, A., & Soria, I. (2021). Human-robot collaborative systems: Structural components for current manufacturing applications. *Advances in Industrial and Manufacturing Engineering*, *3*, 100060. DOI: 10.1016/j.aime.2021.100060

Seo, M. J., & Kim, M. (2019). Understanding the purchasing behaviour of second-hand fashion shoppers in a non-profit thrift store context. *International Journal of Fashion Design, Technology and Education, Taylor & Francis*, *12*(3), 301–312. DOI: 10.1080/17543266.2019.1611945

Shabur, M. A., Shahriar, A., & Ara, M. (2025). From automation to collaboration: Exploring the impact of industry 5.0 on sustainable manufacturing. *Discover Sustainability*, *6*(1), 1–23.

SHAFIK, W. (2025). Navigating Artificial Intelligence and Digital Twin for Smart Cities. Driving Innovation through AI and Digital Twin for 6G Powered Sustainable Ultra Smart Cities, 1-26.

Shahab, H., Iqbal, M., Sohaib, A., Khan, F. U., & Waqas, M. (2024). IoT-based agriculture management techniques for sustainable farming: A comprehensive review. *Computers and Electronics in Agriculture*, *220*, 108851.

Shahin, M., Chen, F. F., Hosseinzadeh, A., & Zand, N. (2023). Using machine learning and deep learning algorithms for downtime minimization in manufacturing systems: An early failure detection diagnostic service. *International Journal of Advanced Manufacturing Technology*, *128*(9–10), 3857–3883. DOI: 10.1007/s00170-023-12020-w

Sharma, M., Paliwal, T., & Baniwal, P. (2024). Challenges in Digital Transformation and Automation for Industry 4.0. In *CRC Press eBooks* (pp. 143–163). https://doi.org/DOI: 10.1201/9781003432319-9

Shen, Z., Ji, W., Yu, S., Cheng, G., Yuan, Q., Han, Z., & Liu, H.. (2023). Mapping the knowledge of traffic collision Reconstruction: A scientometric analysis in CiteSpace, VOSviewer, and SciMAT. *Science & Justice, Elsevier*, *63*(1), 19–37.

Shi, M., Chussid, C., Yang, P., Jia, M., Lewis, V. D., & Cao, W. (2021). The exploration of artificial intelligence application in fashion trend forecasting. *Textile Research Journal*, *91*(19–20), 2357–2386. DOI: 10.1177/00405175211006212

Shirmohammadi, M., Au, W. C., & Beigi, M. (2022). Remote work and work-life balance: Lessons learned from the covid-19 pandemic and suggestions for HRD practitioners. *Human Resource Development International*, *25*(2), 163–181. DOI: 10.1080/13678868.2022.2047380

Shi, Y., Sorrell, S., & Foxon, T. (2023). The impact of teleworking on domestic energy use and carbon emissions: An assessment for England. *Energy and Building*, *287*, 112996. DOI: 10.1016/j.enbuild.2023.112996

Sicari, S., Rizzardi, A., Grieco, L., & Coen-Porisini, A. (2015). Security, privacy and trust in Internet of Things: The road ahead. *Computer Networks*, *76*, 146–164. DOI: 10.1016/j.comnet.2014.11.008

Singh, N., Jena, D., & Panigrahi, R. R. (2025). Digital Intelligence in Supply Chain Management: Driving Economic Diversification and Sustainability. In Fostering Economic Diversification and Sustainable Business Through Digital Intelligence (pp. 83-110). IGI Global Scientific Publishing.

Singh, T., Singh, D., Singh, C. D., & Singh, K. (2023). Industry 5.0. *Factories of the Future: Technological Advancements in the Manufacturing Industry*, 21-45.

Singh, K. A., Patra, F., Ghosh, T., Mahnot, N. K., Dutta, H., & Duary, R. K. (2025). Advancing food systems with industry 5.0: A systematic review of smart technologies, sustainability, and resource optimization. *Sustainable Futures : An Applied Journal of Technology, Environment and Society*, •••, 100694.

Singh, R. K. (2025). Exploring the impact of green supply chain strategies and sustainable practices on circular supply chains. *Benchmarking*, *32*(4), 1387–1409.

Singh, V., & Kumar, R. The Rise of Industry 5.0: how artificial intelligence is shaping the future of manufacturing. In *Artificial Intelligence and Communication Techniques in Industry 5.0* (pp. 26–46). CRC Press.

Slaton, K., & Pookulangara, S. (2022). The Secondary Luxury Consumer: An Investigation into Online Consumption. *Sustainability (Switzerland)*, *14*(21). Advance online publication. DOI: 10.3390/su142113744

Slavic, D., Marjanovic, U., Medic, N., Simeunovic, N., & Rakic, S. (2024). The evaluation of Industry 5.0 concepts: Social network analysis approach. *Applied Sciences (Basel, Switzerland)*, *14*(3), 1291.

Small, H. (1973). "Co-citation in the scientific literature: A new measure of the relationship between two documents", *Journal of the American Society for Information Science*, John Wiley & Sons. *Ltd*, *24*(4), 265–269. DOI: 10.1002/asi.4630240406

Smith, J. D., Hill, A. J., Reeder, L. E., Franke, B. C., Lehoucq, R. B., Parekh, O., & Aimone, J. B. (2022). Neuromorphic scaling advantages for energy-efficient random walk computations. *Nature Electronics*, *5*(2), 102–112.

Smolka, M., Stoepel, L., Quill, J., Wahlbrink, T., Floehr, J., Böschen, S., & Lemme, M. (2024). Transdisciplinary development of neuromorphic computing hardware for Artificial Intelligence applications: technological, economic, societal, and environmental dimensions of transformation in the NeuroSys Cluster4Future. In *Transformation Towards Sustainability: A Novel Interdisciplinary Framework from RWTH Aachen University* (pp. 271–301). Springer International Publishing.

Sondermann, D. (2018). Towards more resilient economies: The role of well-functioning economic structures. *Journal of Policy Modeling*, *40*(1), 97–117. DOI: 10.1016/j.jpolmod.2018.01.002

Soori, M., Arezoo, B., & Dastres, R. (2023). Artificial intelligence, machine learning and deep learning in advanced robotics, a review. *Cognitive Robotics*, *3*, 54–70. DOI: 10.1016/j.cogr.2023.04.001

Soori, M., Arezoo, B., & Dastres, R. (2024). Virtual manufacturing in industry 4.0: A review. *Data Science and Management*, *7*(1), 47–63. DOI: 10.1016/j.dsm.2023.10.006

Soroui, S. T. (2021). Understanding the drivers and implications of remote work from the local perspective: An exploratory study into the dis/reembedding dynamics. *Technology in Society*, *64*, 101328. DOI: 10.1016/j.techsoc.2020.101328

Srai, J. S., Kumar, M., Graham, G., Phillips, W., Tooze, J., Ford, S., Beecher, P., Raj, B., Gregory, M., Tiwari, M. K., Ravi, B., Neely, A., Shankar, R., Charnley, F., & Tiwari, A. (2016). Distributed manufacturing: Scope, challenges and opportunities. *International Journal of Production Research, 54*(23), 6917–6935. DOI: 10.1080/00207543.2016.1192302

Sreelatha, A. S., Pallavi, B., & Ajala, S. O. (2023). Energy Efficiency and Renewable Energy in Industry 5.0. In *CRC Press eBooks* (pp. 107–155). https://doi.org/DOI: 10.1201/9781032686363-6

Sturgeon, T. J. (2019). Upgrading strategies for the digital economy. *Global Strategy Journal, 11*(1), 34–57. DOI: 10.1002/gsj.1364

Sun, K., Ooi, K. B., Wei-Han Tan, G., & Lee, V. H. (2025). Small and medium-sized enterprises' path to sustainable supply chains: Exploring the role of supply chain finance and risk management. *Supply Chain Management, 30*(1), 1–18.

Sutthiphisal, D. (2006). Learning-by-Producing and the Geographic Links Between Invention and Production: Experience from the Second Industrial Revolution. *The Journal of Economic History, 66*(4), 992–1025. DOI: 10.1017/s0022050706000404

Szmelter-Jarosz, A., & Nozari, H. (2025). AI-Driven Decision Intelligence and Human-AI Collaboration in Economic Systems. In Dynamic and Safe Economy in the Age of Smart Technologies (pp. 171-190). IGI Global Scientific Publishing.

Tagliaro, C., & Migliore, A. (2021). "Covid-working": What to keep and what to leave? Evidence from an Italian company. *Journal of Corporate Real Estate, 24*(2), 76–92. DOI: 10.1108/jcre-10-2020-0053

Tanpipat, W., Lim, H. W., & Deng, X. (2021). Implementing Remote Working Policy in Corporate Offices in Thailand: Strategic Facility Management Perspective. *Sustainability, 13*(3), 1284. DOI: 10.3390/su13031284

Tathavadekar, V. P., & Mahankale, N. R. (2025). Neuromorphic Computing-Enabled Digital Twin Framework for Sustainable IT Supply Chain Integration in Smart Urban Ecosystems. *Frontiers in Digital Twin Urban Ecosystems, 1*(1), 1–8.

Testa, D. S., Bakhshian, S., & Eike, R. (2020). Engaging consumers with sustainable fashion on Instagram. *Journal of Fashion Marketing and Management, 25*(4), 569–584. DOI: 10.1108/JFMM-11-2019-0266

Thuraka, B. (2021). AI-Driven Adaptive Route Optimization for Sustainable Urban Logistics and Supply Chain Management. *International Journal of Scientific Research in Computer Science Engineering and Information Technology, 7*, 667–684.

Tian, J., Vanderstraeten, J., Matthyssens, P., & Shen, L. (2021). Developing and leveraging platforms in a traditional industry: An orchestration and co-creation perspective. *Industrial Marketing Management*, *92*, 14–33. DOI: 10.1016/j.indmarman.2020.10.007

Tóth, A., Nagy, L., Kennedy, R., Bohuš, B., Abonyi, J., & Ruppert, T. (2023). The human-centric Industry 5.0 collaboration architecture. *MethodsX*, *11*, 102260. DOI: 10.1016/j.mex.2023.102260 PMID: 37388166

Tranfield, D., Denyer, D., & Smart, P. (2003). "Towards a Methodology for Developing Evidence-Informed Management Knowledge by Means of Systematic Review", *British Journal of Management*, John Wiley & Sons. *Ltd*, *14*(3), 207–222. DOI: 10.1111/1467-8551.00375

Tsur, E. E. (2021). *Neuromorphic Engineering: The Scientist's, Algorithms Designer's and Computer Architect's Perspectives on Brain-Inspired Computing*. CRC Press.

Tusquellas, N., Santiago, R., & Palau, R. (2025). Professional Development Analytics: A Smart Model for Industry 5.0. *Applied Sciences (Basel, Switzerland)*, *15*(4), 2057.

Tussyadiah, I. P., & Pesonen, J. (2016). Impacts of Peer-to-Peer Accommodation Use on Travel Patterns. *Journal of Travel Research*, *55*(8), 1022–1040. DOI: 10.1177/0047287515608505

Tu, X., Ala-Laurinaho, R., Yang, C., Autiosalo, J., & Tammi, K. (2024). Architecture for data-centric and semantic-enhanced industrial metaverse: Bridging physical factories and virtual landscape. *Journal of Manufacturing Systems*, *74*, 965–979.

Vallaster, C., Kraus, S., Merigó Lindahl, J. M., & Nielsen, A. (2019). Ethics and entrepreneurship: A bibliometric study and literature review. *Journal of Business Research*, *99*, 226–237. DOI: 10.1016/j.jbusres.2019.02.050

Van Eck, N. and Waltman, L. (2010), "Software survey: VOSviewer, a computer program for bibliometric mapping", *Scientometrics*, Akadémiai Kiadó, co-published with Springer Science+ Business Media BV …, Vol. 84 No. 2, pp. 523–538.

van Eck, N. J., & Waltman, L. (2007). VOS: A New Method for Visualizing Similarities Between Objects BT - Advances in Data Analysis. In Decker, R., & Lenz, H.-J. (Eds.), *Springer Berlin Heidelberg, Berlin* (pp. 299–306).

Venkatesh, V., Morris, M. G., Davis, G. B., & Davis, F. D. (2003). User acceptance of information technology: Toward a unified view. *Management Information Systems Quarterly*, *27*(3), 425–478.

Verna Allee. (2008, January 18). Value network analysis and value conversion of tangible and intangible assets. *Journal of Intellectual Capital*, *9*(1), 5–24. DOI: 10.1108/14691930810845777

Victor, N., Maddikunta, P. K. R., Mary, D. R. K., Murugan, R., Chengoden, R., Gadekallu, T. R., & Paek, J. (2024). Remote Sensing for Agriculture in the Era of Industry 5.0–A survey. *IEEE Journal of Selected Topics in Applied Earth Observations and Remote Sensing*.

Villani, V., Pini, F., Leali, F., & Secchi, C. (2018). Survey on human–robot collaboration in industrial settings: Safety, intuitive interfaces and applications. *Mechatronics*, *55*, 248–266. DOI: 10.1016/j.mechatronics.2018.02.009

Vineyard, C. M., Severa, W. M., & Aimone, J. B. (2024, July). Strategic Considerations for Neuromorphic Computing. In *2024 International Conference on Neuromorphic Systems (ICONS)* (pp. 161-168). IEEE.

Voropai, O., & Antoniouk, O. (2025). Innovation Ecosystem Models: Defining the Role of the University in the Industry 5.0 Perspective. *Humanities and Social Sciences*, *32*(1), 143–152.

Vrontis, D., Christofi, M., Pereira, V., Tarba, S., Makrides, A., & Trichina, E. (2023). Artificial intelligence, robotics, advanced technologies and human resource management: a systematic review. *Routledge eBooks*, 172–201. https://doi.org/DOI: 10.4324/9781003377085-7

Walsh, I., & Rowe, F. (2023). BIBGT: Combining bibliometrics and grounded theory to conduct a literature review. *European Journal of Information Systems, Taylor & Francis*, *32*(4), 653–674.

Wamba, S. F., Akter, S., Edwards, A., Chopin, G., & Gnanzou, D. (2015). How 'big data' can make big impact: Findings from a systematic review and a longitudinal case study. *International Journal of Production Economics*, *165*, 234–246.

Wang, L., ... (2021). Future of Industry 5.0 in society: Human-centric solutions, challenges and prospective research areas. *Journal of Cloud Computing*. https://journalofcloudcomputing.springeropen.com/articles/10.1186/s13677-021-00279-4

Wang, D., Weisz, J. D., Muller, M., Ram, P., Geyer, W., Dugan, C., Tausczik, Y., Samulowitz, H., & Gray, A. (2019). Human-AI Collaboration in Data Science. *Proceedings of the ACM on Human-Computer Interaction, 3*(CSCW), 1–24. https://doi.org/DOI: 10.1145/3359313

Warner, K. S. R., & Wäger, M. (2019). Building dynamic capabilities for digital transformation: An ongoing process of strategic renewal. *Long Range Planning*. https://api.semanticscholar.org/CorpusID:158197061

Wei, X., Lo, C. K. Y., Jung, S., & Choi, T. M. (2021). From co-consumption to co-production: A systematic review and research synthesis of collaborative consumption practices. *Journal of Business Research, Elsevier Inc.*, *129*(March), 282–294. DOI: 10.1016/j.jbusres.2021.02.027

Whig, P., Remala, R., Mudunuru, K. R., & Quraishi, S. J. (2024). Integrating AI and quantum technologies for sustainable supply chain management. In *Quantum computing and supply chain management: A new era of optimization* (pp. 267–283). IGI Global.

Wicaksono, T., Illés, C. B., & Dunay, A. (2023). Enhancing collaborative apparel consumption model: Quality-driven insights from customers and industry professionals. *Journal of Open Innovation: Technology, Market, and Complexity, Elsevier*, *9*(2), 100077. DOI: 10.1016/j.joitmc.2023.100077

Wu, H., Liu, J., & Liang, B. (2025). AI-driven supply chain transformation in Industry 5.0: Enhancing resilience and sustainability. *Journal of the Knowledge Economy*, *16*(1), 3826–3868.

Xu, X., Lu, Y., Vogel-Heuser, B., & Wang, L. (2021). Industry 4.0 and Industry 5.0—Inception, conception and perception. *Journal of Manufacturing Systems*, *61*, 530–535. DOI: 10.1016/j.jmsy.2021.10.006

Ye, A., Xu, D., Li, Y., Du, J., Wu, Z., & Tang, J. (2025). Neuromorphic energy economics: Toward biologically inspired and sustainable power market design. *Frontiers in Computational Neuroscience*, *19*, 1597038. PMID: 40495879

Yin, S., Liu, L., & Mahmood, T. (2024). New trends in sustainable development for industry 5.0: Digital green innovation economy. *Green and Low-Carbon Economy*, *2*(4), 269–276.

Yin, Y., Stecke, K. E., & Li, D. (2017). The evolution of production systems from Industry 2.0 through Industry 4.0. *International Journal of Production Research*, *56*(1–2), 848–861. DOI: 10.1080/00207543.2017.1403664

Yordanova, Z., & Nozari, H. (2025). Harnessing Cyber-Physical Systems and Digital Twins for Industrial Innovation and Economic Resilience. In Dynamic and Safe Economy in the Age of Smart Technologies (pp. 33-48). IGI Global Scientific Publishing

Yu, D., Xu, Z., & Wang, W. (2018). Bibliometric analysis of fuzzy theory research in China: A 30-year perspective. *Knowledge-Based Systems, 141*, 188–199. DOI: 10.1016/j.knosys.2017.11.018

Zamani, B., Sandin, G., & Peters, G. M. (2017). Life cycle assessment of clothing libraries: Can collaborative consumption reduce the environmental impact of fast fashion? *Journal of Cleaner Production, Elsevier Ltd, 162*, 1368–1375. DOI: 10.1016/j.jclepro.2017.06.128

Zaman, M., Park, H., Kim, Y. K., & Park, S. H. (2019). Consumer orientations of second-hand clothing shoppers. *Journal of Global Fashion Marketing, Routledge, 10*(2), 163–176. DOI: 10.1080/20932685.2019.1576060

Zekhnini, K., Benabdellah, A. C., Bag, S., & Gupta, S. (2024). Supply chain 5.0 digitalization: An integrated approach for risk assessment. *Management Decision*. Advance online publication. DOI: 10.1108/md-12-2023-2329

Zhou, X., Song, M., & Cui, L. (2020). Driving force for China's economic development under Industry 4.0 and circular economy: Technological innovation or structural change? *Journal of Cleaner Production, 271*, 122680. DOI: 10.1016/j.jclepro.2020.122680

Zupic, I., & Čater, T. (2015). Bibliometric Methods in Management and Organization. *Organizational Research Methods, 18*, 429–472. DOI: 10.1177/1094428114562629

About the Contributors

Hamed Nozari is a distinguished researcher and innovator in industrial engineering, supply chain optimization, and artificial intelligence applications. Holding a Ph.D. in Industrial Engineering, he has made significant contributions to the fields of multi-objective decision-making, smart supply chains, and digital twin technologies. His research spans various interdisciplinary areas, including predictive maintenance in green supply chains, AI-driven marketing optimization, cybersecurity in smart economies, Digital twin, and autonomous AI for sustainable last-mile delivery.

***

Abhishek Choudhary is currently a research scholar at Amity Business School, Amity University Rajasthan. He is working as an Assistant Professor at the Department of Fashion & Clothing, Indian Institute of Crafts & Design, Jaipur

Ridhima Goel is a distinguished researcher who completed her Ph.D. at the Institute of Management Studies and Research, Maharshi Dayanand University, Rohtak, India. She brings a rich interdisciplinary approach to her research, combining her business administration and English literature expertise, with an M.B.A. and an M.A. in English from the same institution. As an educator, she imparts knowledge to postgraduate students, teaching open elective subjects such as Fundamentals of Management and Fundamentals of Marketing. Ridhima has published several research articles in Scopus-indexed and Web of Science journals. Additionally, she has contributed to Scopus-indexed book chapters published by IGI Global. Her research interests encompass human resource management, organizational behavior, and occupational health.

Toolika Gupta, the Director of the Indian Institute of Crafts and design, Jaipur since 2017, is a researcher, designer, author, educator and an academic administrator.

After completing her Post Graduation from Lady Irwin College, Delhi University, she began her career as a designer in 1996, joining academics at NIFT, New Delhi in 2005. To follow her research interests, she resigned from NIFT to pursue her PhD at the University of Glasgow, UK, (2012-2016), while being a PhD fellow with the Center for Textile Research, (CTR), Denmark. Back in India, along with likeminded people she formed the Textiles and Clothing Research Center (TCRC), Delhi in 2016. Her research interests include Fashion and textile history, revival of Indian handicrafts and culture, craft cluster initiatives, and craft business incubation. She is on the Board of Studies of many design institutes, Secretary of TCRC and Dean-Product Design of Vishwakarma Skills University Jaipur, Rajasthan. Since 2022 she is also the President of Alliance Francaise of Jaipur.

Amit Jain is currently the President/Vice-Chancellor at Amity University Rajasthan. He holds a PhD in Management and completed FDP from IIM Ahmedabad. He has designed and conducted training programs/sessions for executives of various organizations. He has several publications to his credit and has presented research papers at national and international conferences. He is an editorial board member of the Indian Journal of Training and Development. He is also the Chief Editor of Amity Management Review. His area of interest for research, training and consultancy includes marketing strategy, sales management, digital marketing, marketing communications, retail management, sustainability, and entrepreneurship

Sourabh Kumar is Associate Professor at Anand International College of Engineering, where he brings a wealth of expertise in Human Resource Management (HRM) to his academic role. With a keen interest in understanding organizational dynamics and scholarly impact through bibliometric methods, Dr. Kumar contributes significantly to both fields through research and teaching. His dedication to advancing HRM practices and evaluating scholarly impact underscores his commitment to fostering knowledge and innovation within academia.

Pawan Prabhakar is a nanotech and life science professional working in the area of phytopharmaceuticals, nanotechnology and entrepreneurship. He pursued his PhD degree in ethnomedicinal phytopharmaceuticals from prestigious Indian Institute of Technology Kharagpur, Kharagpur, India. Currently, Dr. Prabhakar is working as an assistant professor of technology, innovation and entrepreneurship, School of Business, Woxsen University, Hyderabad, India. He is also recipient of many awards and grants throughout his academic career including Young Scientist Award, Best Professor Award, Research Excellence Award, Outstanding Paper Award, FEBS and DST international travel grants to visit Germany and USA, Visiting Fellow-TMU,

Taiwan. In addition, he is a member of prestigious professional bodies including Royal Society of Chemistry, UK (RSC), American Chemical Society, USA (ACS), USA and ESDA, India. His activities and accomplishments include conferences, seminar, workshop, training and the publication of research articles, review papers and book chapters in reputed international publishing houses including Elsevier, Springer and Taylor & Francis.

Tejas Shah is MBA and Ph.D. in management. He is the programme chair MBA (Family Business and Entrepreneurship) and faculty in the Marketing area at Institute of Management, Nirma University. He has more than 15 years of experience in teaching and research at post graduate management programs. He is actively involved in research, consultancy and faculty/management development programmes. He has published papers in peer-reviewed journals of national and international repute. He is also reviewer for the journals like Asia Pacific Journal of Marketing and Logistics, Benchmarking: An International Journal, etc. to name a few. He has been teaching and consulting in area of Digital Marketing and retail marketing.

Jagdeep Singla is presently employed as an Associate Professor at the Institute of Management Studies and Research, Maharshi Dayanand University, India. He had also served as a Professor at HPKV Business School, CUHP, Dharamshala. He has more than 28 years of teaching and industry experience after completing his post-graduation. He has more than 35 research papers/articles to his credit, published in national and international journals of repute. He has supervised 11 Ph.D. His areas of Specialization are Production and Operations Management, Supply Chain Management, Marketing Management, Human Resource Management, and Brand Management.

Index

V

W

www.ingramcontent.com/pod-product-compliance
Lightning Source LLC
LaVergne TN
LVHW081535300926
849161LV00006B/1447